Gastronomy

The Anthropology of Food and Food Habits

Editor

MARGARET L. ARNOTT

MOUTON PUBLISHERS · THE HAGUE · PARIS

DISTRIBUTED IN THE USA AND CANADA BY ALDINE, CHICAGO

Distributed in the United States of America and Canada
by Aldine Publishing Company, Chicago, Illinois
ISBN 90-279-7739-9 (Mouton)
202-90025-8 (Aldine)
Jacket photo by Cas Oorthuys
Cover and jacket design by Jurriaan Schrofer
Printed in the Netherlands

General Editor's Preface

The very definition of anthropology — the study of man, all he requires, creates, uses, and how and where he lives — implies that the study of anything so basic to man's survival as food is essential. Anthropology takes for granted the need to provide specieswide information on its history and distribution. Nevertheless, the subject of food, like other items of material culture and technology has apparently become "old fashioned" in past years. Because of this, there has recently been an effort to give this subject renewed and international attention. That effort, which is exemplified in this volume, is succeeding, for of course the knowledge assembled in the 1970's is exceedingly "new fashioned." Indeed, it is even newer than the rapidly advancing sciences from which it comes. It is the genius of anthropology to relate to differing cultural values the knowledge and techniques of the physical, biological, and social sciences, and by doing so to humanize such knowledge for understanding and for use. To such an end, perhaps, we have had to await changes in the world which can render the study of food interdisciplinary as well as international.

Like most contemporary sciences, anthropology is a product of the European tradition. Some argue that it is a product of colonialism, with one small and self-interested part of the species dominating the study of the whole. If we are to understand the species, our science needs substantial input from scholars who represent a variety of the world's cultures. It was a deliberate purpose of the IXth International Congress of Anthropological and Ethnological Sciences to provide impetus in this direction. The *World Anthropology* volumes, therefore, offer a first glimpse of a human science in which members from all societies have played an active role. Each of the books is designed to be self-contained; each is an attempt to update its particular sector of scientific knowledge and is written by specialists from all parts of the world. Each volume should be read and reviewed individually as a separate volume on its own given subject. The set as a whole will indicate what changes are in store for anthropology as scholars from the developing countries join in studying the species of which we are all a part.

The IXth Congress was planned from the beginning not only to include as many of the scholars from every part of the world as possible, but also with a view toward the eventual publication of the papers in high-quality volumes. At previous Congresses scholars were invited to bring papers which were then read out loud. They were necessarily limited in length; many were only summarized; there was little time for discussion; and the sparse discussion could only be in one language. The IXth Congress was an experiment aimed at changing this. Papers were written with the intention of exchanging them before the Congress, particularly in extensive pre-Congress sessions; they were not intended to be read aloud at the Congress, that time being devoted to discussions — discussions which were simultaneously and professionally translated into five languages. The method for eliciting the papers was structured to make as representative a sample as was allowable when scholarly creativity — hence self-selection — was critically important. Scholars were asked both to propose papers of their own and to suggest topics for sessions of the Congress which they might edit into volumes. All were then informed of the suggestions and encouraged to re-think their own papers and the topics. The process, therefore, was a continuous one of feedback and exchange and it has continued to be so even after the Congress. The some two thousand papers comprising *World Anthropology* certainly then offer a substantial sample of world anthropology. It has been said that anthropology is at a turning point; if this is so, these volumes will be the historical direction-markers.

As might have been foreseen in the first post-colonial generation, the large majority of the Congress papers (82 percent) are the work of scholars identified with the industrialized world which fathered our traditional discipline and the institution of the Congress itself: Eastern Europe (15 percent); Western Europe (16 percent); North America (47 percent); Japan, South Africa, Australia, and New Zealand (4 percent). Only 18 percent of the papers are from developing areas: Africa (4 percent); Asia-Oceania (9 percent); Latin America (5 percent). Aside from the substantial representation from the U.S.S.R. and the nations of Eastern Europe, a significant difference between this corpus of written material and that of other Congresses is the addition of the large proportion of contributions from Africa, Asia, and Latin America. "Only 18 percent" is two to four times as great a proportion as that of other Congresses; moreover, 18 percent of 2,000 papers is 360 papers, 10 times the number of "Third World" papers presented at previous Congresses. In fact, these 360 papers are more than the total of ALL papers published after the last International Congress of Anthropological and Ethnological Sciences which was held in the United States (Philadelphia, 1956).

The significance of the increase is not simply quantitative. The input of scholars from areas which have until recently been no more than subject matter for anthropology represents both feedback and also long-awaited theoretical contributions from the perspectives of very different cultural, social, and historical traditions. Many who attended the IXth Congress were convinced that anthropology would not be the same in the future. The fact that the next Congress (India, 1978) will be our first in the "Third World" may be symbolic of the change. Meanwhile, sober consideration of the present set of books will show how much, and just where and how, our discipline is being revolutionized.

This book joins others in the *World Anthropology* series on technology, including volumes dealing with clothing, housing, stone tools, domestication and agriculture, and maritime pursuits, and those volumes on archaeological, biological, psychological, historical, and enthnographic subjects which include materials on gastronomy and nutrition.

Chicago, Illinois SOL TAX
March 26, 1976

Preface

In an age of abundance as early as the 1950's anthropologists were aware of the diminishing supply of food to feed the world's increasing populations. When the VIth International Congress of Anthropological and Ethnological Sciences met in Paris in 1960, a group gathered for the first time to discuss the problems and to plan for the future. From this meeting, some time later Le Comité International pour les Recherches sur le Ravitaillement Populaire, with archives and headquarters in Bern, Switzerland, evolved under the leadership of Max Wärhen. When the VIIIth International Congress of Anthropological and Ethnological Sciences met in Tokyo in 1968, another group of anthropologists, led by some who had been at the 1960 session, met and agreed that the time had come to actively endeavor to bring together scholars from all disciplines who were engaged in the study of any aspect of food habits, including those whose major interest lay not in food, so that information could be centrally located and scholars going into the field could be encouraged to make note of food habits as they observed them. This group organized as the International Committee for the Anthropology of Food and Food Habits and was recognized by the Congress. Since that time, two international meetings of food specialists have been held — one in Lund, Sweden in 1970, and one in Helsinki, Finland in 1973. Additionally small symposia have been set up in various parts of the United States and Canada.

Under the aegis of the International Committee for the Anthropology of Food and Food Habits, this collection of papers, both invited and volunteered, was presented at a session of the IXth International Congress of Anthropological and Ethnological Sciences when it met in

Chicago in 1973. The title, *Gastronomy,* defined as the intelligent examination of whatever concerns man's nourishment, was selected because it seemed to cover all aspects of the subject from studies of prehistoric food patterns as revealed in archaeological excavations, to studies of modern urban food habits and studies of textual terms limited to special areas, as well as studies of ceremonial or folkloristic approaches to food.

In this volume, some aspects of food habits have been only narrowly treated while others have been completely omitted. This merely points up the urgency and quantity of work to be done. Discussions of prehistoric findings in relation to the food of early man, as presented herein, are a limited aspect of a subject which should be carried down to the present day. Plant breeders have long dreamed of finding a superplant that would combine the desirable characteristics of a variety of agricultural crops which have so far resisted nature's crossbeeding and given us variety in food plants. Scientists are searching for a plant that would resist insects, survive drought, and still produce large quantities of highly nutritious food. Some of the new crossbreeding experiments have employed the same drugs that are used when human organs are transplanted, thus crossing biological boundaries. As a result of such research, new kinds of food plants could be the forerunners of wholly new crops that our expanding populations may have to rely upon in the next century.

Hand in hand with such experimentation must go ethnic and geographic studies to determine food preferences and requirements. There is a dire need of ethnic studies to learn how people may be fed, what they will and will not eat, to show what part fast, festival, and status foods play in the total diets, and to know what foods can be called upon to sustain life in times of scarcity. What is famine food? In one culture, for example, the rabbit is considered a delicacy, while in another it is famine food. In still another, the deadly nightshade is eaten without ill effects. Can heretofore poisonous plants be made into food, or are they culturally taboo and so without value for all time — a problem for the anthropologist.

The economics of food is an area quite untouched in this volume, yet it is a subject which affects the eating habits of all the populations of the world. Recently, a college student experimented to find out how cheaply it was possible to eat while still maintaining health and weight. Clearly, this is an area for cooperation between the economist, the food specialist, and the medical anthropologist.

No mention has been made of the psychic phenomena of prayer and music in relation to increased crop production. A few studies exist but many more are called for. Nor have studies been presented about space food, the food of underwater researchers, the use of insects in diet, the new methods of producing high-protein breads, and a host of other recent developments relating to the production, storage, transportation, and preparation of food, all of which require intensive investigtaion.

Food has always been and still remains man's most important concern, and its study should be of crucial importance to anthropologists since it affects all mankind and all man's relationships and activities, but this has rarely been undertaken by them except as a secondary or peripheral study. Newspaper and popular magazine articles about food have appeared regularly, while, buried here and there in odd journals, scholarly studies have been published. The plethora of cookbooks of every description now flooding the market attests to the concern man is experiencing in connection with his eating habits and his ability to obtain food. The 1970's are highlighting the concern felt by some anthropologists in the 1950's, therefore no aspect of the subject of food can be overlooked. Because his food is thereby affected, the changes in weather patterns, the changes in economic conditions, the changes in eating habits all bear heavily on man's very existence.

Gastronomy, a volume in the World Anthropology series, is presented in the hope of encouraging scholarly studies of food habits, not only by anthropologists, who must take the lead, but by environmentalists, economists, missionaries, psychologists, sociologist, folklorists, nutritionists, medical scientist, linguists, geographers, ethnologists, and all others who are engaged in scientific field studies of any kind.

Philadelphia, Pennsylvania
January 1976

MARGARET L. ARNOTT

Table of Contents

SECTION ONE

Ethnobotanic Change

Effects of Environmental and Cultural Changes on Prehistoric Fauna Assemblages

S. BÖKÖNYI

The animal bone sample of a prehistoric or early historic settlement reflects the way the fauna lived in and around the settlement. The question is how true is that reflection? The answer to this question is different from the qualitative and quantitative points of view. From the former view, if the remains of a species are found in the bone sample of a settlement it means that that particular species was kept or hunted by the inhabitants. But, if the remains are not found there it does not necessarily mean that the species did not live there; it only means that it was not eaten or its bones were not used in any form by the human population. From the quantitative point of view, the bone sample — at least in prehistoric settlements — approximately reflects the true ratios of domestic animals. In prehistoric times man ate the meat of all his domesticated species; therefore, all of his domesticated animals came to this end, quite independent of their exploitation. Later, when man did not consume the meat of certain species, he either threw their carcasses into the garbage pits of the settlement (as was the case with small animals) or buried them (if they were larger ones) outside the settlement. The situation is not quite the same with the wild animals. The quantitative composition of the wild bone sample does not reflect the relative numbers of wild species which lived around the settlements. The main difference is that in the bone sample one can find the bones of only those species which were hunted or fished by man. One can state, however, that if the remains of a wild species are found at a site, the well-determined environmental conditions of that particular species must have existed somewhere around that site. As for the ratios of the wild species in the bone sample, they depended not only on the frequency in the wild fauna but also on food preferences, local domestication, etc.

The analysis of animal bone samples of prehistoric and early historic settlements can give an immense amount of information to the archaeologist. It can reveal a lot about the nature of the settlement: whether it was permanently occupied or only at certain seasons of the year; whether it was an agricultural village, refuge, nomadic camp, or town; the way of life of its inhabitants; the origin and wandering route of a culture; its relations to other cultures; the geographical environment; the climate and its changes, etc.

All these problems are far more complicated than one would think, and their complete clarification needs long-range investigation. This investigation has to be many-sided and carried out by teams of archaeologists, zoologists, botanists, climatologists, geologists, geographers, etc.

This paper attempts to discuss a modest part of the problem: the effects of environmental and climatic changes on prehistoric settlement faunas. The investigation is based on animal bone assemblages of prehistoric sites in the Carpathian Basin, the Balkan peninsula and the Near East (southwestern Asia). All bone samples were recently excavated and collected with modern recovery techniques and equipment. In the evaluation of this study material the zoological results were compared with those of archaeology, botanics, climatology, etc.

As for their effects on the fauna, environmental changes can be divided into two main types: (a) either a given culture moves (through migration) into a new environment or (b) the environment of a stationary culture undergoes changes.

When the people of a culture arrive in an environment different from their original one they will try to keep their original animal husbandry also under the changed circumstances. They will do so even if it is not as advantageous and profitable as it was before, and they will try to fill up their loss with more hunting and fishing. This means that while the species ratios in the domestic fauna will be the same as in the original territory of the culture the domestic ratio as a whole will decrease and the wild one increase. On the other hand, hunting will depend more on the local environmental conditions, man will hunt those species which are abundant in the new environment — onager and gazelle in steppes, aurochs and wild ass (*Asinus hydruntinus*) in forest steppes, red deer and wild swine in dense forests, waterfowl in swamps, etc. — and in the well-watered areas the importance of fishing will also generally grow. For this type of environmental change the early Neolithic Körös culture offers a very good example. The origin of this member of the Starčevo-

Körös-complex has not been completely solved yet, nevertheless, one thing is clear: it must have come from the southeast where it had had close contacts with the caprovine (sheep and goat) domestication center of southwestern Asia. Its animal husbandry was based on sheep and goats representing the overwhelming majority of domestic animals. Cattle were much rarer, pigs were even less numerous than cattle, and dogs were completely unimportant. This caprovines-based domestic fauna must have developed somewhere in southwestern Asia, reached the Greek mainland (Boessneck 1962; Higgs 1962) and Crete (Jarman and Jarman 1968), and was possibly completed there with cattle in the millennium B.C. From Greece it found its way through the Balkans as far to the north as the Carpathian Basin (Bökönyi 1968, 1969, 1971).

Table 1. Ratios of animal groups and species in the bone samples of earliest Neolithic settlements of the Balkans and the Carpathian Basin (in percent)

	Wild animals	Domestic animals	DOMESTIC ANIMALS Cattle	Sheep/Goat	Pig	Dog
Argissa Magula (Greece) (Boessneck 1962)	0.92	99.08	4.76	84.15	9.99	0.18
Nea Nikomedeia (Greece) (Higgs 1962)	7.00	93.00	14.55	70.45	14.77	0.23
Knossos (Crete, Greece) (Jarman and Jarman 1968)	0.05	99.95	14.77	66.48	17.44	0.05
Anzabegovo (south Yugo-slavia) (Bökönyi in print)	4.25	95.75	9.38	76.19	8.86	1.32
Ludas-Budzak (Yugo-slavia (Bökönyi 1969)	20.92	79.08	13.13	86.13	0.37	0.37
Maroslele-Pana (Hungary) (Bökönyi 1963, 1969)	32.96	67.04	26.52	70.16	1.66	1.66
Gyálaret (Hungary) (Bökönyi 1969)	26.95	73.05	30.37	63.56	4.67	1.40
Röszke-Ludvár (Hungary) (Bökönyi 1969)	59.18	40.82	17.96	76.41	1.64	3.99
Deszk-Olajkut (Hungary) (Bökönyi 1969)	19.84	80.16	29.39	70.21	0.20	0.20
Tiszajenö-Szárazérpart (Hungary)	8.78	91.22	26.44	72.84	0.48	0.24

One cannot be surprised that a domestic fauna based on the caprovines (see Table 1) could get a footing in Greece. There the environmental conditions were so similar to those of southwestern Asia that sheep and goats bred very well. Also, that fact shows the success of this animal hunsbandry there so that man did not need to hunt and fish much (the wild ratio is always very low in the bone samples of early Neolithic sites in Greece).

The environment was quite similar to that of Greece also in the hot and dry lower Bregalnica Valley in Yugoslavian Macedonia. And the result: in the Starčevo settlement of Anzabegovo sheep and goats were the far more common species in the domestic fauna, and the ratio of wild animals was only slightly higher than in Greece (see Table 1). The only difference in comparison to the early Neolithic domestic fauna of Greece was that in the Yugoslav sites cattle were somewhat more frequent than pigs.

The situation was not the same in the Carpathian Basin. Here this typical domestic fauna of the dry environment got into quite wet surroundings, particularly in settlements located in the inundation areas of the Tisza River and its tributaries. Nevertheless, man insisted on keeping this "dry type" domestic fauna, and since it could not flourish under these circumstances he had to turn to hunting and fishing to a larger extent. In the domestic bone sample of Körös settlements 60–80 percent caprovine bones occur, the ratio of the wild animals is between 20 and 60 percent (see Table 1), and, as the thick shell layers prove, even gathering played an important role in securing animal protein.

Table 2. Ratios of animal groups and species in the bone samples of Baden culture settlements in Hungary (in percent)

	Wild animals	Domestic animals	DOMESTIC ANIMALS Cattle	Sheep/Goat	Pig	Horse	Dog
Budapest-Andor utca (Bökönyi 1959, 1969)	6.81	93.19	34.41	41.72	22.58	—	—
Andocs-Nagytoldipuszta	5.11	94.89	36.47	43.44	14.67	0.14	5.38
Tiszasöllös-Csákányszeg	9.96	90.04	15.42	74.11	8.30	—	2.17

A similar phenomenon can be observed in the case of the Baden culture. This culture of southern origin also introduced an animal husbandry (see Table 2) into the Carpathian Basin and stuck to it in spite of the unfavorable environmental conditions. Unfortunately, there is little known about the original fauna of this culture due to a lack of identified animal bone samples. Nevertheless, it is quite clear that such an animal husbandry was alien and therefore could not develop in the Carpathian Basin. Of course, the new environment exerted its effects on the animal husbandry, though only after a certain time. Domestic animals which were suited to the new conditions were developed in a primitive type of animal husbandry by keeping species which preferred the new environment. Since the stimulus to this came from the domestic fauna, one can say, in other words, that the latter adapted itself to the new environment.

In this respect the animal bone sample of Obre II in Bosnia, Yugoslavia gives a good example. In the site a Yugoslav-American team carried out large-scale excavation, that yielded rich archaeological material containing about 28,000 identifiable animal remains. In the whole site only one single culture was represented, the middle and late Neolithic Butmir culture; however, its development in the site could be divided into three phases. This culture had strong southeastern roots (e.g. one of its main components was the local form of Starčevo culture) which means that it took a dry climate domestic fauna into a wet, heavily forested, well-watered valley system of central Bosnia. Although in this fauna cattle were already the leading species due to the influence of local conditions on the precursors of the culture (in the fauna of Obre I also cattle appeared rather more often than the caprovines), sheep and goats were quite common, taking second place. This domestic fauna adapted itself to the wet environment in the following way.

At the beginning of its life in the site (phase I of Obre II) caprovines were in the second place but outnumbered pigs by almost 100 percent. In phase II the situation thoroughly changed as pigs, that typical species of the wet environment, with a very good food basis in the deciduous forests, surpassed caprovines and in phase III outnumbered them by almost 50 percent. In this last phase of the settlement the frequency of sheep/goat was half of the initial figure. The ratios of cattle and dog remained unchanged during the whole life of the settlement, and that of the wild animals increased a little, probably due to a slight local climatic change proved by the increase among the wild fauna of dense forest, even swampy forest, species (see Table 3).

Table 3. Ratios of the most important species in the bone sample of Obre II

	Phase I	Phase II	Phase III
Cattle	71.74	67.91	65.97
Sheep/Goat	11.15	7.57	5.76
Pig	5.39	12.45	12.60
Dog	0.06	0.60	1.13
Aurochs	4.37	3.35	3.14
Red deer	4.25	3.79	6.90
Roe deer	0.82	1.27	1.07
Wild swine	1.97	2.45	2.54
Other wild animals	0.25	0.63	0.89
Domestic animals	88.34	88.53	85.46
Wild animals	11.66	11.47	14.54

The other type of environmental change affecting the settlement fauna is when the climate changes markedly and exerts its influence on the fauna of a given settlement. Climatic changes affect the wild fauna first of all, either directly or through changes in the geographical environment. Each wild animal species has its well-determined habitat in which it has the best chance to live and breed. The habitat is determined through its soil flora/food/fauna/food — competing species/ and climate. The wild species are able to tolerate smaller changes in their habitat; it is particularly true for the carnivores, since their food basis, meat, remains practically unchanged. Nevertheless, if the changes reach a certain degree they will give up their original habitat and withdraw from it, if they can.

The domesticated animals cannot do the same. Since they are bound to man they cannot move out of an unfavorable environment. Fortunately, since the appearance of the domestic animals, our area has not seen such drastic climatic and environmental changes as, for example, those of the Pleistocene (though they certainly occurred in some parts of Central Asia and North Africa) and therefore the domestic animals did not face the danger of extinction. Nevertheless, environmental changes affected the domestic fauna in a small degree. On the one hand the environmental change forced man to reorganize his animal husbandry in favor of species which bred better under the new conditions (as one could see at the point where a culture arrived in a new environment). The other type of change was that the domestic species tried to adapt themselves to the new environment. According to palynological and even archaeological data, a large-scale climatic change took place in Europe during the Bronze Age and reached its climax at the end of the period. Its essence was that the warm and dry climate of the Neolithic became gradually more wet and cold. In the animal bone sample the wild fauna reflect this change very well: the ratio of the elements of the dry environment decreased and that of the dense forest and swamps increased. At the climax of the deterioration of the climate even subarctic species occurred in central Europe, e.g. the wolverine in Remete Cave, near Budapest, Hungary (Bökönyi 1959).

The animal bone sample of the 1948 excavation of Tószeg, Hungary, a site occupied through almost all of the Bronze Age demonstrates

Table 4. Changes in the ratios of dry climate and wet climate animals in the successive phases of Tószeg (Hungary) during the Bronze Age

Phase	Domestic animals of the:		Wild animals of the:	
	dry climate	wet climate	dry climate	wet climate
C	86.3%	13.7%	10.5%	89.5%
B	93.4%	6.6%	17.6%	82.4%
A	92.4%	7.6%	35.7%	64.3%

the effects of this climatic change on the wild fauna very well (see Table 4).

As for the domestic fauna the most important change effected by this deterioration of the climate was the decrease in the caprovine ratio (Bökönyi 1968, 1971), sometimes connected with a small-scale decline of cattle, e.g. in Greece (Boessneck 1962) and the increase in the pig ratio (which later was supported by the large-scale domestication of wild pigs abundant in the swampy forests around the sites). As regards the changes within the species as a result of environmental changes, the case of Bronze Age horses is the best example. From the center of the first horse domestication in the Ukraine (Bibikova 1967) masses of domestic horses got to the different parts of eastern and central Europe at the beginning, or at least in the first half, of the Bronze Age. They were narrow-hoofed steppe horses. When the wet climate produced swampy soils in these areas, they underwent an adaptation, and their hooves became wide and flat. (In other words the steppe form transformed into a forest form.) In this way they could move more easily on the soft soil. This process was not limited to Europe, but spread over also to the southwestern part of Siberia (Zalkin, personal communication).

The cultural changes affect the domestic fauna much more than the wild fauna. It will be quite clear if one considers that the different cultures generally hunted the same wild fauna (the only exception being when, during the abundance of wild game, they hunted large animals that supplied them with more meat, or when, in the interests of domestication, they killed adults of domesticable species first, this being the only way they could capture and domesticate their young). It was more common that the importance of hunting changed in the different cultures. On the other hand, since the different cultures represented different ethnic groups with different animal-keeping traditions, on different economic levels, coming from different ecological areas, their animal husbandries were quite different from each other. (And all these are reflected by the bone sample of their domestic fauna in their settlements too.) How could one explain, after all, the differences in the domestic fauna of different contemporaneous cultures in the same environment? And how could one explain that cultures following each other in the same environment had different domestic fauna?

In this respect, the Hungarian Neolithic offers a good example. In the Middle Neolithic, the animal husbandry of the Zseliz group of the Linear Pottery and that of the Tisza culture are well known (Bökönyi 1959, 1968, 1971). And although the two cultures lived in practically the same environment, their domestic fauna were quite different. In both of them, cattle was the most common species; in the Zseliz group caprovines were in second place, while in the Tisza culture pigs were in second place (see Table 5). There was a difference also in the importance of the hunting; however, the ratios of the main wild species

Table 5. Ratios of animal groups and species in the Zseliz group and the Tisza culture (in percent)

	Wild animals	Domestic animals	DOMESTIC ANIMALS Cattle	Sheep/Goat	Pig	Dog
Györ-Pápai vám (Zseliz group of Linear Pottery (Bökönyi 1959, 1971)	10.36	89.64	73.49	14.77	11.21	0.53
Neszmély-Tekerespuszta (the same) (Bökönyi 1968)	13.33	86.67	56.06	29.22	14.72	—
Szegvár-Tüzköves (Tisza culture) (Bökönyi 1959, 1971)	43.60	56.40	68.47	6.48	18.14	6.91
Lebó (the same) (Bökönyi 1959)	36.90	63.10	91.24	2.28	3.15	3.33

were similar in the two cultures. In the Zseliz group, hunting was rather unimportant (with about 10 percent wild ratio in the bone sample), on the other hand it played an essential role in the economy of the Tisza culture (in whose bone samples the wild ratio nearly reached the domestic one). In the Late Neolithic of Hungary, through the high wild ratio, the two main cultures of the period can be distinguished. While the animal husbandries of the two cultures are quite similar with cattle as the leading species, followed by pig, caprovines, and dog (in this order) in the Herpály culture of east Hungary, hunting connected with

Table 6. Ratios of animal groups and species in the bone samples of Herpály and Lengyel culture settlements in Hungary (in percent)

	Wild animals	Domestic animals	DOMESTIC ANIMALS Cattle	Sheep/Goat	Pig	Dog
Berettyószentmárton (Herpály culture) (Bökönyi 1959, 1971)	77.38	22.62	62.72	6.88	28.80	1.60
Berettyóujfalu-Herpály (the same) (Bökönyi 1959)	76.06	23.94	54.26	16.28	24.81	4.65
Polgár-Csöszhalom (the same)	69.58	30.42	68.63	6.44	21.09	3.84
Zengövárkony (Lengyel culture) (Bökönyi 1959, 1971)	39.48	60.52	85.29	1.04	11.70	1.97
Aszód-Papi földek (the same) (Bökönyi 1971)	47.51	52.49	77.92	2.83	15.45	3.80

large-scale cattle domestication was the main economic activity, much more important than animal-keeping; in the Lengyel culture of west Hungary, the latter clearly surpassed hunting (see Table 6). At the same time the hunting of the Lengyel culture was based on aurochs, in that in the Lengyel culture aurochs and red deer were of about the same frequency.

As mentioned in the introduction, the aim of the present paper was to raise the question of the effects of environmental and cultural changes on prehistoric settlement fauna, i.e. animal husbandry and hunting. As the picture outlined above shows, some of these effects and their interactions can already be clearly seen. Nevertheless, these processes are not simple nor free from side effects that can disturb and complicate them. It is needless to enumerate all of them here, but one has to mention local domestication, inner evolution of the cultures, influence of neighboring cultures, increase of density of the human population, small-scale local geographical differences, and climatic changes, etc. as factors which can and must be taken into consideration. And one needs that close cooperation between archaeologists and natural scientists mentioned at the beginning and — last, but not least — the collection of data through the study of carefully recovered large animal bone samples from prehistoric sites excavated by modern techniques.

REFERENCES

BIBIKOVA, V. I.

1967 Studies of ancient domestic horses in East Europe (in Russian with English summary). *Bull. Moscow. Ispit. Prirod. Otd. Biol.* 72: 106–118.

BOESSNECK, J.

1962 "Die Tierreste aus der Argissa Magula vom präkeramischen Neolithikum bis zur mittleren Bronzezeit," in *Die deutschen Ausgrabungen auf der Argissa Magula in Thessalien.* Edited by V. Milojcic, J. Boessneck, and M. Hopf, 27–99. Bonn: Habelt.

BÖKÖNYI, S.

1959 Die frühalluviale Wirbeltierfauna Ungarns. *Acta Arch. Hung.* 11: 39–102.

1963 The vertebrate fauna of the sites of the Lengyel culture (in Hungarian with German summary). *Jan.Pann. Muz. Evk.* 73–101.

1968 The historical development of animal husbandry in Central and Eastern Europe (in Hungarian with German and Russian summary). *Agrártört. Szle.* 10:278–342.

1969 "Archaeological problems and methods of recognizing animal domestication," in *The domestication and exploitation of plants and animals*. Edited by P. J. Ucko and G. W. Dimbleby, 219–229. London: Duckworth.

1971 The development and history of domestic animals in Hungary. *Amer. Anthrop.* 73:640–674.

ERDÉLYI, I.

1969 Steppe — Klima — Völkerwanderung. *Móra F. Muz. Évk. Szeged* 139–145.

HIGGS, E. S.

1962 The fauna (of the early neolithic site at Nea Nikomedeia). *Proc. of the Prehist. Soc.* 28:271–274.

JARMAN, M. R., H. N. JARMAN

1968 The fauna and economy of early neolithic Knossos. *Ann. of the British School of Archaeology at Athens.* 63:241–264.

The Archaeobotanical and Palynological Evidence for the Early Origin of Agriculture in South and Southeast Asia

VISHNU-MITTRE

The Far East (south and southeastern Asia) has, in recent years, risen in prominence as a center for early domestication and cultivation of plants dated by radiocarbon as having existed prior to 5000 B.C. (Chang 1970; Solheim 1971; Gorman 1969; Singh 1971). This claim of the Far East as a center, largely derived from archaeobotanical and pollen analysis investigations supported by the C^{14} assay, is welcome in view of the fact that de Candolle (1959) and Vavilov (1950) had long ago suggested that south or southeastern Asia was probably a center for the origin of rice and root crops. From a synthesis of all sources of available information in the tradition of de Candolle, and by elaborating five comprehensive criteria for the recognition of centers and noncenters of origin of cultivated plants, Harlan (1971) finds that agriculture may have originated in discrete centers or evolved over vast areas without a definite center. Harlan further holds that it is imperative that either wild progenitors of a cultivated plant, or plants, or else archaeobotanical records must be found to establish the center, in the event that the progenitors no longer exist today. The distribution areas of the progenitors might have changed because of past climatic and floristic changes.

The archaeobotanical evidence largely depends upon careful recognition of the remains of wild species or cultivars. More often the materials are fragmentary, in the form of impressions or carbonized remains, and the absence of essential characteristics usually stands in the way of their specific identification. No morphological criteria have yet been discovered to distinguish among the fragmentary, or ill-preserved but complete, spikelets or kernels of rice both in the living and the subfossil state of the various wild and cultivated species of *Oryza*. Statistical criteria have, however, been discovered, based upon modern materials from various parts of south and southeastern Asia. The $l/b \times t$ index (l, length; b, breadth; t, thickness of kernels and spikelets) seems to distinguish the various species of *Oryza* distributed in south and southeastern Asia (Vishnu-Mittre 1974b). The indexes for various species are given below:

O. perennis	2.20
O. officinalis	2.36
O. rufipogon	2.64
O. sativa var. *spontanea*	1.77
O. sativa var. *indica*	1.71
O. sativa var. *japonica*	1.70

How far these indexes can be reliably applied to archaeobotanical materials remains to be demonstrated, for these materials have shrunk in dimensions. However, the indexes of carbonized materials have permitted the recognition of some Oryza species in Neolithic and other contexts in India (Vishnu-Mittre 1974b).

The seeds of *Triticum sphaerococcum*, whose origin was believed (de Candolle 1959; Vavilov 1950) to have been located in the extreme western part (India, Pakistan, and Afghanistan) of south Asia, are indeed much different in morphology and size from those of the other species of *Triticum*.

The other criterion is the large size of the remains of cultivated plants, viz., fruits, seeds or pollen grains, which distinguishes them from those of the wild ones. How far this "gigantism" should be stretched in its application for distinction between the wild and the cultivated plants should be approached carefully, for "gigantism" may not always suggest the well-recognized concept. It can be illustrated through the case of pollen grains. The pollen of cultivated millets is much smaller than the average-sized pollen of a cereal. A large number of wild grasses have pollen as large as the average-sized cereal pollen or even the largest size attained by them (Vishnu-Mittre 1971). Such a comparison could well be applied to seeds and fruits of wild species. Gigantism thus should not be taken blindly to suggest domestication or cultivation.

Pollen evidence, apart from indicating the large size of cereal pollen, should be accompanied by shifts in plant populations or communities in the pollen diagrams as a registration of the farmers' activities, namely, their clearance of a vegetated area, farming, and abandonment of it — typical characteristics of early nomadic tribes of the Neolithic time (Iversen 1941).

The importance of the archaeological provenance in regard to the event of earliest domestication has its own bearing upon the problem. Radiocarbon investigations have made possible the absolute dating of the event. How far the absolutely dated event of the earliest domestication concerns the Neolithic period, as recognized apart from other criteria on the evidence of the commencement of agriculture, is often not taken seriously.

This paper reviews critically the recent evidence from south and southeastern Asia of the earliest domestication, from biological and cultural viewpoints, and attempts to determine to what extent recent research has successfully made a case for this part of the world as a center of the origin of early agriculture.

EVIDENCES FROM THE INDIAN SUBCONTINENT

The Neolithic period in the Indian subcontinent did not commence until about 2700 B.C. though it began a few centuries earlier in neighboring Afghanistan. A strange contemporaneity of the Neolithic with the highly advanced Harappan culture should be noted here. In the context of the history of cultivated cereals, as known from western Asia, the time bracket 3000 B.C. to 2500 B.C. has witnessed the diffusion of hexaploid wheat, *T. aestivum*, from the Fertile Crescent to the lands outside it. Was shot wheat, *T. sphaerococcum*, evolved by the highly advanced Harappans living in the Indus Valley in about 2300 B.C. or by the Neolithic peoples at Chirand, Bihar (Vishnu-Mittre 1974a, 1974b)? Or was it a natural evolution as a result of the adaptation of *T. aestivum* to the environment of drought then prevailing there? An important fact that must be pointed out here is that the kernels of carbonized wheat are variable, some approaching shot wheat and the others *T. compactum*. Has this variability anything to do with the origin of shot wheat from *T. aestivum* or *T. compactum*? The evidence does not go beyond suggesting that this shot wheat was cultivated by the Harappans and the Neolithic peoples in northwestern and northern India.

The situation regarding rice is more or less the same. The great variety of *Oryza* spp. existing in eastern India is rarely accompanied by finds of Neolithic rice which are known so far from Kuchai in Orissa and Singhbhum and Chirand in Bihar (Vishnu-Mittre 1968, 1974b).

Oryza perennis, recognizable at the Neolithic site Kuchai, is believed to date from about 1500 B.C. The Chirand rice dating from about 3000 B.C. (several C^{14} dates are erratic) includes kernels of *Oryza sativa* var. *spontanea (O perennis). O. sativa* is the only species identified at Singhbhum. Can we look upon these evidences of wild rice in a Neolithic context as indicating domestication of rice? Or should we safely conclude that wild rice grew as a weed in the fields cultivated by Neolithic peoples in eastern India? It has not been possible to determine whether the three impressions of rice spikelets from Lothal (Harappan context) in Gujarat belong to wild or cultivated species (Vishnu-Mittre 1968, 1974b).

It is unnecessary to discuss the Neolithic and Chalcolithic records of *Sorghum*, *Pennisetum*, and *Eleusine* dating from 2000 B.C. to 1500 B.C. (Vishnu-Mittre 1968, 1974b) and their possible domestication in India in view of the strong cytogenetical and phytogeographical evidences for their origin in Africa. These were very likely diffused here from Africa, although their archaeobotanical records have not yet been found there.

The Indian palynological evidence deserves special mention. That it is not possible to distinguish cereal pollen from that of wild grass pollen in south and southeastern Asia, and that the Neolithic in India is not older than 2700–3000 B.C., a period of time corresponding with the sub-Boreal climatic period, have already been stated elsewhere in the paper.

In view of the above, the earliest landnam phase recognized in the Haigam pollen diagram from the Kashmir valley cannot be older than 2300 B.C. (C^{14} dating of the Neolithic site of Burzahom in the valley: Vishnu-Mittre and Sharma 1966; Vishnu-Mittre 1968; 1974b), though the corresponding vegetational pattern seems to compare rather strangely with that of Boreal times in the European pollen diagrams. That this comparison may be too farfetched is proven by the fact that the alleged Boreal phase in the Kashmir pollen diagram is preceded by a warm temperate declining broad-leaved forest of ash, alder, and oak woods rather than by the late glacial arctic/subarctic vegetation as observed in the European pollen diagrams. However, the first landnam phase provisionally dated as being in the Neolithic has yet to be absolutely dated.

The other pollen evidence comes from Rajasthan (Singh 1971). Here the event of the first appearance of the alleged cereal pollen appears at a level dated by C^{14} at 6000 B.C. There is no corresponding shift in pollen curves suggesting phases of clearance, farming, and abandonment of the area. A small hump in the curve of microscopic remains of charcoals is interpreted as a strong evidence suggesting burning together with cultivation (cereal pollen). The palynological evidence here is not beyond doubt; Singh is aware of the overlap in size of cereal and wild grass pollen; there is no shift in pollen curves suggesting a landnam phase; the microscopic remains of charcoals suggest nothing more than burning and were probably derived from long distance transport; fire was not unknown to the Mesolithic peoples who lived around 4000 B.C. in Rajasthan; and the Neolithic in Rajasthan is dated 2800 B.C. by radiocarbon. This alleged pollen evidence of early agriculture in Rajasthan dated to 6000 B.C. would have us believe that the early Mesolithic or perhaps the dwindling late Palaeolithic were practicing agriculture in Rajasthan, and this can by no means be acceptable to the archaeologists and anthropologists.

There is still more pollen evidence worthy of mention here. Apart from the beginning of the alleged cereal pollen curve, all the palynological criteria of a landnam phase can be made out in the lower part of the pollen diagram from Kakathope, Ootacamund, Madras, dated by C^{14} at 23000 B.P. (Vishnu-Mittre and Gupta 1971). By no stretch of the imagination or reasoning can we justify this as evidence of the earliest farming known in the world.

THE SINO-JAPANESE EVIDENCE

Preserved as grains and rice husks in baked clay, the cereals identified tentatively in Neolithic contexts in China include *Setaria indica* var. *germanica* and *Panicum miliacium* from the Yang Shao sites in Shenshi and southern Shansi, and rice, *Oryzo sativa*, from Ya Shao Tsun in Honan and from Liu Tzu Chen in Shansi (Watson 1969: 398). The Neolithic context of Honan evidence is indeed doubtful (Watson 1969).

Rice known from the eastern part of the Yangtze basin is believed to date from possibly a little before the Shang Bronze Age, around 1650 B.C. (Yuch-Ch'ien 1957; Chim-chu and Chiang 1955; cf. Watson 1969). *Oryza sativa* spp. *spontanea*, from baked clay discovered at Chaiang Han Plain, Hupei, is dated in the late Neolithic period. Both wheat and *Sorghum vulgare* are also known from the Neolithic of China. The latter is a highly advanced form; the specific nature of the former is not known.

In the absence of absolute dates or even developed relative chronology of the Neolithic period in China, it is certainly not possible to appreciate the significance of these discoveries. The primitive strain of rice from Hupei is certainly of interest and its late Neolithic context deserves to be absolutely dated. Further, it would be of interest to know the criteria employed to identify the specimens to subspecies before anything meaningful is made of this discovery. One could repeat the conclusion arrived at on the Indian evidence, namely that this wild strain grew along with the cultivar as a weed.

Pollen analyses of lake Jihuuch Tan in Taiwan by Tsukada (1966, 1967) have brought to light charred woody fragments at the lake bottom and a gradual but decisive growth of a secondary forest dated 12,000 B.P. A similar phase is noted around 4200 B.P., corresponding with the farming activity of the Lungshanoid peoples. Whereas the latter phase may be tenable, the former could be due to climatic change (a worldwide change in the temperate regions recognized at 12,000 B.P.). There is, however, no evidence of farming except human interference with forest vegetation. Whether it resulted from natural fires or those caused by the late Palaeolithic peoples is a question which should be looked into.

In Japan the pottery-using Jomon culture subsisted for some six millennia (radiocarbon evidence: Watson 1969: 397). We have absolutely no idea about their plant economy. As a first cereal, rice is known to have arrived in Japan in the second century B.C. Whether it was a cultivar or a wild strain of rice remains to be determined systematically. A recent report of the discovery of subfossil pollen of *Oryza* dated to about 3200 B.C. in the Chikaoka remains in Kanazawa city, central Japan (Fugi 1971) is of interest, though it remains to be established if the *Oryza* pollen really belongs to the cultivated or to a wild species. Personal discussions with Dr. Fugi at Novosibirsk in the Soviet Union during the Third International Palynological Conference revealed that Dr. Fugi was not certain if the subfossil *Oryza* pollen belonged to a cultivated or wild species.

I have, however, no personal experience in examining either the Chinese or Japanese materials; my comments are largely based upon my experience with the pollen of cereal and wild grasses and the difficulties encountered in specific determination of archaeobotanical remains, more particularly of rice.

The material from the Philippines, received through the kind courtesy of Professor W. G. Solheim of Hawaii, consists of fruits of some wild shrubs or trees and are as yet unidentified.

THE THAILAND EVIDENCE

My examination of the Non Nok Tha impressions on potsherds dated to 3500 B.C. and referred to as *Oryza sativa* by Solheim (1971 and personal communication) has revealed that the imprints of rice are too fragmentary to permit any specific determination. They could as well belong to any cultivated or wild species of *Oryza*. Gorman's recent discovery of "quantities of rice" dated to about 5000 B.C. in a cave in Thailand near the Burmese border (personal communication) would be worth examining. The material, being carbonized, is sure to permit detailed biological and statistical study towards specific determination.

The other tantalizing discovery is from the Spirit Cave in the north of the provincial center of Mae Hougson in extreme northwestern Thailand (Gorman 1969). It is dated to 11,500 years. The botanical identifications are tentative and to the generic level only. The plant remains include nuts of *Madhuca, Canarium, Terminalia, Aleurites* (candle nut), and betel nuts, pepper, bottle gourd, *Phaseolus, Vicia*, peas, cucumber, almond, and *Trapa*. The array of material is indeed interesting and deserves a fuller botanical investigation before any meaningful significance can be obtained. Their large size led the excavator to suggest a case of domestication. Most tentatively identified genera have species occurring in the forests today. A more cautious and plausible explanation could have been inferred from the nature and composition of the forest. The plant remains indeed reveal an assemblage of tropical and temperate (or subtropical) species some of which would be ecological misfits in a reconstruction of a plant community from tropical genera. It is nonetheless unsafe to reconstruct a plant community without the exact specific identification and individual frequencies of its members. A rough estimate can however be made, as follows:

The forests probably consisted of trees of *Madhuca, Canarium, Terminalia*, and *Aleurites* among which betel nut and *Piper* also flourished. Species of *Phaseolus* and *Vicia* occurred in the open areas fringing the forests, whereas *Trapa* occurred in the ponds in the vicinity. It is not possible to fit into this assemblage the other tentatively identified remains such as cucumber, almond, and bottlegourd.

The early Thais living at that time amidst this forest environment must have been at the gatherer-hunter stage, as the time interval 10,000 to 15,000 years ago would also indicate. There is no evidence of domestication or cultivation as the excavator would have us believe.

DISCUSSION

A critical examination of the archaeobotanical and pollen records in south and southeastern Asia reveals that definite evidence exists of highly evolved cultivars dating to about 3000 B.C. The records predating this are not carefully documented. The evidence of shifting cultivation from the pollen record is not based upon sufficient and convincing data, and certain other local factors involved are overlooked. The cerealia pollen or cerealia-type pollen alone cannot be used to infer former cultivation in view of the overlap of its characteristics with those of the large-sized pollen of wild grasses, unless accompanied by the pollen of weeds associated with crops and by shifts in pollen curves in a well-determined Neolithic context. The earliest evidence from southeastern Asia suggests a gatherer-hunter stage rather than domestication. The earliest evidences in India, dating from 6000 B.C. and based upon pollen-analytical records, cannot be upheld owing to difficulties in identifying cereal pollen and lack of shifts in pollen curves.

Continued efforts and a more cautious approach may bring out evidences of domestication in south and southeastern Asia — a recognized center for the origin of rice and root crops.

REFERENCES

CHANG, KWANG-CHIH

1970 The beginnings of agriculture in the Far East. *Antiquity* 44:175–185.

CHIM-CHU, HSIEH, CHU CHIANG

1955 Examination of the Neolithic site at Hsien Li Tun in Wu Hsi Kiangsu. *Wen Su* 8:48–59.

DE CANDOLLE, A.

1959 *Origin of cultivated plants* (second edition). New York: Haffner.

FUGI, N.

1971 "Principle for palynological research on the origin of rice agriculture and its practical application in Japanese Islands," in *Proceedings of the Third Palynological Conference in Novosibirsk, USSR.*

GORMAN, CHESTER, F.

1969 Hoabinhian: a pebble tool complex with early plant associations in Southeast Asia. *Science* 163:671–673.

HARLAN, J. R.

1971 Agricultural origins: centres and noncentres. *Sciences* 174:468–474.

IVERSEN, J.

1941 Land occupation phase in Denmark's Stone Age. *Danmarks Geologiske Undersøgelse* 2:1–66.

JAN-CHANG, YIN, LI CHUNGI

1960 Preliminary report on the second season of excavations on the site of San Li Tun, Hsin I Hsien, Kiangsu. *K'ao Ku* 7:20–22.

SINGH, G.

1971 The Indus Valley culture seen in the context of postglacial climatic and biological studies in north-west India. *Archaeological and Physical Anthropology in Oceania* 6:177–180.

SOLHEIM, WILHELM, G.

1971 The "new look" of Southeast Asian archaeology. *Fifth Conference on Asian History,* IAHA, Manila.

TSUKADA, M.

1966 Late Pleistocene vegetation and climate in Taiwan (Formosa). *Proceedings of the National Academy of Sciences* 55:543–548.

1967 Vegetation in subtropical Formosa during the Holocene and Pleistocene glaciations. *Palaeogeography, Palaeoclimatology, Palaeoecology* 3:49–64.

VAVILOV, N. I.

1950 The origin, variation, immunity and breeding of cultivated plants. *Chronica Botanica* 13:1–366.

VISHNU-MITTRE

1968 Protohistoric records of agriculture in India. *Transactions of the Bose Res Instituto* 31:87–106.

1971 "Cereal vs. noncereal grass pollen and the inference of past agriculture," in *Proceedings of the Third International Palynological Conference in Novosibirsk, USSR.*

1974a Neolithic plant economy at Chirand, Bihar. *Palaeobotanist* 21.

1974b "Palaeobotanical evidence in India," in *Evolutionary studies in world crops: diversity and change in the Indian subcontinent.* Edited by Sir Joseph Hutchinson. Cambridge: Cambridge University Press.

VISHNU-MITTRE, B. D. SHARMA

1966 Studies of postglacial vegetational history from the Kashmir Valley. I. Haigam Lake. *Palaeobotanist* 15:185.

VISHNU-MITTRE, H. P. GUPTA

1971 The origin of Shola Forest in the Nilgiris, South India. *Palaeobotanist* 19:110–114.

WATSON, WILLIAM

1969 "Early cereal cultivation in China," in *Domestication and exploitation of plants and animals.* Edited by Peter J. Ucko and G. W. Dimbleby. London.

YING, TING

1959 Examination of rice husk found in red baked earth of the Neolithic period in the Chaiang Han Plain. *K'ao Ku hsueh pao* 4:31–34.

YUCH-CH'IEN, HU

1957 Reconnaissance of Neolithic sites in Anhui. *K'ao Ku hsueh pao* 1:21–30.

Pre-Columbian Maize in the Old World: An Examination of Portuguese Sources

M. D. W. JEFFREYS

Various accounts are available which provide information on the crops observed by the Portuguese and others on their early exploring voyages to Africa and to Asia. Among these crops is a cereal mentioned under various names such as *milho de Guynee*, *milho zaburro*, *milho maçaroca*, *milho marroco*, *milho*. A knowledge of the differences between maize and sorghum tolerance in high rainfall regions, maturation times, and size of grain allows a ready identification of the grain in numerous and important references. Lists of local cereals and various native names provide corroborative evidence.

It appears that maize was introduced into Portugal in pre-Columbian days not only from Morocco but also from Guinea. An examination of numerous references to a grain under various names showed a consistent equivalence to maize, a point overlooked, for instance, by Sauvageot (1961: 135) when he held that "the presence of maize in Africa must be rejected."

Maize is an American plant without any feral varieties, a point recorded by Moll (1747: 663) when he wrote of New England "No INDIAN corn grows wild now...." This plant is incapable of self-propagation. Consequently wherever found its presence there is due to the "green-fingers of man." Mangelsdorf and Reeves (1939: 8), after discussing the wide range of maize

I am indebted for help in translation from the French to Mrs L. Lambert, Dept. of Psychiatry, General Hospital, Johannesburg, and to Miss E. Verdier, Vice-Principal of the Girls' High School, Pretoria.

For help in translations from the Portuguese I am indebted to Mrs Hatenbach, Librarian to the Ernest Oppenheimer Portuguese Dept., University of the Witwatersrand, Johannesburg, and to Dr A. T. Quintanilha, University of the Witwatersrand, Johannesburg.

varieties, are satisfied that maize is a single species of American origin. They wrote:

> In spite of this overwhelming diversity of form, all the main types of corn known today were already being grown by the Indians when America was discovered and all of them are classified by botanists within a single species, *Zea mays*, L. ... All varieties of corn known today are readily hybridized with each other and the hybrids are, almost without exception, completely fertile. All evidence from botany, genetics or cytology has, until recently at least, pointed to a common origin of all varieties of corn which exist today.

MAIZE AND SORGHUM IN HIGH RAINFALL REGIONS

Rainfall Tolerance

Areas of 1,000 millimeters to over 2,000 millimeters of rainfall per year occur roughly between the Tropics of Cancer and of Capricorn, according to Semple (1911: 484). In all these areas maize flourishes. In Africa this region of high rainfall lies roughly within 10° north and south of the equator and is the rainforest region.

Sorghum is not found in the high rainfall areas, where high humidity is inimical to its fruition. Thus Irvine (1953: 104) wrote when "the seeds begin to form they are sometimes attacked by moulds and other fungous diseases, particularly when the humidity is high or the weather is rainy." Dalziel (1937: 545) lists five varieties of smuts that attack sorghum but lists none for maize. Irvine (1953: 102) wrote that sorghum "is indispensable to those countries... which are too dry for maize...." Bascom (1951: 46) wrote: "sorghum... and bulrush millet... are important north of the forest zones." Wild (1958: 176), writing of Rhodesia, remarked: "... [*Sorghum caffrorum* Beauv], known to Europeans as Kaffir corn... does well under most conditions except those of high rainfall." Snowden (1936: 21), a leading authority on sorghums, wrote: "West Tropical Africa is particularly rich in types [of sorghum], but they are found mainly in the hinterland away from the coastal area and often at 1,000 feet or more above sea-level." Burtt-Davy (1914: 42) wrote:

> Major Whitlock observes that guinea corn [*Sorghum vulgare* var.], an annual plant, is the staple cereal of the natives on the plains of Nigeria, at about 1,400 feet above sea-level, from Lake Chad almost to the foot of the watershed plateau between the Benue and the Cross Rivers. South of this plateau, however, where the country is clothed with forest, no more guinea corn is seen ...

Ittmann, of the Basle Mission at Buea in the rainforest belt of the former

German Cameroons, kindly sent me in 1939 the names for maize among the seven African tribes in his mission field but no names for sorghum, remarking: "Guinea corn is not found in the forest area." Madam Dugast, for many years at Ndiki among the Banen in this same forest belt, sent me the name *ambasak* for maize in this tribe and added that there was no name for sorghum because it did not grow there.

Maize, on the other hand, grows in the heavy rainfall areas and is the only cereal observed growing in this region. Of the cathedral rainforest belt of Nigeria, the Landers (1832: III, 183) wrote: "The Eboe people... cultivate yams, Indian corn, and plantains only." Bascom (1951: 45) said of the Yoruba: "Corn or maize [*igbado, agbado*] *Zea mays* is the only grain grown in Ife." Baumann and Westermann (1948: 29) describing the rainforests of western Africa, remarked: "The great humidity that the rain brings at all seasons creates a luxuriant vegetation. The permanent cultivation of the fields is possible there, and, in the first place, that of root crops; maize is the only grain that is well adapted to this climate."[1] (Original texts given in Notes.)

In a review of the food crops of Nigeria, Faulkner and Mackie (1933: 25, 134, 136) stated:

> In the south, yams and maize are the staple food crops; but the northern farmer lives chiefly on millet ['gero', *Pennisetum*] and guinea corn ['*dawa*', *Sorghum*] ... Maize is grown to some extent everywhere in Nigeria and the Gold Coast except in the extreme north; in the districts within 90 or 100 miles of the coast it is the only cereal crop ... Guinea corn [*Sorghum vulgare*] is the main food crop of the north. Although it can sometimes be grown successfully as far south as Ibadan the climate there is really a little too wet for guinea corn. Thus its cultivation in Nigeria is, in practice, confined almost entirely to the Northern Provinces.

Personal observation as an administrative officer in the British Colonial Service in southern Nigeria allows me to confirm these observations on maize and on sorghum. Among my special duties was the preparation of reports on the crops and agriculture of the local inhabitants. I can say that no sorghum grows in Nigeria in regions with a rainfall of 65 inches and over. The only cereal that grows in regions with a rainfall in excess of 65 inches is maize. During the twenty years that I spent in the Calabar province where the rainfall ranged from 140 inches at Opobo to 95 inches at Ikot Ekpene, I saw two crops of maize harvested a year but never any sorghum.

The suggestion that maize had replaced sorghum in places in the rain-

[1] "La grande humidité que la pluie apporte à toutes saisons crée une végétation luxuriante. La culture permanente des champs y est possible et, en premier lieu, celle des tubercles; le maïs est l'unique graminée bien acclimatée."

forest belt of west Africa is untenable in view of the fact that sorghum will not grow in the rainforest. Willett (1962: 7) has made this suggestion in the expression of his view that maize was post-Columbian in Africa. He wrote: "In Sierra Leone the replacement of sorghum has caused *nyon* to be transferred to maize. Similarly in Liberia Vai *nyoro* and Malinke *nyon* refer now to maize but formerly to sorghum, which has disappeared from use." As sorghum never grew in these rainforest areas it could neither have been replaced by maize nor have disappeared from use.

Maturing Times

The maturing time of maize was frequently noted by early travellers both in America and in Africa. The time is comparatively short.

Peter Martyr in his letter of 1514 referring to maize in America, according to MacNutt's (1912: I; 225) translation, wrote: "This maize is harvested twice yearly..." Moll (1747: II, 602, 608, 633, 694) noted of Guatemala: "in many Parts of the Country the Soil bears INDIAN Corn thrice a Year..."; of Tabasco in New Spain, "they have three or four Harvests of Maize in a year..."; of Florida, "There are almost every where two, and in some Parts of the Country, three Crops of INDIAN Corn in a Year"; of the Bahamas, "They sow Pease and INDIAN Wheat, the first of which is fit to gather in six Weeks, and the last in twelve." Heriot, according to Rhys, (1907–1909: VI, 173) was in Virginia in 1584–1587, and remarked about maize as follows: "There are three sorts, of which two are ripe in eleven and twelve weeks at the most, sometimes in tenne, after the time they are set... The other sort is ripe in fourteene, ... every head conteining five, sixe, or seven hundred graines, within a few more or lesse." Boxer (1952:179) pointed out that when Friar Juan Pabre Zamora went from Mexico to the Ladrone Islands and landed there he planted maize and according: "to his own account the grain ripened in from 40 to 60 days." Osborne (1745: II, 927) quoted Warren's description of the crops grown in Surinam: "The corn grows upon a stalk like a reed, commonly six or seven foot high, and two ears upon a stalk: the grain is about the bigness of a pea, which becomes ripe in four months. They have two crops in a year, and the increase is at least five hundred for one."

In West Africa one finds that maize has not altered its characteristics. Thus Meredith (1812:179) writing of Agoona on the Gold Coast remarked: "The chief vegetable productions here are maize (of which there are two crops in the year)..." Adandé (1935: 226), a native of Dahomey, reported that certain varieties of maize, known as *Agogo ume* and *Kito*, matured in two and a half to three months. The other types, for which he also gave names, mature in three and a half to five months. Bowen (1858: xvii–xviii) reported that the Yoruba of Nigeria raised two crops of maize annually. Around Minna in northern Nigeria, according to Dudgeon (1911: 149), the only variety of maize grown: "is apparently a three-months' crop ... thus giving two crops in the year in some localities." Irvine (1953: 84) dealing with agriculture in Nigeria wrote that maize: "takes from three to four months after planting to reach maturity, some varieties yielding seed within ten or twelve weeks ... In many parts of West Africa two crops of corn are raised during the year." Bumpus (1951:44) stated that in parts of Oyo, southern Nigeria: "it is possible to obtain two maize crops each year ..." Martin (1956:8) recorded that in the Uyo district of the Calabar province, southern Nigeria, maize was planted in February and again in June.

Sorghum, in comparison with maize, has a lengthy maturing time. Sorghum, indeed, usually produces only one crop a year as most varieties require at least six months to mature.

Schweinfurth (1878: I, 102–103) in Khartoum remarked: "I could not help being astonished at the length of time which most of the kinds [of sorghum] take to ripen." He had also remarked that: "In Sennaar and Taka, sorghum requires five or six months to come to maturity, but in this district it rarely takes less than eight months." Dudgeon, (1911: 146), in his survey of West African agricultural products, lists eleven kinds of sorghum grown in northern Nigeria. Seven of these varieties: "are grown as six-months' crops. ..." The eighth matures in three months, but he notes that the "grain is much smaller than the others"; the ninth is found far inland around Lake Chad. The other two varieties are not grown for human consumption. Duncan (1847: II, 249), when at the inland Dahomian town of Jallakoo, noted that Guinea corn, which he contrasted with quick ripening Indian corn or maize, took nearly seven months to ripen. Irvine (1953: 102), in his text book on West African agriculture, wrote that many varieties of sorghum: "are long-seasoned and take six months to mature, being planted in April and harvested in October when the rains cease. Others [varieties] are quicker in ripening, one variety taking only three months to mature. This three-months variety is much smaller seeded than the six-months varieties, its seed somewhat resembling that of bulrush millet." Godinho (1963: 36) wrote: "The maturation of sorghum is much longer than that of maize, it can only be harvested once a year, as it takes six to seven months (maize three to four)."[2]

[2] "A maturação do sorgo, é muito mais longa do que do maiz, apenas é possível, daquele, uma colheita por ano, pois leva seis a sete meses (o maiz três a quatro...)."

Grain Size

The large size of the maize grain is an important characteristic, noted frequently by early travellers in America.

MacNutt (1912: I, 64), in his translation of Peter Martyr's epistle of November 1493, records that the islanders of Hispaniola "...easily make bread with a kind of millet, similar to that which exists plenteously among the Milanese and Andalusians. This millet is a little more than a palm in length, ending in a point, and is about the thickness of the upper part of a man's arm. The grains are about the form and size of peas." A letter written by Syllacio at Pavia in Italy on December 13th, 1494, dealing with Columbus's discovery of America, reads, according to Thacher's translation (1967: II, 249), "There is here, besides, a prolific sort of grain of the size of a lupin, round like a vetch, from which when broken a very fine flour is made." Sturtevant (1919: 613) noted: "When Cartier visited Hochelaga, now Montreal, in 1535, that town was situated in the midst of extensive corn fields, the grain, 'even as the millet of Brazil, as great and somewhat bigger than small peason'." Taylor (1932: 154), editing Barlow's travels in Brazil in 1540–1541, recorded that: "In this countrie thei have no corne but a certeine seede thei call *abati* ... The seede is ... as big as a good pease. ..." Lopez de Gómara in his history of the Indians of America, of 1552 according to Finan (1950: 153) "describes the maize of Guatemala as being very large. ..." Hawkins, on his second voyage, off the mainland of America at Cumana in 1565, according to Rhys (1907–1909: VII, 22) wrote: "Neere about this place, inhabited certaine Indians, who the next day after we came thither, came down to us, presenting mill and cakes of breade, which they had made of a kind of corne called Maiz, in bignesse of a pease, the eare whereof is much like a teasell, but a spanne in length, having thereon a number of granes." Heriot in Virginia, 1584–1587, wrote, according to *Hakluyt's Voyages* as edited by Rhys (1907–1909: VI, 173): "Pagatowr, a kinde of graine so called by the inhabitants: the same in the West Indies is called Mayz: Englishmen call it Guiny-wheat or Turkey-wheat, according to the names of the countreys from whence the like hath beene brought. The graine is about the bignesse of our ordinary English peaze, and not much different in form and shape: but of divers colours..." According to Markham's (1880: II, 229) editing of Grimstone's translations of de Acosta's account of Peru between 1570 and 1587, one reads of maize that: "It grows vpon canes or reedes; every one beares one or two *mazorcas*, to which the graine is fastened, and although the graine be bigge, yet finde they great store thereof, so as in some *mazorcas*, I have told seven hundred graines."

The largeness of maize grains was also commented on when first it appeared in the Old World. Arber (1943: 28) remarked:

Maize was first reported in the herbals in the work of the German herbalist, Jerome Bock (1539: XXI–XXII)... The plant he explains is new in Germany and probably came from India. "Because we have no written proof, we want to name it *Frumentum Asiaticum* [wheat of Asia] because in Assyria such a fruit is found whose grains or kernels grow as large as olives and that I can easily believe. I myself have seen four or five such grains at a country merchant's — grains similar in shape and colour to these discussed here. When I made a thorough enquiry about such a fruit I was told it came from India."

Botanists are also agreed on the large size of the maize grain. Weatherwax (1954: 196) wrote: "In the range of size and form of the grain, maize far surpassed all other cereals." Towle (1961: 20) wrote: "Maize, the largest of the cereals, is a coarse annual grass with solid, jointed stems and long, broad, two-ranked blades with wavy margins." Gode (1950: 20) comments: "... *Makkā* [maize] is a variety of *yāvanāla* ... [Holcus sorghum] or *Jondhlā* or *Jawar*. ... The Maize plant looks like the *Jondhlā* plant but the seeds of the Maize are bigger than those of the *Jondhlā*. ..." The late Professor E. Roux, when Professor of Botany in the University of the Witwatersrand, Johannesburg, wrote to me in a letter (November 4, 1962): "Though different varieties of maize do vary in the size of their grains, the differences are not so striking as the differences between maize grains and, e.g. those of sorghum or other so-called millets."

Sorghum, in sharp contrast with maize, is a cereal with small seeds.

Baker (1868: 76) when in Abyssinia describing sorghum remarked: "Each grain is about the size of hemp-seed. I took the trouble of counting the corns contained in an average-sized head, the result being 4,484." Hartwig (1886: 166) wrote:

In light sandy soil, under the scorching rays of the sun, and in situations where sufficient moisture cannot be obtained for the production of rice, numerous varieties of millet [*Sorghum vulgare*] are successfully cultivated in many tropical countries — in India, Arabia, the West Indies, in Central Africa, and in Nubia, where it grows almost to the exclusion of every other esculent plant. Though the seeds are by much the smallest of any of the cereal plants, the number borne upon each stalk is so great as to counterbalance this disadvantage, and to render the cultivation of millet as productive as that of any other grain.

Hill (1952: 324) classified the sorghums with the small grains. Ogilby (1670: 493), quoting from Andrew Battel who was in Angola in 1590, wrote that in the kingdom of Lovango "grows both great and small Mille, the first is call'd *Massa-Manponta*; and the other *Massa-Minkale*." These are vernacular names for maize and sorghum respectively. Johnston

(1908: II, 605) writing of the Congo remarked: "The ear of corn [*Andropogon sorghum*] is a little like a diminutive cob of maize, with the seeds more numerous and growing less closely to the main stem. The grains are the size and shape of flattened buckshot." Kidd (1904: 323) describing the inhabitants of Zululand, wrote: "the staple food grown consists of mealies (Indian corn) and Kafir corn, which is a small round russet-coloured grain about the size of hempseed." Kaffir corn is the South African name for sorghum. Nicholls (1913: 56), writing of the people of Dongolla in 1698, remarked that they: "eat no other bread than that of Dora [Sorghum], which is a small round grain...."

The distinction made brings into prominence the importance, for instance, of the comment by Fernandes in 1506 when describing the crops on the Senegal river. According to Monod, Teixeira da Mota, and Mauny (1951: 54) Fernandes noted that: "*milho zaburro* was large. ..."[3]

MILHO DE GUYNEE

Guynee, to use the early Portuguese spelling, was an ancient kingdom whose northern boundary was the river Senegal and which was bounded on the west by the Atlantic ocean. It was the first African kingdom which travellers met along the Guinea coast, noted by the Arab geographer, Ibn Said, circa 1275, according to Major (1868: 114), and by a Franciscan Friar in the middle of the fourteenth century, according to Markham's translation (1912: 28).

The name Guinea, however, came to be used by navigators and travellers for the coast of Africa from the Senegal to the Congo. This coast, except for a short stretch between Accra and Whyda on the Gold Coast and Togoland, lies within the great tropical high rainfall forest belt.

The only cereal which will grow on these high rainfall coasts is maize. As Joyce (1934: 167) noted: "maize in England was called Guinea-corn because it came to us from west Africa."

Early users of the term Guinea wheat or its variants explain it with some care, or use it for maize in the West Indies.

The Hollander, Hans Stade, about 1550, during his captivity in Brazil, according to Sturtevant (1919: 611) "speaks of maize under the names of *abaty* [the Tupi name for maize] ... or *milhe de Guine*." On Stade's use of the word *abaty*, Burton (1874: 49) who knew both the Guinea coast and Brazil, commented that the word *abaty*: "is applied to the *milho de Guiné*,

[3] "Milho zaburro he grãde...."

in old Portuguese *zaburro*, Zea mays. ..." Ralph Lane writing from Virginia in 1585 remarked, according to Rhys (1907–1909: VI, 140): "And now within these few dayes we have found here Maiz or Guinie wheate. ..." Moll (1747: II, 746) in his description of the island of Barbados remarked that though no English grain is sown: "the Poor, who spare most of their Ground for the Cultivation of *Indian* or *Guiney* Corn, sell it to the Rich. ..." In 1613, Harcourt, writing of his visit to Guiana in the West Indies, remarked, according to Harris (1928: 94): "There is a kind of great wheat called Maix, of some it is called Guinea wheat." Pretty, who accompanied Cavendish in his circumnavigation of the earth, 1586–1588, described when at the island of Sant Marie off the Chilian coast the victuals they procured there, according to Rhys (1907–1909: VIII, 217) "... and Guinie wheate, which is called Maiz." Andrew Battel, who, from 1590, was eighteen years in Angola, remarked, according to Purchas (1625: 985), that the Negroes have: "the great Guiney wheat, which they call *mas-impota*." He then describes *mas-impota* as maize. In the Cape Verde islands, off the coast of Guinea, Sir Richard Hawkins noted after his visit to Fuego in 1593, according to Drinkwater (1847: 48) that some of the bread made there was composed "of mayes, which we call Guynee wheate." Rhys (1907–1909: VIII, 8) recorded that Sir Walter Raleigh, while in the Carribean in April 1597 wrote that the locals: "brought to us such infinite store of potatoes, and Guiney-wheate, that the stewarde sayd wee had no stowage for them. ..." Of the island of Lororinha, Sir Edward Michelbourne in 1605 is reported by Moore (1785: I, 355) as writing: "Here is also abundance of maiz, or Guinea wheat. ..."

The Portuguese also used this term for maize both in America and in Africa. Burtt-Davy (1914: 19) noted that "the forms in which the word milho are applied to maize include milho de Guine (Brazil)."

The early Portuguese and also the British and the Dutch, on reaching the Americas, found there an indigenous cultivated grain. This grain, however, they called *milho de Guynee*, Guinea corn or Guinea wheat. The use of such a name implies that these early navigators had already seen this cereal on the Guinea coast when they first arrived there circa 1442.

MILHO ZABURRO

A second term used by early travellers for a cereal found on the Guinea coasts is *zaburro*. This term, many scholars maintain, refers to maize; others dispute this claim on the grounds that if maize was first introduced by Columbus, it could not, for instance, be an export crop from Guinea to São Tomé in 1502 as Fernandes reported.

It is of little use attempting to resolve this dispute by starting with a dispute. What is important, however, is to note that *zaburro* has consistently meant maize in Portuguese from today back to the early years of the sixteenth century.

Recent Portuguese dictionaries, without exception, record that *zaburro* means maize (de Paiva Boléo 1946: 42; Vieira 1874: II, 1020; and Bluteau 1716–1721: VIII, 625.)

Sixteenth-century references to *zaburro* may be readily identified with maize in the works of experienced historians, travellers and administrators. Soares de Sousa (1878: 162), a Portuguese colonial administrator, who had been in charge of the Gold Coast fort of São Jorge da Mina and then was sent to Brazil, noted: "In all Brazil there is an indigenous plant which the Indians call *ubatim*, which is *milho de Guinee* and which in Portugal is called *zaburro*."

The Portuguese historian João de Barros had wide experience and first-hand knowledge of Guinea. According to Crone (1937: 103) he "was commander of S. Jorge da Mina from 1522 to 1525; Treasurer of the *Casa da India e Minia*, 1525–1528, and Factor in 1532." The first *Decade* of his *Asia* was published in 1552. According to the reprint of the *Asia* by Cidade and Murais (1945: 108), he wrote: "as for *milho de masaroca* which we call *zaburro*, it is the main sustenance of these natives, the Guynee negroes." The common Portuguese name for maize, *milho de maçaroca*, is discussed under the relevant heading in this paper. De Barros also has an interesting note on *zaburro* and climatic conditions on the west coast. According to Crone's (1937: 139) translation, de Barros, after mentioning *zaburro* as cultivated by the Jolofs, noted: "They do not grow wheat or the other seeds we use; it seems that the climate would not allow them to ripen, for the soil, especially near the Gambea, is very damp."

Bluteau (1716–1721: VIII, 625) in his discussion of *milho zaburro* expressed disagreement with the Barros, quoting Alvares in Abyssinia as saying: "the common nourishment of those people is *milho maçaroca*, which we call *zaburro*." It is to be noted, however, that de Barros himself saw nothing extraordinary in the fact that *zaburro* should have been quoted as a staple crop in Abyssinia when Alvares travelled extensively there between 1520 and 1526.

Alvares, the Portuguese friar, made other references to a grain identifiable with maize. According to the edition of his travels published by Machado (1943: 117), he noted that: "bread is made from *milho zaburro*, and barley and other seeds which they call *tafo*, a small black seed." Here *milho zaburro* is distinguished from barley and from a grain with a small black seed. Beckingham and Huntingford (1961: I, 135–136) in their translation of Alvares's travels wrote: "We travelled five days through country entirely depopulated, and through millet stalks as thick as canes for propping vines." The editors explain in a footnote that Alvares's phrase of 1540 was *canas de milho* which was translated by Ramusio in 1550 as *migli zaburri.* They note: "Milho is the Latin milium, 'millet'; *zaburro* is now used as an adjective only in this phrase, or by itself with the same meaning, i.e. 'zaburro millet', which is the modern Portuguese for 'maize'. Stanley translated it as 'maize canes.' But it is unlikely, on general grounds, that maize had reached Ethiopia as early as 1520. Nevertheless, the expression 'as thick as canes for propping vines' does suggest (to a maize grower) maize rather than millet. ..." The editors call attention to a similar passage: "we set out from this town, and travelled through thick millet fields, as tall as large cane brakes..." and the editors (1961: I, 191) noted that Ramusio translated *milharadas* as *migli zaburri.* On *milharadas,* Da Marais Silva (1945: VI, 793), who gives *milho* as the popular name for *Zea mays* L., wrote: "Milharada, S.F. (of maize). Plantation (or field) of maize; the same as *milheiral.* Ter. de Avis. A quantity of maize cobs which are taken to the granary."[4]

I have not found any other meaning for "a field of maize" attributed to the Portuguese word *milharada.* There seems enough evidence to interpret *zaburro* in Abyssinia as maize.

Between 1520 and 1545, an anonymous Portuguese pilot from Villa do Conde, according to Serge Sauvageot (1961: 123), paid five visits to São Tomé, an island in the Bight of Biafra. On one of these visits he noted, according to Lains e Silva (1958: 63) that the Negro slaves there were fed on *zaburro*: "which we call maize in the western islands and which is like chick peas."[5] Lains e Silva remarked that *zaburro* certainly did not refer to sorghum but to *Zea mays*: "whose grains can roughly be compared with those of *Lathyrus cicera* which is indigenous in the south of Europe and therefore known to the author."[6] This pilot's account of the island of Santiago (Cape Verde Islands) was cited by Ramusio in 1554; Blake's translation (1942: I, 149) runs: "At the beginning of August they [the islanders] begin to sow grain, which they call *zaburro*, or, in the West Indies, *mehiz* [maize]. It is like chick pea, and grows all over these

[4] "Milharada, S. F. (de milho). Sementeira de milho; o mesmo que milheiral. Ter. de Avis. Quantidade de espigas de milho, que se transportam para a eira."

[5] "Que se chama maiz nas Illhas Ocidentais' e se parecia com chícharo branco."

[6] "... Cujos grãos podem grosseiramente ser comparados aos de *Lathyrus cicera*, espontâneo no sul da Europa e, portanto, conhecido do autor."

islands [Lit. this island] and all along the African coast, and is the chief food of the people. It is harvested in 40 days."

In this key passage the staple cereal of the rainforest African coast is clearly indicated. Not only is *zaburro* identified with *mehiz* of the West Indies, but it is also identified as maize according to size, maturing time, and climatic locality. In addition, it must be noted that the Portuguese pilot referred to sorghum in a passage in which he compared sorghum with melegueta pepper, which according to Dalziel (1937: 471) is called *Aframonum melegueta* K. Schum. It is indigenous to Guinea and has small aromatic seeds about the size of the grains of *Sorghum vulgare*. Blake's translation (1942: I, 151) from Ramusio reads: "A kind of plant called melegete, very like the sorghum of Italia, but in flavour like pepper, grows on this coast." It is thus quite clear that this anonymous pilot knew the difference between sorghum and maize and did not confuse these two cereals.

Furthermore, in support of the Portuguese pilot's claim that maize was the chief food of all the African tribes along the coast is the Yoruba proverb quoted by Bowen (1857: 47) who noted: "The Yoruba esteem this grain so much, that they have a proverb which says, INDIAN CORN is the Chief support of man." The Yoruba claims that corn had been grown and used by them from time immemorial exasperated Bascom (1951: 45) who noted: "The belief that corn was known and used in Nigeria long before first European contact is so deep-rooted and widespread among the Yoruba, that it is necessary to state that the accepted scientific position is that corn ... was unknown outside of the New World before the time of Columbus."

The usages which have been quoted are all unequivocal in meaning maize and there is no indication in Portuguese literature that the term *milho zaburro* underwent any sudden change in meaning. It is in the light of these uses of the term that other passages may be read although these provide fewer details in the context. The light thrown on the meaning of *zaburro* allows other passages to be more confidently interpreted.

Fernandes, for instance, according to the edition by Monod, et al. (1951: 14, 18, 54, 136) mentioned *milho zaburro* several times. In describing the Gyloffa [or Woolofs] of the old kingdom of Guynee, he noted they had plenty of *milho zaburro*, and that these Woolofs ate "rice, milk, *milho zaburro* ..." He noted that in the Kingdom of Guynee the *milho zaburro* was of large size.

Within this kingdom and just south of Cape Verde lay the slave victualling port of Beziguiche where, by the Ordinances of King Manuel who died in 1521, slave ships were allowed to take in provisions. Concerning these Ordinances, Blake (1937: 92) wrote: "The Ordinances of King Manuel provided that those ships, which were sent to embark slaves at São Thomé, O Principe and Annobon might by special permission purchase maize and meat on the outward journey at Beziguiche and its hinterland, and this suggests that some local trade was organized before 1521 in Upper Guinea."

The aim in controlling this trade in maize was to ensure that from it revenue accrued to the King's treasury. Blake (1942: I, 118) translating from the Portuguese, reproduced the three year audit of Gonçales Lopez's accounts dated 17 December, 1514. Among the items audited were: "25 quintals, 2 arrobes, 19 arrats and a quarter of red corn, which he received from the contractors of Sierra Leoa, as the twentieth of 513 quintals." In all, Lopez had received from the local African middlemen at Sierra Leone 513 quintals of red corn. As a quintal is a measure of 100 pounds, Lopez had received 51,300 pounds of red corn, and this quantity did not exhaust the local crop. Neither sorghum nor European corn will grow in Sierra Leone, but maize will.

Further north, on the Senegal, in the land of the Woolof, Alvarez D'Almada in 1554 recorded the probable presence of maize, as reported by Portères (1958–1959: 128) who considered it to have been red maize.

Finally, Fernandes speaks of *milho zaburro* as being brought from Guinea to San Tomé in 1502. Fernandes according to Monod, et al. (1951: 137) wrote:

> *Milho zaburro* grows here and it was never grown before 1502, as they used to bring it by ship from Guynee. And it grows exactly like the one we grow here, except that it grows high and the grain is compact and not loose like ours. To get milho, they clear the ground, and all the year it is reaped. They sow it in November and December and they reap it in March, and in the same way they sow it in May and June and reap it in September.[7]

Lains e Silva (1958: 62), a Portuguese botanist, has offered a careful analysis of this passage:

> The *milho zaburro* grew as well as the daca, that is as well as the *Panicum mileaceum*, from which it could be distinguished by having greater height — which could be said of *Sorghum vulgare* — and, which is most important, the "corn is in mass, and not spread out as ours" — which can only possibly be said of *Zea mays*. *Maça* is an archaic Portuguese word, native to, or derived

[7] "Milho zaburro naçe aqui e nũca he semearõ se nõ ãno de 1502 primeyro ca sempre o trazia em nauios de Guynee. E naçe proprio como ho daca se nõ q̃ naçe grãde e o milho e hua maça e nõ aspalhado como o nosso. Para este milho roça e semea e naçe todo ho ãno, e todo o ãno colhẽ. Semeã-no no nouẽbro. E no março colhem e assi mayo e junho semeã e colhem no setẽbro."

from, Godo, and which means *clava*. *Maça* or *clava* is figurative of the form of the cob of *Zea mays*, and cannot correctly be applied to the panicle of sorghum. Besides which the vegetative cycle took ninety to one hundred and twenty days, seeing that, planted in November and December, it ripened in March, and equally so if planted in May or June it ripened in September. Although certain varieties of sorghum ripen in from one hundred and seven to one hundred and twenty three days they more often have longer vegetative periods of one hundred and sixty seven to one hundred and ninety eight days, that is from four and a half months to more than six months. With an ordinary vegetative cycle of three months, it is more likely that reference was made to *Zea mays*.[8]

It is interesting to note that Ogilby (1670: 722–723), reporting on São Tomé island in the Gulf of Guinea, wrote: "corn never attains its full growth because of the over-fatness of the Soil, and the exceeding moisture, hinders the due Ripeness... Turkey Wheat or Maize may be had there...."

The term *milho zaburro* also appears in early Portuguese records of contacts with African tribes on the east coasts of Africa. The Portuguese vessel, the *S. Bato no Cabo da Bona Esperança*, in 1554 was wrecked on the South African coast. One of the survivors, Manoel de Mesquita Perestrello, wrote an account of this shipwreck and of the subsequent adventures of the survivors. Peres (1942–1943: I, 140) reproduced this account in Portuguese of which the relevant passage runs: "... after wandering for a couple of days we reached the mouth of the Pescaria rivier in Latitude 28¾° ... we met two of Manoel de Sousa's slaves ... who remained with the natives of the country who brought us fish for sale ... and some *milho zaburro*."[9]

Fernandes writing from Goa in India in 1562 and describing the food of the inhabitants of the African kingdom of Inhambane in Mozambique, wrote according to Theal (1898: II, 140): "... otherwise their provisions are only beans and millet (milho zaburro) such as is eaten in Lombardy though it is of better quality there." The natives of Inhambane are Thonga

[8] "O milho zaburro nascia *próprio como o daca*, isto é, desenvolvia-se como o *Panicum mileaceum*, do qual se distinguia por ser de maior porte — o que podia dizer-se também do *Sorghum vulgare* — e, o que é importantíssimo, *o milho ẽ hũa maça e nõ espalhado como o nosso* — o que só é possível dizer-se do *Zea mays*. *Maça* é palavra do português arcaico nativa ou derivada do godo e que signigicava *clava*. Maça ou clava é bem figurativa da forma da espiga do *Zea mays*, e não pode aplicar-se correctamente à panícula do sorgo. Além disso, o ciclo vegetativo durava noventa a cento e vinte dias, visto que, semeado em Novembro e Dezembro, amadurava em Março, assim como, semeado em Maio e Junho amadurecia em Setembro. Embora certa variedade de sorgo haja amadurado de cento e sete a cento e vinte e três dias, são mais comuns períodos vegetativos muito mais longos, de cento e trinta e seis a cento a sessenta e sete, ou de cento e sessenta e sete a cento e noventa e oito dias, isto é, de quatro meses e meio a mais de seis meses. Com ciclo vegetativo vulgar de três meses é mais natural se tratasse de *Zea mays*."

whose name for maize is *sibela*, a word in no way connected with the Portuguese.

There appears to be general agreement among scholars today that the term *zaburro* refers to maize consistently in the early chronicles.

Lains e Silva (1959: 314) noted: "*Milho* — *Zea mays* — L. Milho [*mi* in Creole] has been cultivated in São Tomé for a very long time. Valentim Fernandes calls it *milho zaburro* of which he gives so perfect a description that it may be admitted that maize was already known to the African peoples before the Armada of Columbus brought it from America."[10] Portères's (1958: 128) comments on the unchanging use of the word *zaburro* are cogent. He wrote: "Reporting on the voyages on the Guinea coast, the sixteenth century chroniclers also give the word *zaburro* as a synonym for *milho de maçaroca*, always used, it seems, to designate maize."[11]

Monod (1960: 71) has lately reversed his disagreement, for he wrote on the meaning in 1501 of this term: "Nevertheless *milho zaburro* in Valentim Fernandes, and at San Tomé must be maïs. ..."[12]

Furthermore Godinho (1963: 33–35) in 1963 noted that: "an inventory of the 15th century and early 16th century of Portuguese sources showed not only Barros but all others identify *milho zaburro* with maize from Antilla and America and with *abati* of the Indians of Brazil; ..."[13] He deals with the possibility of an interpolation here by Ramusio into the account of the Portuguese Pilot about Santiago by pointing out that: "J. Moquet, in 1604, confirmed that it was maize which was cultivated in the Cape Verde Islands and we have Thevet writing in 1575 about S. Tomé: 'that the slaves plant a millet which they call *zaburro*, the local Arabs, *Alahassel*, and the west Indians *mahic*."[14] In addition, according to Godinho, Brandão in 1618 noted: "This third (type of food) is the maize cob which

[9] Peres has: "Depois disto caminhámos dois dias, no fim dos quais chegámos à barra da Pescaria, que está em 28 graus e três quartas, ... e ali achámos dois escravos que foram de Manoel de Sousa ... e fizeram com os da terra que naquela noits nous trouxessem a vender peixe ... a algum milho zaburro ...."

[10] "Milho — *Zea mays* L. O milho (*mi* em crioulo) é cultivado em São Tomé de há longa data. *Milho zaburro* lhe chamou Valentim Fernandes, que dele faz tão perfeita descrição que permite admitir ser o *Â. mays* ja conhecido dos povos africanos antes de a armada de Colombo o ter trazido da America."

[11] "Les chroniques du XVI siècle, relatant les voyages sur la Côte de Guinée, donnent aussi le terme de *zaburro* comme synonyme de *milho de maçaroca*, employé toujours semble-t-il, pour désigner le Maïs."

[12] "Bien que *milho zaburro*, dans Valentim Fernandes, et à São Tomé, soit le maïs...."

[13] "Por outro lado, o inventário das fontes Portuguesas quinhentistas e de começos de seiscentos mostra que não apenas Barros mas todas elas identificam o milho zaburro com o maiz antilhano e americano e com a abati dos Indios do Brasil."

[14] "J. Moquet, em 1604, confirma que é o 'maïs' que é cultivado nas ilhas de Cabo

in Portugal is called *zaburro* and in the west Indies *mais*, and among the native Indians *abati*."[15]

Godinho has pointed out a particularly early use of the word *zaburro*. He noted that the Portuguese had reached the Guinea coast before 1470, and that: "in the *Cronica do Conde D. Pedro de Meneses de Zurara* we read in respect of Cencem (8 leagues from Ceuta): 'Fields of milho zaburro,' this chronicle, which was begun in 1458, was completed in 1464. The word *zaburro* was, therefore, used in Portugal before the Portuguese had reached the Gulf of Guinea."[16]

Sauvageot (1961: 135) though denying that *milho zaburro*, as used by Valentim Fernandes in 1506, could refer to maize admits that circa 1545 when the anonymous Portuguese pilot wrote of *milho zaburro* being present in Santiago, *milho zaburro* must be maize because it ripens so rapidly. Sauvageot wrote: "As far as the present reference of the Pilot is concerned *miglio zaburro* from Santiago must be maize, for this plant, in contrast with "mils", which require at least 90 days, ripens in approximately 2 months."[17]

MILHO DE MAÇAROCA

Milho de maçaroca or grain of the cob is another Portuguese term for maize which appears in early chronicles.

It is not a name for sorghum, although the term *maçaroca* may be. Mullet (1866: 77) in his translation of a treatise in Arabic on agriculture by D'Ibn-al-Awan of Seville in 1158, noted that D'Ibn-al-Awan mentioned *dourah* as the Arabic name for sorghum which in Italy was called *sorgho* and in Portugal *maçaroca*.

De Paiva Boléo (1946: 42) listed *milho maçaroca* as a Portuguese name for maize. Viterbo (1865 [1792]: 43) in 1798 wrote: "*milho zaburro, milho*

Verde (Liv. 2. p. 77). E temos Thevet, em 1575 (*Cosmographie* Liv. III, Cap. 13), a propósito de S. Tomé: Ils (escravos) sement le millet (qu'ils appellent *zaburro*, les Arabs du pais Alahassel, et les Indiens Occidentaux mahic) ...".

15 "Mais peremptórios, os testemunhos de Ambrósio Fernandes Brandão (*Dialogos des Grandezas do Brasil*, 1618: 4°, 192 dà ed J. Cortesão): 'Este terceiro (modo de mantimento) é o milho de massaroca, que em nosso Portugal chamam zaburro, e nas Indias Occidentais maïs, e entre os indios naturais de terra *abati;*'...."

16 "Ora na *Crónica do Conde D. Pedro de Meneses de Zurara* (Liv. II, Cp. XXXIV) lemos, a propósito de Cencem (a 8 léguas de Ceuta): 'Emilharda de milho zaburro': esta crónica, cuja feitura foi iniciada em 1458, foi terminada em 1464; a palavra zaburro era, pois, usada em Portugal antes de se entrar no golfo de Guiné."

17 "Pour la présente référence du Pilote, le *miglio zaburro* de Santiago doit bien être le maïs, car cette plante, au contraire des mils, auxquels il faut au moins 90 jours, mûrit en 2 mois environ."

grande, milho graûdo, milho maiz, milhão, ou milho grosso, è milho de maçaroca." Here Viterbo is stating that these names all mean *milho de maçaroca*, that is maize. Bluteau (1714–1721: VIII, 625), the Portuguese lexicographer, gave *milho maçaroca* together with *milho grande, milho da India* as alternatives to *zaburro*.

In the seventeenth century Manuel Severin de Faria, according to Ribeiro (1941: 657), stated that *milho grosso de masaroca* "comes from Guinea." Ribeiro has also shown that *milho de masaroca* is *milho americāno* or maize.

Alvarez D'Almeida, for instance in 1554, according to Portères (1959: 128), cited *milho maçaroca* as being cultivated by the Wooloffs of Senegal and Portères noted: "this *millet maçaroca* is maize or else *mil de chandelle* (bulrush millet) probably the former."[18]

De Barros (1945: 128), in the first decade of his *Asia* in 1552, as reprinted by Cidade and Murais, discussing the Jolofs, noted: "There is a *grain of the cob* which we call *zaburro* and is the main food of these natives....[19] Only maize grows on a cob.

It matters not whether one of the great compilers and historians, such as de Barros, was quoting earlier sources. The fact is that men, experienced in the trade of the coast, saw nothing extraordinary in claiming maize for the west coast and under unambigious names. A claim, such as that brought by Ribeiro, that sorghum was being referred to does not stand up to the climatic evidence, the maturing times, and the size of the grain.

One of the earliest commentators to use the term leaves no doubt as to its meaning. According to Lains e Silva (1958: 64), "at the beginning of the sixteenth century Fernandes Brandão identified *milho de maçaroca* with *milho zaburro* and said that its name was maize in the West Indies."[20]

MILHO ON THE EAST AFRICAN AND GUINEA COASTS

The term *milho* is the common name for maize in Portugal at the present day. Wright (1949: 63) noted: "the ordinary word now used in Portuguese to describe *Zea mays* [is] *milho* which has passed into the English, mealie, through the Cape Dutch, milje." The Portuguese authors J. and M. Dias (1964: II, Figure 68) give illustrations of maize cobs which they refer to as *milho*.

[18] "Ce millet maçaroca est le 'maïs' ou 'mil de chandelle', probablement le premier."

[19] "E para dar os *milhos de maçaroca* a que chamamos *zaburro* que é o comum mantimento daquels povos."

[20] "No princípio do seculo XVI, Fernandes Brandão identifica o milho de maçaroca com milho zaburro, e diz ser seu nome *mais* nas Indias Ocidentais."

Milho is also one of the key words in establishing the presence of pre-Columbian maize in the Old World; it is essential to apply the usual criteria and, in addition, in places where sorghum will grow, an extra check on local terms for sorghum is necessary.

The first Portuguese to sail round the Cape and up the coast of Africa was Vasco da Gama. On his way to Malinde in 1498, according to Ravenstein's (1898: 33ff.) edition, he chased two *barcas* or ocean going vessels: "In the one we took we found seventeen men, besides gold, silver, an abundance of maize [*milho*] and other provisions." On arriving at Malinde, Vasco da Gama reported that: "on the landside are palm-groves, and all around it maize [*milho*] and vegetables are being cultivated." Stanley (1869: 26) has also translated *milho* as maize in his rendering of da Gama's visit to Malinde.

There is evidence which indicates that maize is the correct rendering of *milho* in these passages, and that maize was growing on the east coast when da Gama arrived.

At Mombasa, for instance, da Gama, according to Ravenstein, received on April 8, 1498, among other items, "*trigo tremez*" or corn that ripens in three months, and maize is the only cereal that matures thus quickly. Mention has been made of D'Almeida's remark, according to Axelson (1940: 232) in 1505 that Kilwa "had plenty of *milho* like that of Guinea." Gann (1964: 13) noted that "Maize, oranges, lemons and onions ... were cultivated at Kilwa as early as 1505, the year in which the Portuguese first captured the fort." Ogilby (1670: 613) describing the kingdom of Quiloa [Kilwa] wrote: "Osorius praises it as being watered with many Fountains, so enriching the Soyl, that it produces all sorts of grain and Fruits with little Labor, especially Maiz, Rice, Oranges, Citrons and Lemons ... Their usual food is Maiz, Rice and other Grains, Carrots and a variety of wild Fruits, a fit Diet for such poor people."

Further material is forthcoming in the first four volumes covering the years 1497–1516 of the projected twenty-four volumes of *Documents on the Portuguese in Mozambique and Central Africa 1497–1840*. This is a work of Portuguese scholarship. The editors are A. da Silva Rego, who is Professor of the Higher Institute for Overseas Studies and President of the Center for Overseas Historical Studies, Lisbon, and T. W. Baxter who is Director of the National Archives of Rhodesia and Malawi, Salisbury, Rhodesia.

The references are generally found in requisition orders and are given in *alqueires*. An *alqueira* is the equivalent of a bushel and a bushel of grain weighs about 55 pounds.

The editors (1962: I, 332–335, 466–467) of this work translate the

Portuguese word *milho* as maize and with some reason, as other crops are easily identifiable, including sorghum for which an adaption of the local native name is used.

Rice, for instance, is mentioned under the name *arroz* at Sofala on December 20, 1505 in a requisition for "thirty four *alqueires* of rice for the maintenance of the people..."[21] The editors add a footnote to the effect that "it was not often that rice was consumed. Maize was usually given to the local population."[22]

Flour is distinguished from *milho* or maize in a list of maintenance payments for May, 1506, in the fortress of Kilwa: "Item, I order you to give for my use and for the use of all those entitled to rations two *alceires* of flour and another two of maize... you shall likewise give to each of the men-at-arms and to the men of the brigantine four *alceires* of maize. ..."[23]

Chick peas according to Rego and Baxter (1962: 3) are distinguished from maize in an entry for Sofala on 2 January, 1517: "Joam Vaaz d'Allmada, provost of this fortress of Sofala, ... order you Cristoram Çalema, the factor, to deliver to Pero Lopez ... three hundred and fifty *allqueires* [*sic*] of maize and a further one hundred and fifty *alquires* [*sic*] of chick-peas ..."[24]

An interesting entry including rice, maize, and sorghum or Kaffir-corn appears according to Rego and Baxter (1962: 142–143), on September 1, 1511: "Bertolameu Perestrello, factor of this fortress of Sofala ... order you Troylos Bramdam ... to give ... to these forty nine people ... four hundred *alqueires* of unhusked rice and fifty four *alqueires* of maize and nine *alqueires* of kaffir corn ..."[25]

The translators have rendered the word *mexoeira*, or variants of it, by Kaffir-corn. The word also occurs in the accounts of the survivors of the wrecks of the *San Tomé* in 1589 near Saint Lucia Bay in Lower Zululand, according to Boxer (1959: 108), and the *Santo Alberto* in 1593 a few miles south of Mazeppa Bay, according to Juta (1968: 39, 40). Diogo do Conto

[21] "... Almoxarife dos mantimentos trimta e quarto alqueires d'arroz para mantimento da jemte ...."

[22] "Item, vos mando que des pera mym e pera todos os da(s) raçoes dous alceires de farinha e outros dous de mylho... E asy dares a todos os homens d'armas e do barga(n)-tim a cada huum quatro alceires de mylho...."

[23] "Não era normal o consumo de arroz, porque em geral se distribuia milho de produção local...."

[24] "Joam Vaaz d'Allmada, allcaide moor desta fortaleza de Çofala ... mando a vos Cristoram Çalema feytor que entrequees a Pero Lopez ... trezentos e cinquoenta *allqueires* [*sic*] de milho e mais cento e cinquo enta alquires [*sic*] de grãos ...."

[25] "Bertolameu Perestrello feytor desta forteleza de Çofala ... mando a vos Troylos Bramdam ... pag(u)ees a estas corenta e nove pessoas ... quatrocentos alqueires d'arroz por pylar e cinquoenta e quatro alqueires de milho e nove alqueires de mexoeira ...."

of the San Tomé wrote, according to Theal (1898: 206) that the African chief: "gave orders to his people to bring food, and they returned directly with two baskets of a kind of pulse which they call *ameixoeira* and a goat. ..."[26] João Baptista Lavanha, of the *Santo Alberto*, kept a record of the journey of the survivors, according to Juta (1968: 39). The record runs, according to Theal (1898: 317), that the survivors camped near a native village, but: "It did not seem too far for the negroes, for they brought a quantity of millet, cakes made of the flour of a grain resembling our millet in size and colour, which they call ameixoeira. ..."[27]

Both writers state that the Negroes called a local grain *ameixoeira*, which indicated that it was not a Portuguese word. It was Junod (1914: 156) who in his discussion of Lavanha's use of *ameixoeira* remarked: "it is, if I am not mistaken, the Sorghum, ...": he identified it in a footnote: "The word *ameixoeira* or *mexoeira* nowadays designates the small grey kaffircorn in Lourenço Marques. ..." There is no reason to suppose that the word *ameixoeira* used in the early decades after 1500 at Sofala does not refer to the same grain. The local Maconde name for maize is quite different, and J. and M. Dias (1964: II, 38) note that *Zea mays* or *milho* is called *dindjele* among them.

There is thus considerable assurance to be gained from the records quoted that the Portuguese about 1500 distinguished between rice, chick-peas, a type of sorghum, and maize.

There are some further interesting references. At Sofala, as early as December 12, 1506, according to Rego and Baxter (1962: I, 332–335, 466–467), is the following entry in the King's Treasury that certain: "merchandise and items were spent in buying one hundred and seventy-seven bags of maize with fifteen heads of maize to each bag for the maintenance of the people of the fortress."[28] The indigenes would not sell their total crop to the Portuguese, and it is to be recalled that D'Almeida had noted in Kilwa: "plenty of *milho* like that of Guinea."

The extent to which maize was supplied to the Portuguese by the local natives also appears in two other entries at Sofala. There is the list of merchandise received by Troilos Brandão as keeper of Stores of Sofala,

[26] "E logo deo recado aos seos pavo lhes trouxessem alguma couza de comer. Os quaes tornarão logo dous balayos de hum leguma a que chamaõ Ameixoeira, e huma cabra ..." (171).

[27] "Não lhes pareceo longe aos negros para virem a elle ver os nossos, trazendo muito milho, e bolos feitos da farinha de huma semente do tamanho e cor do nosso milho, chamada delles Ameixoeira ...."

[28] "... Quaes mercandarias e cousas se gastaram em compra de cemto e setemta e sete sacos de milho de quinze capos de milho cada saco pera mantimento da jemte desta forteleza."

September 30, 1512, which included: "Ninety six lances and twelve thousand five hundred and seventy six *alqueires* of maize and a hundred and nine *alqueires* of kaffir-corn. ..."[29] There is also the list of monies and merchandise received by Pero Vaz Soares whilst factor at Sofala 1513–1514 which included the following entries: "In maize twenty thousand 758 *alqueires*. In Kaffir-corn 593 *alqueires*."[30] In this last list the maize alone is about 572 short tons.

The word *milho* appears also in the records of Pacheco Pereira. Pereira, according to Kimble (1937: xiii) had been employed by King John II of Portugal in African waters, whence: "in company with others of the King's captains, he discovered 'many places and rivers along the coast of Guinea'." It would appear that in 1482 on the Gold Coast "Pereira was associated with Diogo d'Azumbuja in the founding of the castle of S. Jorze da Mina." Further travel was undertaken when in: "1503 King Manuel sent Pereira to India with the Albuquerques...", a voyage which, it should be noted, necessitated a call on the east coast of Africa. Pereira returned to Lisbon in 1505 and never visited Africa again. By 1509 he had compiled his *Esmeraldo de situ orbis*. Two points are important. First, he was well acquainted with the Guinea coasts and the trading there. Second, he would have called in at some of the Portuguese ports on the east coast where the custom was to refer to maize as *milho*.

Pereira, when noting a cereal in the high rainfall areas of the west coast, uses the term *milho*. The following extracts are from notes ranging from Sierra Leone to Cape Lopez on the Guinea coast littorals, the only areas known to Pereira on the West Coast. In these areas the climatic conditions preclude the cultivation of any crops other than rice or maize. The extracts are taken from Mauny's reproduction (1956: 86, 72, 76, 124, 156). As the Portuguese dictionaries give *milho* as maize, in my translation, Pereira's *milho* is invariably rendered as maize.

Near Cape Ledo, Sierra Leone, Pereira noted: "Among these mountains can be obtained much fish, rice, maize. ..." Of the Guogueliis and the Beafores of the Rio Grande, subjects of the Mandingo king, Pereira noted: "These people have a great abundance of rice, maize, yams. ..." Of the Joalungas, Pereira noted: "They live on rice, maize, and other vegetables. ..." Describing the fortresses at Elmina and at Axim, Pereira noted that the natives thereabouts: "live on maize and palm wine," and of the people around Cape Lopez he notes: "They live on meat, maize and sugar cane."[31]

[29] "Novemta seis lamças e douza mill quinhemtos setemta e seis alqueires demilho e cemto nove alqueires de mexoeira ..."

[30] "De milho vinte mill 758 alqueires d'ameixoeira 593 alqueires."

Two interesting adaptions of the Portuguese term *milho* by the English, one from the west coast and one from the east coast, are on record. Purchas (1625: 650) has: "The Guineans ... stamp their milia as we do spice ... and grind it ... till it is dowe, which they temper with water and salt, and make rolls thereof. ..." May, in October 1591 at Quintongane, a few leagues north of Mozambique, mentioned the capture of a Portuguese *pangaia*, a type of local boat, and noted, according to Rhys (1907–1909: 157): "In this pangaia we had certain corn called millio..." Pearce (1920: 14–15), who concentrated on East Africa, the region where *milho* is frequently noted in the Portuguese records, came to the conclusion that maize had been imported before the arrival of the Portuguese:

Maize (Indian corn), which in many parts of Africa is the staff of life is only grown spasmodically [in Zanzibar]. ... It is generally understood that the Portuguese introduced maize into Africa, but, like the coconut and orange, it appears likely that it was an importation of the Arabs or Indians long before the Portuguese ever ventured into the Indian Ocean. Its introduction into the African continent was probably the work of the Indian trader, or his Islamised negro agents, for the Portuguese did little in the way of real colonization in East Africa. The Swahili name for maize is *muhindi*, which is itself suggestive.

Pearce has added a footnote to the term *muhindi* which raises the question of local names for maize. These are connected with the Arabs who had been driven off the coasts by the Portuguese. Pearce said: "It may be worthy of note that the Chinyanja — that is the language of the Lake people, spoken by the Bantus of the Nyasa region — for maize is *chimanga*. The word *Manga* in Swahili means 'Arabia' or 'Arab'. May it be surmised that maize was introduced into Zanzibar from India, and into Nyasaland by the Arabs?" I have shown that *hindi* in *muhindi* does not refer to India but to an old name for the Hadramaut (1920: 198–201). There is a name of similar associations on Madagascar, indicating that the island had gained its maize from the Arab colony of Pemba. In addition, there is a report by visiting Portuguese of maize on Madagascar before 1515. When the island was first sighted in 1500 by Diogo Diaz and named St. Lawrence for the day of the saint, all the ports were controlled by "Moors" and no attempt was made to colonize the island. Corsali, however, who had been in Mozambique in 1514, seen by Soares in the Red Sea in 1515, and then reported from Goa in a letter early in 1516, wrote, according to Dames (1921: II, xxix): "During our stay at Mozambique,

[31] "... É em toda esta serra há muita pescaria e arroz e milho ... (86). esta gente tem muita abastança d'arroz, milho e ynhames ... (72). e estes se mantêm d'arroz e milho e autros legumes ... (76). Os negros d'esta terra se mantêm de milho e vinho de palma ... (124). Mantêm-se de carne e milho e canas de açuquar ..." (156).

we found two small Portuguese vessels which came from the island of St. Lawrence ... Here are likewise silver, ambergris, ginger, Turkey corn and cloves. ..." Maize, thus reported as a noteworthy crop in 1514, in Madagascar takes its name from *Tsaki-Tshaki*, according to Portères (1959: VI, 74), the capital and principal port of Pemba which was, at the date of the arrival of the Portuguese, an Arab colony. The names *chimanga*, *muhindi*, and *tsaka-tsaka* all indicate an Arab introduction of maize around the littorals of the Indian ocean.

MKATE AND ISINKWA

In 1505, Martin Fernandez de Figuerra noticed of the natives of Sofala, according to Rego and Baxter (1962: III, 600) that: "they make bread out of maize, they bake it in pots and not in ovens." Of the natives of Mozambique he noted: "... they have no corn though they have rice and maize from which they make bread. ..."

Dos Santos reached Sofala in 1586, and according to Theal (1898: VII, 190), wrote: "The bread commonly eaten in Sofala is made of rice and millet mixed and made into cakes which they call *mocates*."[32] Here Theal was in error in translating *milho* by millet, for in *mocates* one recognizes the present Manganja word *mkate*, a maize loaf. According to Scott (1892: 345): "the real *mkate* is a roll compounded of maize flour mixed with bananas and honey." The word would have been in existence when the maize loaf was observed in 1505. The Manganja language is spoken in Mozambique and down the valley of the Zambezi to Sofala. The word *mkate* for a maize meal loaf is also found in Swahili.

A similar type of roll made with sorghum has a different name in Manganja where it is called *nsima*.

A corresponding name for a maize loaf among the Zulu of Natal is *isinkwa*. Concerning it Bryant (1907: 4), the Zulu historian, noted: "Mealie (maize) grains having been crushed or ground on the stone, with a sprinkling of a little water, the moist damp dough so formed is wrapped as a large lump within mealie-spathes and so boiled for about three hours, and then eaten."

A tribe far inland from the sea and hence far from European contacts, the Venda of the northern Transvaal, according to Van Warmelo (1937: 280) have a similar name for the maize loaf. Among the Mashona of Rhodesia, according to Dale (1968: 123), their word for bread is *zingwa*.

32 "O pão ordinario que se come en Sofala é de milho e arroz misturado, do que fazem uns bolos, e que chamam mocates."

It is evident that this word for maize meal bread is spread over many tribes.

That the term was in use when the Europeans first contacted the Bantu and owes nothing to European influence is clear from its appearance in the records of the survivors of the *Santo Alberto* disaster, when the ship was wrecked in 1593 on the Transkei Coast, according to Juta (1968: 40). Theal (1898: II, 310) renders Lavanha's diary as follows: "In exchange for a few tacks (actually ships nails) they [the Negroes] gave a quantity of milk and cakes of millet which they call *sincòa*."[33]

Sincòa is an attempt to render into Portuguese the Zulu word, *isinkwa*, for a maize loaf. As the Zulu had here for the first time encountered Europeans, this word could not refer to the wheaten bread of the Europeans, If this stiff loaf had been made of sorghum, the survivors would have recorded a word like the *isigwamba* of the Zulu, according to Doke and Vilakazi (1948: 282), or the *amazimba* of the Xhosa, according to Kay (1833: 122).

MILHO GROSSO

The size of the maize grain is frequently reflected in descriptive terms in many parts of Europe where maize is labelled as "the great millet." It is known as *gros millet des Indes* in France, "great wheat" in Britain, *miglio grosso*, *frumentone*, and *granone* in Italy, where the last term according to Muratori (1952: 79) is an augmented form of the common name for wheat and means "big or thick corn."

This type of descriptive term appears in general European records.

Nicholay Daupninais, who visited Tripoli in North Africa about 1551, noted, according to the translation by Washington (1585: I, xvii, li): "Instead of corn they sow Maith which is a kind of grosse Mill." Bosman (1907: 296) on the coast of Guinea in 1690 observed: "The large *Milhio* is by most taken to be Turkish wheat. ..." He also remarked of the crops grown at Benin: "The Fruits of the Earth are first Corn or great *Milho*; for they have none of the small sort." Crow (1830: 256), who was slave trading at Bonny on the Niger delta in 1790, wrote that the local natives: "sow their large and small millet, the former of which is what we call Turkey wheat..."

The large size of the grain is also reflected in the term used in Portu-

[33] "... A troco de muy poucas tachas dèraõ muito leite, e bolos de milho, que traziaõ, chamados delles sincòa."

guese. In Portugal today *milho grosso*, as any good modern Portuguese dictionary will reveal, is still in current use as a name for maize. Martins (1910: 68–83), for instance, published an article in 1910 entitled *Milho grosso* [*Maize*] *in Portugal and its enemies.* Boxer (1952: 178) referring to Bluteau's *Vocabulario Portuguez e Latino* of 1712–1721, which he called the "oldest good Portuguese Dictionary" noted *maiz* as being "the name given in some parts of Portugal to *milho grosso.*" Boxer noted that the fact that *maiz* is the name used "throughout all Castile," implies that the Portuguese word *maiz* was borrowed from Spain. It would appear that the use of the term *milho grosso* preceded the use of the word *maiz.* When Bluteau added (1716–1721) that *milho grosso* was also called *milho da India,* the implication is that again the use of the term *milho grosso* preceded that of *milho da India. Milho grosso,* indeed, is possibly a term of some antiquity, only later superseded by other names for maize. Boxer (1952: 178) noted: "I dare say there are earlier references to *milho grosso* than 1712 but so far I have not found them." The term, however, was used unequivocally by Duarte Ribeiro de Macedo (1817: 117) who stated in 1675 that *milho grosso* was the food of the Indians in America and from there it was brought to Spain.[34]

In the records of travel are three instances of the term. In 1831 the two Portuguese African explorers, Monteiro and Gamitto, left Tete on the Zambezi to visit the court of Muato Cazembe. They observed the presence of *milho grosso* which Burton in his translation of the account of their journey (1873: 17) rendered as maize. Duarte Barbosa, who controlled Portuguese interests in the Orient from 1500 to 1516, left a record of his administration. Dames (1918: I, 155) in his translation gave Barbosa's account of the merchandise exported from Guzarat as including: "abundance of wheat and of great millet [*milho grosso*]." Cadamosto, the famous Italian who entered the Portuguese service, visited the Senegal River in 1456. He describes the farming activities of the Negroes along the banks of the river and his text, reproduced by Ramusio in 1554 and translated by Crone (1937: 42) reads as follows: "It appears that they grow various kinds of millet, small and large, [like chick peas, and] beans, and kidney beans, which are the largest and finest in the world."[35]

Godinho (1963: 15; 35), in his survey of the field, said: "It is perhaps already to maize that Cadamosto refers when describing what he saw on

[34] "O milho grosso for achado na America como sustento dos Indios, e de la trazido a Hespanha."

[35] "Laqual non è quelli paesi; ma la viuanda sua è di meglio di diuerse sorti, cioé minuto & grosso, come ceseri, & di fana & fasoli che nascono, che sono piu grossi & piu belli del mondo."

his voyage of 1455–1456 beyond the Senegal river: 'la vivanda sua è di miglio di diverse sorti, cioé minuto, e grosso como ceci...'"[36] He points out that the comparison "como ceci" could be a Ramusian interpolation, seeing it does not occur in the earlier text, but the distinction between *milho miudo* and *milho grosso* stands out. On referring to Crone's (1937: 42) translation of this passage one finds that it runs: "It appears that they grow various kinds of millet, small and large, beans and kidney beans, which are the largest and finest in the world. ... They are sown in the months of July, and harvested in September. ... They sow and harvest within three months." The translation is ambiguous. One cannot be sure whether it is the beans that are sown in July and harvested in September or whether this remark applies to all crops. The rainfall in Senegambia is suitable for both maize and sorghum, but no large-grained sorghum is known to ripen in three months, whereas maize, a large-grained cereal, does.

Those who know the area and the complications of the text are best fitted either to dismiss the point of the three months harvest as irrelevant to the *miglio* or to give it further consideration.

ASIA

There are a number of historical references to maize in Asia but only two that are Portuguese. One refers to maize in southern Arabia and the other to maize in China. Each of these references to maize indicates that maize was there prior to the arrival of the Portuguese and its presence was not due to any activity of the Portuguese.

Describing the city of Muscat, Dalbuquerque wrote, according to Birch (1875: I, 83): "It is a very elegant town, with very fine houses, and supplied from the interior with much wheat, maize, barley and dates for lading as many vessels as come for them."[37]

Dalbuquerque (1875: I, 84), also remarked of Muscat: "In this land, which these lords hold, there are many horses, which the farmers breed for sale; there is also great abundance of wheat, maize, and barley. ..."[38]

Dalbuquerque (1875: I, 93), according to Birch, said of the Arabian

[36] "É talvez já ao maiz que se refere Cadamosto, ao descrever o que viu nas suas viagens de 1455–1456 para além do rio Senegal: 'la vivanda sua è di miglio diverse sorti, cioè minuto, e grosso como ceci'...."

[37] "É lugar muito gracioso de casas muito boas, vem lhe do sertão muito trigo, milho, cevada, e tamaras para carregarem quantas náos quiserem."

[38] "Nesta terra, que estes senhores tem, ha muitos cavalos, que os lavradores criam, para vender: tem muita abastança de trigo, milho, e cevada ...."

port of Soar: "great quantities of dates and of maize are exported hence."[39]

Finally, Dalbuquerque (1875: I, 100) leaves one in no doubt that his use of *milho* refers to maize and not to sorghum when, according to Birch, describing Orfaçao, a large town in the kingdom of Ormuz, he wrote: "... in the fields is much straw and stubble, as in Portugal, and there are many maize fields."[40] Dalbuquerque's use of the word *milharadas* in this passage is conclusive. The term is used for fields of maize and for no other cereal.

Early Chinese encyclopedias state that maize reached China overland from the west. Thus Ho (1955: 195) wrote: "It is fairly certain that maize was first brought to Peking as tribute by ... western tribesmen before the middle of the sixteenth century, hence the early Chinese name for maize, *yü-mai* [Imperial wheat] and its early vulgar name, the homonym *yü mai* [jade wheat]."

A Portuguese emissary to China in 1575, Martin de Rada, is quoted by Boxer (1953: 277) in his translation as recording that among the taxes paid in kind as tribute to the Chinese emperor was one of "another kind of grain, 139,535 quintals." Boxer (1952: 179) also noted:

> Mendoza, OSA, *Historia de las cosas notables ritos y costumbres del gran Reino de la China* ... in a list which he gives of the tribute paid annually to the Emperor of China by his subjects, after mentioning rice, 'trigo como el de España' and milho [modern *mijo*] is an item — 'De trigo clamado maiz, veinte millones doscientas cincuenta mil fanegas,' which implies that a great quantity of maize was grown in China as early as 1575, which was the year in which Mendoza's informants had visited China.

The tribute, amounting to 20,500,000 *fanegas* or bushels of maize, paid in 1575 did not represent the whole maize crop. Even if the tribute were as high as one third of the crop it would mean that something like 60,000,000 bushels of maize had been harvested. Boxer (1953: 277), commenting on 20,500,000 *fanegas* paid as tribute, remarked: "This seems to be rather an early date for the large scale cultivation of maize in China, but Gonzales de Mendoza refers elsewhere to its growth — 'between these trees they sow maize, which is the ordinary food of the Indians of Mexico and Peru'." From the reference to Mexico and Peru it is clear that de Mendoza knew what grain he had in view. Boxer was highly sceptical of the alleged recent introduction of maize into China and claimed: "The spread of maize from the New World to the Old World merits further study." For

[39] "Carrega-se neste porto muitas tamaras, e milho."

[40] "... Pelos campos muitos rastolhos de trigo, como o de Portugal, muitas milharadas."

maize to have been used in Peking in eastern China in such quantities as tribute in 1575 and to have been brought by "western tribesmen" before 1550, maize must have been a well-established crop in countries west of China long before these dates, say by 1510. But this in turn indicates a long period of cultivation in the locus of diffusion still further west, certainly going back to 1490. In the distribution of a foreign annual crop, such as maize, it is necessary to have half-a-year at least for the production of seed, while propagation methods also have to be learnt. The western route into China involves a journey of some nine thousand miles from the Iberian Peninsula. The people along the route were not in contact with Spain or Portugal. The route was controlled from the Turkish Empire, then in the ascendant. The evidence points to Turkey as the locus of diffusion and to a date earlier than that of the return of Columbus.

MAIZE ENTERS THE IBERIAN PENINSULA

In the history of the Iberian peninsula it is evident that there have been not one but several entries of maize at pre-Columbian dates. The evidence here can be based on surviving tradition and early records, but is supplemented by calling attention to names which connect maize with its introduction from Africa and the Old World. This last point is a curious anomaly if the first introduction came straight from the New World.

Godinho (1963: 34), a Portuguese scholar of distinction, has summarized and commented on the greater part of the available information on early maize. An interesting reference in Portugal is noted from the poems of Rui Moniz, writing about 1492, and mentioning popcorn maize: "which means that before the 1515 edition of Moniz's poems, it is probable that at the end of the fifteenth century maize on the cob was eaten in Portugal, and so commonly that a poet referred to it."[41] Godinho concluded: "It cannot be excluded that in metropolitan Portugal the cultivation of maize was introduced through Moroccan sources, in their turn from Negro sources."[42] I do not subscribe to Godinho's conclusion that maize was also indigenous to Negro Africa, but the conclusion in no way

[41] "Numa poesia de Rui Moniz, cuja actividade poética se situa à volta de 1492 (Costa Pimpao, Idade Media, 347), refere-se a 'maçaroca fryta' (Cancioneiro Geral, II, 136–137): quer dizer que antes de 1515 (data de ediçao) e provàvelmente já em fins do século XV se comia milho de maçaroca em Portugal — e tão correntemente, que um poeta se lhe refere."

[42] "... Não é pois de excluir que em Portugal metropolitano a cultura do milho tenha sido introduzido em provenciência de Marrocos, por seu turmo em proveniência do mundo Negro."

invalidates his evidence for pre-Columbian maize in Africa and its early introduction to Portugal. Godinho (1963: 37, 38) was finally forced by the limited chronology to suggest two origins for maize, one in the New World, another in the Old. Such a proposition is not accepted by botanists, and the views of such experts as Kempton and Mangelsdorf and Reeves have been quoted that: "Maize is everywhere identical."

Other scholars have been interested in the early appearance of maize in the Iberian peninsula, for instance, Merrill (1954: 373) noted: "Messedaglia, a well informed though somewhat hasty and uncritical author, was convinced that maize was in cultivation in Spain and in Italy before Columbus discovered America."

Milho marroco or Moroccan grain was a term known fairly early in Portugal as Ribeiro (1941: 659) admits. The name has a parallel in Catalan Spain, where, according to Sauer (1960: 780) maize was formerly known as *blat de Moro*, and a parallel in Sardinia, where, according to Muratori (1952: 79) maize is called *triticu moriscu.* The term indicates that maize was being cultivated in Moorish North Africa before it crossed the Mediterranean carrying the name of the source from whence it came.

A tradition of the entry of maize under this name is recorded by Gomez who was in Monomatapa about 1645. According to Axelson's translation (1959: 155–242) he wrote: "Everyone has a hankering to make wine and so the Cafres also appear with a brew which they call *pombe*, which is made of *milho* with the large cob of which there is some along the banks of the Duoro and Mondego, between the Duoro and the Minho it is called *milho marroco*, milho which comes from the Morrocos, it is a tradition among the farmers that the Moors when they took possession of Spain brought it with them."[43]

There were several Moorish invasions; the last and greatest was that of the Almodes who, according to Haydn (1910: 42): "entered Spain and took Seville, Cordova, and Granada, 1146–1156 and founded a dynasty and ruled Spain till 1232." The Moors were finally evicted from Spain in 1492. The tradition then may go back to 1232, and certainly goes back before 1492.

The scenes of the Moorish conquest, Seville, Cordova, and Granada, are all in Andalusia, the province nearest to Morocco. There is evidence of maize growing in Andalusia from Peter Martyr who chronicled

[43] "Toda a naçao aspirou a fazer vinho, os Cafres tambe sayraõ cõ sua emuençao, chamão lhe elles *pombe*, este se fas de farinha de milho, de milho de espiga grande, q̃ ao longo do douro e Mondego, há algũ, chamão, lhe entre douro, e minho maroco, milho q̃ veo marôcos, assy he tradição dos lavradores, q̃ os mouros, quando se apoderauão de Espanha, o trouxerão consigo."

the return of the ships from America. In a letter written to Cardinal Sforza in Milan on the Ides of November 1493 after the return of the caravels, he wrote, according to MacNutt's translation (1912: I, 64), of the inhabitants of the Caribbean islands: "The islanders also easily make bread with a kind of millet, similar to that which exists plenteously amongst the Milanese and Andalusians. ... The grains are about the form and size of peas. While they are growing they are white, but become black when ripe. When ground they are whiter than snow. This kind of grain is called maize." Weatherwax (1954: 10) has pointed out that the last sentence was an addition made twenty years later, circa 1516, but the sentence merely adds the name. The description is clearly that of maize, for no other cultivated cereal is indigenous to the Americas. The size and color are, as reported for instance by the anonymous explorer who accompanied Cortez and, according to Saville's translation (1917: 35), noted of the inhabitants of Mexico: "The grain with which they make the bread is a kind of pea, and there is white, crimson, black and reddish." On the report of maize in Milan, one may quote Bon (1924–1932: 970) as saying: "The time when maize was first reported in Italy was about 1500."[44] Peter Martyr also interviewed Antonio Torres who, according to Duff (1936: 320), arrived at Medina having been sent by Columbus in April 1494 and bringing specimens of the various plants with him. Peter Martyr sent to Cardinal Sforza "some of those black and white seeds" of which the American Indians "make bread."

Peter Martyr's mention of maize in Andalusia throws light upon the letter of Columbus, mentioning maize in Castile, and hitherto ambiguous. Pim (1910: 11) drew attention to the passage as early as 1910:

> In *The History of a voyage which Don Christopher Columbus made the third time that he came to the Indies (1497) when he discovered Terra Firma, and which he sent to their Majesties from the island of Hispaniola*, the following passage occurs: 'y asimismo debo de maiz, ques es una simiente qua hace una espiga como una mazorca de que llevé yo alla, y hay ya mucho en Castilla, y parece que aquel que lo tenia mejor lo traia por mayor excelencia, y lo daba en gran precio.' This is translated or perhaps mistranslated as follows: 'The most reasonable inference is that they use maize which is a plant that bears a spine like an ear of wheat, SOME OF WHICH I TOOK WITH ME FROM SPAIN, WHERE IT GROWS ABUNDANTLY.'

Pim adds a footnote to the effect that: "The word maize is recorded in European literature here for the first time." The ambiguity has been dealt with in detail elsewhere.[45]

[44] "All' epoca in cui in Italia si connobe questo grano, nel 1500 circa ...."
[45] Jeffreys (1965).

Milho marroco was also given as the name of a new crop cultivated in 1531 by Rui Fernandez near the village of Lamego in Portugal, according to Ribeiro (1941: 659) who commented on the list of crops as follows:

Milho marroco appears here clearly distinct fro m *milho miudo* and from *painço* the detailed way in which they describe the very tall cane with a cob and its grain leaves no doubt that it is maize ... Marroco may mean foreign, (cf. *trigo de Indias, blé d'Espagne, grano turco* — all names for maize) and shows without a shadow of doubt that it is a cereal of exotic origin ...[46]

The views of Godinho on the introduction of maize from Morocco into the Iberian peninsula are unequivocal. Godinho (1963: 37, 38) after being satisfied that *milho zaburro* meant maize, wrote:

This *milho zaburro* is grown in Morocco from 1523 at the latest: the *Varzea of Conde* near Arzile, was covered with it (Bernado Rodrigoes, *Anais do Arzila* I, 422). But it was not only the Portuguese who cultivated it. In 1540 Bastiao de Vargae saw fields sown with *milho zaburro* in native Morocco, even around Fez and he says 'In Africa much *milho zaburro* is produced and it is good quality' (Sources Inédites de l'Histoire du Maroc, III 290). The following year he tells the king that had it not been for the *milho*, people would die of hunger in the kingdom of Fez (III, 547) ...[47]

In view of the evidence of Moroccan introduction, one ought to find an Arab name for maize which would be the name used by the Moors and the name introduced into the invaded territories. Curiously enough *milho de maçaroca* is itself such a term. Wiener (1920: I, 110) remarked that the Portuguese term for cob millet was not of Portuguese origin: "*maçaroca* is an old word for it is recorded in Spain as *mazorca*, 'the distaff with its flax,' in Alcala, where it is also given as an Arabic word. Whatever its origin it is older than the discovery of the New World...." It appears to be a name long used by the Arab world for maize. Portères (1958: 752) noted

[46] "*O milho marroco* aparece aqui claramente distinto do *milho* (muido) e do painço, e a minucia em que se descrevem 'canas muito altas', a espiga e os respectivos grãos, não deixa dúvidas que se trata do maiz ... Marroco pode estar na acepçao genérica do estrangeiro (cf. *trigo de Indias, blé d'Espagne, grano turco,* nomes dados ao milho) e mostra sem sembra de dúvida que se trata de um cereal de origem exótica ...."

[47] "Ce milho zaburro est cultivé au Maroc dès 1523 au plus tard: la Varezea do Condes, près d'Arzila, en était couverte (Bernado Rodriques, Anais de Arzila, I, 422). Mais ce n'étaient pas seulement les Portugais qui le cultivaient: En 1540 Bastião de Vargas a vu des champs semés de milho zaburro dans le Maroc indigène, même autour de Fès, et il dit: en Afrique il se reproduit beaucoup de milhos zaburro, de bonne qualité (Sources Inédites de l'Histoire du Maroc, III, 290). L'année suivante il raconte au Roi que s'il n'y avait pas eu de milhos, on crèverait de faim dans le royaume de Fès (III, 547) ...."

that in the languages spoken in the Arab influenced area of Lake Chad are the following names for maize: "Among the Shuwa Arabs, *massakua*; among the eastern Fulani of Nigeria, *maskuweri*; among the Fulani of the Cameroons, *muskuari*; among the Housa, *masakuwa* and *mazakua*; among the Kanuri, *masakwa*." Portères claimed that all these maize names derive from the Arab word *maqzul* meaning a fuse or a tassel and that they have the same primary meaning that the Spanish-Arab word *mazorka* has.[48] It appears that the descriptive Arab word *maqzul* was applied to maize before the Arabs entered Spain, and that they took their name with them, and that the name was adopted for general use on the peninsula. It is highly unlikely that a Spanish term would be transported to the depths of Africa.

There is evidence that one line of the importation of maize into Portugal was via Guinea and the West African coasts and at a pre-Columbian date. Thus Viterbo (1865 [1792]: I, 68), a Portuguese himself, in his *Supplement* to the *Elucidario* of 1798 noted under the word *maçaroca* that in the time of King John II (1481–1495): "on the discovery of Guinea, so say some writers, the Portuguese discovered the *milho grosso de maçaroca* and brought it to Portugal ..."[49] In the seventeenth century Manuel Severin de Faria according to Ribeiro (1941: 659) stated that *milho grosso de masaroca* "comes from Guiné" and Ribeiro established that *milho de masaroca* was *milho americão* or *maize*. Ribeiro has also cited M. N. Martins 'O milho grosso em Portugal e seus imigos' (1910: IX, 68–83) as saying that: "the statement by Rui Fernandes agrees with the passage quoted from De Barros and Rui Fernandes maintains that maize came to Portugal from Africa."[50] Support for the claim of such an introduction of pre-Columbian maize has lately come from Sauer.

Godinho (1963: 37, 38) stated:

> I incline to the following interpretation: milho zaburro, milho grosso, milho de maçaroca, milhao, milho marroco, maize, are all one and the same. The centre of diffusion has been Guinea. Introduced as early as 1502 to the island of São Thomé, during the first twenty years of the sixteenth century it established itself in the Cape Verde islands (unless it started there a little earlier) and in

[48] "Dans les parlers circumtchadiens on relève des termes comme: arabe shuwa massakua; peul oriental de Nigeria *maskuweri;* peul fulfulde du Cameroun *muskuari;* housa *masakuwa* et *mazakuwa;* kanuri *maskwa.* ... Tout ces termes d'origine arabe (maqzul 'fusée) ont ici le même sens que dans l'hispano-arabe *mazorka.*"

[49] "No tempo d'El Rei D. João II, e no descubrimento da Guiné, dizem alguns, descubrirão os Portuguezes, o *Milho grosso de maçaroca,* donde o trouxeram a Portugal; ...."

[50] "... Conjuga com o passo aludido de Barros o Testemunho de Rui Fernandes e sustenta que o milho nos veio de África" (M. N. Martins 1910).

Morocco. From Morocco — indirectly then — and from Guinea, directly, it reaches Portugal.[51]

The Cape Verde islands mentioned by Godinho were not restricted to trading in their own produce, but had been trading with Upper Guinea, the coast from the Senegal to Mount Cameroons, since before 1466. Discussing the early maritime trade from Santiago, Blake (1937: 91) pointed out that in addition to the trade with Portugal: "there was a little local trade in West Africa. The Santiagians early opened up a trade with the mainland of Guinea. This commerce was encouraged by the special privileges granted the islands in 1466. ..." He went on to note: "During the year 1514 at least nine caravels left the island carrying hides, skins, rice, ivory, wax, wooden-bowls, and millet (milho), products which had been purchased in Upper Guinea." Prestage (1933: 145) confirmed this, pointing out that it was not until about 1500 that the other Cape Verde Islands were colonized: "but already in 1513 and the two following years the island of Santiago exported a considerable amount of slaves, hides, skins, rice, ivory, Indian corn, wax and cotton." Indian corn, or maize, had been purchased in Guinea and was being exported to Portugal. Prestage is quoting from a Portuguese source, Barcello's *Subsidias pava a historia de Cabo Verde e Guiné* (1899: 72–75).

Similar introductions of maize from Guinea could be made into Spain, for the Portuguese sailors were not the only traders on the west coast. Blake (1937: 92) wrote: "Unquestionably evidence exists that a fleet of Andalusians went to Senegambia in 1454; it is equally certain that Andalusians frequented the whole of West Africa between 1475 and 1480." He also notes: "The link between Castile and Guinea dated back ... at least to 1454. There can be little doubt about spasmodic Castilian voyages between 1454 and 1475."

Viterbo (1865 [1792]: 89) in the *Elucidario* quoted: "milho zaburro, milho grande, milho graùdo, milho maiz, milhão, ou milho grosso, è milho de maçaroca." In his entry under *milhom* (from which the present word *hilho* is derived) he noted a will dated 1289 reading: "'to Stevdo Johannes de Parafita, or to his heirs, a *quarteiro* of *milhom*'" and added: "from which we could infer that at this date maize was already in

[51] "Je penche donc vers l'interprétation suivante. Milho zaburro, milho grosso, milho de maçaroca, milhão, milho marroco, maïs: c'est tout un. Le centre de diffusion en a été la Guinée. Introduit dès 1502 à l'île de São Tomé, pendant les deux premières décades du XVIe siècle il s'installe aux îles du Cap Vert (à moins qu'il n'y ait commencé un peu plus tôt) et au Maroc. Du Maroc — indirectement, donc — et de la Guinée, directement, il gagne le Portugal ...."

[52] "'... *A Stevdo Joannes de Perafita, on a seos herées, hum quarteiro de milhom.* Daqui se poderia inferir, que já então havia em Portugal milho maiz."

Portugal."[52] Bonafous (1836: 15) remarked: "Such an inference is in accord with the opinion of Valcarcel and other authors, who accepted that Arabs brought maize into the Spanish peninsula." An introduction in the thirteenth century would be compatible with Marques (1944: II, 12) listing *milho* as among the imports through the port of Antonguia between the years 1223–1279.

The known characteristics of the introduction of a new crop, the localized cultivation and the slow initial production, can be said to apply to any introduction of maize. Ribeiro (1941: 655) has noted: "Perhaps even in the fifteenth century it was introduced into Europe: in 1500 there was already in Seville some grains of it that served as experiments for a new crop. Its spread did not occur immediately afterwards and for some years it was confined to the valley of the Guadalquivir. ..."[53] This is the pattern to be expected from the cultivation of maize grains brought back by Columbus to Castile after his second voyage. But the widespread reports of maize in various localities about 1500 and the amount produced can only be explained by earlier introductions. The early reports of maize in Castile, Andalusia and Milan, as well as in Portugal, together with reports of its extensive cultivation in Morocco and in West and East Africa, are only compatible with an introduction into Africa about the twelfth century and an introduction into Spain about the thirteenth century. An early account of maize recorded by Ribeiro (1941: 655) is interesting in revealing a post-Columbian local introduction into a country where maize was evidently already known. The popularity attributed to the crop of one farmer was in actuality the result of earlier maize cultivation:

Duarte Ribeiro de Macedo (1675) says: '*Milho grosso* was found in America as the food of the Indians and from there was brought to Spain. From Cadiz a Portuguese of Campo de Coimbra brought less than an alqueire (so said the farmers of that Campo) and sowed it in one of his fields and it throve with such luxuriance that it is not easy to explain its abundance and the wealth which accrued to the realm from the rustic curiosity of this private individual.'

Cuna Coutenho suggests that the date of this introduction was 1515–1525. 'At first these exotic crops were prohibited from being sown and survived as small plots in gardens and kitchen gardens; soon, however, the planting of maize began to spread rapidly through all the northern provinces and this American grain became so highly appreciated by our farmers that already in 1533 it had ousted in the markets barley and sorghum.'[54]

[53] "Talvez ainda no século XV fôsse introduzida na Europa: em 1500 havia já em Sevilha alguns grãos que seriam para ensaiar a nova cultura. A propogação dela não se fez imediatemente e durante alguns anos esteve confinada ao vale do Guadalquivir; foi dai que a trouxeram para Portugal."

[54] Diz Duarte Ribeiro de Macedo (em 1675): "O milho grosso foi achado na America

The case of De Acosta is illuminating. The very fact that he considers maize to have been imported into the Indies, his inability to realize that it is indigenous to the New World, and his lack of connection of maize in Europe with Columbus, all argue that maize had long been an established crop in the Old World. He had lived in Peru between 1570 and 1587 and published his *Historia* as early as 1588 in the Andalusian city of Seville. He had been interested in the recent intercontinental traffic in plants, according to Purchas's translation (1905–1907: 122): "The Indians have received more profit, and have been recompensed in plants that have been brought from Spain, than in any other merchandise, for those few that are carried from the Indies into Spain, grow little there, and multiply not, and contrariwise the great number that have been carried from Spain to the Indies, prosper well and multiply greatly." Of the Peruvians he noted, according to Purchas (1905–1907:106): "We find not they had any kind of wheat or barley, nor any other kind of grain which they use in Europe to make bread withal: instead whereof they used other kinds of grains and roots, amongst the which mays holds first place, and with reason, in Castile they call it Indian wheat, and in Italy they call it Turkey grain." According to Markham (1880: II, 231), in his rendering of Grimstone's translation of 1604, De Acosta voiced his queries as follows: "I will aske sooner than I can answer it, whence Mays was first carried to the Indies, and why they do call this profitable graine in Italie, Turkie graine? For in truth I doe not find that the Antients make any mention of this graine...." A thirteenth-century introduction of maize into Europe would explain De Acosta's belief that the grain had been taken from Europe as a boon and a blessing to the American Indian, while it would also explain the lack of any reference in "the Antients".

Terms for this cereal are numerous, the word rendered as maize, however, only appeared with Columbus and is not found in early works. Nowhere along the southern coasts of the Mediterranean is maize known by a name connecting it with Europe, but several names along the northern coasts indicate that maize crossed the Mediterranean from south to north. The herbalists use names indicating an eastern origin. Boek was the

como sustanto dos Indios, e de lá trazido a Hespanha. De Cadiz trouxe hum Portuguez do Campo de Coimbra menos de hum alqueire, (dizem os Lavradores daquelle Campo) e o semeou em huma terra sua, e produziu com tanto excesso, que não he facil de explicar a abundancia, utilidade e riqueza, que se seguio ao Reino desta rustica curiosidade de hum particular."

"Cuna Coutinho propõe, como data da introdução, 1515–1525. Proïbidas a princípio aquelas sementeiras exóticas, reduzidas a paucos pés, nas hortas e jardins, em breve se divulgara a cultura de milho por tôdas as provincias do Norte; e por tal forma foi apreciada essa gramínea americana pelos nossos agricultores que já em 1533, havia suplantado, nos mercados, o centeio, a cevada e o milho miudo."

first to mention the plant, according to Bonafous (1836: 11) and in 1532 said that the plant was brought: "from Arabia Felix to Germany and that it was named wheat of Asia. ..." Bonafous quotes Fuchs as saying: "This wheat came from foreign parts, from Asia and from Greece it passed into Germany where it is called Turkish wheat; ... it is because of the country from which it was introduced that the Germans call it Turkey wheat."

CONCLUSION

The records of Portuguese investigation of the west coasts of Africa by a variety of observers between 1502 and 1510 make frequent and consistent mention of a grain grown in quantity as one of the staple foods of the local inhabitants. From the descriptions the grain cannot be identified as sorghum, for there is no species of sorghum which is simultaneously large grained, quick maturing, and tolerant of the high rainfall of the forest belt which virtually, with one small break, covers the Guinea coasts from the Senegal to Mount Cameroon. There is no evidence today that sorghum is cultivated in these areas or that it has ever been grown there. The descriptions, on the other hand, are characteristic of maize, a New World plant, which is today a staple food of the inhabitants of West Africa and which has an ancient history among them. The now universally used modern term "maize," originally a local American Indian word, was only introduced by Columbus. It has been necessary to establish at some length the exact meaning of other, and probably older, names for the grain, including *milho de Guynee*, *milho zaburro*, *milho de maçaroca* and *milho*. This has been done by reference to the descriptions given and by noting that these names were used of maize when it was first seen in America.

On the East Coast of Africa records from the first arrival of the Portuguese in 1498 exhibit the same interest. Under the word *milho* a grain is similarly recorded as existing in large quantity and shown as distinct from *mexoiera* or sorghum; also, early arrivals speak of a grain similar to that of Guinea, while Pereira uses the term *milho* for a grain both on the East and the West Coast.

Portuguese observers also noted a grain which can clearly be identified as maize in Muscat in 1515 and also in China as early as 1575, areas not controlled by European trade. This point indicates that the Turkish Empire had obtained maize and was acting as a locus of diffusion. The vast areas served and the quantities of grain cultivated in Africa and in China indicate that maize had been in the Old World for some time and certainly at a date incompatible with an introduction into Castile after 1492.

In the Iberian peninsula itself the introduction of maize cannot be clearly traced to a date after the return of Columbus. A letter from Columbus himself can be read as stating that he had taken maize to America and that there was much in Castile when he wrote. Peter Martyr, who met the returning ships, noted that the maize grains were the same as those used by the Milanese and the Andalusians. Early Portuguese historians were of the opinion that maize had been brought from Guinea, an opinion confirmed by the Portuguese term of *milho de Guynee*. Another tradition connects maize on the Douro with a Moorish introduction, and the term *maçaroca* is in itself a word of Arab provenance. Morocco, under Arab domination, has also been an unquestioned source of maize.

This linguistic study has been undertaken to establish the presence of maize in the Old World before the return of Columbus from America and by this means to alert archaeologists to the fact that the presence of maize cannot be used to date a site as post-1500. It is a contribution to the larger problem of trans-Atlantic contacts in the centuries immediately preceding the European discovery of the New World.

REFERENCES

ADANDÉ, A.

1935 Le maïs et ses usages dans le Bas Dahomey. *Bulletin de l'Institut français d'Afrique noire* 15:220–282.

ANONYMOUS

1929 "Albuquerque, Alfonso D'," in *The Encyclopedia Britannica* (fourteenth edition). London: Encyclopedia Britannica.

ARBER, A.

1943 *The graminae: a study of cereal, bamboo and grass.* Cambridge, Massachusetts: Schenkman

AXELSON, E.

1940 *Southeast-Africa 1488–1530.* London: Longmans, Green.

1959 Viagem que fez o Padre Ant. O Gomes, da Comp. A de Jesus, ao Imperio de de [*sic*] Manomotapa; e assistencia que fez nas ditas terras d. E Alg'us annos. *Studia.* 3:155–242.

BAKER, S. W.

1868 *The Nile tributaries of Abyssinia and the sword hunters of the Hamran Arabs* (third edition). London: Macmillan.

BASCOM, W. R.

1951 Yoruba food. *Africa.* 21:41–53.

BAUMANN, H., D. WESTERMANN

1948 *Les peuples et les civilizations de l'Afrique suivis de les langues et l'education.* Translated by L. Homberger. Paris.

BECKINGHAM, C. F., G. W. B. HUNTINGFORD

1961 *The Prester John of the Indies*, two volumes. Cambridge: Hakluyt Society.

BLAKE, J. W.

1937 *European beginnings in West Africa 1454–1578*. London: Longmans Green.

1942 *Europeans in West Africa 1450–1560*, two volumes. London: Hakluyt Society.

BLUTEAU, R.

1716–1721 *Vocabulario Portuguez e Latino*, eight volumes. Coimbra: Collegio das Artas de Companhia de Jesu.

BON, M.

1924–1932 "Mais," in *Enciclopedia Italiana*. Rome.

BONAFOUS, M

1836 *Histoire naturelle: agricole et économique du maïs*. Paris: Huzard.

BOSMAN, W. A.

1907 *New and accurate description of the coast of Guinea* (reprint of 1690 edition). London: Ballantyne Press.

BOWEN, J. T.

1857 *Central Africa*. New York: Sheldon, Blakeman.

1858 *Grammar and dictionary of the Yoruba*. Washington: Smithsonian Institution.

BOXER, C. R.

1952 Maize names. *Uganda Journal* 16:178–179.

1953 *South China in the sixteenth century*. London: Hakluyt Society.

1959 *The tragic history of the sea 1589–1622*. Cambridge: Hakluyt Society.

BRYANT, A. T.

1907 *A description of native foodstuffs and their preparation*. Maritzburg: Times Printing and Publishing.

BUMPUS, E. D.

1951 Agriculture in Nigeria. *Proceedings of the Rhodesia Scientific Association*, 43:40–49.

BURTON, R. F.

1873 *The lands of Cazembe*. London: John Murray.

BURTON, R. F., *editor*

1874 *The captivity of Hans Stade*. Translated by A. Tootal, annotated by R. F. Burton. London: Hakluyt Society.

BURTT-DAVY, J.

1914 *Maize: its history, cultivation, handling and uses*. London: Longmans Green.

CRONE, G. R.

1937 *The voyages of Cadamosto*. London: Hakluyt Society.

CROW, H.

1830 *Memoirs of Captain Hugh Crow*. London: Longman, Rees, Orme, Brown and Green.

DALBOQUERQUE, A.

1875 *The commentaries of the great Afonso Dalboquerque*, four volumes. Translated by W. de Gray Birch. London: Hakluyt Society.

DALE, D.
1968 *Shona companion*. Gwelo: Mambo Press.
DALZIEL, J. M.
1937 *The useful plants of west tropical Africa*. London: Crown Agents.
DA MARAIS SILVA, A.
1945 *Grande dictionario da lingua Portuguesa* (tenth edition). Lisboa: Moreno, A. Cardosa, Jn., J. P. Machado.
DAMES, M. L.
1918–1921 *The book of Duarte Barbosa*, two volumes. London: Hakluyt Society.
DE BARROS, J.
1945 *Asia* (reprinted edition). Lisbon: A. Cidade and M. Murias.
DE CENIVAL, P., T. MONOD
1938 *Description de la côte d'Afrique que de Ceuta au Sénégal par Valentim Fernandes (1506–1507)*. Paris: Libraire Larose.
DE PAIVA BOLÉO, M.
1946 Introduçao ao estudo da Filologia Portuguesa. *Biblos* 22.
DIAS, J., M. DIAS
1964 *Os Macondes de Mozambique*, three volumes. Lisbon: Junta de Investigaçoes do Ultramar.
DOKE, C. M., B. W. VILAKAZI
1948 *Zulu-English dictionary*. Johannesburg: Witwatersrand University Press.
DRINKWATER BETHUNE, C. R.
1847 *The observations of Sir Richard Hawkins Knt. on his voyage into the South Sea in the year 1593*. London: Hakluyt Society.
DUDGEON, G. C.
1911 *The agricultural and forest products of British West Africa*. London: John Murray.
DUFF, C.
1936 *The truth about Columbus*, London: Grayson and Grayson.
DUNCAN, J.
1847 *Travels in Western Africa in 1845–1846*, two volumes. London: Richard Bentley.
FAULKNER, O. T., J. R. MACKIE
1933 *West African agriculture*. Cambridge: University Press.
FINAN, J. J.
1950 *Maize in the great herbals*. Waltham, Massachusetts: Chronica Botanica.
GANN, L. H.
1964 *A history of northern Rhodesia, early days to 1953*. London: Chatto and Windus.
GODE, P. K.
1950 "The history of maize (makā) in India," in *Commemoration volume* M. M. Prof. D.V. Potdar, 14–25. Poona.
GODINHO, V. M.
1963 O milho maiz — origem e diffusão. *Revista de Economia* 15:33–38.
GREAT BRITAIN EAST AFRICAN ROYAL COMMISSION
1953–1955 Report (Cmd 9475). London: Her Majesty's Services Overseas.

HARRIS, C. A.

1928 *A relation of a voyage to Guiana by Robert Harcourt 1613*. London: Hakluyt Society.

HARTWIG, G.

1886 *The tropical world* (new edition). London: Longmans Green.

HAYDN, J.

1910 *Haydn's dictionary of dates and universal information* (twenty-fifth edition). London: Ward Lock.

HILL, A. F.

1952 *Economic botany*. New York: McGraw-Hill.

HO, PING-TI

1955 American food plants in China. *American Anthropologist* 57:191–201.

IRVINE, F. R.

1953 *A text-book of West African agriculture* (second edition). Oxford: Oxford University Press.

JEFFREYS, M. D. W.

1956 Muhindi or grain of Arabia. *The Uganda Journal* 20:198–201.

1965 Maize and the ambiguity in Columbus's letter. *Anthropological Journal of Canada* 3:2–11.

1970 Maize names round the Indian ocean. *Anthropological Journal of Canada* 8:2–15.

JOHNSTON, H. H.

1908 *George Grenfell and the Congo*, two volumes. London: Hutchinson.

JOYCE, T. A.

1934 "The use and origin of Yerba maté," in *The advancement of* science. Aberdeen: British Association Meeting.

JUNOD, H. A.

1914 The condition of the natives of South Africa in the sixteenth century according to early Portuguese documents. *South African Journal of Science* 10:137–161.

JUTA, C. J.

1968 The wreck of the 'Santo Alberto', 1593. *Africana Notes and News* 18:39–42.

KAY, S.

1833 *Travels in Caffraria*. London: John Mason.

KIDD, D.

1904 *The essential Kaffir*. London: Adam and Charles Black.

KIMBLE, G. H. T., *editor*

1937 *Esmeraldo de situ orbis*. Written by Pacheco Pereira in 1509. London: Hakluyt Society.

LAINS E SILVA, H.

1958 São Tomé e Principe e a cultura do café. *Memõirs da Junta de Investigaçoes do Ultramar* (second series). 1:57–69.

1959 Nomes vulgares de algumas plantas de São Tomé e Principe. *Garcia de Orta* 7:293–323.

LANDER, R., J. LANDER

1832 *Journal of an expedition to explore the course and termination of the Niger*, three volumes. London: John Murray.

DE MACEDO, D. R. DE
1817 *Obras ineditas*. Lisbon.

MACHADO, A. R.
1943 *Verdadeira informação des terras do Presto João das Indias pelo Padres Francisco Alvares: 1520* Lisbon.

MACNUTT, F. A.
1912 *De orbe novo: the eight decades of Peter Martyr D'Angera*, two volumes. New York: G. P. Putnam's Sons.

MAJOR, R. H.
1847 *Select letters of Columbus*. Hakluyt Society.
1868 *The life of Prince Henry of Portugal, surnamed the navigator*. London: A. Asher.

MANGELSDORF, P. C., R. G. REEVES
1939 The origin of Indian corn and its relatives. *Texas Agricultural Experiment Stations Bulletin* 574.

MARKHAM, C. R.
1912 *Book of knowledge of all the kingdoms, lands and lordships that are in the world...* London: Hakluyt Society.

MARKHAM, C. R., *editor*
1880 *The natural and moral history of the Indies by Father Joseph de Acosta*, two volumes. London: Hakluyt Society.

MARQUES, J. M. DA SILVA
1944 *Descobrimentos Portugueses*, twelve volumes. Lisbon: Instituto de Alta Cultura.

MARTIN, A.
1956 *The oil palm economy of the Ibibio farmer*. Ibadan: Ibadan University Press.

MARTINS, M. N.
1910 O milho grosso em Portugal e seus inimigos. *Brotéria Ser. Bótanica* 9:68–83.

MAUNY, R.
1956 *Esmeraldo de situ orbis côte occidentale d'Afrique du sud Marocain au Gabon par Duarte Pacheco Pereira (vers 1505–1508)*. Bissau: Centro de Estudos da Guiné Portuguesa.

MEREDITH, H.
1812 *An account of the Gold Coast of Africa*. London: Longman, Hurst, Rees, Orme and Brown.

MERRILL, E. D.
1954 *The botany of Cook's voyages and its unexpected significance in relation to anthropology, biography and history*. Waltham, Massachusetts: Chronica Botanica.

MOLL, H.
1747 *A complete system of geography*, two volumes. London: William Innys, et al.

MONOD, T.
1960 Notes botaniques sur les *îles* de São Tomé et de principe. *Bulletin de l'I.F.A.N.* 22, series A:19–83.

MONOD, T., A. TEIXEIRA DA MOTA, R. MAUNY
1951 *Description de la côte occidentale d'Afrique (Sénégal au Cap de Monte, Archipels) par Valentim Fernandes (1506–1510)*. Bissau: Centro de Estudos da Guiné Portuguesa 11.

MOORE, J. H.
1785 *A new and complete collection of voyages and travels*, two volumes. London: Alexander Hogg.

MULLET, J. J. CLEMENT
1866 *Le livre de l'agriculture ou Kitab Al-Felahah par D"Ibn-al-Awan* 2 (1): 77 Paris.

MURATORI, C.
1952 Maize names and history: a further discussion. *The Uganda Journal* 16.

NICHOLLS, W.
1913 *The Shaikíya*. Dublin: Hodges, Figgs.

OGILBY, J.
1670 *Africa*. London: T. Johnson.

OSBORNE, T.
1745 *The Harleian collection of voyages and travels*, two volumes. London: T. Osborne.

PEARCE, F. B.
1920 *Zanzibar, the island metropolis of eastern Africa*. London: T. Fisher Unwin.

PERES, D., B. GOMES DI BRITO
1904 *Historia tragico-maritima*, volume one. Lisbon: Escriptoria.

PIM, H.
1910 *A plea for the scientific study of races inhabiting South Africa (with a digression on the history of maize)*. Johannesburg: Native Affairs Society of the Transvaal.

PORTÈRES, R.
1958–1959 Les appellations des céréales en Afrique. *Journal d'Agriculture Tropicale et de Botanique Appliquée*. 5 and 6.

PRESTAGE, E.
1933 *The Portuguese pioneers*. London: A. and C. Black.

PURCHAS, S.
1625 *Purchas his pilgrimes*, five volumes. London: Henrie Fetherstone.
1905–1907 *Hakluyt's posthumus or Purchas his pilgrimes* (First printed *1625–1626* London), twenty volumes, 15:122. Glasgow: James Maclehose and Sons.

RAVENSTEIN, E. G.
1898 *A journal of the first voyage of Vasco da Gama 1497–1499*. London: Hakluyt Society.

REGO, A. DA SILVA; T. W. BAXTER
1962 *Documents on the Portuguese in Mozambique and Central Africa 1497–1840*. Lisbon: Centro de Estudos Históricos Ultramarinos.

RHYS, E., *editor*
1907–1909 *Hakluyt's voyages (Everymans Library)*, eight volumes. London: Dent and Sons.

RIBEIRO, O.
1941 Cultura do milho economia agraria e povomento. *Biblos.* 17: 645–663.
SAUER, C. O.
1960 Maize into Europe. *Akten des 34 Internationalen Americanisten-kongresses* 778–784. Vienna: Verlag Ferdinand Berger, Horn.
SAUVAGEOT, S.
1961 Navigation de Lisbonne à l'île Sào Tomé par un pilote portugais anonyme (vers. 1545). *Garcia de Orta* 9:123–138.
SAVILLE, M. H.
1917 *Narrative of some things of New Spain.* New York: The Cortes Society.
SCHWEINFURTH, G.
1878 *The heart of Africa*, two volumes. London: Sampson Low, Marston, Searle and Rivington.
SCOTT, D. C.
1892 *A cyclopedic dictionary of the Mang'anja language.* Edinburgh: Foreign Mission Committee of the Church of Scotland.
SEMPLE, E. C.
1911 *Influences of geographic environment.* New York: Henry Holt.
SNOWDEN, J. D.
1936 *The cultivated races of sorghum.* London: Adlard and Sons.
SOARES DE SOUSA, G.
1878 *Tratado descriptio do Brazil em 1587.* Rio de Janeiro: Companhia editora Nacional.
STANLEY, E. E. J.
1869 *The three voyages of Vasco da Gama.* London: Hakluyt Society.
STURTEVANT, E. L.
1919 Notes on edible plants. *New York State Department of Agriculture 27th Annual Report* 2.
TAYLOR, E. G. R.
1932 *A brief summe of geographie by Roger Barlow.* London: Hakluyt Society.
THACHER, J. B.
1967 *Christopher Columbus, his life, his work, his remains as revealed by original printed and manuscript records together with an essay on Peter Martyr of Anghera and Bartolomé de las Casas, the first historian of America*, three volumes. New York: Ams Press, Kraus Reprint.
THEAL, G. M.
1898 *Records of south eastern Africa*, nine volumes. Capetown: Government Printer.
TOWLE, M. A.
1961 *The ethnobotany of pre-Columbian Peru.* Chicago: Aldine.
VAN WARMELO, N. J.
1937 *Tshivenda-English dictionary.* Pretoria: Government Printer.
VIEIRA, D.
1874 *Grande dictionario Portuguez au thesauro da lingua Portugueza*, five volumes. Porto: Chadron e de Maraes.

VITERBO, SANTA ROSA DE
1865 [1792] *Elucidario*, two volumes. Lisbon: A. J. Ferdinand de Lopes.
WASHINGTON, T.
1585 *Nicholay's voyages*. London.
WEATHERWAX, P.
1954 *Indian corn in old America*. New York: Macmillan.
WIENER, L.
1920 *Africa and the discovery of America*, three volumes. Philadelphia: Innes and Sons.
WILD, H.
1958 "Botanical notes relating to the Van Niekerk ruins," in *Inyanga*. Edited by R. Summers, 173–179. Cambridge: Cambridge University Press.
WILLETT, F.
1962 The introduction of maize into West Africa: an assessment of recent evidence. *Africa* 32:1–13.
WRIGHT. A. C. A.
1949 Maize names as indicators of economic contacts. *Uganda Journal* 13.

The Origin of Grape Wine: A Problem of Historical-Ecological Anthropology

GAETANO FORNI

HISTORICAL-ECOLOGICAL LAYOUT

For ecologists (Odum 1965), each living organism constitutes a part of an ecosystem. This is made up of nonliving and living components that interact among themselves resulting in the creation of an ecological balance. This develops with the evolution of the individual components (each component being endowed with a specific and variable evolutionary force) and with the accumulation of the long-range effects of their characteristics and nature.

Such evolution becomes highly dynamic in the ecosystems of which man is a part. Man in fact manifests a kind of behavioral change in which an exceedingly fast cultural evolution is associated with a biological one.

The result of this double evolution is an ever-growing reciprocal adjustment between the human species and its ecosystem. We can thus see that while initially the human species is ACCIDENTAL — i.e. that its presence is not a determining factor with regard to the structure of the ecosystems in which it exists (the hunter-gatherer stage in which use was made of natural crude implements) — yet, within contemporary industrial society the human species is outstandingly dominant. That means that the structure of the ecosystems in which man moves, i.e. the situation in which he dominates, is more or less completely determined by him, consciously (agriculture, gardening) or unconsciously (species that die out even if man has nothing to do with it). The transition from accidentality to ecological dominance is marked not only by substitution, even if only partial, of the hunting-gathering economy by that of an agricultural-pastoral one, but also by a complex of changes in customs, beliefs, and social structures. This paper aims to examine the evolution of a sector of human alimentation, the sector which deals with fermented beverages as found among peoples living in the eco-systems of ancient times, and thereafter during the transition (described above) from the stage of accidentality to that of ecological dominance. The course of our research will lead us to examine the history of the definite prevalence of wine in the Mediterranean and surrounding areas, and, at the same time, the evolution from wild to cultivated grapevines, that is, to a plant which is strictly symbiotic with man and genetically modified through this cohabitation.

There are three sources from which the historian can draw to reconstruct the original phases of the use of fermented beverages: (a) archaeological records; (b) customs and habits of peoples presently living on an analogous ecological level; (c) the traditions that remain among ecologically dominant peoples.

DIRECT AND INDIRECT ARCHAEOLOGICAL RECORDS

As far as archaeological records are concerned we have direct and indirect proof at our disposal.

DIRECT PROOF is the residues of fermented beverages such as dregs and seed clusters, related to the must of sugary fruits, etc. This obviously cannot take us back very far into antiquity for the simple reason that these residues have a very limited capacity for preservation. Clark (1955: 309) speaks of evidence of birchbark containers sewn with bast fiber: in the bottom of these containers, residues of dregs of a fermented drink were found. The containers were uncovered at a tomb in Egtved (Denmark) and date back to the Bronze Age. Also from the Bronze Age, even if chronologically older, are clusters of cornial cherry seeds (Landi 1962) found in northern Italy, proof of production of a fermented drink made from these fruits, and records of grape wine found in the eastern regions of the Mediterranean (Logothetis 1970; Renfrew 1973). Records of the production of grape wine then become general for the Mediterranean world during the Iron Age (Negri 1934; Renfrew 1973).

INDIRECT PROOF can be derived, on the other hand, from general verification, that is, where inventions have been made for a certain technological process resulting from existing technical, economic, social, and natural conditions. It is for this reason that the electric motor, the combustion engine, the telephone, the radio, etc. boast of different inventors — and contemporary ones among them at that. The fact is, we are dealing here in effect with a process of a physical-biological nature, for, in different localities which are distant from each other, we have similar kinds of ecosystems and even similar kinds of living species, even if they do not descend from an immediate common ancestry.

For this reason, when we have archaeological records in a given prehistoric period of (1) raw material, (2) the technical know-how regarding the preservation of liquids, (3) favorable economic-social conditions, we can consider we have indirectly proven the existence of a production of fermented beverages for the period in question.

It is obvious, nevertheless, that indirect proof cannot be held as certain but should be considered as probable.

Demonstration of (1) is easy in that in temperate Europe and the Mediterranean regions any treatise on vegetable paleontology will point out the presence of juicy, sugary fruits, of sprouts (palms, etc.), and of barks (maple, birch, etc.) which, when broken or incised, produce a large amount of sugary sap which is highly nourishing. Examination of (2) allows us to clarify (1) even more; in fact it is evident that only the possession of containers for holding liquids allows for the utilization, in a generalized and determinant way, of such drinks. Moreover, only sufficiently spacious and efficient containers permit the preservation of these beverages for the entire fermentation period.

In turn, (3) enables us to clarify (2); in fact, among the nomadic or seminomadic tribes of food-gatherers or hunters, it is rather difficult to ascertain the usefulness of preserving for a long time beverages that are not absolutely necessary.

An overall analysis, embracing the technical difficulties compared to the usefulness gained and the existing socioeconomic, technical, and natural conditions in the way considered above, enables us to establish the following:

a. Utilization of sugary sap derived from cut-up sprouts directly sucked out by mouth or gathered in concave leaves was probably widespread among gatherers in prelithic times.

b. A higher technical level (possession of sharp flint knives) is needed for incising bark (maple, birch, etc.) for the purpose of forcing the sugary sap to seep out. Such technical ability can be ascribed to hunters of the more recent Paleolithic period of Western Europe, for example. Such peoples were also able to make containers out of bark, or baskets plastered with resin or clay, or rudimentary skin bags for temporarily preserving these sugary liquids. But these could not preserve the juices for long periods of time, especially as the low sugar content found in these juices brings about a rapid, initial, and spontaneous fermentation (for which such beverages were in fact generally partially fermented), not the formation of wines, not even of the short-duration kind. In the tropical countries, among contemporary populations on an analogous technical level, containers are made out of strips of internodal bamboo (transversely cut in half with the pith removed) or, more easily, out of coconut or pumpkin shells. The sap taken from the apex cut from palm trees was preserved in these small containers and remains the custom of primitive peoples today.

c. It is only with the widespread development of the formation of settlements in the Epipaleolithic, Mesolithic, and above all, in the Neolithic periods that the technique of making containers for keeping liquids for long periods of time was perfected. This took place first of all with the introduction of ceramics. It is only then that one can detect at the bottom of the containers in which fruit juices were preserved the accumulation of a sugary liquid, derived from pressing of overripe fruits, in the fermentation stage.

d. With the differentiation of cultivated or domestic grapevines, and with the abundant production of grapes rich in juice and sugars, the production of grape wine which could be preserved for a long time came into being.

Since archaeological records concerning cultivated grapevines go back only to the late Neolithic (Bronze Age), it is clear that the production of grape wine in the area of southwestern Asia and in the Balkans can only be proved to go back to the Bronze Age.

ANALOGICAL PROOF AND THE LOGIC OF RESEARCH

The premise stated above, that is, that with given natural, economic, and social conditions, different human communities which are independent among themselves probably bring about the invention and hence the possession of a given technique which directly depends on those conditions, can be verified and studied more thoroughly by using contemporary illiterate populations found in analogous conditions. In fact, Werth (1954: 229) and Maurizio (1970: 1) cite as evidence of this gatherers and hunters of California who, before the predominance of the white man, made use of sap taken from maple, birch, and sugar pine. In the same way, other contemporary, very primitive peoples, either hunters or gatherers such as the Bushmen and the Pygmies of the Congo, the Weddas of Ceylon, the Semangs of Malacca, use juices derived from barks of different plants, as well as drinks prepared from wild honey and fruits. The Tungusi hunters of northern Asia use wine made from birch, while Australian hunters use flowers rich in nectar (Baxia) as well as juice taken from Mangrove sprouts; Patagonian and Chaco hunters use succulent and sugary fruits. The more rudimentary the technical level of such peoples, the less efficient the available containers are, and the faster the sugary drinks are used while undergoing only the inevitable initial fermentation. This is the case with the Weddas, the Semangs, the Pygmies, and the Bushmen. On the whole we have thus confirmed the interpretation of the archaeological data according to the evolutionary process which we have already illustrated.

It could be said that we are dealing with demonstrations of a probable as well as statistical nature, and hence that it is easy to draw rash conclusions. But even in historical and anthropological research, Popper's logic (1959) seems valid. His logic states that the researcher must, on the basis of available data (of whose certainty and validity he must be aware), draw up hypotheses concerning the occurrence of an event. These then will never be able to be shown as being true (some data imply only probability), but only a falsification of events. This will take place when data are pointed out which show that the event never took place or that, if it did take place, it did so differently from what was believed. In other words, the rejection of determining data on the basis that they deal only with probability is not wise because it would unduly impoverish our knowledge.

TRADITION AS EVIDENCE

The rural populations of Europe, especially those found in secluded regions, still adhere to the very ancient traditions of making wine from birch. Invaluable documentation of this is given for peasants of Baltic Europe by Ligers (1953: 31). Similar customs are common in the forest of Bohemia, in Carinthia, the Balkan, and Russia. Besides birch, beech and maple are used (Werth 1954: 229). Besides making a cut into the bark, the techniques are based on the more primitive technique of cutting the sprouts and then leaving them to drip. This practice is often used by young boys (Tolstoi 1970). Here we can see how an economic activity of the late Paleolithic is preserved on a "game" level: we do not say "degraded" because, as was rightly pointed out by Huizinga (1964), everything was a "game" in the beginning.

After the sugary liquid has been gathered in great quantities, it is left to ferment in big wooden vats, at times with aromatic herbs added, or honey or other alcoholigens.

What is the value of these data handed down to us by tradition? The difficulty in using them lies in separating that which is original (breaking up sprouts, incisions made in the bark with sharp stones) from that which was added little by little. Thus the use of large wooden vats in Latvia is without a doubt, according to Sereni (1964), a contribution derived from a protohistoric age, via different mediators, which originally came from the Celts.

In the reports on production of wine from birch, maple, and beech, etc., we are also presented with documentation on the Classical Age: the cult of Dionysus Phleos, which was diffuse among the ancient Greeks (Werth 1954: 229). He personified the spirit of the tree that produced sugary sap which, with preservation, transformed itself little by little into an inebriating drink. This was the divinity whose cult had, without a doubt, for a millennium after the Ice Age, preceded that of Dionysus, the god of wine.

THE CIVILIZATION OF THE FRUITGROWERS AND THE ORIGIN OF CULTIVATING GRAPEVINES

From the historic-evolutionary scheme described above we arrive at the following ecological-cultural correlations:

1. Human communities that are ecologically accidental (pre-Paleolithic): fracturing of sprouts and the immediate utilization of the sugary sap that drips out.
2. Ecologically dominant human communities (Neolithic): preservation for relatively long periods by means of fermentation of sugary sap kept in large-sized, leak-proof containers made of terracotta or of other materials.
3. Ecologically dominant human communities which are socially stratified and have a reasonable level of technology (Bronze Age): pressing of sugary fruits, and fermentation by elaborate techniques of the resulting must, with consequent prevalence of grape wine (Mediterranean Europe).

But where can we pinpoint the origin of the cultivated grapevine, the producer *par excellence* of succulent and sugary fruits? Perhaps, marginally, it could be found among the Neolithic and copper civilizations of the Mediterranean area, which were known to be outstanding cereal producers. It does not seem so, however, certainly not in an influential way. The paleobotanic studies by Zoller (1967) of alpine Europe, and by Vavilov (1930) Neubauer (1952), and Capus (1884) for the Caucasian area, pointed out that, in such mountain communities, through slow, prolonged activity in cultivating for protection (Forni 1961), nuclei of semispontaneous orchards were formed, beginning from wild, fruit-bearing trees which were spread sporadically in the alpine forests and in the original Caucasian forests. It was in this way that in the alpine hills, chesnut forests were formed during the pre-Roman and Roman periods; pollen analysis has shown that these forests did not exist earlier. In the same way, in and around Caucasia woods of apple trees, pear trees, plum trees, peach trees, apricot trees, and grapevines sprung up and even today they fill the traveler with wonder.

Protective cultivation consists not only of the elimination of certain species of trees and shrubs that are not as useful as others, but also of the unconscious dissemination of useful trees so that seeds and other materials accumulate near places of habitation. This created spontaneous introgressive hybridization (Anderson 1968) which determined the appearance of new features, some of which were useful (for example, vines with bigger, sweeter, and more succulent grapes) in the resultant selection of trees. This hybridization consisted of deliberate and nondeliberate fostering of the useful trees and hence also the vines, favoring those bearing higher quality fruits. The hybridization done by these civilizations — which in many ways were in an epipaleolithic stage (no consistent archaeological traces were left by them) — was applied by fruitgrowers (who acquired proteins for nourishment, most likely by hunting, sporadic animal raising, and from leguminosae: peas, broad beans, etc.) from the neighboring Neolithic, copper, and bronze civilizations. The result was that the copper and bronze civilizations were able to boast of having acquired semidomestic fruit trees, and one of them was the grapevine.

In this way archaeological diggings demonstrate the almost sudden appearance in the western Mediterranean and temperate Europe, at the end of the Bronze Age or more frequently the Iron Age, of domestic grapevine seeds and, somewhat earlier, of the domestic apple and pear. In the Mediterranean regions and the area surrounding the eastern Mediterranean their development was more gradual because of the geographical proximity and there was a continual influx from the protofruitgrowers' civilization, as pointed out by paleobotany, that probably had a part in stimulating a local semidomestication process.

GRAPE WINE, PALM WINE, AND BEER: GEOGRAPHIC DIVISION BEFORE EUROPEAN COLONIAL EXPANSION AND THE RECIPROCAL HISTORIC, ECOLOGICAL, AND GENETIC INFLUENCE

The area of diffusion of palm wine expanded during precolonial times throughout the entire tropical belt (Africa, Asia, Oceania, America) of the hoe culture, each region having one or more specific kinds of palms near which other plants eventually appeared (banana trees, sugar cane, agave, etc.); but at the same time the area of diffusion of grape wine extended over a zone that was much more limited, immediately to the north of the area in which it had previously existed from southern Europe to southwestern Asia. It is appropriate to point out here that precisely in the area where the two zones touched on each other, that is, in the southwestern part of Asia, date palms (*Phoenix dactylifera*) are common; from them the Phoenicians got their name (date eaters). In the beginning this plant was grown for its sugary sap which was extracted from the central sprout. The fact that we do not know the direct wild ancestor of this plant implies, according to Ames (1939), that its domestication occurred a very long time ago, that it is certainly much older than its archaeological record would indicate, and that it almost certainly can be ascribed to the Epipaleolithic-Mesolithic Age. If we consider that use of its sap as a sweet beverage, and thereafter as wine, has since remotest antiquity reached such importance as to imply a very radical domesticating process, and that its area of diffusion in the eastern Mediterranean (Palestine, etc.) coincides with that of the most ancient of the developed civilizations which have left archaeological records, then it is evident that, in these subtropical districts which lack birch, maple, and beech trees, equipment and techniques for alcoholic fermentation of sugary liquids had been developed to make palm wine and later on were used to produce grape wine. This wine then would be the ancestor of the wine made from bark (birch, maple, etc.) in the temperate regions and of the wine made from palms in the subtropical regions.

The production of beer, though dating back to more recent times, must have exerted a striking influence on the historic genesis of grape wine. In fact, only rudimentary and sporadic production of beer goes back to the Neolithic period, to the time of a cereal-eating civilization equipped with ceramics, in which the custom of eating soups made from cereal was widespread. When the soups were not eaten right away, they began to ferment. If at first the peculiar acid flavor acquired by this did not appeal, in the end it certainly became delicious for refined palates, as is the case today with moldy cheeses such as the Italian Gorgonzola and French Camembert. This flavor turns out to be particularly strong when the caryopses of the cereals are partially germinated, as is the rule with cereals preserved in primitive granaries dug in the often moist ground. From this "spoiled" soup, a dish perhaps sought after by gourmets, we have the original derivation of beer, a drink typical of the countires which lacked grapevines during the period following that of making wine from birch. But, as pointed out by Werth (1954), the evolution, even if similar to the evolution of wines made from birch (in this respect we must have dealt with sweet drinks "going bad"), is in the case of beer more complex — certainly much more so than that with wines made from sugary fruits that (obviously) require pressing and squeezing in addition to fermentation, in order to be produced. In the case of beer, in fact, the raw material used to acquire alcohol is not the sugar of the juice but the starch of the cereal which is not directly broken down by the fermentation but by the enzymes that come into being only during the process of germination. As a result, only populations with a highly evolved level of technology were able to produce beer in quantities sufficiently large for consumption by the entire community. This took place only among peoples who used the plow in their agricultural activities. Among these peoples methods other than germination were used in order to break down the starch so as to be able to expose it to fermentation. In many places in Africa, for example, cereals are chewed and then the wad, saturated in saliva, is spat into a bowl. In this way the enzymes in the saliva cause the starch to break down and render it fermentable.

The people who made beer in central northern Europe (in particular the Celts), as was indicated previously, exercised with their technique of preservation a particular influence on the peoples who produced wine. It seems, in fact, that the construction of large barrels was perfected by the beer-producing populations in central northern Europe, and in particular by the Celts (Sereni 1964).

SUMMARY AND CONCLUSIONS

A problem such as the origin and evolution of alcoholic beverages, and in particular grape wine, cannot be examined from the paleobotanic standpoint only. One must investigate in historical perspective the continuous and diverse interrelations and dynamic behavior of two groups of factors: (1) factors relative to natural environment, particularly to plant that produce sugary saps; and (2) factors relative to human communities which, due to their social, technical, and economic development, are able to produce grape wine.

To do this type of research it is imperative not to confine ourselves to direct archaeological data; it is necessary to integrate these data with indirect data and with similar types of records drawn from the examination of contemporary prehistoric civilizations. Even data obtained from European traditions should be considered valuable.

On the basis of all the available data gathered and correctly evaluated in this way, we can hypothetically reconstruct the facts that are of interest to us.

It will be the task of future critical research to "falsify" (if we may borrow Popper's terminology here) the results of this reconstruction.

In our study, using the methods described we were able to ascribe to the prelithic period, that is, several hundreds of thousands of years ago, among human populations which were still accidental from the ecological standpoint, the practice of cutting the apex of sprouts of particular plants for the purpose of obtaining sugary saps which were immediately consumed as a drinkable beverage. During a long transition phase, which lasted hundreds of millennia, these drinks began to be preserved for short periods by a less nomadic people using rudimentary methods. Thus they had arrived at a more evolved paleolithic stage from the stage of the production of birch wine, or palm wine in the subtropical regions.

It was only among the ecologically dominant peoples, and specifically among the Neolithic peoples, that preserving methods were improved by the invention of wine vats made of ceramic and nonceramic (wood, etc.) materials, so that long and reliable preservation of the liquids was possible. The preservation of such fermented sweet drinks was futhered by the fact that the communities became progressively more settled. At the present time among the mountain peoples of the Caucasian region who practice cultivation and protection of plants which bear spontaneous fruits, with resultant introgressive hybridization, and selection from it, we can see the generation of semidomestic grapevines. In ancient times, this method would be acquired by neighboring populations who were at a more advanced technological level and were more socially stratified, so that they were able to substitute grape wine for birch or palm wine.

REFERENCES

AMES, O.
1939 *Economic annuals and human cultures.* Cambridge, Mass.: Botanical Museum of Harvard University.

ANDERSON, E.
1968 *Inrogressive hybridizaion.* New York and London: Hafner.

CAPUS, C.
1884 Sur les plantes cultivées qu'on trouve à l'état sauvage ou subspontané dans le Thian-Schan occidental. *Annales des Sciences Naturelles.*

CLARK, J. C. D.
1955 *L'Europe préhistorique — Les fondements de son économie,* pp. 309ff. Paris: Payot.

DANTRINE, M.
1937 *Le palmier-dattier et les arbres sacrés.* Paris: Librarie Orientaliste Paul Geuthner.

EVREINOFF, V. A.
1956 Contribution à l'étude du dattier. *Journal d'Agriculture Tropicale et Botanique Appliquée* 3:328–329.

FORNI, G.
1961 Due forme primordiali di coltivazione. *Rivista Storia dell'Agricoltura* 72.

GUYOT, A. L.
1949 *Origine des plantes cultivées,* page 99. Paris: Presses Universitaires de France.

HUIZINGA, J.
1964 *Homo ludens.* Milan: Il Saggiatore.

LANDI, R.
1962 A distanza di millenni si ritrovano semi che rivelano la civilità dei primi agricoltori. *L'Italia Agricola.* Rome.

LEVADOUX, L.
1956 Les populations sauvages et cultivées de Vitis vinifera L. *Annales de l'Amélioration des Plantes* (1956):73.

LIGERS, Z.
1953 *L'économie d'acquisition: la cueillette, la chasse et la pêche en Lettonie,* pp. 31ff. Paris.

LOGOTHETIS, B.
1970 *L'evoluzione della vite e della viticoltura in Grecia secondo i reperti archeologici della regione.* Salonica: Aristoteleion Panepistemion Tessalonikes. (In Greek.)

MAURIZIO, A.
1970 *Geschichte der gegorenen Getränke*, pp. 1ff. Wiesbaden: M. Sändig.
NEGRI, G.
1934 "Viti fossili e viti preistoriche in Italia," in *Storia della viti e del vino in Italia*. Edited by A. Marescalchi and G. Dalmasso, volume one, page 10. Milan: Arti grafiche Gualdoni.
NEUBAUER, H. F.
1952 Über ein ursprüngliches Vorkommen der wilden *Vitis vinifera* L. in Ost-Afganistan. *Mitteilungen Klosternenburg* 2(4):109–146.
ODUM, E. P.
1965 *Ecologia*. Bologna: Zanichelli.
POPPER, K.
1959 *The logic of scientific discovery*. London.
1969 "Problemi, scopi e responsabilità della scienza," in *Scienza e filosofia*. Turin: Einaudi. (Italian translation.)
RENFREW, J. M.
1973 *Palaeoethnobotany*. London: Methuen.
SERENI, E.
1964 Per la storia delle più antiche techniche e delle nomenclature della vite e del vino in Italia. *Atti dell'Accademia Toscana di Scienze e Lettere* 29:92. Florence: La Colombaria.
TOLSTOI, L.
1970 "I meli," in *I quattro libri di lettura*. Turin: Einaudi.
VAVILOV, N. I.
1930 "Wild progenitors of the fruit trees of the Turkestan and the Caucasus and the problem of the origin of the fruit trees," in *Proceedings of the Ninth International Horticultural Congress*. London.
WERTH, E.
1954 *Grabstock, Acker und Pflug*, page 229. Ludwigsburg: E. Ulmer.
ZOLLER, H.
1967 Pollenanalytische Untersuchungen zum Kastanienproblem am Alpen-Südfluss. *Pflanzensoziologie und Palynologie*. The Hague: W. Junk.

Monophagy in the European Upper Paleolithic

LUIGI SAFFIRIO

The characteristics of human feeding habits in the European Upper Paleolithic pose some dietetic problems which also have an important bearing on cultural development. We shall briefly try to clarify these problems here.

Archaeological evidence shows that the feeding system of Paleolithic man in the last Ice Age, living in an arctic or subarctic environment, was founded almost exclusively on the big game hunting of that period, that is, reindeer, horses, mammoths, and bisons among others. Numerous sites in various parts of Europe from west to east, have preserved impressive quantities of remains of these animals, often showing thousands of them having been slaughtered.[1] On the basis of the abundance of game and the skill of the hunters as indicated by this evidence, we can consider this form of hunting profitable. How profitable can only be established if we know, apart from the number of animals slaughtered, how many mouths were fed by the game and the length of time the data refer to. Even then, however, the reckoning would not be definite, for the number of bones lost would have to be taken into account.

Fishing and bird hunting would seem to have been of fairly limited importance since the evidence is either scarce or confined to just a few areas. Whatever importance they had, however, the fact remains that

[1] This has long been been known in regard to sites such as Solutré, Meiendorf, Predmost, and others; as to further examples we will confine ourselves here to mentioning two sites written about fairly recently, both located in southern Russia: Amvrosievka, with the remains of a thousand bisons, and Bokhaia Akkaria, which has supplied 5,000 bone fragments of *Bison* sp. or *Bos* sp.(Mongait 1964: 99, *Amvrosievska ossuarium*; and Boriskovski 1965).

these two activities supplied even more meat in addition to the big game source.

It is evident that, for an adequate diet, this massive supply of meat would have to be balanced by a sufficient supply of vegetables. The vegetation of the last Ice Age was generally of limited extent, poor in vigor and variety, and was comparable over much of central and western Europe to that of the polar regions today;[2] we can therefore exclude the possibility that this was able to guarantee an adequate supply of vegetable foods, especially from the quantitative point of view. The tundra vegetation, i.e. the fruticoses, suffruticoses, lichens, and moss which covered a good portion of the zones indicated, could not be expected to guarantee such a supply. The situation on the steppe could have been somewhat better if the inhabitants of this phase of the Stone Age had known how or had wanted to exploit for nutritional purposes the gramineae common to this vegetal formation. But this is a conquest, if we wish to consider it as such, which in the Upper Paleolithic (late phase) is amply documented elsewhere, particularly in Africa (Nile Valley), but not in Europe.[3]

Excluding any notable contribution from vegetables, it is clear that the food of Paleolithic man consisted almost exclusively of meat; meat was in practice the only means of sustenance that could be relied on. Hence the problems mentioned above.

We are led in fact to wonder (1) whether such a monophagous diet could give the Paleolithic hunter's organism a balanced, adequate supply of the protids, lipids, glucides, vitamins, and salts needed for wholesome nutrition; (2) whether this diet was able, at least potentially, to furnish an adequate supply of calories to an Ice Age man whose caloric requirement was certainly very high because of the climate and the activity he carried on; (3) bearing in mind this situation, whether

[2] Maurizio (1932: 9) points out that polar populations can avail themselves of a very poor vegetation and that there are only 112 vascular plants reaching or bypassing 80° North latitude. From a table published by Pignatti (1964: 708) it emerges that there are 110 vascular plants subsisting at the Spitzbergen (77–81° North latitude), dwindling to 25 in the Franz Joseph archipelago (79–82° North latitude).

[3] Of course we know that episodes of milder climate occurred during the last Ice Age. As to how such episodes might have influenced vegetation, we can deduce that in southern regions, during this period, there was some improvement in availability of edible plants. This may be hinted by any flora found in tufa in Provence, associated with Magdalenian flints, which includes *Vitis vinifera* and *Pistacia terebinthina* (Furon 1966: 91).

On the exploitation of wild gramineae in the Nile valley in this period see Vignard 1923; Wendorf (ed.) 1968, especially pp. 941–946, 1051; Birket-Smith 1955; Gessain 1958; Stefansson 1958; Collins 1964; Taylor 1966.

the organism was able to withstand the eminently proteic and lipidic composition of this diet without damage to health and to the biological equilibrium of the population.

DISCUSSION

ESKIMO PATTERN. The conditions of life and natural environment of the Upper Paleolithic people in Europe, at least in the west central zones, have been often equated with those of Eskimos in Arctic lands; the climatic situation was, in fact, in these zones very similar to that experienced by Eskimos today. Even the form of sustenance presents analogies, sometimes very close, and these are worth examining.

The information available derives from both ethnology and archaeology. We find in outline a range of economies which have a common root but take on different aspects, some being founded mainly on the hunting of sea mammals (seals, walrus, cetacea), others on the hunting of caribou, and others occupied in both forms. Further sources of supply are the hunting of other great mammals (musk-ox and bear, for example), fowling, fishing, gathering eggs, and any edible vegetation offered by the environment. It should be pointed out straightaway, however, that the part played by vegetables in food supplies as a whole appears to be quite secondary. In summary, food is based almost exclusively on products of animal origin, generally similar in this respect to that of our European Upper Paleolithic man. If we go into greater detail, however, it is clear that we must look for closer analogies not among sea mammal hunters or fishermen but among those Eskimos of the hinterland who specialize in hunting caribou. Here we can avail ourselves of the information contained in a publication by Mowat in which feeding habits and related problems are dealt with at length.[4]

Mowat reported that the Inhalmiut, an Eskimo population of northern Canada whose habits of life he personally shared for some time, lived exclusively on the meat and fat of the caribou. This animal can, in fact, at least during the autumn hunt when it is in its best physical condition, provide considerable quantities of fat which is largely used as nourishment, fat being an essential component of the diet of the peoples living at such northern latitudes. It should be enough to say that, when the fat is available in sufficient quantities, the rule with the

[4] Mowat (1954a).

Inhalmiut is to take three mouthfuls of meat and one of fat. It must be added that if the hunt was good they fed daily on a striking amount of meat — several kilos a day per person[5] — thus an enormous load of proteins, fat, and calories and apparently an unbalanced alimentation, if one takes into account the lack of any vegetable food.

From Mowat's report, instead, such alimentation turns out to be borne without dangers and even to be quite suitable for this arctic population, considering their physical environment and their way of life.

Moreover, Mowat advances good arguments to demonstrate that a different diet would be injurious to the health as well as to the survival of either Eskimos or Indians living in the northernmost parts of the American continent. For example, he mentions the case of the Idthen Eldeli Indians of Manitoba (Canada), who in 1860 still formed a community of 2,000 individuals and lived by hunting caribou, following them in their migrations and feeding exclusively on their meat. Today, because of a change in their diet (consisting almost exclusively of flour and fish), they are reduced to a population of only 150 individuals, far indeed from being endowed with the physical resistance and exceptional vigor of their ancestors.

To summarize, if the parallel with Eskimos is valid, it would seem quite natural that the prevailing meat diet of Upper Paleolithic people in the Ice Age environment was not dictated by external circumstances alone (i.e. favorable hunting conditions), but also depended on the physiological needs imposed by the physical environment.

UPPER PALEOLITHIC MAN'S ALIMENTATION. Mowat's news about his Eskimos' diet, and other quotations from the same book we refer to alter, present many points in common with Von Stokar's specific study of man's alimentation in the second half of the last glaciation.[6] Mowat starts from the premise that this man was physiologically like present-day man: his food needs can, therefore, be evaluated by today's scientific criteria. For his study he takes into consideration the reindeer, the typical game of those times. By calculating the daily need of proteins, fats, and carbohydrates for a normal man living mostly in the open air, at an average yearly temperature of 5°C (which is the temperature of the Arctic Circle now, but corresponding to the climate

[5] To be more exact we shall say that Mowat tried to calculate the amount of meat that one of his Eskimo mates could eat in a single day: ten to twelve pounds (i.e. approximately to ten kilos; Mowat 1954a 96). In lean priods of course, the amount of meat available was less or even totally lacking, so that such an intake of meat cannot be considered as a constant daily occurrence.

[6] Von Stokar (1957: 59–62).

at 50° of latitude along central Europe in the Ice Age) Mowat calculates that a hunter of the Ice Age needed as much as 8.5 kilograms of reindeer meat a day. This figure is certainly impressive but it is worth pointing out that it is not too far from the amount quoted by Mowat as regards his Eskimos (see Note 5). Keeping in mind, as mentioned by Von Stokar, that the caloric value of reindeer meat is rather low (100 grams = 100 calories) the above recorded 8.5 kilograms of reindeer meat corresponds more or less to 8,000 calories, enough to secure, with a fair margin, the daily caloric need of a hunter living a very active life in the open air. Mowat maintains in fact that for this hunter 6,000 calories are needed at an average annual temperature of 5°C, and 7,500 at a temperature of –10°C. As we noted about Eskimos, and as Von Stokar in fact confirms, people living in polar regions can ingest great quantities of meat without the health troubles that might be caused elsewhere by this habit.

Following Von Stokar's paper, it is of particular interest to remark that the reindeer hunter of the Ice Age ate lean meat, fat, viscera, etc., everything except the tegument and bare bone. This accounts for the fact that from such a specialized diet he could nevertheless get sufficiently balanced nourishment as far as nutritive principles are concerned. In fact, carbohydrates are provided by the liver, which has "a high glycogen content," as well as by the blood and stomach of the animal; the liver, moreover, "contains the whole range of vitamins."[7] This is substantially in agreement with what was observed by Mowat about the Inhalmiut people: "they believe that only by eating all parts of the deer can they achieve a satisfactory diet. So the heart, kidneys, intestines, liver and other organs are greatly esteemed and often eaten."[8]

However, going back to Upper Paleolithic man, it is fully acceptable that he could, even despite the scarce vegetation of the Ice Age, find a way of getting some supply of carbohydrates and vitamins from certain plants. In this connection Von Stokar mentions, among other plants, *Cetraria islandica* and *Empetrum (nigrum)*, containing both carbohydrates and vitamins (Von Stokar 1957). In our opinion, however, vegetal food, quantitatively at least, could only play a quite minor role, not altering the fundamental monophagic character of the diet of Upper Paleolithic man living in the tundra and steppe zones.

For our part we should also like to mention the mineral salts of calcium, phosphorus, potassium, sodium, chlorine, magnesium, iodine, iron, fluorine, and others, the deficiencies of which can give rise to

[7] Von Stokar (1957: 61–62).
[8] Cited from the English text: Mowat (1954b: 80).

pathological conditions. Here, of course, we are interested in cases which might have been of outstanding importance on a general biological level. We shall therefore consider essentially calcium, iron, iodine, and fluorine, the deficiencies of which are respectively responsible for rickets, anaemia, thyroid dysfunction (goiter), and dental troubles which can take on an endemic character. There is some uncertainty about whether the Paleolithic diet would be able to fulfil the calcium requirement, as calcium is rather scanty in meat. Nor would Paleolithic men be able to obtain their calcium from animal milk for, as far as we know at present, they were not aware of this source of alimentation. We must bear in mind, however, that these populations lived primarily in the open air and therefore benefited from considerable exposure to the sun. As utilization of calcium is related to vitamin D, there is no doubt that the sun's rays could certainly have assured an abundant supply of the vitamin and, therefore, the maximum utilization of calcium. Assuming that there was adequate sunshine in the Ice Age, the existence of endemic rickets would therefore seem to be improbable.

Iron presents no problem as it is sufficiently present in meat. Iodine, however, is rather scarce in meat. Its main vehicle for man would seem to be water. It is a well-known fact that among other possible causes it is iodine-deficient water which gives rise to endemic goiter. There are no problems here either, nor are there for fluorine, which is also supplied by water, provided of course that a sufficiently mineralized water was drunk. At the general level, of course, we should not ignore the other salts, particularly calcium, magnesium, and sodium, which can be provided by water.

It is worth saying a word about the habit common to almost all peoples of adding salt (sodium chloride) to food. In line with the general opinion that such a custom was followed among Paleolithic peoples, it might be thought that there was a lack of this salt; however, the experience of people who do not use it shows that it is possible to live by using only the sodium chloride obtainable from food.[9]

To conclude, mention must be made of secondary foods. These include birds' eggs (rich in salts), salmon (fished by the Magdalenians) and edible vegetation.

MONOPHAGY AMONG CAMEL DRIVERS IN SOMALILAND

Here we would like to mention another unusual example of high

[9] Cf. Grottanelli (1965: 445).

protein and fat diet which is apparently unbalanced and yet accepted without inconvenience by the population which practices it; the fact that it concerns a climate totally different from those described above supports our general conclusions. The case was described in a report of a scientific expedition sent out by the Institute of Medical Pathology of the University of Florence to study nomadic camel herdsmen in Somaliland.[10] These herdsmen nourish themselves almost exclusively on camel's milk, drinking from 5 to 10 liters a day.[11] This diet, even at the above minimum of 5 liters, corresponds, according to the assessments made by these researchers,[12] to 355.5 grams of lipids, 236 grams of protids, 231.5 grams of lactose, equivalent to a total of 5,222 calories. If to this already high figure we add the calories supplied by the relevant quantity of cane sugar which these camel breeders consume daily with tea (200 to 250 grams = 1025 calories), we obtain a daily ration of 6,247 calories, about twice that considered normal for an adult man.[13]

However, clinical examinations of 203 males between eleven and seventy years of age led to completely different results from those which one might expect from such a hyperlipidic (and hyperproteic, hypercaloric) diet. Suffice it to say that measurements of the cholesterol blood level among these herders has yielded a mean of 147.25, showing it to be rather low, and that no pathological effects were detected to be due to their kind of alimentation.

Lapiccirella, et al. interpret these results as being presumably due primarily to an atavistic physiological adaptation (homeostasis) as well as, among other factors, to the advantage of the very intense muscular activity connected with the nomadic life of these herders (1962).

CONCLUSION

While the case of Somali herders is perhaps a unique and localized one,

[10] V. Lapiccirella, R. Lapiccirella, Abboni, and Liotta (1962).

[11] The only variation to diet being represented by cane sugar, as reported in the text, and twice a month (at least from December to March) by a little goat's or camel's meat. It may be added that as spices they use clove, cardamom, and resins like incense and myrrh ("... girofle, cardamom, résines comme l'encense et la myrrhe") (Lapiccirella, et al. 1962: 683).

[12] It is to be noted, as stated by the authors, that camel's milk has a fat content (7.11%) about twice that of cow's milk (3.50%).

[13] The authors, keeping in mind the high local temperature (mean 30° C) and consequent reduction of calorie requirement, calculate the local ration as 2,880 calories *pro die* i.e. slightly below normal (Lapiccirella, et al. 1962: 683).

related to a diet based on milk, the adjustment of the Eskimos to their diet rich in fat and proteins is widespread, recorded not only among the Inhalmiut but also common to all Arctic populations. In both cases we have definite evidence of a hypercaloric, unbalanced diet which under normal conditions would lead to negative and even pathological results in individuals who rely on it. However, the instances cited indicate that particular conditions of existence and natural environment, as well as phenomena of physiological adaptation, can be such that a diet of this kind can be tolerated without harmful effects. In evaluating prehistoric food habits, then, we must keep these facts in mind, for some of their aspects may arouse perplexity from the point of view of nutrition itself.

This is valid for the case in question — that is for Upper Paleolithic men in Europe. Moreover, the information that can be drawn from their culture as well as from their fossils allows us to believe not only that a meat diet did not cause harmful effects, but on the contrary, it yielded very good results from a biological standpoint.

We are permitted to hold this view because many of the aspects of Upper Paleolithic cultures show the enterprising nature and strong dynamism of these populations, which are signs of good nourishment. Their skeletal remains, moreover, demonstrate that they belonged largely to a particularly strongly built people, the Cro-Magnon race.

This allows us to think that the possible signs of malnutrition noticed on some skeletons can be considered either as sporadic cases or due to alimentary deficiencies caused by famine which even the hunters of the Upper Paleolithic in Europe, no matter how enterprising, certainly could not escape during the 20,000 to 25,000 years of their existence.

REFERENCES

BIRKET-SMITH, K.
1955 *Moeurs et coutumes des Eskimos.* Paris: Payot.

BORISKOVSKI, P. J.
1965 A propos des récens progrès des études paléolithiques en U.S.S.R. *L'anthropologie* 69:5–36.

BOULE, M., M. V. VALLOIS
1952 *Les hommes fossiles* (fourth edition). Paris: Masson.

BREUIL, H., R. LANTIER
1951 *Les hommes de la pierre ancienne.* Paris: Payot.

BUILDER, A.
1939 *L'eau potable.* Paris, Liège: Ch. Beranger.

BUOGO, G.
1958 *Igiene e industrie dell'alimentazione.* Milan: Ceschina.

CHILDE, V. G.
1954 *What happened in history* (revised edition). Harmondsworth: Penguin Books. (Reprinted 1964, 1965, 1967.)
1965 *Man makes himself* (fourth edition). London: Watts.

CLARK, J. G. D.
1952 *Prehistoric Europe: the economic basis.* London: Methuen.

COLLINS, H.
1964 "The Arctic and Subarctic," in *Prehistoric man in the New World.* Edited by J. D. Jennings and E. Norbeck. Chicago: University of Chicago Press. (Published for the William Marsh Rice University.)

DAY, M. H.
1965 *Guide to fossil man.* London: Cassell.

Documenta Geigy
1955 *Documenta Geigy. Tables scientifiques* (fifth edition). Paris.

FURON, R.
1966 *Manuel de préhistoire générale* (fifth edition). Paris: Payot.

GESSAIN, R.
1958 *Gli eschimesi dalla Groenlandia all'Alaska.* Translated by M. Bertini. Turin: S.A.I.E.

GROTTANELLI, V. L.
1965 *Ethnologia. L'uomo e la civilità,* volume two. Milan: Edizione Labor.

LAPICCIRELLA, V., R. LAPICCIRELLA, F. ABBONI, S. LIOTTA
1962 Enquête clinique, biologique et cardiographique parmi les tribus nomades de la Somalie qui se nourissent seulement de lait. *Bulletin of the World Health Organization* 27:681–697.

LAVOCAT, R., *editor*
1966 *Faunes et flores préhistoriques de l'Europe Occidentale.* Atlas de Préhistoire 3. Paris: N. Boubée.

MAURIZIO, A.
1932 *Histoire de l'alimentation végétale.* Translated by F. Gidon. Paris: Payot.

MONGAIT, A.
1964 *Civilità scomparse.* Translated into Italian by C. Valenzano Parlato. Rome: Editori Riuniti.

MOVIUS, H. L., JR.
1960 Radiocarbon dates and upper Paleolithic archaeology in central and western Europe. *Current Anthropology* 1:355–391.

MOWAT, F.
1954a *Il populo dei caribù* (second edition). Translated into Italian by A. Zorzi. Milan: Rizzoli.
1954b *People of the deer.* London: Readers Union, M. Joseph.

PIGNATTI, S.
1964 "Fitogeographia," in *Botanica* (second edition). By C. Cappelletti. Turin: UTET.

PRADEL, L.
1967 La grotte des Cottés commune de Saint-Pierre de-Maillé (Vienne);

Moustérien-Périgordien-Aurignacien. Datation par le radiocarbone. *L'Anthropologie* 71:271–277.

SCHWARZBACH, M.
1963 *Climates of the past.* Translated and edited by R. O. Muir. London: Van Norstrand.

SECCHI, G.
1967 *I nostri alimenti.* Milan: Hoepli.

STEFANSSON, V.
1958 Eskimo longevity in northern Alaska. *Science* 127:16–19.

TAYLOR, W. E., JR.
1966 An archaeological perspective on the Eskimo economy. *Antiquity* 40:114–120.

VAUFREY, R.
1933 *Le Paléolithique italien.* Archives de l'Institut de Paléontologie Humaine Memoir 3. Paris: Masson.

VIGNARD, M. E.
1923 Une nouvelle industrie lithique, le Sébilien. *Bulletin de L'Institut français d'Archéologie Orientale* 22:1–76.

VON STOKAR, W.
1957 Über die Ernährung in der Eiszeit. *Quartär* 9.

WENDORF, F., *editor*
1968 *The prehistory of Nubia,* volume two. Dallas: Fort Burgwin Research Center and Southern Methodist University Press.

ZEUNER, F. E.
1958 *Dating the past* (fourth edition, revised and enlarged). London: Methuen.

SECTION TWO

Dietary Change

On Determining Food Patterns of Urban Dwellers in Contemporary United States Society

NORGE W. JEROME

INTRODUCTION

Consistent with the holistic approach of data gathering, ethnographers have provided information, understandably with varying scope and depth, on the dynamics of food procurement and food use among members of traditional and posttraditional societies. For those societies, there exists a large body of data describing the dynamic processes of food procurement, storage, processing, preparation, distribution, consumption, and waste disposal; modes of adaptation to environmental influences, especially to periods of food abundance and scarcity, have received special attention. We lack similar information on modern societies.

Adaptive responses to cycles of food abundance and scarcity in traditional and posttraditional societies range from gorging and force-feeding to irregular repletion and inanition. Adaptation to the uncertainties of food procurement is also manifest in the social rhythms of daily life; harvest is accompanied by physical and social activities (e.g. work and festivals) and these functions precede or follow the relative inactivity of famine periods. This cyclical patterning of physical and social activities in relation to the agricultural cycle and primitive forms of food technology effectively demonstrates how closely a community or society's food supply and level of technology influence the rhythm of food consumption.

Where social and environmental conditions severely limit the food supply, diet and consumption patterns assume some degree of seasonal or

This research was supported by USDA Grant No. 12-14-100-9907 and by special Grant Awards from the Kansas Regional Medical Program and the National Dairy Council.

daily uniformity. By contrast, DIET INDIVIDUATION emphasizing personal preferences seems to typify the food consumption practices of individuals in modern, industrialized societies with stable, regular food supplies. But this hypothesis must be tested.

Little attention has been paid to the types of food consumption rhythms and cycles developed by modern man as he adapted to a regular and abundant food supply. However, data from my studies on the dynamics of food use in contemporary society provide indications that in an affluent society, food security, as derived from food abundance, fosters simultaneous EXPANSION/STABILIZATION of the core diet and EXPANSION/VARIATION of the noncore diet and may result in individuated dietary formulations. The process appears to involve a CONTINUOUS TWO-PHASE CYCLIC INCORPORATION of foods into the diet. It commences with item experimentation through tentative incorporation of noncore items into the diet at a low-frequency rate (expansion/variation) and is followed by continuous incorporation of the preferred items into the established diet (expansion/stabilization).

This paper discusses the cyclical patterning of food among members of an American (United States) urban community. It places emphasis on methodological approaches to the study, specific instruments designed to obtain the data, and aspects of food procurement and selection relevant to the process of cyclical food patterning.

Hypothesis

It is hypothesized that diets with relatively large numbers of core and ceremonial/marginal dietary items as compared with secondary core and peripheral[1] noncore items, when measured by the relative frequency of

[1] The terms "core," "secondary core," and "peripheral" used to describe the cyclical patterning of food into the diet were borrowed from Bennett (1942:651–652). However, the description of the diet pattern according to the above terms differs substantially from Bennett's and is included below.

a. CORE. The essentials of the diet, e.g. those foods and beverages consumed from two to three times per week to two to three times per day by at least twenty-five percent of the respondent households. The respondents perceive the foods falling under this rubric as the preferred and most important items of the diet and generally refer to them as COMMON, REGULAR, or ORDINARY foods, or foods that must be included in the diet and consumed regularly alone or as ingredients.

b. SECONDARY CORE. Those foods consumed approximately once per week by at least twenty-five percent of the respondent households. As perceived by the respondents, the function of these foods is to add variety to the diet or to assist in realizing an established weekly food consumption routine, e.g. beef roast on Sunday afternoon. It

item consumption, express a TWO-PHASE CYCLIC INCORPORATION of foods into the established diet pattern and may serve to further express diet individuation.

The National Food Setting

The variety of items carried in the modern supermarket has increased dramatically during the last four decades. In 1928, grocery stores carried an average of 867 items; the number of items increased to 3,470 in 1950, to 6,600 in 1962, to 7,525 in 1968. Some stores now carry over 10,000 items (*Progressive Grocers* 1969: 58). It has been predicted that some 32,000 items will be carried by some stores in the 1970's (Ullensvang 1970: 240). Interestingly, this increase in food item offerings has not been matched by an increase in food energy consumption.

Actually, there has been a decline in per capita energy consumption. Between 1909 and 1965 energy consumption per capita had decreased by 400 calories (United States Department of Agriculture (USDA), 1959: 602, 1970: 10; Food and Agriculture Organization (FAO) 1971: 762). It is obvious, then, that an increase in the number of dietary items, while encouraging expansion of the individual's food repertoire, has been accompanied by a decrease in energy consumption.

This type of dietary change may be effected in numerous ways. It seems reasonable to speculate, however, that as the core diet expanded to include certain traditional nonstaples (e.g. tossed salads, tomatoes, evaporated milk), other traditional nonstaples (e.g. lunchmeat and orange juice) were

---

is important to note that no beverage falls within this classification.

c. PERIPHERAL. Those foods consumed approximately once or twice per month by at least twenty-five percent of the respondent households. Foods within this category may be referred to as "special interest foods." These are the foods which are considered essential by certain, but by no means all, members of the family, and are perceived as being "less common" or "more expensive" than the core and secondary core foods. Foods in this category function in adding variety to the diet and in fulfilling individual wishes and preferences. Again, it is interesting to note that no beverage meets the criteria for inclusion in this category.

d. CEREMONIAL/MARGINAL. These foods and beverages are on the borderline of either being completely excluded from the diet or only included on very few occasions by at least seventy-five percent of the respondent households. The foods and beverages included in the diet are considered "special occasion" or "ceremonial" items and consumed no more than six times per year. These include fruit salad, turkey, fruit cake, eggnog, waffles, and hard rolls. Foods and beverages completely excluded from the diet include lobster, lamb chop, peach nectar, skim milk, powdered milk, and liquid diet foods; although defined as food by the group, they are generally considered "food for others but not for me."

added to the diet initially on an experimental basis but followed by high-frequency usage, until a large number of traditional nonstaple favorites had become incorporated into the core diet. The diet could be expanded to accommodate a large number of nonstaple items without increasing food energy consumption (in relation to energy input) only through a rhythmic inclusion/exclusion/replacement pattern developed by each individual or family to promote diet variation.

Organizing Framework

To test the hypothesis, an ethnographic study emphasizing the dynamics of food procurement and use was conducted in a low-to-middle income urban community of a large north central metropolitan center (population, 1,253,916). Basic anthropological techniques of participant observation were combined with the more formal sociological method to achieve the research goals. This combination of methods permitted the collection and systematic recording of data that can only be derived from direct observation and participation in the daily routine of the respondents. It also enabled four fieldworkers to collect and organize data gathered from a fairly large urban population.

Because preliminary field studies had revealed numerous access routes to food and a wide variety of food items marketed in the community, it became important to develop methodological approaches and instruments to capture and unravel the complexities of food use and consumption practices within the community. To be effective, these instruments must identify those foods and beverages included in the respondents' diets as well as those completely or almost completely omitted from their diets. The instruments must also assist in identifying the lay food classification system, as well as the cyclical patterning of food as revealed by frequency of use patterns.

METHODOLOGY

Instruments

Between September, 1969 and February, 1970, we conducted five sets of preliminary field studies among forty-two households in three different urban communities in the greater Kansas City area. As a result, we developed food-habits research tools for securing and recording observational and interview data on the dynamics of food use. Two of these tools, a Precoded Structured Interview Schedule (hereafter referred to as PSIS) and a Supermarket Simulator (SS), are salient to this paper.

The former instrument, PSIS, consisting of 178 questions and space for field observations, permitted recordings of field observations and responses to open-ended, free-flowing interviews on individual and family (at home and away from home) food consumption practices.

The latter instrument, SS, displayed *bona fide* labels of 223 foods and beverages arranged according to 35 lay-designated categories in four catalogs (Table 1). Pictorially, the SS reproduced arrangements of selected

Table 1. Thirty-five lay food categories

Beverages	Meat/seafood salad
Broths and consommé	Milk products
Candy	Nuts
Casseroles	Pastas
Cereal products	Pies
(bakery and nonbakery types)	Preserves and condiments
Cheeses (natural and processed)	Puddings
Desserts	Salads
Eggs	Sandwiches
Fats	Sauces
Frozen ices	Sausages
Fruits	Seafood/fish
Game/wild meats	Snack foods
Jams and jellies	Soups
Legumes	Stews
Lunchmeats	Sugars and syrups
Meats and poultry	Sweeteners (other)
Meat and nut spreads	Vegetables

foods and beverages observed in modern supermarkets. Ninety percent of the items displayed in the SS were available in supermarkets located within the target community; while the remaining 10 percent were marketed in supermarkets located outside the community.

One section of the PSIS, the Food Data Sheet (Table 2), was used in conjunction with the SS to obtain and record detailed data on food procurement, technological state of food purchased, and the frequency of use of every item included in each respondent household's food repertoire.

Procedure

Between March and December, 1970, 150 households, a 5 percent random sample of the households in the community described below, participated

Table 2. Food data sheet

			Food	V/P	Frequency	S	P/S	Freq.	R	How obtained	Where obtained	Tech. st.	Prep. meth.
CC 1–34	001	(——)	——	–	–.–/–	–	–	–.–/–	–	—..	—..	—..	—..
CC 35–68	002	(corn)	0045	1	2.5/3	2	3	2.5/4	1	19..	01..	01..	01..
	↓ 100 food items												

Codes:

Item 1, Food...........	food name and four-digit food code.
Item 2, V/P	1 = response volunteered, 2 = response probed.
Item 3, Frequency.......	frequency of use (two to three times per week).
Item 4, S	season (to determine if used only in season or a particular season).
Item 5, P/S	personally determined season (to determine personal idiosyncracies in establishing seasonal intake).
Item 6, Frequency.......	frequency (two to three times every four months).
Item 7, R	regularity (to determine, where indicated, an individual respondent's definition of regularity for a particular item).
Item 8, How obtained ...	in relation to money exchange.
Item 9, Where obtained .	source of food supply.
Item 10, Tech. st.	technological state of purchase (e.g. frozen or fresh).
Item 11, Prep. meth.	preparation method.

in the phase of the study which required use of the instruments described above.

The PSIS was administered to each of the respondent households until all relevant data had been collected. An initial contact and informal visit designed to establish rapport with members of the target households was followed by a series of close interactions with the individuals involved. Without limiting our efforts, we concentrated on those individuals who had identified themselves as the ones with major roles in various aspects of household food management.

Thus, we were afforded numerous opportunities for observing and recording ongoing events directly and indirectly related to food use with respondents, members of their immediate families, and all identified "significant others." We continued close and continuous relationships with them for as long as it was mutually convenient until all data had been collected and recorded in the PSIS. In many instances, the relationship continued many months after the pertinent data had been recorded.

The interview schedule included six major sections arranged according to the division of labor for food activities. Thus, depending upon individual household organization, a maximum of six respondents in each household could provide information on food use. Some interviews began as early as 7:00 A.M. and others ended as late as 11:00 P.M. on a scheduled or nonscheduled basis, depending upon the type of relationship developed with a particular respondent household. Although we used a structured interview schedule, all interviews were free-flowing and informants were encouraged to follow their own thought patterns and their own organizational format in discussing their dietary practices. In cases where anticipated data were not volunteered, respondents were asked specific questions until responses to the 178 questions were obtained.

THE COMMUNITY

North Central City, (a fictitious name for the target community) located in the heart of two well-defined and locally recognized communities in Kansas City, Kansas, is encompassed by three census tracts (Kansas City 1969). Physically and socially, the area encompasses what may be termed the best and worst of urban living. One very small area has many of the characteristics of suburbia, another seems almost rural, one strip is said to be the vice district, and most of the area is officially defined as the "inner city."

Many of the services obtained in North Central City are much like those obtained in United States urban communities of similar age, structure, history, and population characteristics. The services are limited in quality and quantity and distinctly inferior to those found in modern neighborhood or community service centers. Residents rely upon mass communications media and the larger social system for certain basic information and services. However, many services of a social and personal nature may be obtained in the immediate area. Often, these are small outlets of national or regional commercial enterprises and branches of governmental agencies.

Individuals and families must decide whether to rely on North Central City and its adjoining communities for some or all of their consumer services or go elsewhere to obtain them. The final decision is usually based upon an individual or household's world view and life space, and upon the available transportation facilities. As far as food is concerned, most residents must select from among the foods and beverages marketed in the supermarkets and small independent grocery and snack stores within the local community.

Of the two defined communities spanning North Central City, one, Community A (approximately two-thirds of North Central City), possesses many of the external characteristics of an "inner city" and is, in fact, the locus of a Model Cities Program. The condition of single-family residential structures which predominate in this particular community vary from good to fair in one section and from poor to those slated for clearance in another. The majority of the population in this community consists of young and middle-aged black adults; the white minority consists mainly of middle-aged and "retired" adults.

The community is served by a number of small shopping strips located primarily along major vehicular routes. These strips usually consist of one or two national chain stores, one or two independent grocery stores, a number of grocery-variety stores, liquor stores, and laundromats. Other businesses include barber and beauty shops, drive-in "eateries," food carry-out shops, gasoline service stations, and hardware-variety stores. These business places serve as communication centers and informal meeting places for residents and nonresidents alike. However, structured community social activities take place in the numerous Protestant churches located in the community.

Educational facilities include one junior high school, eleven elementary schools and many Head Start and adult job-training centers, which are fairly new to the community. Health services in the community include a Children and Youth Project and a few physicians' offices. Well Child Clinics are conducted once or twice per week in churches, in other community service centers, and in the offices of physicians.

One-third of North Central City is located in the other defined community, Community B. The greater part of this community's population is white; the racial-ethnic distribution varies considerably from sector to sector. Although the area has many of the physical and social features of suburbia, due to recent annexations, it is generally considered part of the "inner city."

This section contains very few neighborhood stores and has no major shopping areas. Drive-in restaurants, barber shops, beauty shops, and food carry-outs are found along the major vehicular routes which are fairly well removed from the residential areas.

Educational facilities in the community include nine elementary schools, three junior high schools, and one senior high school. Health facilities within the community boundaries are virtually nonexistent; residents must seek health care in other areas of the city.

North Central City is a community in the sense that it is welded by its own social institutions, network of friendships, family ties, mutual obligations, and dependence. Many people refer to three generations of kinsmen who live within walking distance of each other, and a majority of the residents relate to at least one other generation living in close proximity. There is little out-migration in North Central City; most of the single-family dwellings are owned or are being bought by the residents.

Social and Economic Characteristics of Respondents

Insofar as race, ethnicity, household structure and composition, occupation, income, housing, and regional background influence the character of a community and its methods of food acquisition and use, details on the socioeconomic characteristics of the respondents will be discussed.

Of the 150 households studied, the racial/ethnic distribution was 112 Afro-American, 37 Euro-American, and 1 Mexican-American. (A household is defined as the group which usually inhabits a common domicile and regularly shares its resources to provide food and shelter for its members.) Of the 575 individuals in these households, 453 were Afro-American, 116 Euro-American, and 6 Mexican-American. Except for a few selected meat and vegetable items, race and ethnicity did not influence the food procurement and consumption practices of the respondents. For example, the gathering and consumption of wild greens and the inclusion of boiled "greens," other than cabbage and spinach, into the diet was unique to the Afro-American. Tripe and tortillas for Sunday breakfast was singular to the Mexican-American family, and lard sandwiches unique to the Euro-American. Because of the small number of people exhibiting these practices, it is difficult to ascribe racial/ethnic exclusivity to any of these practices.

One hundred and twenty households consisted of nuclear families. Of the remainder, 17 were lineally extended and 13 were laterally extended.

Of the 137 households consisting of more than one individual, 92 were headed by a male and 37 by a female. In 8 instances the households consisted of persons not related by blood or marriage. Size of the households is summarized in Table 3, and formal education attainment of the person interviewed (female in 138 of 150 instances) and the spouse is presented in Table 4. Among the 575 individuals included in the study, there were 316 adults or individuals over sixteen not attending high school; 180 children, six to sixteen years of age, and teen-age minors attending school full time; and 79 children less than six years of age. Nearly all of the children less than six years of age were Afro-Americans.

Household structure and composition exert a powerful influence over

Table 3. Distribution of respondent households by size

Household size	Number of households	Household size	Number of households
1	13	8	7
2	42	9	4
3	32	10	1
4	11	11	1
5	18	12	1
6	10		—
7	10	Total	150

Table 4. Formal educational attainment of respondents and spouses

Number of years of formal education	Respondents	Percent	Spouses[a]	Percent
1–6	11	07.3	5	05.7
7–9	28	18.7	15	17.2
10–11	23	15.3	21	24.2
12, completing high school	88	58.7	46	52.9
Totals	150	100.0	87	100.0

[a] Because a majority of the respondents are female (138 of 150), the spouse column refers to males, essentially.

food procurement and selection. The food preferences of individual members are recognized and respected during the food quest and in the preparation and serving of food. Food is viewed as something to be enjoyed, and the major function of the food provider is to obtain and prepare only those items which are liked by the individuals in the household. Children and adolescents are especially influential in the decision-making process involving food procurement, preparation, and consumption.

The labor force status of the 316 adults and individuals over sixteen not attending high school was as follows: 209 were employed; 68 were unemployed retired; and 39 were unemployed nonretired. The occupational classification[2] of the head of the household (male or female) could be specified for 143 of the 150 households: 43 unskilled workers, 32 skilled manual, 31 semi-skilled, 13 lower-level professional, 9 sales or clerical, 8 technicians, and 7 managers.

On the basis of data from the Bureau of Labor Statistics, U.S. Department of Labor, for the Kansas City (Missouri-Kansas) area for spring, 1970, 60 households were below the lower budget cost, 32 were within the

[2] Occupational classifications were derived from Strauss and Nelson (1968:2); professional levels were based on the years needed to complete professional training and the prestige accorded to the occupation by American Society.

lower budget cost, 24 within the intermediate budget cost, and 34 within the higher budget cost. One hundred and twenty-one households owned or held equity in their dwelling, 27 rented, and 2 lived rent-free. Most of the households (143) occupied a single-family house, three lived in a two-family house, two in a three-family house, and two in an apartment building. The dwellings of 85 households had more than six rooms, the dwellings of 63 households had four to six rooms, and the dwellings of two households had one to three rooms. The regional backgrounds of the respondents (usually female) and spouses are presented in Table 5.

Table 5. Regional background of major informants on food practices

U.S. regions[a]	Respondents	Spouses[b]
North-central	87	70
South	67	32
Northeast	4	1
West	3	0
Total	161	103

[a] Refers to area in which individual resided from birth to age sixteen. Only rarely did an individual claim more than one region.
[b] Because the majority of the respondents are female (138 of 150), the spouse column refers to males, essentially.

Income and occupation influenced food procurement and use only to the extent that the secure feelings brought about by an assured and secure income permitted individuals to incorporate dietary noncore items into the established diet at a relatively high frequency rate. Except for ceremonial occasions, regional background did not appear to exert strong influences on food consumption practices. The informants seemed to be responding to the stimuli of the immediate environment.

THE ACQUISITION AND SELECTION OF FOOD FOR USE AT HOME

Residents of North Central City take steps to ensure the presence of at least a week's supply of dietary staples and nonstaples in the home. The routineness of food acquisition — time of week and day, source of food, method of transportation — is altered by planned diversions. Although the amount and type of staples to be obtained is known, additional money is always included either for self-indulgence and family catering or simply for experimental purposes. Emphasis is always placed on securing only those items relished by household members; this approach is designed to please, but no one fails to recognize the economic benefits of securing foods "for the stomach and not for the garbage."

Food Acquisition for Use at Home

CHANNLES THROUGH WHICH FOOD ENTERS THE HOME. Food enters the home through a variety of channels; however, purchasing represents the major channel through which food is obtained. Every respondent household purchases some or all of the food and beverage items consumed. One-third of the respondents supplement their grocery purchases by maintaining small vegetable gardens, by gathering wild greens and mushrooms, by fishing, and by hunting small game. These "home-grown" items are considered a delicacy.

A relatively small number of households (16) participate in the commodity food distribution program. However, through an intricate system of exchange a majority of the respondents receive and use one or more of the food items generally referred to as "commodity foods." Another minority (17 households) have certain foods and beverages delivered to their homes.

FOOD PURCHASING PRACTICES. The supermarket serves as the major locus of food procurement (144 households). Of less importance in terms of numbers utilizing the resources are small farms, discount food stores, corner grocery stores, drive-ins, small independent food markets, specialty stores, e.g. bakery and meat stores, farmer's market, liquor stores, PX stores, and "Quick Stop" outlets. Not one respondent household held membership in all-purpose Food Service Plans.

Trips to the supermarket within and outside the community for major grocery purchases are spaced according to the household needs; however, the trend is either once each week or twice each month (Table 6) coinci-

Table 6. Frequency of major grocery shopping

Frequency	Number of households	Frequency	Number of households
Daily	2	1 time per month	16
2 to 3 times per week	6	3 times per year	1
1 time per week	91	No set pattern	1
2 times per month	33	Total	150

dent with the pay-day cycle. However, many respondents volunteered that it is not uncommon to have members of the family pick up bread, milk, and lunchmeats almost every day at either the supermarket or corner store. In households with small children, approximately 25 percent of a week's food purchases is obtained through this type of supplementary shopping. Five respondents reported that household members purchase their food individually rather than communally.

Although one-third of the respondent households (51 households) obtain food items by maintaining small vegetable gardens and by hunting game and fishing, there is essentially little seasonal variation in their food purchasing practices (Table 7).

Table 7. Number of respondent households purchasing "almost all" food items consumed in each of the four seasons

Season	Number of households (n = 150)
Spring	133
Summer	123
Fall	135
Winter	134

Food Selection for Use at Home

In the majority of cases, the female head of household[3] (104 respondents; 76 percent) assumes the major responsibility for grocery shopping. However, actual shopping and food selection represent a cooperative venture for members of 83 households (60 percent of respondents). In the remainder of households, the food shopper is unaccompanied by household members or "significant others" residing outside of the household.

However, even when the food shopper is unaccompanied by others, the foods selected always include the stated preferences of household members. Various household members—adults (male and female), adolescents, youth, and children assist in selecting foods for the household between the regularly scheduled grocery shopping trips.

Decisions on how much is to be spent on food vary among households. In 25 percent of the households "all family members" participate in the decisions. Among the remaining 75 percent decisions are made by either the male or female head of household. The data show equal distribution in each category. Forty percent of the respondent households knew in advance the lower and upper limits of money to be expended on food for a given food shopping cycle. Although the remaining 60 percent did not set limits in advance, they always operated within a certain dollar range

[3] There were 137 respondent households with more than one individual.

rather than a set figure. The establishment of a range rather than a set figure is consistent with the flexible approach to food shopping.

Food selection in the supermarket is viewed as both an expedition and an important social occasion by a majority of the respondents. Ninety percent of the respondents described their visits to the supermarket in terms of a grand tour. Supermarket cart in hand, they travel from aisle to aisle and pick up the food and beverage items they customarily get or have an urge to try. Aisle-to-aisle shopping seems directly associated with the development of lay food categories (Table 1).

Further analyses reveal that three factors defined by the respondents as NEED, LIKE, and TRY, greatly influence the food selection process. Foods defined as "needed" and those known to be "liked" by individual household members essentially form the core and secondary core of the diet, while the "try" foods are well represented in the peripheral core and ceremonial/marginal categories.

Marketing a wide variety of foods at relatively low cost permits the selection of NEED/LIKE foods on a consistently high frequency basis and TRY foods on a low frequency basis. When a TRY food meets an individual or family's goal for food acceptability, it gradually moves from the TRY to LIKE category and later becomes incorporated into the NEED/LIKE highly preferred foods category. The individual is moved to "try out" new and different foods by television and grocery store advertisements. Of equal importance as food item attractants are food packaging and merchandising techniques and verbal endorsements by relatives, friends, and colleagues.

Although cost of food also functions to further define and clarify the NEED, LIKE, and TRY concepts, 75 percent of households indicated that neither the price tag nor the lure of "weekly specials" persuaded them from the dominant influences of their twin perceptions — NEED and LIKE in selecting foods.

Two-thirds of the respondents admitted that they customarily buy food items advertised on TV "just to try them out to see if we like them" during the shopping expedition. One-half of the respondents "buy things that look real good on the shelves," although they did not originally plan to get those items. Usually, these are new or different foods. For 80 percent of shoppers, snacks turned out to be more popular "splurge items" than "nonsnacks."

The Cyclical Patterning of Food and Beverages Used at Home

What is consumed at a given time in the home environment depends on what is available when one has the urge to eat. In selecting food for home consumption, care is taken to provide for the preferences and basic and special needs of household members; these preferences and needs are expressed in food consumption frequencies.

It had been hypothesized that a large number of core items (those with a very high frequency of consumption scores) and ceremonial/marginal dietary items (those foods receiving very low frequency of consumption scores) as compared with secondary core items (with intermediate frequency ratings) and peripheral core items (those with low frequency scores) express a TWO-PHASE CYCLIC INCORPORATION of foods into the established diet and may serve to further express diet individuation.

The data appearing in Table 8, obtained from the combined use of the SS and Food Data Sheet (Table 2), will be used to test the hypothesis.

Of the 318 food and beverage items yielding frequency-of-use responses (233 items were displayed in the SS and 85 were volunteered by respondents), only 76 (24 percent) were consistently used at specified frequency intervals by the respondent households to warrant their being considered truly integrated into the diet (i.e., consumed at frequencies of at least once per month). It is obvious, then, that a large majority of the respondents consumed a large number of items, a total of 242, with such irregularity that one must conclude that the food-ways of the respondents appear to demonstrate a strongly individualistic style.

Of the 76 items fully integrated into the diet, 51 (67 percent) were used with a high degree of frequency; 9 (12 percent) were used at a lower order of frequency, and 16 (21 percent) were used at an even lower order of frequency.

Of the 242 items falling outside of the predefined core, secondary core, and peripheral diets, 84 items (35 percent) were deemed marginal to the diet, i.e. they were rarely included in the diet. The remainder, 158 items (65 percent), were used so eclectically that it was difficult to determine how they were patterned into the diet.

The data lead one to accept the hypothesis of CYCLIC INCORPORATION as expressed by the presence of a large number of dietary items in the highest and lowest frequency categories, 51 and 84 items, respectively; and a relatively low number of items in the intermediate and low frequency categories, 9 and 16 items, respectively. Inability to classify 158 items by the frequency-of-consumption criteria selected for this study, forces one to conclude that there exists a high degree of variableness in the frequency consumption of a large number of items by a large number of people, suggesting a strong individualistic trend in the food consumption pattern.

Table 8. Cyclical patterning of food and beverages[a]

Food category	Core	Secondary	Peripheral	Marginal
Candy				
	Candy/candy bar (variety)[b]	→→→	→→→	→→→
Casseroles				
	Spaghetti and meat sauce[b]	→→→	→→→	→→→
	Macaroni and cheese[b]	→→→	→→→	→→→
Cereal products				
	Dry cereal (variety)			Corn (white)
(Bakery and nonbakery types)	Enriched white bread	Hot biscuits	Pancake	Blueberry muffins
	Toast	Cream of wheat		Blueberry turnover
	Corn (yellow)			Hard rolls
	Cornbread			Waffles
	Rice			Fruit cake
	Oatmeal			Honey buns
Cheeses				
(Natural and processed)	American cheese[b]	→→→	→→→	→→→
	Cheddar cheese[b]	→→→	→→→	→→→
Desserts				
	Jello[b]	→→→	→→→	→→→
Eggs				
	Egg	— — —	— — —	Baked custard
Fats				
	Shortening	— — —	— — —	— — —
	Butter	— — —	— — —	— — —
	Margarine	— — —	— — —	— — —
Frozen ices				
	Ice cream	— — —	— — —	— — —

Fruit	Apple Orange Banana Watermelon (in season)	— — —	Fruit cocktail	Figs Cherries Dates Blueberries Tangerines Mixed fresh fruit Tangelo Cranberry Plums Mandarin oranges Apricot halves Honeydew melon
Jams and jellies	Jellies (variety)	— — —	— — —	— — —
Legumes	— — —	Green peas	Black-eyed peas Lima beans	— — —
Lunchmeats	Lunchmeat (variety)[b]	→→→	→→→	→→→
Meats and poultry	Bacon (pork) Ground beef Chicken[b] Wiener Beef	Pork chop Beef roast Chicken[b]	Ham Pork spareribs Beef liver	Lamb chop Turkey
Meat and nut spreads	Peanut butter	— — —	— — —	Spam spread
Puddings	— — —	— — —	— — —	Lemon pudding Butterscotch pudding

[a] Item listed in order of predominance in each catagory.

[b] Item represented in every food catagory.

Table 8. (Continued) [a]

Food category	Core	Secondary	Peripheral	Marginal
Salads	Tossed salad	— — —	— — —	Citrus salad Fruit salad Macaroni-meat-vegetable salad
Sandwiches	Sandwich (variety)	→→→	→→→	→→→
Sausages	Sausage (variety, excluding beef)	→→→	→→→	→→→
Seafood	— — —	Fish (variety) fresh or frozen	Tuna	Crab/crabmeat Lobster Salmon
Snack foods	Snacks[b] (variety)	→→→	→→→	→→→
Soups	Soup (variety)[b]	→→→	→→→	→→→
Sugars and syrups	Sugar	— — —	— — —	— — —
Vegetables	Potatoes Tomatoes Lettuce Onions Green beans[c] Celery Green pepper Cucumber	Green beans[c] Greens	Cabbage Sweet potato/yam Broccoli Mixed vegetables Cauliflower Beets Sauerkraut Spinach	Tomato wedges (canned)

Food category	Core	Secondary	Peripheral	Marginal
Beverages				
	Coffee	— — —	— — —	Cranprune juice
	Whole milk			Peach nectar
	Carbonated beverages (variety)			Orange-apricot drink
	Orange juice			Gelatin drink
	Kool aid			Pineapple-apricot drink
	Iced tea			Apricot nectar
	Hot tea			Eggnog
	Evaporated milk			Liquid diet food
	Beer			Mixed vegetable juices
				Cream
				Instant breakfast
				Orange plus
				Pineapple-grapefruit juice drink
				Funny face
				Wine (carbonated)
				Pineapple-orange juice drink
				Brandy
				Powdered milk
				Gin
				Rum
				Vodka
				Wine (noncarbonated)
				Skim milk

[a] Items listed in order of predominance in each category.
[b] Item represented in every food category.
[c] Equally distributed in both categories.

CONCLUSION

In contrast to small, nonindistrialized, nonaffluent, and relatively homogeneous societies and communities, the contemporary urban United States presents a special challenge to the ethnographer interested in elucidating diet patterns of the community's inhabitants. Among other considerations, the researcher must account for the wide variety of foods (and beverages) always available in the market place, the living patterns of the heterogeneous groups residing in these urban communities, and the numerous socioenvironmental stimuli — including food and nutrition promotional programs — which influence food selection and use.

With few restrictions on his attractive and stable food supply, the individual has become very selective in his choice of food and has learned to cater to his personal food preferences. The development of individuated dietary patterns, apparently a characteristic response to sustained food abundance, is very difficult to capture in traditional ethnographic research.

The methodological approach discussed in this paper which combines participant-observational techniques with interviews and special instruments is being recommended as one way of capturing the complexities of food use in modern urban centers. Through this approach, it was possible to capture the cyclical patterning of individual foods as they were incorporated into the diet on a nonseasonal basis; it was also possible to identify the dynamics involved in the structure of the diet pattern.

On the basis of observed food behavior, the major finding, which suggests a continuous two-phase process in the cyclic patterning of food, seems tenable. This process accounts for the large and varied food supply and the varied food consumption pattern of individuals and families. The process is also compatible with societal goals which emphasize the benefits of food variation, self-fulfillment, and achievement.

If, indeed, this method is sensitive to food behavior in modern, urban communities with a regular, constant supply of food, this method should be refined to capture the specific sociocultural and psychological factors which catalyze rapid turnover in the food system.

REFERENCES

BENNETT, JOHN W.
1942 Food and culture in southern Illinois. *American Sociological Review* 7:645–660.

FOOD AND AGRICULTURE ORGANIZATION (FAO)
1971 *Food balance sheets 1964–1966*, page 762. Rome: FAO.

KANSAS CITY
1969 *Community renewal program: an analysis of community needs and renewal potential; northeast community 13*. Kansas City: Kansas Planning Department.

Progressive Grocers
1969 *Progressive Grocers* (April): 58.

STRAUSS, M. A.; J. I. NELSON
1968 *Sociological analysis: an empirical approach through replication*. New York: Harper and Row.

ULLENSVANG, LEON P.
1970 Food consumption patterns in the seventies. *Vital Speeches* 36:240–246.

UNITED STATES DEPARTMENT OF AGRICULTURE (USDA)
1959 *The yearbook of agriculture*, page 602. Washington, D.C.: U.S. Government Printing Office.
1970 Dietary levels of households in the northeast, spring, 1965. *Household Food Consumption Survey 1965–66*, *Report 7*, page 10. Washington, D.C.: U.S. Government Printing Office.

UNITED STATES DEPARTMENT OF LABOR
1970 Bureau of Labor Statistics, data for spring, 1970, for Kansas City (Missouri – Kansas).

Nutrition Behavior, Food Resources, and Energy

M. M. KRONDL and G. G. BOXEN

Cultural anthropologists regard nutrition behavior as a part of a set of customs that are learned and constantly changing. They observe them thoroughly without being specifically concerned about their effect on health. Nutritionists, on the other hand, rarely link nutrition behavior with the value system of culture and instead concentrate on the implications of the behavior on health.

Because of the different approaches of these two disciplines, there is seldom any exchange of ideas between them. Nutrition behavior is a complicated issue; thus even their joint efforts would be insufficient. Many other disciplines have to become involved.

The objective of the authors is to present a conceptual framework for a complex study of nutrition behavior. We hope to relate nutrition behavior with food resources and energy, on the one hand, and with cultural values, on the other hand. The origin of our interest in this idea dates back to the 1950's when the senior author, having studied the results of nutrition surveys, recognized a wide degree of diversity of foods in different economic regions of Central Europe (Smrha and Skopkova-Krondlova 1957: 232). In mountainous regions the quality and quantity as well as the variety of foods was poor. Only cities offered a full range of food choice in sufficient quantity. Rural areas were in between. Similar findings in the 1970's are now well known and fit into the stratification pattern of society defined by Lenski (1966). His societal types are arranged according to increasing social complexity. They range from the simplest form of hunting and gathering society, through early and advanced horticulture to the agrarian type, and finally to industrial society. This pattern has been widely used as a basis for later research.

For example Quick (1970: 133–152) has suggested that the societal pattern has geographical applications. He has also observed that with the increase of social complexity there occurs a change in the relationship between food resources and man's general behavior. We have found these hypotheses stimulating but insufficient to explain the degree of diversity of foods found in different types of society. In these days of ecological awareness the most important factor in this connection seemed to us to be energy (Figure 1).

ENERGY ——→ FOOD RESOURCES

Figure 1. Food resources are dependent on energy

We began to appreciate the fact that there is a close tie between the quantity of available food and the energy input. Food resources in primitive society depend almost entirely on photosynthesis and man's energy (Figure 2).

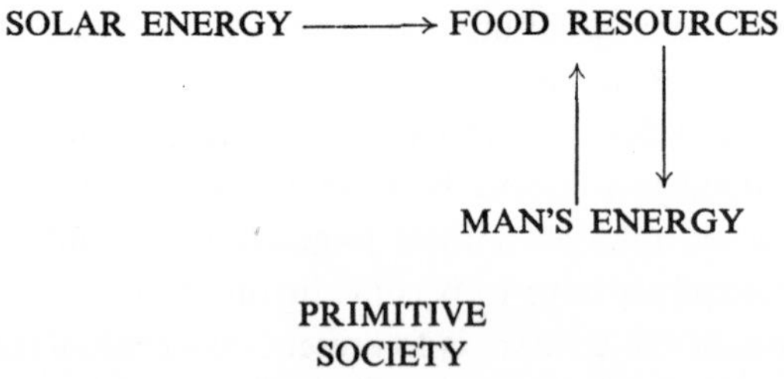

Figure 2. Relationship of solar energy, food supply, and man

In the agricultural society the available energy is reinforced by the addition of energy sources such as wind, water, and animals (Figure 3).

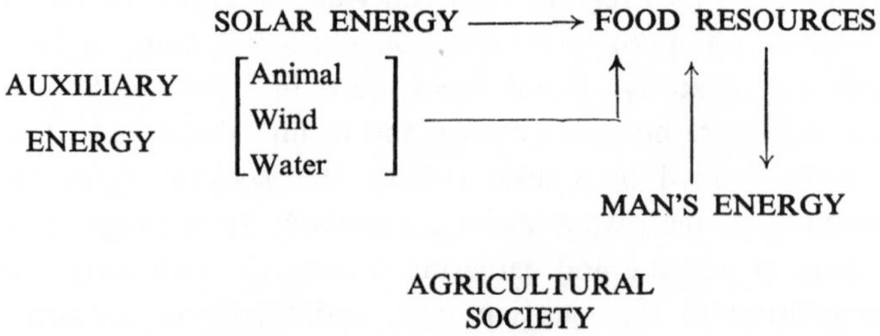

Figure 3. Solar energy is supplemented by auxiliary supplies

In the industrial society other sources of energy such as fossil fuels, hydropower, and atomic energy step in (Figure 4).

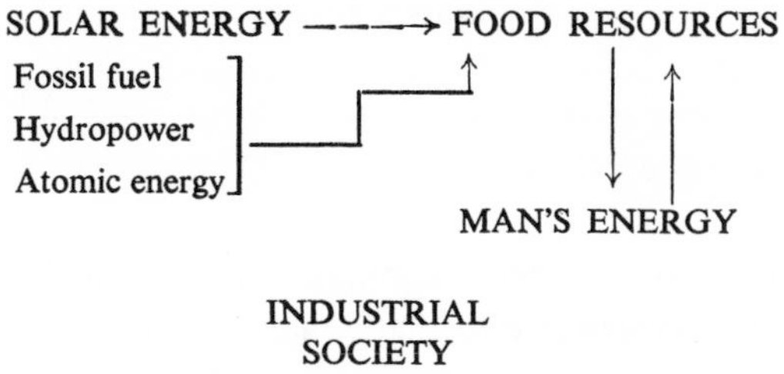

Figure 4. Newer energy sources further supplement solar energy

Simultaneously the extra energy disturbs the natural ecosystem. As man contributes less of his own energy to the creation of his food resources, he starts to break out of the natural food chain. The biological relationship between man's physical output, energy needs, and food resources becomes lost. This detachment is apparent in the changing diversity of plants and wildlife. The efficient use of energy in cultivation of food resources necessitated narrowing this diversity and caused the extinction of a great number of species. The increased supply of energy created a NEW FORM OF FOOD DIVERSITY by means of transportation, storage, and eventually by means of technological processing. Thus, in the industrial society we have a new type of food variety, which reflects very little of its origin. In view of the above hypothesis, the first part of our conceptual framework began to acquire shape; energy and food availability (which we may call utility stimuli) influence nutrition behavior (Figure 5).

ENERGY→FOOD RESOURCES→NUTRITION BEHAVIOR

Figure 5. Energy influences nutrition behavior by controlling food resources

We shall now discuss the alternate set of variables which influence nutrition behavior — the cultural values. Our research on the nutrition behavior of obese populations (Beal 1970; Boxen 1972) has convinced us that more than just utility stimuli are involved, although the origins of the stimuli can be tracked back to the extra energy intervention. The energy input affects not only food resources, but simultaneously spares man's energy for activities other than basic survival. New energy empowers achievement in technology, which in turn changes man's life-style and cultural values. These are reflected in man's general behavior, which includes NUTRITION BEHAVIOR (Figure 6).

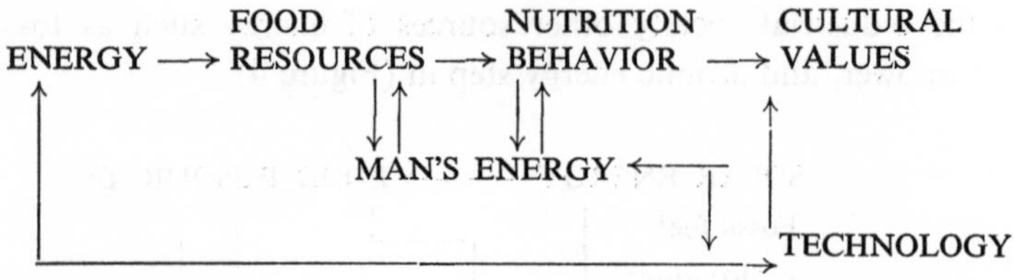

Fig. 6. Auxiliary energy allows man to devote more energy to nonsurvival activities

As a result, food takes on new meanings and uses, which gradually affect the INTERNAL MECHANISM that regulates man's food intake. The physiological system in his body reacts to the expenditure of energy. The food intake that should counterbalance the energy output is controlled by the hypothalamus gland. We have designated information, supplied to this brain center by the physiological changes in the body, as "internal cues." Thus, it can be argued that nutrition behavior is basically regulated by a physiological mechanism using these internal cues as monitors in accordance with the amount of energy used for work. In the primitive society, food intake is almost entirely dependent on physiological signals, on internal cues. With the increase of extra energy input accompanied by the increased complexity and the changing food resources of our society, the influence of utility stimuli on nutrition behavior diminishes. Cultural values, thus, appear to create a secondary mechanism affecting food intake. Schachter (1967: 117–144) has indicated the presence of a whole range of environmental, nonphysiological nonutility stimuli, such as time, advertising, sensory perception, all of which are related to nutrition behavior. He has termed them "EXTERNAL CUES." The existence of some of these external cues encourages technologists to tamper with foods so that they are more appealing to the senses. To sell his new food product even if it is devoid of nutritional value, the manufacturer attempts to manipulate cultural values and create new associations. Because people today are less concerned with basic survival than their ancestors in primitive society were, nutrition behavior is very much influenced by cultural cues through a feedback mechanism (Figure 7).

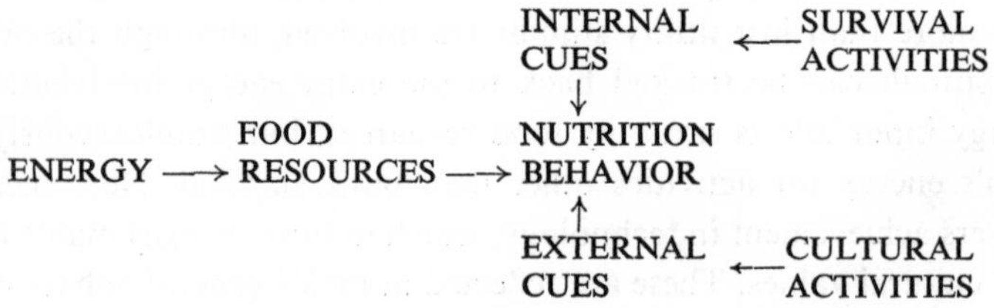

Figure7. Control of nutrition behavior by internal and external cues

In the most advanced technological society the external cues are of such importance that the mechanism to maintain energetic homeostasis often cannot adapt adequately. Because man's energy needs have decreased and food intake is not limited, obesity is the result. Strangely enough, man seems to have an adaptation system regulated by internal cues that functions for intermittent harmonic starvation (Young and Scrimshaw 1971: 14); but he seems to lack the ability to reinforce his response to an abundant food intake by external cues.

Our findings from research on nutrition behavior (Boxen 1972) are in accordance with those of Schachter, supporting his observations that obese persons are more dependent on external than on internal cues. Thus, our final conceptual framework includes as basic variables for nutrition behavior, food resources (utility stimuli), on one side, and cultural values (nonutility stimuli), on the other side (Figure 8).

ENERGY ⟶ FOOD RESOURCES (US) ⟶ NUTRITION BEHAVIOR ⟵ CULTURAL VALUES (NS)

where US = utility stimuli
NS = nonutility stimuli

Fig. 8. Nutrition behavior is dependent on both food resources and cultural values

We have come to believe that nutrition behavior is basically energy. On one hand, this energy causes a disruption in the external environment that directly affects the food supply and, in this way, nutrition behavior. Indirectly, this energy enhances man's activities and, in turn, affects the internal mechanism influencing his nutrition behavior. In the end man becomes more dependent on external cues than on internal cues.

We believe that this conceptual framework will primarily be useful in developing methods for the study of nutrition behavior. It is now possible for us to set the variables controlling nutrition behavior into the form of a continuum (Figure 9). The stimuli can be arranged according to their utility and nonutility values. The operation of utility stimuli depends essentially on physiological need or internal cues. Nonutility stimuli function to fulfill cultural needs and therefore depend on food acceptability. The characteristics of these stimuli are wellsummarized by Gifft, et al. (1972). Essentially, physical availability suggests merely the presence of food. A second type of availability is the economic means to acquire food. Awareness presumes knowledge of the existence of certain foods and their effect on health, so important in this age of intensive world nomadism (Savage and Krondl 1972: 55). In some instances superstition,

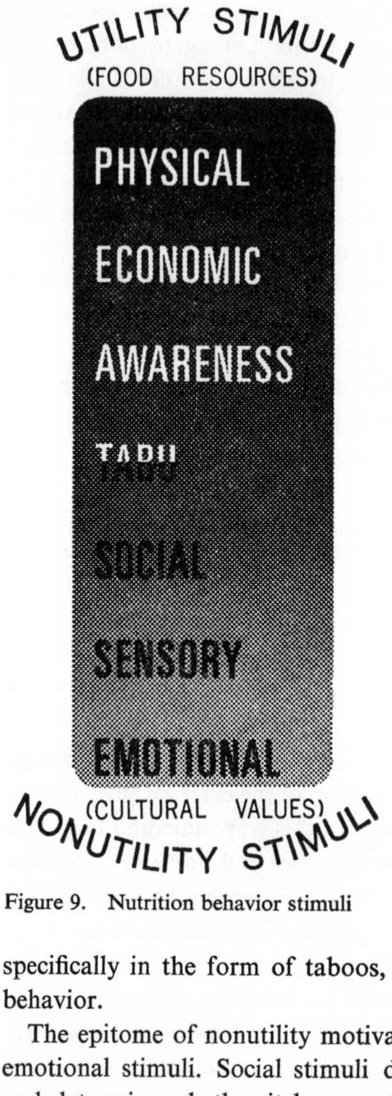

Figure 9. Nutrition behavior stimuli

specifically in the form of taboos, is a factor in determining nutrition behavior.

The epitome of nonutility motivation is found in social, sensory, and emotional stimuli. Social stimuli define the meaning and use of food and determine whether it has prestige, sex, or health value. Individual relationships to food depend on the response to sensory stimuli and emotional attachments to food, to its use as a crutch or as a source of satisfaction.

The methods used so far in assessing nutrition behavior have been restricted mainly to examining food resources without considering the energy input (Figure 10). Food balance sheets are used by the government food policy makers; economists and nutritionists predominantly use food inventories; health personnel, including nutritionists, rely basically on

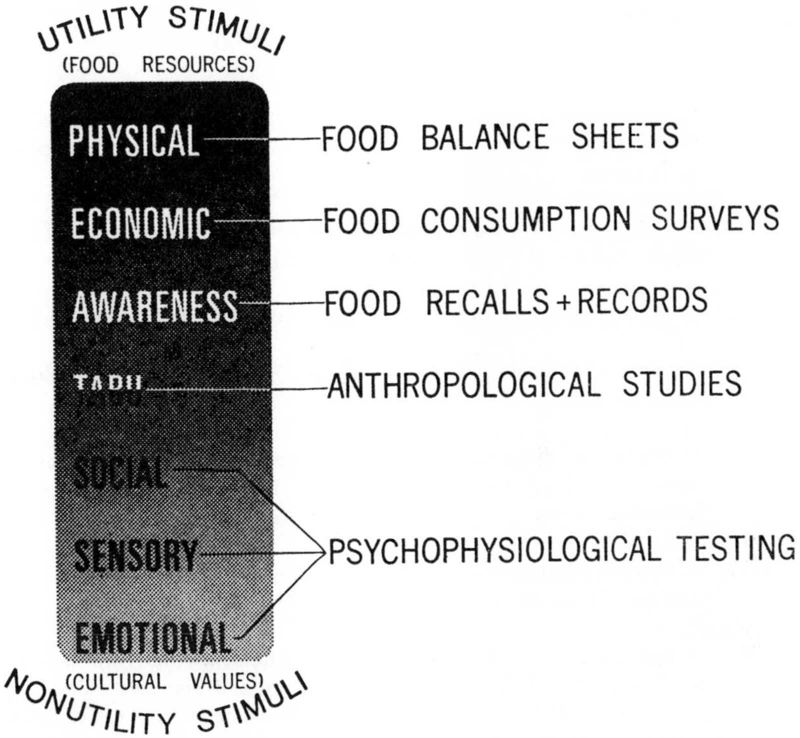

Figure 10. Methods of assessing nutrition behavior stimuli

food recall and food record methods; observation methods are used by nutritionists and, to an even greater extent, by anthropologists in research of food taboos; sensory stimuli are much explored and exploited by food technologists. The emotional aspects of nutritional behavior are beginning to be investigated by psychophysiologists through experimental testing and personality inventory. No specific method of approach has been used to assess the social role of food. Our own efforts have been devoted to the integration of the various approaches and to the further development of methods for assessing the nonutility stimuli.

The significance of this integral approach should be obvious. The dominant factors in a particular society can be determined and the stimuli that have detrimental effects can be adjusted. The obvious ideal condition for understanding the complex stimuli of nutrition behavior is a close interaction between those concerned with man as a species and with his ecological aspects from the point of view of energy and food resources and those who view man in terms of his cultural values and their impact on human behavior. Both anthropologists and nutritionists seem to qualify.

REFERENCES

BEAL, M.

1970 "Environmental influence on the nutritional status of obese subjects." Unpublished Master's thesis, Faculty of Food Sciences, University of Toronto.

BOXEN, G. G.

1972 "Extrinsic and intrinsic factors in obesity." Unpublished Master's thesis, Faculty of Food Sciences, University of Toronto.

GIFFT, H. H. *et al.*

1972 *Nutrition, behaviour and change.* Englewood Cliffs: Prentice-Hall.

LENSKI, G. E.

1966 *Power and privilege, a theory of social stratification.* New York: McGraw-Hill.

QUICK, H. F.

1970 "Geographic dimensions of human ecology," in *Dimensions of nutrition.* Edited by J. Dupont, 133–152. Colorado Associated University Press.

SAVAGE, W. E., M. M. KRONDL

1972 A nutritional investigation of Canadians parasitized in the tropics. *Journal of Canadian Dietetic Association* 33: 55.

SCHACHTER, S.

1967 "Cognitive effects on bodily functioning: studies in obesity and eating," in *Biology and behaviour: neurophysiology and emotion.* Edited by D. C. Glass, 117–144. New York: The Rockefeller University Press.

SMRHA, O., M. M. SKOPKOVA-KRONDLOVA

1957 The impact of food consumption levels on the development of food industry. *Premysl Potravin* 8: 232.

YOUNG, V. R., N. S. SCRIMSHAW

1971 The physiology of starvation. *Scientific American* 225: 14.

The Risks of Dietary Change: A Pacific Atoll Example

NANCY J. POLLOCK

The question of how dietary changes come about is receiving increasing attention. Data from an atoll community in the Marshall Islands in the Central Pacific demonstrate that new foodstuffs (mainly of Western origin) are added to a repertoire of indigenous foods rather than substituted for those indigenous foods. On Namu atoll the diet in 1968 was made up of locally produced breadfruits, pandanus, coconut, and fish, as well as purchased foods such as rice, flour, tea, and sugar. A policy of economic caution suggests that adding to the existing range of foodstuffs certain unfamiliar purchased foods produces greater variety in the diet and at the same time less likelihood of hunger. Namu people fear hunger greatly. Thus while maintaining the subsistence pattern with which they are familiar and for which they can calculate many of the risks, they can become acquainted with a range of purchased foodstuffs that are subject to many factors beyond their control.

As we do not have adequate documentation of past dietary changes on atolls, we can approach the problem by delineating three types of atoll[1] food-producing ecosystems:

1. An atoll not regularly inhabited because food supply is considered inadequate to support a population, e.g. Kili before the Bikini people were relocated there.
2. An inhabited atoll where the local flora and fauna have been used to

Fieldwork was conducted on Namu atoll from February 1968 to January 1969 and was supported by a National Institute of Mental Health research grant 1/T01/MH/-11300-01.

[1] Atoll is used here to include low reef islands that lack a lagoon.

support a population over several generations, as indicated by the established useful flora and by oral history, e.g. Namu.

3. An inhabited atoll (hypothetical) where foodstuffs must all be imported because the population is too dense to allow space on which to grow subsistence foods (e.g. Ebeye islet, Kwajalein atoll).

The selection of (2) over (1) by ancestors of the present atoll inhabitants indicates an awareness of the margins of a food-producing area that are necessary for survival. The difference between (2) and (3) is the degree of dependence on an extra-atoll agency for provisioning the inhabitants. According to the Nathan Report (1966), if the scattered peoples of Micronesia were consolidated on a few key islands, then food could be readily supplied from the vacated islands. This paper will demonstrate why this is an economically irrational statement.

Because (3) is a hypothetical case, we will concentrate our attention on (2). To do this we must subdivide (2) into two types of subsistence:

a. entirely locally derived food; and
b. local plus purchased foods, with varying dependence on each.

Then we can contrast (2a) with (3) in order to demonstrate why (2b) is the economically rational mode of subsistence.

By first investigating the ecosystem of locally produced foodstuffs, we can set out the risks involved and the strategies by which the Namu people cope with them. We can then examine the risks involved when purchased foods are used for subsistence.

The term RISK is used here to apply to a situation where outcomes are so uncertain that an action may be considered to have dangerous repercussions; in this case, these repercussions would be upon the unavailability of foodstuffs and would thus bring about hunger. The question of certainty/uncertainty lies in the people's knowledge of the economic system within which they must operate. Where many generations have been growing foodstuffs in the same type of environment, they can be said to have "adapted," i.e. to have learned to handle that environment and how it affects them. They have learned to expect certain phenomena such as high winds, too much or too little rainfall, etc., though they cannot tell exactly when these events will occur. From their forebears they know that there are certain risks in their world and that there are time-worn methods of coping with them to avoid dire hunger. A full stomach indicates a state of great satisfaction and thus has a very positive value to a Namu inhabitant.

Coping mechanisms to deal with adverse effects upon the food supply have become incorporated into the society's value system. For the Namu people there is a strong ethic that no one household should be allowed to go hungry as long as any other household in that community has some food. Similarly, certain foods are considered good for a sick individual. These socially approved tactics ensure that drastic hunger is not a common phenomenon and that everyone in the community is at the same level of fortune. They are also part of a philosophy that things, though bad now, will get better soon.

LOCALLY PRODUCED FOODSTUFFS

Risks

1. Natural calamities such as typhoons, tidal waves, droughts, or very strong winds: Although each is rare (the Marshall Islands lie outside the normal typhoon belt [Wiens 1962]), they have been known to have disastrous effects on subsistence. The memory of such an event lingers on in oral tradition, and with the memory is handed down the method by which the people pulled themselves out of the trouble. Because Namu is a large atoll, twenty-five miles long by fifteen miles wide at its broadest point, and because there are numerous small islets, particularly on the southeastern rim, it is likely that not all parts of the atoll would be equally affected by a natural calamity. Thus, when the food supply has been depleted on the islets on which most people reside, small, uninhabited islets to which people have rights may be utilized.

The local crops appear to be resistant to most disasters. A breadfruit tree is likely to lose its leaves, fruit, and some branches in a high wind, but the trunk is usually very stout. Taro can be adversely affected by inundations of salt water, so that this staple may be forced out of usage temporarily. Coconuts and fish are very resilient in all but the very worst disasters, and the Namu people cited these as the very rock-bottom staple foodstuffs.

2. Pestilence and crop disease: These are extremely unlikely to reach annihilation levels where the biotic communities are relatively static and where communication with foreign biota is minimal. The coconut rat and *Pingelap* disease of breadfruit trees are two of the major known dangers.

3. Human inundation: The risks of being attacked by outside predators are well documented in the oral history. War parties were particularly devastating on Namu and tended to clean off all the produce from the large islets (Erdland 1914). The problems of the current population increase are less clearly recognized. In precontact times social controls existed to cope with this problem: each couple was allowed to have only

three live children, and the rest had to be drowned. But with mission influence and modern Western medicine, such controls have been forbidden. Yet these Western agencies have not demonstrated how the extra mouths are to be fed.

Strategies

Means of coping with the threat of food shortage are not consciously reasoned. The suggestions here are derived from the writer's observation of atoll life, rather than from answers to questions, and are not necessarily listed in order of importance.

1. Namu, because of its large lagoon in proportion to its land mass (135:0.72 square miles), and thus its scattered range of human habitats, offers a variety of small environments. Resources vary from islet to islet according to size, orientation to the northwest trade wind, ready access to the open ocean, availability of fresh water in the Ghyben-Herzberg lens, and length of occupancy. The coconut palm is found on almost all islets except the smallest sandbars. Breadfruit, pandanus, papaya, and banana are indications of the length of human occupancy. Wet taro (*Cyrtosperma chamissonis*) pits are found only on the two largest islets, where there are only two pits each today. The people say they are too much trouble to look after. Dry taro (*Alocasia macrorrhiza*) grows wild on the largest islets but is only eaten in times of extreme hunger. Arrowroot (*Tacca leontopetaloides*) grows wild and is utilized but not replanted. Fishing is good off the northernmost and southernmost islets, but poor off the easternmost islet, and this is noted by the Namu people when comparing islets. Thus, within the atoll food resources vary and offer a certain range of choices of habitat and therefore of diet.
2. Mobility of the population ensures that resources are not completely exhausted in any one area. Namu people move around very freely within their atoll in order (now) to make copra, be with a sick parent or sibling, or help in a "family" task (for further discussion, see Pollock n.d.a). Food shortage was never given as a direct reason for a move, but it was implied. Thus household composition changes frequently and with it the drain on resources.
3. Resources are available on the islets not regularly inhabited. In particular, birds and crabs are less regularly exploited on these uninhabited islets; they therefore increase and are readily caught once a year or more when an occasional party visits the islet.
4. Kin links with neighboring atolls through intermarriage enable those

people who have suffered a depletion of food resources on one atoll to use these ties to obtain temporary access to such resources on another atoll.

5. Trading up and down the chain, which was particularly common in precontact times, enabled the various atoll populations to increase the range of foodstuffs available to each. From north to south through the Marshalls the annual rainfall increases. Thus the drier northern atols were able to trade turmeric and arrowroot for breadfruit and other fruits that grew more profusely in the wetter southern atolls. Navigational skills, for which the Marshallese are renowned, were of great assistance in this broadening of the resource base of any particular atoll.

6. On Namu twenty-four locally named varieties of pandanus are recognized. They differ in time of maturation of fruit, as well as in shape, color, and size of the fruit, and are thus spread over a four-month consumption period. This range may have been increased by trading or other human means because the plant requires human interference to propagate edible varieties.

7. Wet taro can be left in the ground as a "last resort food."

8. Some resources (e.g. breadfruit, taro, Pandanus, etc.) were considered as more suitable for food than others, and these were labeled "food," i.e. items for everyday consumption. Other resources (e.g. dry taro, woody stems, and hermit crabs) were considered "starvation foods," for emergency use only.

9. Appeals were made to the supernatural through rituals such as the annual fertility feast, which was apparently converted into a Christmas celebration upon missionization. Lacking detailed accounts of the earlier fertility feasts, we can only surmise that they were concerned with ensuring the general welfare of the population. The present-day Christmas celebrations place much importance on abundance of food (Pollock n.d.b).

10. A strong ethic of community survival was apparent among the Namu people. If one family did not have enough food, then other members of that community, whether closely related to them or not, were morally bound to supply them with some food. In that way all of the community remained at the same level of hunger or fullness. It would be considered highly unacceptable for one person to have a lot of food while others had little. The one exception to this ethic is the paramount chief; however, he too had to dispense food gifts widely among the community. This emphasis on generosity and sharing may thus be seen as a major strategy in the constant and equitable distribution of resources.

11. We can hypothesize that the Namu people may have become

physiologically adapted to a low protein, high carbohydrate diet, as has been found in New Guinea (Oomen and Corden 1969; Hipsley 1969). If an atoll population, too, is able to fix nitrogen in the intestine, then a high protein, high fat diet may be not only unnecessary but even harmful (Oomen and Corden 1969). Energy levels appeared (subjectively) to be adequate for the normal pace of the daily round of atoll life.

These strategies, taken in combination, indicate the ways in which the Namu people obtain their foods from the local resources using various mechanisms within their social system as safeguards. Each strategy has some latitude within it that allows for the various risks to be countered.

PURCHASED FOODSTUFFS

Money to buy food comes mainly from the sale of copra on Namu. Only eleven men received regular salaries for their services as teachers and health aides; five other men each received a small honorarium for his services to the Atoll Council. Income for 1968 averaged 110 dollars per active adult male. Of the copra income, 91 percent of the money never left the trading ship. It was immediately exchanged for food supplies. Nonfood purchases comprised less than 2 percent of all purchases. Four items made up the bulk of the food purchases: rice, flour, tea, and sugar, with cooking fat, matches, cigarettes,[2] and yeast being other important items. Carbohydrates were thus of marked importance in the expenditures. The Namu people stated that these were essential because they made a person feel full, and therefore content.

Risks

The Namu people felt that there were many uncertainties connected with buying food, of which shipping ranked in the forefront. They have been using money for ninety years and know that it will bring in additional food, but just how much they can never be sure.

1. Changing political control. With political control of the Marshalls changing from Spanish, to German, to Japanese, and now to United States control in the last 100 years, there have been concomitant changes in control over who buys the copra and who supplies the goods to the

[2] Cigarettes are considered as "food" by the Namu people in the sense that they are vital to getting work done. The adjectival type *kijen* is used both for food and cigarettes.

outer islanders. Different ideas have been matched with different policies. There are more than a Namu person can figure out.

2. Price fluctuation of copra. With changes in political control, as well as changing world market prices for vegetable oils, there have been marked price fluctuations within the lifetime of a Namu person. In 1937 they received 14 cents per pound; during World War II no copra was sold; in 1968, 4.5 cents was the rate to outer islanders; in 1971 the rate dropped to 1.7 cents per pound. This copra price is completely outside the control of the producer. He cannot withhold whatever copra he has, as he must buy foodstuffs each time a ship appears and he has no storage facilities. Worse still, copra tends to dry out too much when stored for any length of time, thus losing value in weight. The producer must sell his copra whatever the going price.

3. Fixed price of foodstuffs. Despite the fluctuations in copra price, foodstuffs have remained at the same price or increased in price; in 1968 5 dollars bought a 50-pound sack of flour, 8 dollars a 50-pound sack of sugar. These were essential items and each household bought as much of these as its copra returns would allow. Thus the amount of foodstuffs purchased is determined by the price of copra, as set far away from Namu atoll. The purchaser can endeavor to obtain the most rational return given what is available to him.

4. Shipping and communications. Sale of copra depends on a trading ship calling at the atoll to purchase as many bags as have been made. Prior warning of a ship's movements through the various atolls is given over the radio. If the gap since the last ship is too long, the radio batteries may be worn out. Ships are subject to many interruptions on their trading routes, e.g. emergency medical calls and restricted movement into Kwajalein lagoon (a United States Army testing site) during missile tests. When a ship announced it was leaving for Namu, the men of each household planned their copra work carefully to ensure that as many bags as possible were ready for sale when the ship eventually arrived. Delays in shipping sometimes meant an extra few bags of copra could be made, but it also meant that earlier bags were drying out and losing weight. Shipping was particularly irregular in the period from February to May, the stormy season. This also happens to be the period each year when food is short because the pandanus his finished bearing and the breadfruit is not yet ready. The risks attached to too much reliance on obtaining foodstuffs from shipping are thus extremely high.

5. Population increase. With Western medicine to aid both pregnant mothers and tiny infants, together with the ban on infanticide, the population of Namu atoll has trebled in the last fifty years (see Pollock

n.d.a). These introduced practices seem to the Namu people not to be infallible, that is, some sick mothers and infants die despite Western medicine, but many do survive. Again, with changing political control, the emphasis on health care on the outer islands has varied greatly, with a result that the Namu people still practice a considerable amount of "Marshallese medicine" to work alongside Western medicine. The people recognize that the population of the atoll is increasing alarmingly, but they also note that at times counteracting measures by the various controlling governments have allowed Namu adults to live and work for at least part of their lives on other atolls (e.g. Kwajalein). These policies fluctuate wildly. For example, the edict from the High Commissioner of the Trust Territory in 1967 stated that all persons living on Kwajalein atoll but not born there or actively working there must return to their home atolls. Projections of population size of Namu ten or fifteen years hence are extremely difficult, but some of the men recognize that the continuing increase in population is severely taxing the food resource base.

Strategies

1. The Namu people maintain a minimal reliance on purchased foods. Because they never know when a ship will call, nor what it will bring for them to buy, nor how long what they buy will have to last, they have not given up eating breadfruit pandanus, etc.

Coconut is a staple of the economy. They can eat it, drink it, burn it, build houses with it, OR sell it. It is a multipurpose crop they have been dealing with for generations, and therefore not to be lightly discarded or replaced. The Agriculture Department has had considerable difficulty in getting people to cut out old trees and replant new ones because they fear loss of returns in the interval. Fish can be obtained under either system. If someone can save enough money to buy a boat with an outboard engine, he can range further afield to fish; however, the boat with an outboard has not replaced but rather is used in addition to the paddle and sailing canoes on Namu.

3. On special occasions such as parties and feasts a high value is placed on local foods together with purchased foods. Thus donuts, bread, and rice balls are featured at a feast alongside the breadfruit, taro, and fish. But for personal gifts only local foods are given. This may be seen as a social mechanism to maintain interest in local production.

4. New foods tend to be introduced as sauce for local or other foods (for example, spaghetti noodles on rice, or corned beef in breadfruit and coconut cream soup).

5. When sick, people prefer pandanus or breadfruit to rice.
6. Whereas frequent changes of residence between islets within the atoll and fewer frequent changes between atolls were formerly means of alleviating the population pressure on resources, with the ever-increasing numbers, not only on Namu atoll but on all atolls throughout the Marshalls, available land is becoming utilized to somewhere near its maximum. With the population increase, the pattern of mobility is altering as the land becomes filled up.
7. The writer found on Namu a self-contained polity characterized by a sense of self-support and self-reliance. This appeared to have been maintained despite modern communications and some political efforts to unite all the Marshallese atolls. Reliance on factors and assets within the atoll itself appears to be based on the uncertainties of the world beyond the atoll. Intrusions into Namu's way of life are considered, tolerated, even accepted at one level, but with a little skepticism. Part of this overall ideology is the belief that not too much reliance should be placed on outside, nonlocal foodstuffs. If they fail to arrive, that means hunger, i.e. disaster.

CONCLUSION

Weighing up the risks and strategies of the two types of subsistence, locally derived and purchased foodstuffs, it is apparent that there are uncertainties in each sphere. However, with local foodstuffs the risks can be calculated with some degree of accuracy, whereas with purchased foodstuffs there are too many incalculables. The result is that new adaptations are ADDED TO old subsistence foods, not substituted for them. Moreover, as atoll resources are extended in use, so social mechanisms are developed to ensure that everyone gets some of whatever food is available. We can thus argue that this process of addition of new foodstuffs to the existing diet, rather than replacing the old with a new foodstuff, is a cautious strategy to ward off the ever-present fear of hunger.

REFERENCES

ERDLAND, AUGUST
1914 *Die Marshall-Insulaner*. Munster.
HIPSLEY, E.
1969 *Metabolic studies in New Guineans*. South Pacific Commission Technical Paper 162.

NATHAN REPORT

1966 *Economic development plan for Micronesia.* Washington, D.C.: Robert R. Nathan Associates.

OOMEN, H., MARGARET CORDEN

1969 *Metabolic studies in New Guineans.* South Pacific Commission Technical Paper 163.

POLLOCK, N. J.

1970 "Breadfruit and breadwinning on Namu atoll, Marshall Islands." Unpublished doctoral dissertation, University of Hawaii.

n.d.a "Demography of Namu atoll." Unpublished manuscript.

n.d.b "Christmas ritual celebrations on Namu, Marshall Islands." Unpublished manuscript.

WIENS, HAROLD

1962 *Atoll environment and ecology.* New Haven: Yale University Press.

Nutrition in Two Cultures: Mexican-American and Malay Ways with Food

CHRISTINE S. WILSON

Mexican-Americans and Malays live nearly half the world apart, and few rural dwellers in either group are aware of the existence of the other, yet they share a remarkably similar inventory of foods and several food-related customs which probably originated for both in similar ideologies.

That many of the same basic foodstuffs should be found in such widely separate locales should not surprise students of culture or history. The adventurers of the Age of Exploration ranged worldwide — a kind of fifteenth-century "international set," which used galleons and sail in place of jet airplanes. Europeans (the Portuguese) settled on the Malay Peninsula at the same time that Spaniards and others were exploring the New World. After the discovery of America, foods of American origin spread swiftly to the Far East. Table 1 gives a partial list of foods common or unique to the areas under consideration, and Table 2 presents some New World foods that are used today by Malays in many parts of the Peninsula.

Other investigators have already documented the travels of individual foods (Burkill 1966; Verrill 1950). The intent of this paper is to contrast the cuisines that have developed in the Mexican-American and Malay cultures, which have similar larders and common food ideologies.

Data for Malaysia were collected during two periods of one year each in a Malay fishing village, or *kampong*, on the east coast of the Malay

This work was supported by the following grants from the National Institutes of Health: predoctoral fellowship GM 35,001-3 to the author for a portion of the research in Malaysia; postdoctoral fellowship AM 53619-01 to the author for the study of the Mexican-American community; and AI 10051 to the Department of International Health, University of California, San Francisco, through the UC International Center for Medical Research and Training (UCICMRT) at the Institute for Medical Research, Kuala Lumpur, for the rest of the Malaysian research.

Table 1. Partial list of foods shared by or unique to Mexican-Americans and Malays

Common vegetables	*Common fruits*	*Common spices*	*Other common foods*
Maize corn	Plantains, bananas	Coriander	Rice
Tomatoes	Papaya	Chilis	Fish, fresh and dried
Manioc [tapioca]	Limes, sour	Onions	Shrimp and prawns
Potato	Persimmon	Garlic	Brown sugar
Sweet Potato	Mango	Cumin	Peanuts
Yams	Pineapple	Cinnamon	Coconuts
Squashes, gourds	Watermelon	Cloves	
Beans and bean products		Anise	
		Lemon grass	

Foods unique to Mexican-Americans	*Foods unique to Malays*
Nopales and *tunas*	*Belachan* [fermented prawn paste]
Avocado	*Durian*
Menudo [tripe soup]	Glutinous rice

Table 2. Foods of New World origin consumed by Malay villagers

Manioc [tapioca] (*Manihot utilissima*)	Sweetsop (*Annona squamosa*)
Potato, white (*Solanum tuberosum*)	Cashew (*Anacardium occidentale*)
Potato, sweet (*Ipomoea batatas*)	Guava (*Psidium guajava*)
Chilis (*Capsicum annuum*, and *frutescens*)	Passionfruit (*Passiflora laurifolia*)
Tomato (*Lycopersicum esculentum*)	Sapodilla (*Achras zapota*)
Maize corn (*Zea mays*)	Star apple (*Chrysophyllum cainito*)
Soursop (*Annona muricata*)	Pineapple (*Ananas comosus*)
Cherimoya (*Annona cherimola*)	Peanut [groundnut] (*Arachis hypogaea*)
Custard apple (*Annona reticulata*)	Pumpkin (*Cucurbita pepo*)
	Peanut Pumpkin

Source: Burkill 1966.

Peninsula. The Mexican-American information was obtained from a year's study in a long-established *barrio*, or neighborhood, of an urban community in southern California.

The techniques used were participant observation and modifications of methods used by dietitians to determine food intake. The investigator observed preparation of meals and recorded their components for several families for one week. Amounts of foods consumed by family members were noted during meals. Facsimiles were weighed, and the nutrient content was calculated using appropriate food composition tables. A 12-hour recall of foods served or consumed that day was used to study both families and individuals. A few persons were "followed" for a waking day to record snack food intakes and food eaten away from home as well as at home meals.

Tables 3 and 4 give sample menus for one day, and the calculated nutrients that each of these day's intakes would provide.

THE DIETS — CONTRASTS AND SIMILARITIES

Daily Foods

Mexican-Americans and Malays share rice as a common diet item. For Malays, a meal is not so defined if rice has not been a part of it. Mexican people once surrounded corn with cultural meanings beyond nourishment. Religious rites were involved in its planting and harvest. Similar activities still surround rice cultivation in Malaysia today, where its consumption is believed to have great benefits for soul as well as body.

Rice is the principal staple of Malays. Boiled without seasoning it is usually served with a number of side dishes which supply other needed nutrients, but are considered by the consumer as pleasing accompaniments to help the rice go down. Mexican-Americans (hereafter referred to as Mexicans) do not always eat rice daily. When they do, it is merely one constituent of the meal, browned with onion in oil or lard, and then boiled with tomatoes and hot chilis or tomato sauce, stock, and salt.

A ceremonial meal of rice marks important landmarks throughout life for the Malay, such as circumcision, marriage, or a house-raising. A sticky or glutinous variety called *pulut* is the usual rice of these special meals. Rice or rice flour is the commonest constituent of the cakes the Malay eats for his first meal of the day, or of those served on special occasions, such as the feasting days following the fast of Ramadan.

While the Mexican diet in the United States is now a blend of traditional foods and those of the surrounding culture, maize corn is still an important component of the persisting foods of Mexico. The *nixtamal* or *masa*, which forms the basic dough for most of the corn products, is prepared commercially as a rule, as are the corn *tortillas*, thin, flattened pancakes which are the bases of many Mexican dishes familiar in the U.S. The hominy (corn grains soaked in lime water) from which the *masa* is made is occasionally eaten as part of a dish cooked with pork.

The *tortilla* has many guises. Cooked on an ungreased griddle, it can be served as bread for a meal. Fried in oil before or after folding in other components, it becomes a *taco*. When fried until crisp and used as a plate for other ingredients it is a *tostada*. Unbaked *tortillas* become *quesadillas* when stuffed with a filling and formed into turnovers fried in hot oil. *Tortillas* serve as the cases of *enchiladas*, which are baked in a sauce of chilis and cheese. *Tamales* are corn dough stuffed with various fillings and then steamed in corn husks until done.

Malays also eat maize corn, but only as an occasional snack. Prepared at home or by sidewalk vendors, it is boiled on the cob and eaten without condiments.

Wheat is a less common staple for both groups, although *tortillas* of wheat flour are almost as prevalent in the United States Mexican household as those of maize corn. Wheat flour bread is widely consumed by Mexicans in the United States. Malays may buy bread from itinerant vendors as a morning or daytime snack. *Galletas* or *biskut* [cookies] are another wheat-based snack shared by both groups. None of these wheat products, with the exception of the *tortilla*, has cultural associations of importance to either group.

Both Mexicans and Malays like fish. The Malays depend upon it heavily as their chief protein source. Both use small fish preserved by salting and drying as seasoning in other dishes. Malays eat many varieties of fish — stewed, curried, fried, or roasted. In the United States today Mexicans eat fish less commonly than their relatives to the south. When they do, it is most often canned tuna.

There is no counterpart in the Malay cuisine to the Mexican pinto bean. These are boiled until done, then reheated by frying in hot lard, into which onions, *chorizo* [Mexican sausage] and hot chilis are sometimes incorporated. For the Mexican, beans are almost equal in importance to maize corn *tortillas*. He feels hunger, or feels as though he hasn't eaten, if he has not had one of these foods. The same may be said of the coastal Malay offered a meal lacking fish. Malays do eat bean products such as bean sprouts and bean curd.

Meat is an important protein food to the Mexican. Pork is a particularly prominent diet item. Besides roasts and stews, meats are included in *tacos*, *tostados* and *enchiladas*, and served with beans. (Mexicans also like hamburgers, hot dogs, and bologna sandwiches.) Meat is festival food for the Malay, served at weddings and other occasional feasts, although it is bought for meals of a special sort during the fasting month. It is expensive for them, and not so readily obtained as fish. Malays, being Muslims, avoid pork.

The most important food which both groups share is the hot red chili pepper. There are many varieties of chilis, especially in Mexico and the southwestern United States. Those which are found in both Malaysia and the United States are the tiny, inch-long fiery red bird pepper and the slightly larger red pepper. Both may be obtained in either locale, fresh or dry. Only a few examples of the many uses of the chili by each society are presented here.

A meal lacks a certain essential verve for both Mexicans and Malays without the presence of this vegetable/spice which is an almost daily component of their diets. Chili is an integral part of the sauces such as those which are used in preparing Mexican rice, or to cover the *enchilada* before baking. Hot sliced pounded chilis are part of *chile con carne* [ground meat]. The Mexican sausage, *chorizo*, is seasoned with chili. Pickled small chilis are often eaten as a side dish or condiment at meals. A larger green chili, also hot, is filled with cheese and fried in deep fat, the *chile relleno*. Both Mexicans and Malays like hot sauces sprinkled over cooked food. Chilis are largely responsible for this "heat." For both groups, fresh chilis are seldom served alone, but rather are mixed with other spices in sauces or other dishes.

Among its uses in a Malay kitchen, the chili is an integral part of the coconut milk sauce in which curries are boiled, a condiment added to boiled or stir-fried vegetables, and a side dish pounded with fresh fruit such as mango and a fermented prawn paste. Pounded chilis are usually included in fried rice or fried noodles among Malays, and a hot sauce of chilis pounded with peanuts and other spices and boiled with coconut milk is served as an accompaniment to broiled cubes of meat.

Mexican and Malay meals are dissimilar in the dishes making them up, but the hot taste of each cuisine is reminiscent of the other, the thread of likeness being the hot chili pepper.

The tomato is integral to many Mexican dishes (rice, soups, *tamales*, stews), or is an ingredient of sauces, or part of the contents of *tacos* and *tostadas*. Malays sometimes eat the tomato, mainly as catsup. Of other seasonings, onion and garlic are used daily in food preparation by both groups. Mexicans use *cilantro*, the leaf of fresh coriander, as well as the seed, in numerous dishes. Malays pound cumin and coriander seeds for various kinds of curries. Cumin is another common Mexican flavoring.

Both Mexicans and Malays eat stews. Those of the former are usually composed of beef, potatoes and other vegetables, and seasonings, including onion, garlic and chili, and are served fairly frequently. Malays make several kinds of stews or *bubor*, which are infrequently used as a meal, more often being consumed as a between-meal snack. These may be sweet stews of maize corn, or of some fruit such as durian, boiled in sweetened coconut milk. Another kind of Malay *bubor*, of rice, wild greens, fish, spices, and coconut milk, is made only in the fasting month. This is not sweet, and may be part of a meal, or a meal in itself.

For both Mexicans and Malays, fruits tend to be snack foods. The fruits which both groups share will vary for the Mexican in the United States depending on his proximity to the source of such tropical natives as papaya, mango, and pineapple; in southern California these can all be obtained from the markets, although they may often be too expensive for the Mexican to purchase. Other fruits which grow readily in California and Malaysia include loquats and persimmons. Malays will eat watermelon or pineapple as a side relish with a meal. All other fruits are taken at odd times between meals.

The Malay has access to a host of fruits peculiar to Southeast Asia. These have been described elsewhere (Wilson i.p.). However, one favorite Malay fruit originated in Latin America — the cashew, which is seasonal in Malaysia. Properly speaking, the fruit is the stem from which the nut hangs. The Malays eat this portion both as a fresh fruit or cooked in coconut milk as a vegetable. They also roast the nut.

Both groups eat root vegetables of American origin. Malays use the white or sweet potato and the yam either as snack foods or for breakfast. Mexican candy made from sweet potatoes can be purchased in small groceries in California. Another food which is similar in the two cultures is brown sugar. The Mexican brown sugar is known in Spanish as *panoche*, and can be bought as a kind of candy in the U.S., made from raw sugar from sugar cane. The egg custard or *flan* of Mexico often has a topping of this sugar. In Malaysia, the source of the brown sugar, called *manisan*, is the sap of the coconut palm, boiled down and crystallized. It is used to make cakes, or to sweeten the sweet *bubor* mentioned above. Sugar-cane is an occasional snack food for children in both cultures.

Special Foods

It is probable that the foods of which people are most proud are those which are used on special occasions. It may be that they are foods representative of times past which have been preserved in this way. The reader is probably familiar with some of the special Mexican foods. For example, the *quesadillas*, *enchiladas*, and *tamales* mentioned earlier are time consuming to prepare, and are tending to become chiefly reserved for special times like fiestas. Other special foods are Mexican bride's cookies, and many of the foods of the Christmas season.

Another food relished by Mexicans may be categorized as special since it is mainly seasonal, and regarded with pride. This is the leaf and the fruit of the prickly pear. The leaf, or *nopal*, is boiled and served as a vegetable or salad, or cooked with onion, tomato and chilis, as is done with other green vegetables. The fruit, called a *tuna*, may be taken fresh, or frozen to eat as a kind of ice cream.

Avocado is a food Mexicans regard well, eaten alone or as part of the sauce *guacamole*, made with chilis, tomato, and onion, or some other raw vegetable. A popular fiesta food which is sometimes part of Mexican meals is fried pork skin, or *chicharrones*. Other special Mexican foods are barbecued heads, chiefly pork, and *menudo*, or tripe soup, to which curative powers are sometimes ascribed.

A uniquely Southeast Asian food Malays enjoy is the durian, a fruit that smells and tastes like a combination of soft cheese and onion or garlic. It is seasonal and much prized. The excitement among Malays when the fruit is available surpasses that of the Mexicans at the time of the availability of the *tuna*.

To preserve the catch of fish for another season, Malays make a variety of fish products. Many of these have been described in a previous publication (Wilson i.p.). One which has been mentioned above is *belachan*, a paste made by fermenting and pounding together whole small prawns. It is used in curries and sauces, as well as in side relishes for a meal.

Of the many cakes which Malays make for special occasions, such as weddings or feast days, the two most common are made from steamed glutinous or sticky rice (*pulut*). For the *ketupat*, which is also eaten for breakfast from time to time, the rice is then mixed with coconut milk, wrapped in a leaf triangle, boiled, and finally fried without oil. An even more popular cake which is made chiefly at the end of the fasting month is *tapai*. A locally made yeast is sprinkled over the steamed glutinous rice, which is placed in cones made of rubber tree leaves and kept covered in a warm place for three days. At the end of this time the alcoholic content of the cakes is three to four percent. They are considered a great delicacy.

Food Intakes and Nutrient Status

Table 3 presents a hypothetical "typical" day's diet for an adult male of each of these two ethnic groups and the nutritive value of each. The recommended dietary allowances of the countries concerned for an adult male are included for comparison.

It is evident that these diets meet or exceed calorie and protein needs in both groups. The Mexican-American diet provides other nutrients in excess of recommendations, with the exception of the B-vitamins thiamine, niacin, and riboflavin, and calcium. The Malay diet, on the other hand, is rather seriously lacking in many essential nutrients, judging by the recommended dietary allowances (which are set lower for these generally smaller people). These menus are not actual, observed one-day intakes, but generalizations from observations in a number of households. Actual intakes of individual foodstuffs would of course vary from day to day, with items of greater or lesser nutritional value being included at other

Table 3. Hypothetical day's menu for an adult male, Mexican-American and Malay

	Mexican-American	*Malay*
Morning meal	2 fried eggs, 3 slices bacon 3 tortillas (wheat) Coffee with cream and sugar	Rice cake with fish Coffee with sweetened condensed milk
Midday meal	Soup with noodles Rice (Spanish) Refried beans Canned chilis Cola drink	Rice Fried fish, fish stew Boiled pumpkin Prawn paste relish, cucumber relish Water
Evening meal	Beef stew with vegetables Refried beans 3 *tortillas* (corn) Lettuce and tomato with chilis Soda	Rice Fried fish Cucumber relish Prawn paste relish Tea with sugar
Snacks	2 beers, potato chips, 1 banana	2 rice cakes, coffee with sugar

Table 4. Hypothetical day's nutrient intakes for an adult male, Mexican-American and Malay

	Calories	Protein g	Fat g	Calcium mg	Iron mg	Vitamin A IU	Thiamine mg	Riboflavin mg	Niacin mg	Vitamin C mg
Mexican-American[1]	2,864	87.0	76.5	661	18.6	8,500	0.9	1.2	14.5	73
RDA[2]	2,800	65	...	800	10.0	5,000	1.4	1.7	18.0	60
Malay[3]	2,447	78.1	32.7	294	7.2	302	0.7	0.5	13.7	19
RDA[2]	2,500	55	...	450	10.0	4,500	1.0	1.4	16.5	30

[1] *Sources:* Church and Church 1970; Leung and Flores 1961.
[2] Recommended dietary allowances.
[3] *Source:* University of Malaya 1968.

times. It should be remembered that, with the exception of ascorbic acid (vitamin C) and the B-vitamins, most nutrients can be stored in the body. A dish of greens can supply more than one day's needs for vitamin A, as well as calcium, so that nutrient requirements may have been met for several days at an earlier time.

The excess intake of protein in both groups may be reflected in some of the obesity observed. The high fat content of the Mexican-American diet is certainly echoed in obesity among adults. For those nutrients tested, blood levels of vitamin A and its precursor carotene were equivocal in a small sample tested in the Malay village, and there were some blood indicators of anemia in that population (Wilson, et al. 1970). Similar biochemical measures are not yet available for the Mexican community. Dental decay and tooth loss were widely prevalent among Malays of all ages. Mexican-Americans, having access to reparative dentistry, have suffered less in this regard.

CUSTOMS AND BELIEFS RELATED TO FOODS

Mexicans and Malays both believe that certain foods have innate "heating" or "cooling" qualities. Among Latin Americans these beliefs are descended from the Galenic system of the hot and cold, wet and dry humors thought to rule the body (Foster 1967: 185–193). It is possible, though not yet proven, that the same set of beliefs reached the Malay Peninsula by way of the Arabs (Hart 1969). While these beliefs are fading from the minds and customs of younger Mexicans in the United States, they are still in full effect among Malays. Although there are great individual variations in the classification of foods as "hot" or "cold," both groups have generally considered vegetables and fruits "cold" or "cooling." Onions, garlic, and, not surprisingly, chilis are considered "hot" by both these ethnic groups. Meat tends to be categorized as "hot" by both (Clark 1970; Wilson 1971).

Both Mexicans and Malays believe that "air" or cold wind can enter the body from various causes, including the eating of "cold" foods, and cause damage to body tissues. Among Mexicans in the United States this belief too is lessening, but by Malays it is still strongly held, as it once was by Mexicans, that "air" and "cold" foods are extremely dangerous for the new mother for a forty-day period following childbirth.

The diet culturally prescribed for the Mexican woman during lying-in is less restricted in nutrient quality than is the ritual postpartum diet of the Malay woman. Whereas the latter may have no fruits, vegetables, sauces, gravies or fried things, and exists on rice, roasted fish, dry spices and an occasional egg, the former may eat any meats but pork, and is encouraged to take toasted *tortillas*, broths, and milk. Fruits and their juices, beans, and some fresh vegetables such as tomatoes may be forbidden the new Mexican mother, especially if she is nursing. Many young Malay mothers suffer from borderline anemias as a result of the socially dictated diet taboos of the postpartum period (Wilson, et al. 1970).

Food taboos in pregnancy among present-day Mexican women seem to be few, although some mothers say hot chilis should not be eaten at this time. Malay women have no observable food taboos during pregnancy.

Mexicans and Malays both use foods as medicines, for folk-diagnosed illnesses (Clark 1970; Wilson 1971). Many of the "treatments" are topical. Mexicans consider mint and other herb teas good for gas in the stomach. Malays avoid a wide variety of foods such as eggs, pineapple, or chicken, during self-diagnosed illnesses or minor afflictions such as cuts or headaches, and are afraid some fruits or vegetables would be toxic if eaten while they are taking pills given by the doctor (Wilson 1971). If they were "eating" the root or bark medicines of the local medicine man, consuming these same foods would not be harmful.

One social custom regarding food practiced by both groups is the sharing of food, especially at holiday times. In both cultures, adults take presents of food to elderly relatives and receive other foods in exchange. Among Malays especially, this social custom is followed to the extent that it assures no person in the family or community goes hungry. Malay children are trained from the earliest age to share their sweets and other snacks with other children.

Mexican and Malay mothers alike do not force their children to eat any food they do not want. This cultural practice sometimes results in a Malay child going hungry for hours, and for both him and the Mexican child it may lead to increased snacking. The present-day Mexican-American child does have an advantage in living in a society from which he can choose widely if not well. Mexican-American mothers seem to be sufficiently nutrition-conscious to have on hand enough kinds of foods which are good for him. While children of neither culture like vegetables as a rule, psychological eating problems of children seem extremely rare in these cultures.

DISCUSSION OF METHODS USED

The techniques for doing these studies varied in the two communities. For both, the general picture of foods selected from what was available was obtained by casual questioning, listening to conversations, and observations of markets. In both cases this last was a useful and valuable method.

Meal patterns, number of meals eaten a day, and definitions of foods as distinguished from snacks were also determined by questioning and observation. For the Malay villagers the investigator obtained permission to drop in at meal times to record every food item each person ate. Thus both quantitative and qualitative aspects of eating habits were observed. The technique included watching meal preparation to note the kinds and amounts of the ingredients of each dish.

At a Malay meal, each person eats from his own bowl of rice, and takes spoonfuls or handfuls of the side dishes which are set out for everyone in the middle of the floor. While a family was eating, the investigator recorded food intakes, counting and writing the number of spoonfuls or handfuls of every dish that each person took. The amount of rice served to each person was gauged visually and recorded, as were additional amounts taken during the meal.

The investigator ate the same kinds of food as the local people, prepared in the same manner, and was thus able to make and weigh replicas of these foods at home with the competent assistance of the local woman doing her cooking, approximating the amounts of each ingredient. The investigator purchased all food in the local markets, and recorded weights of individual items as obtained.

In the Malay study family meals were observed for approximately a week for each of five different families chosen from the middle socio-economic level of the community. Local tables of nutrient composition of Malaysian foods were used to calculate nutrient intakes of each member of a family for each day (University of Malaya 1968). Totals for each person were then averaged to obtain daily intakes.

Because of the prevalent Malay custom of snacking, foods eaten at meal times do not give an accurate picture of total daily intake. Therefore, two other methods were tried. The first was an extension of the meal-watching principle. Since health authorities considered toddlers to be the group whose nutritional status was most likely to be equivocal, several postweaning, preschool children were chosen for study. Each was followed for one whole day, wherever he went from the time he got up until he went to sleep at night. Everything he ate was recorded, wherever he happened to be, including meals at home. Results of these studies have been presented elsewhere (Wilson, et al. 1970). The calculations gave expected calorie and protein intakes for the size and age of the child. The technique was simple and satisfactory, its chief drawback being that it was time consuming and it limited data to one person per day.

A second method was devised to take into account that Malay men eat the first meal of the day in nearby coffee shops. Their calorie and protein intake from this source was therefore estimated by questioning the coffee shop owners as to daily numbers of cups of coffee or tea sold, whether it was served with sugar or sweetened condensed milk, and the approximate number of cakes sold each day. This gave an approximation of a man's principal snack source (the number of cups sold per day was equated to the number of men breakfasting in the shop).

The all-day-watching method was later applied to learn the diet in pregnancy of one young Malay woman and the lying-in diet of several. These data, too, have been reported elsewhere (Wilson 1972).

The technique of family meal watching used in Malaysia had to be modified for the more sophisticated Mexican-American community. There were other problems in studying the diet of this group. The present-day Mexican-American diet is a complicated mixture of the Anglo-American diet and traditional Mexican foods, varying individually with income, tastes, and market resources. In addition to snacking, Mexicans in the United States eat many meals outside their homes. Children can buy lunch at school, provided under a government-supported program. Pre-school children receive snacks in nursery school or Head Start programs. Taco and hamburger stands and roving ice cream vendors cater to teen-agers and younger children. Pocket money can be exchanged for soda pop, candy, or popcorn without the mother's knowledge.

In both cultural groups a household census proved an effective method for obtaining a general picture of the diet. Housewives interviewed were asked approximately how much they spent on food and what their principal purchases were. For the Malays, whose money supply was limited, all purchases were easily recounted, and other foods not raised were reported as gifts or exchanges.

For the Mexican-Americans, dropping in at meal time gave an idea of patterns of foods chosen and amounts consumed. The women indicated the different kinds of foods their families preferred and the extent to which they consumed traditional or manufactured foods.

With both Malays and Mexican-Americans the twelve-hour recall of diet, backed up with occasional observations of actual meals, gave good quantitative results per capita. The current day's meals served in the house were recounted, as were the numbers of people eating at each meal. This, of course, did not allow for snacking. An individual twelve-hour recall of all food eaten that day by the person questioned was used for pregnant and postpartum women in both groups. Thus questioning an individual was more likely to elicit information about between-meal eating. If queries are carefully worded, the person interviewed replies giving definite amounts so that food tables may be used to determine nutrient intakes.

The greatest value of studies such as those outlined here seems to lie in their ability to suggest to health authorities cultural factors which should be given greater consideration in planning nutrition programs. One point that emerges is the basic importance to traditional and primitive peoples of a particular diet pattern or food. This explains why it would be extremely difficult to persuade them to give it up. It also shows how certain combinations of foods that taste good to people are sometimes more valuable nutritionally than those same foods eaten separately. It also reveals that the pattern of three square meals a day eaten at set times every day is culturally superimposed and does not fit the actual eating habits of most of the world's people.

A participant-observer study of food and nutrition gives a far broader picture of what is eaten and why than the dietitian can obtain by the traditional method of entering homes to weigh and measure the foods prepared and eaten three times a day. The meal-watching technique is valuable to indicate general distribution in kinds and amounts of foods among family members and to learn which family member gets the choice foods. The participant observer can also note the sharing of foods, the give-and-take among neighbors and relatives. He learns which foods are important and meaningful, and which the people are proud of.

I do not wish to seem to criticize the dietitian. She endeavors to obtain true values for food intake. She uses scales accurate to a tenth of a gram. She weighs, measures, and records, then calculates the nutrients provided by these foods from tables of nutrient composition that have been established by accurate chemical analyses in more than one laboratory. These methods have now been used by several generations of nutritionist-dietitians. An anthropologist who wishes to study nutrition quantitatively in the field should keep them in mind. The innovative anthropologist who desires to study diet will do well to adapt these quantitative methods to obtain the kind of information that both nutritionists and anthropologists would like to have on the nutrition of the world's population, especially traditional and primitive peoples.

REFERENCES

BURKILL, I. H.
1966 *A dictionary of the economic products of the Malay Peninsula.* Kuala Lumpur: Ministry of Agriculture and Cooperatives. (Originally published 1935.)

CHURCH, C. F., H. N. CHURCH
1970 *Food values of portions commonly used* (eleventh edition). Philadelphia: J. B. Lippincott.

CLARK, M.
1970 *Health in the Mexican-American culture* (second edition). Berkeley: University of California Press.

FOSTER, G. M.
1967 *Tzintzuntzan.* Boston: Little, Brown.

HART, D. V.

1969 *Bisayan Filipino and Malayan humoral pathologies*. Southeast Asia Program, Department of Asian Studies Data paper 76. Ithaca: Cornell University Press.

LEUNG. W.-T. W., M. FLORES

1961 *Tabla de composición de alimentos para uso en America Latina*. Guatemala City: Institute of Nutrition for Central America and Panama.

UNIVERSITY OF MALAYA

1968 "Food composition tables compiled for use in West Malaysia". Unpublished manuscript, Faculty of Medicine, Kuala Lumpur.

VERRILL, G. P.

1950 *Foods America gave the world*. Boston: L. C. Page.

WILSON, C. S.

1971 Food beliefs affect nutritional status of Malay fisherfolk. *Journal of Nutrition Education* 2:96–98.

1972 "Food taboos of childbirth: the Malay example," in *Abstracts of short communications, Ninth International Congress of Nutrition, Mexico, D.F.*, 168.

i.p. "Rice, fish, and coconuts: the basis of the Southeast Asian diet."

WILSON, C. S., J. C. WHITE, K. S. LAU, Y. H. CHONG, D. A. MC KAY

1970 Relations of food attitudes to nutrient status in a Malay fishing village. *Federation Proceedings* 29:821.

SECTION THREE

Tropical Foods

Indigenous Food Processing in Oceania

D. E. YEN

Methods of food preparation are often a part of the ethnographic record of indigenous peoples. But these processes, the steps by which raw foods are converted to edible forms, have been largely ignored in favor of topics of more important and direct sociological interest. This is probably the basis of one plea (Freedman 1968) for more detailed study of "ethnoculinary" materials, because food processing does indeed show some influence on social organization within communities, some definite contrasts between groups in its practice, and some significance in the general issue of change in man's history. Biologically, Schwanitz (1966: 38) has indicated that the ability to process to an edible state those plant products with undesirable taste characteristics gathered by primitive man was important as a forerunner to conversion by domestication and genetic selection. A direction of technological evolution, however, is suggested by the fact that the products of domestication, the cultigens, are still subjected to processing of considerable complexity. This is especially so with some of the grains of the Old World, where milling and dehusking are only the beginning in the steps of alternative methods of preparation toward palatability. Thus necessity as the first spur to food technology is replaced by elaboration for variety and the exercise of preference.

In Oceania, agricultural subsistence relies on the starchy products of root crops and trees as staples. The variety of methods used to process

This paper is a partial result of a study of the southeastern Solomon Islands' prehistory and agriculture, financed by the National Science Foundation, Washington D.C. (Grant no. GS-2977). I have benefited by informal discussion with Alan Howard and Marshall Sahlins, but errors in the data and interpretations are my responsibility.

these foods is rather restricted, compared with Asia for example, but the range is categorized by Barrau and Peeters (1972: 148) for cultivated and gathered species in Pacific island diets:

1 – tel que cueilli, ramassé ou récolté.
2 – après traitement destiné à l'élimination ou à la transformation de substances:
  2a – toxiques,
  2b – déplaisantes,
  2c – indigestes, à l'aide de procédés faisant appel à:
    2.1 – la division et/ou
    2.2 – l'eau et/ou
    2.3 – la chaleur
3 – après conservation par 3.1 – séchage
  3.2 – fumae
  3.3 – confisage
  3.4 – fermentation

This classification brings out one of the further and perhaps ultimate results of the development of processing — the rendering of preservation ability to plant parts otherwise unstorable or difficult to store.

In their main objective of relating vegetable food preparation methods to historical and prehistorical perspectives of Oceania, Barrau and Peeters (1972: 147) offer two generalized propositions from Oceanic and other observations in indigenous societies:

... plus la plante est sauvage, plus complexe est la mode de préparation qui permet son utilisation alimentaire.

[and] ... le progrès technologique en matière de préparation des aliments végétaux a dû précéder, et de loin, celui ayant trait à la production, autrement dit à la domestication et àla culture de ces derniers.

They further develop these statements in terms of the Oceanic range of food technology of primitive and complex to more highly developed and simple — suggesting that Oceania has the aspect of a niche, in which ancient and more primitive practices are preserved, but which is not necessarily the area of origin. Thus like Barrau's earlier thesis of remnant cultigen species in Oceania as "witnesses of the past" (Barrau 1965a), methods of preparation, especially of wild species, are contemporary evidence of a similar and perhaps earlier time.

Undoubtedly agriculture based on tuberous crops was adventive in the Pacific (Barrau 1965b), and those who transferred it followed earlier non-agricultural peoples into the western region, where the subsistence bases were fishing and gathering in insular or coastal environments and hunting and gathering in inland situations. The food treatments of agricultural crops could have been the derivatives of earlier techniques on the gathered plant products; they could also have been cultural transfers with the later agriculture. Here we examine food technology of the cultigens on distributional and environmental bases, and suggest, at least, that developments in food technology could just as well have been responses to the variable environments in which the "new Oceanians" found themselves. Further, we inspect some aspects of agricultural and social control in the ecology of food technology.

METHODS AND DISTRIBUTION

The main method of preparing foods for consumption in indigenous Pacific societies is the simple cooking of raw tubers, fruits, or fish by roasting in fire embers. Although boiling with the help of metal pots is now rather common, the old method of boiling with red-hot stones thrown into water may have been restricted to such food items, or, more properly, condiments, as the oil extracted from grated coconut. The writer, at least, has never been successful in having this method demonstrated on high bulk foods like taro or yam. In reviewing the more elaborate methods, we extend the table of Barrau and Peeters into three main products of the processes that they enumerate: the pounded or "pudding-like" foods, the fermented foods, and the dried foods. For all of these, as with even the gathered *Cycas* seeds, whose toxicity is reduced, many of the preparatory methods used to achieve the final products are common.

Pounded Foods

Through most of Polynesia, Micronesia, and island Melanesia, the tubers of taro, yams, *Cyrtosperma*, and the fruits of breadfruit and banana are cooked in the oven, peeled, and then reduced by pounding with wood or stone implements until they form smooth, yielding pastes. According to varying recipes, mixtures of species may then be made; coconut cream or grated coconut are commonly added, and the mixtures, which are then often shaped into balls or leaf-wrapped bundles, are cooked again in an earth oven. Coconut cream or oil, fish, and occasionally pork and chicken are some accompaniments to the final dish. These products then go through a sequence after harvest of cooking, dividing and pounding, and recooking for consumption; but the intervening compounding of various ingredients, the subject of separate procedures, confers a greater complexity on the process than might be recognized by the use of any formulation. The grating of peeled raw tubers or fruits is an alternative preparation that obviates pounding and cooking for a second time.

In the New Guinea highlands the ripe fruits of *Pandanus conoideus* are used to prepare a sweet concoction after oven cooking. While not pounded, the pulp is extracted by hand, and the saucelike product is a popular accompaniment of meals during the fruit-bearing season. The plant is cultivated, e.g. by the Tsembaga (Rappaport 1967: 55).

In this class of food no storage ability is conferred by its preparation methods, and these foods are features of the menus on occasions of celebration.

The famed Hawaiian *poi* made from taro falls into this category, but the addition of water during pounding adds to the "formula" of preparation. Furthermore, according to Pukui (1968: 429), the spontaneous fermentation of *poi*, which occurs when it is kept after manufacture seems to indicate some temporary storage ability, which, nevertheless, does not equal that of the cooked or raw harvested taro corm.

Fermented Foods

The fermentation and storage of breadfruit had wide application in the Pacific. Its recording was one of the earliest substantive ethnobotanical observations made by early Spanish voyagers to the Marquesas and Marshall Islands (Yen 1973a). Archaeological evidence from Samoa (Green 1969: 121) suggests that the process was used at the time of early settlement. Ethnographic evidence covers all the Polynesian tropical islands as well as the Marshall and Caroline groups of Micronesia. In Melanesia, however, it has only been recorded in Santa Cruz, the population of which is in close contact with Polynesian societies of the outliers.

The method of preservation entails dividing cooked and peeled fruit and packing it into ground pits lined with a variety of leaves, e.g. breadfruit, coconut, banana, *Heliconia, Alpinia.* Semianaerobic fermentation continues under a sealing of leaves and stones packed on the surface, and some people turn the sour mash periodically to maintain "freshness." In some parts of Polynesia, Samoa, and Tahiti, the ensiling of bananas in this way is said to be practiced without, however, prior cooking. In Fiji taro and *Tacco* are also included (Capell 1968: 130). In Anuta and Tikopia, Polynesian islands within the British Solomon Islands Protectorate, the range of species is considerably extended; for as well as breadfruit and banana, *Cyrtosperma* and taro tubers and the fruit of *Burckella obovata*,

Tacca, sago, and the aroid Alocasia are, with some methodological variations, also conserved. Sharing dominance in the quantity of this product made on these two islands, however, are taro and manioc; the latter, of course, is an American plant of recent introduction. The methods enabling a high proportion of standing crops to be conserved are described by Yen (1973b).

Dried Foods

Although the drying of foods directly with little pretreatment is recorded in Polynesia and Micronesia, e.g. coconut meat (not for copra) and banana (Barrau 1961), it is rarely encountered. In the past, however, some species were probably subjected to drying by the sun or smoking over fires, e.g. Tahitian chestnut, which Barrau (1961: 55) records as being stored in the ground in Polynesia and Micronesia.

In Melanesia, the practice of drying with or without prior smoking is common today. Two species of *Pandanus*, *P. julianetti* and *P. brosimus*, are conserved by smoking in the highlands of New Guinea; while in the Solomons, where nuts of the genus *Canarium* appear to have had an important role in former indigenous diets, *P. dubius*, one of the largest seeded of the *Pandanus*, is also stored. In the eastern Solomons, the sea almond (*Terminalia catappa*) and two species of *Barringtonia* must be added to *P. dubius* and *Canarium* in the roster of stored tree crops that form a part of an arboricultural complex uncommonly full for the Pacific (Yen 1973c).

Dried foods requiring more complex pretreatments involve three tree genera: breadfruit (*Artocarpus altilis*), *Pandanus*, and *Metroxylon* or sago palm. In the Santa Cruz Islands in the eastern Solomons, breadfruits are sectioned after earth-oven baking and peeling and are then dried by the sun to yield a biscuitlike product of portability and long-lasting properties. In Kapingamarangi, a more flourlike food is derived from the same species by pounding the peeled, sectioned, and oven-cooked fruit, drying, and then wrapping the fruit up into storable leaf packages (Buck 1950: 35). Also Murai, Pen, and Miller (1958: 20) report that among the Marshallese fermented breadfruit is further processed by pressing, drying, and wrapping in leaf bundles for storage. Apparently the already high storage ability of fermented breadfruit is enhanced in this way, or else the flavor of the product, long kept in pits, is less favored here than in Polynesia.

Of the *Pandanus* cultivars of Micronesia, whose identities are still the subject of contention and investigation (Stone 1963; Fosberg 1946), two dried foods are manufactured: a partially dried paste and a dried flour. Murai, Pen, and Miller (1958: 72) describe these processes. The paste is made by first baking the syncarps or "keys" of ripe fruits, then scraping the pulp on to leaves for drying over hot stones. A high keeping quality is claimed for the wrapped packages, as it is for the flour made from the cut ends of the syncarps cooked in the earth oven, pounded, then dried.

Pandanus flour is made in the Gilbert Islands and Kapingamarangi, while the paste is known so far only in the Marshalls.

For the marsh dwellers of coastal and riverine New Guinea, the great staple is sago, the flourlike food extracted from the inner pith of the *Metroxylon* palms (Barrau 1959; Coenen 1962). After mature palms are felled, the inner sections are exposed and pounded to produce a fine broken fibrous material that is subjected to crushing with the addition of water, into which the flour is precipitated, then reclaimed by evaporation. The product is storable damp, or it may be heated over fires to make briquettes that last for months.

Minor variants of this process occur over the area of distribution of the genus in its varying species forms (Barrau 1959: 154), in New Britain and New Ireland, the Solomons, the New Hebrides, and the western Polynesian islands of Rotuma and Futuna. In these Polynesian areas, the palm is undoubtedly a cultigen, but in Melanesia the generally accepted feral status and therefore "gathered" nature of the derived food may be questioned in some areas where planting has been recorded. Serpenti (1965: 46), for example, defines sago on Frederik Hendrik Island as a cultivated rather than as an exploited natural resource. *M. salomonense* is regarded as a cultigen in Kolombangara in the western Solomons, Santa Cruz in the eastern Solomons, on the Polynesian islands Anuta and Tikopia, and in Futuna.

The three major food types that are elaborated from the predominantly starch plant products may be further grouped; the pounded foods, which do not have real storage value above the raw material itself, form one category, while the fermented and dried foods together form the storage foods category. We have indicated nearly pan-Pacific distribution for pounded foods, but it is the storage foods that have some quite marked differences. Correlation of presence of the plant with distribution of processing methods holds for the gathered *Cycas* and the gathered or cultivated sago, which is largely restricted to the western Pacific. In simple drying techniques, e.g. with *Canarium*, westerly distribution of plant and process stops at the eastern border of Melanesia, but in the more complex procedures, e.g. with breadfruit, the plant is distributed over the whole of the Pacific, including Indonesia and the Philippines; but in these two archipelagos and Melanesia (excluding Santa Cruz), elaborations of the plant utilization not only do not occur, but the fruit is a secondary, largely unimportant food. Then there is the *Pandanus* which is little used for manufacturing flour and paste although the genus occurs in all parts of the Pacific.

There are two further interesting facets of distribution:

(1) In Micronesia, we have not mentioned food technology for the Marianas. Pounding and grating of tuber crops and breadfruit are reported (Sproat 1968), and it might be suggested that whether or not storage techniques existed early in settlement, they were superseded by the introduction of rice from Asia. Certainly references to rice on Guam occur in the early literature about the island (Thompson 1945: 29), although not in the narrative of Magellan's discovery (Pigafetta 1969). There is also archaeological evidence for irrigated fields on Rota, which Yawata (1963) identifies as Chamorro rice paddles.

(2) The New Guinea Highlands seem poor in food technology. We have the simple storage of nuts and one *Pandanus* sauce preparation, which parallels the first steps in the manufacture of Micronesian paste or flour but, unlike them, has no storage value. Within the gathering sectors of highlands subsistence there may be some equivalents to the rendering edible of *Cycas* and *Brugiera* (Barrau and Peeters 1972), but present evidence (Bulmer and Bulmer 1964: 49) suggests that among the rich flora, there is a sufficient number of plants, fruit, and nuts, which may be eaten raw or cooked by simple means.

THE IMPLICATIONS OF FOOD TECHNOLOGY

We have not considered the subject of the origin of Pacific peoples and its influence on agricultural manifestations, i.e. the founding endowment, because it is a subject of too great a magnitude to explore fully. In the case of New Guinea, however, it may be profitable to give some thought to the proposition. The continental highlands there represent the first phase of Oceanic settlement (White 1971), and the archaeological evidence indicates a classical development from hunting and gathering to agriculture over thousands of years. It would seem that technological development in agriculture took AGRONOMIC pathways because the crop processing methods seem "deficient." Today, the highland populations seem helpless in the face of disastrous forest fire and drought damage; those measures which exist for storing food reserves are unable to cope with the crop loss.

In insular Oceania, however, we have not only a situation of varying founder populations (Rappaport 1963), but also the limiting factor of area of land surfaces of coralline, volcanic, and mixed geological origin for subsistence development. Vayda and Rappaport (1963: 137) have stressed this aspect beyond the more obvious ecological restrictions in distributional terms; they have suggested that: "There may also be the development of certain social forms and usages that help to get people to resources and resources to people." To their exemplifications of these phenomena, we may perhaps add the development of processes of food technology, especially the techniques of converting plant products to storable forms; in such forms, the social control of distribution becomes more certain and the product becames more flexible in its modes of disposal. The organization of the processes themselves employs labor beyond the normal concentrations of intensification — the upward influence of such organization on work per unit-area ratios. Food processing, then, takes its place with other agricultural technologies that may not necessarily increase production or output (Brookfield 1972: 31–33) as a sign of intensification. The elaborations of storage techniques, manifest in their variety on small Pacific islands, may reflect the intensification effects of increasing populations in environments of low natural carrying capacities.

This does not deny the general hypothesis of Barrau and Peeters (1972) of an evolutionary regression of preparation techniques, with the progress from plant domestication to agriculture in its early stages. The directional nature of the hypothesis, however, requires some modification because some allowance must be made for amplitudinal fluctuation for the Pacific data. Some of the inventive methods of dealing with food, especially to achieve storage ability, were probably a later addition to agriculture.

It may be noted that the more complex methods of food processing in Oceania are exercised largely on the adventive genera of wide distribution, e.g. breadfruit and taro. It has recently been posited that the non-Austronesian speakers, as the first human arrivals (Yen 1973d), were the possible instigators of the domestication of a range of tropical economic plants — the Australimusa banana, sugar cane, various vegetable greens of the New Guinea Highlands, and a number of fruit and nut trees. If this hypothesis holds true, domestication by these Oceanic peoples, originally without agriculture, proceeded without the stimulus of any food technology of greater complexity than simple drying.

The nonhistorical implications of Pacific food technology may now claim our attention:

The elaboration of raw food into puddings offers a transformation into alternate forms of distinct taste preference. However, such forms tend to be eaten irregularly, and are considered luxury dishes to be savored, as we have noted, on special occasions. This is due not so much to the fact that more of the basic material is required, but to the labor and its organization that have to be invested. The technology of storage foods has similar effects because, while they are not always feast items, such foods provide further dietary changes of different tastes and textures with the investment of group labor. The partibility and storage ability make them available to be used as emergency foods, as stores for journeys by land and sea, and as a trade item where there is a surplus and an external demand. In the case of copra production in modern Oceania (Oliver 1961 [1951]: 186), the common but seldom-practiced indigenous knowledge of drying coconut meat as an emergency food is simply extended to meet an external demand, which did not exist before.

Agronomically the effect of storage practices is to even out production of seasonal surpluses, and this is especially marked in the tree crops. Breadfruit in Polynesia and Micronesia, especially in its fermented form, is almost universally used to provide some stability of food supply in normal between-season and inclement periods. Unless a breadfruit crop fails, the maturation of trees (whose varieties have some degree of maturity spread) precipitates decisions that have to be made on the basis of the crop yields. There is usually a surplus over immediate needs, and the fruit cannot be kept long; a large surplus makes the use of fermentation and drying methods worthwhile; a small surplus may be disposed of by sharing out the fruit (for which later reciprocity is expected) and by the small group manufacture of pudding forms, again shared.

Thus, with fruit crops, which ripen quickly and have low storage ability, there is an element of urgency about disposing of the harvests which is not so obvious for field crops, which will stay days and indeed weeks without spoilage. The planning of field crop disposal for storage and indeed of all agricultural operations is seemingly much more deliberate and predictable than in the tree crops. The PLANNING for a surplus by planting numbers of plants or areas is obvious in cases where such crops are used in storage; but because tree crops are perennial and occupy the ground for many years, their replenishment and the reasons for it are seldom a part of the ethnographic record.

The field crops which are subjected to processing for storage, have similar agronomic requirements to those that are stored without modification. Because of bulk harvesting, fields are generally monocrop or single species in plant composition; they are planted at one time, and harvesting, apart from first fruits and occasional harvest for immediate use, comes to an abrupt halt with the lifting of the crop for storage. This is generally applicable in Melanesia where *Dioscorea* yams and their storage are dominant in agriculture. In the tropical areas such a harvesting procedure allows for much clearer and more recognizable cropping cycles and crop rotational practices.

In many areas of latter-day Oceania, ritual and magic in gardening survive largely in the minds of a few old people, but the practices that they accompanied remain in the subsistence sectors of economies. For instance, the occasions on which the pounding of feast foods is required still depend on the leaders or chiefs within the societies. Rites of passage and Christian holidays are such occasions. In the cases of storage that I have had the opportunity of studying, however, intervention from leadership does not occur at the preparatory stage, but rather at the time of disposal. Food surpluses converted to storable form allow the organization of distribution more readily than fresh garden produce, because their long keeping qualities not only may be exploited for agronomic reasons of seasonal production, fluctuation, and emergency, but they endow them with some of the qualities of artifacts by which trade and exchange are effected. Centralization, or at least concentration of these resources, and partability are factors contributing to the possibilities of distribution along communal lines, but the agency of leadership is implied in such organization.

The decisions that are taken in gardening production are very much within the province of the individual and, as Malinowski (1966 [1935]: 35) showed, even within the ritual-bound system of the Trobriands, the amount of gardening that an individual undertook was a matter of personal inclination sometimes overriding mere necessity. In the processing of plant food for storage there seems to be a similar latitude of decision making, but, because of the labor requirement over a short period, more than the individual or his household are involved. Once the individual decides that his trees bear sufficient fruit or that his crop is mature enough to process, he consults the group that he largely works with on such projects, generally his kin. A schedule is organized, firmly in the case of tree crops but with more latitude to fit into other activities in the case of field crops.

In furthering this discussion of differentiation between production and distribution of processed foods, we will proceed to inspect briefly two geographically close examples, in which such provisions play major roles in economies. The Santa Cruz Islands represent a conglomerate of societies of diverse cultural origins, with trade dependence among speakers of non-Austronesian, Melanesian, and Polynesian languages, while Anuta has a virtually self-sufficient subsistence.

PRODUCTION AND DISTRIBUTION — TWO EXAMPLES

Santa Cruz, Eastern Solomon Islands

Melanesian trade patterns between island groups demonstrate something of the role of food as an item in exchanges that generally feature more permanent artifacts of material culture, such as shells or money, pottery, and the like. Sago figures, among the foods traded in the islands of eastern New Guinea, with yams, coconuts, and taro (Tueting 1935); but in the longer-distance trading carried out across the Vitiaz Strait, between the Rai coastal area of New Guinea and New Britain, Harding (1967: 31) specifies sago and coconuts as the only foods carried by the Siassi Islander traders, even though taro, sweet potato, and other crop products, and dried fish are included in the shorter distance exchanges. In the eastern Solomons, the traditional trade cycles of the Santa Cruz group have been delineated by Davenport (1964: 58, 62–64). The Duff Islanders, Polynesian speakers, provided the Reef Islands with ocean-going canoes and sago, and received in payment the red-feather money acquired from trade with Santa Cruz island (Ndeni). Ndeni purchased women from the Reef Islands with feather money and food. Some specialties from the Reefs, including coconut fiber, turtles, and sharks, were also traded in this part of the cycle. As a result of inquiries made on Santa Cruz in 1971 it was learned that the main food items produced and traded by Ndeni were dried and fermented breadfruit, sago, and nuts. Interestingly, the southerly extension of Ndeni trade routes, to Vanikoro and Utupua, did not include food; Davenport has reported that shell-disk money (some made on Ndeni, some from exchange from the Reefs) went south, where red feathers of the small *Myzomela* bird were acquired for the manufacture of the feather money. As Davenport further pointed out, these specializations were the product of ecological adjustments to the environmental variations within the whole island group. In terms of subsistence adequacy, the high islands of Utupua and Vanikoro were probably self-sufficient but the smaller Duffs of volcanic origin had to rely on transfers of food from the Reef Islands; the central and large island of Ndeni was able to provide the food that the Reefs themselves, as a conglomerate of low uplifted coral islands and atolls, probably lacked. If present population levels of the Reefs are any reflection of earlier times when the trade cycle was fully active, then population density may have been a pressure that forced the trade of valuable marine commodities and women for staple foods. In 1970 the population density of the Reef Islands was estimated at 135 per square mile on some thirty square miles. As a comparison,

Vanikoro and Utupua combined (ninety square miles) had an equivalent density of three and eight, respectively, while Ndeni with 200 square miles had a density of seventeen (Honiara Statistical Office 1970).

Davenport (1964: 67) stressed the role of men's associations identified with men's houses in food distribution during feasts accompanying various rites and in interisland trading decisions. Today, the government-sponsored council at Graciosa Bay tends to govern weightier social decisions, but questions involving subsistence are still decided in the more traditional manner. The scheduling of feasts to celebrate Christian holidays, births, or deaths is still the responsibility of the relevant men's association, and the activity that accompanies such celebration places the onus of preparation on the men. This is the major incursion of men into food preparation at the village level, because after women harvest the tubers of taro or *Cyrtosperma* and men the bananas or breadfruit (the women help carry), only incidental help is afforded by the women. The processes of building and tending the oven, the pounding of food, the recooking in leaf packages, and the sharing out are all within the province of the men's association, and much is done within or in the environs of the house itself.

Preservation of breadfruit by drying sectioned cooked fruits is based on the assessments of men and women and is incidental to hunting and gardening activities. Since the fruit of village trees is usually used for direct consumption and, formerly, for preservation by fermentation, the groves inland are visited as the season nears, and crop prospects are examined by the individuals who claim the trees as their right. Household groups varying from two to four families leave the village for sojourns of some days in garden houses. Men climb the trees and help carry the fruit to the houses, where they prepare the earth-ovens, as many as three per house. They then continue the tree harvesting, while the women cook, peel, section, and dry the product. It is usual for the men to go hunting or return to the village before the women, leaving them to carry the dry product. Dried breadfruit was preferred to fermented for trading because in the season it could be made ready for transport within a few days. Fermented breadfruit takes a month to prepare and preferably longer to reach the edible and transportable state. While local consumption of preserved products, (for instance yam) took place without ceremony, in cases in which display and gifts were former practices the assemblage of material for trade with the Reefs was handled by the men's houses and was the main objective in manufacture. The governing factor in trade was said to be the weather. The main seasons for breadfruit in Santa Cruz, August and February-March, neatly avoid the main cyclone season in November-January.

Apparently the baskets of dried breadfruit allocated for a trip were assembled in the men's houses. Each association had its equivalent trading partner in the Reefs, as Davenport (1964: 67) has already indicated; exchange and mutual hospitality were thus facilitated. Leadership of association was nonhereditary, and indeed the identities of the individual houses were not permanent. As such, authority was attained by individual effort, commercial success being one of the criteria. Political leadership was therefore akin to the "big man" type, described by Sahlins (1963) as widely applicable in Melanesia, and was in contrast with the hereditary chieftainship of Polynesia, as represented in Anuta.

Anuta

The two most easterly of the small Polynesian outlier islands in Melanesia are Tikopia and Anuta. Their almost exclusively subsistence economies, described by Firth (1939) and Yen (1973b) respectively, involve accents on food processing, especially the storage by pit fermentation of the wide range of fieldcrop and tree species already mentioned. Various concoctions of pounded root crops or breadfruit with coconut oil, gratings, or milk are the culinary staples of feasts, with fish caught from ocean-going sailing canoes, while preserved items are among the important sea stores for inter island voyages. Now however, the fermented *ma* is principally an emergency food for the aftermath of cyclones that decimate the islands' floras; furthermore, they are foods of preference, adding to the varietal range of the plant and fish diet. It is notable that the often large catches of fish are not preserved for storage.

On Anuta, an island of one-fifth of a square mile and populated by some 180 people, field agriculture is the most intensive that this writer has encountered in Polynesia. Permanent, dry (unirrigated) fields are cultivated in an incessant annual rotation of taro and manioc, assisted with regular applications of mulch but without significant fallow periods. Within the individual fields, plants are uniform in maturity, being planted within the span of one to two days. Some full-grown corms are used fresh, but it is estimated that one-half to two-thirds of such crops are ensiled in ground pits for storage after simultaneous harvest.

The intensity of cultivation of the perennials and trees is less obvious, thus fishing must be regarded as next to field culture in labor intensity in the subsistence system. The remaining area of the island that is not devoted to taro and manioc raising is covered with trees and *Cyrtosperma* and is divisible into zones of dominant species; this is so much so that there is little floral area on the island that can reflect the natural vegetation — the terrestrial environment is virtually the agricultural system.

The agricultural study, by which these conclusions were reached (Yen 1973b), also illustrates some controls and variants that may be discussed:

AGRONOMY. Once the perennials and trees are established, production is largely under natural control, i.e. nonintensive in regard to labor requirements. In the cultivation of the annuals, however, the area controlled by an individual is adjustable within the limits of the total amount of suitable land. A man with a large family may negotiate with another man, usually related and with a smaller number of dependents, for additional field area on a temporary basis. Also individual effort in cultivation, especially in weeding and mulching phases, is a variation quite apparent among Anutan gardeners. There is no immediate correlation with size of family, however, because some men prefer fishing to gardening.

HARVESTING. The amount of taro or manioc to be eaten from a given garden is the decision of the gardener himself, and the harvesting is done by his family. Consumption has to be measured as a depletion of the amount of food that can be ensiled at the main harvest of the field, and is influenced by the productive state of the other crops under the family's control. A large seasonal crop of breadfruit or *Burckella* virtually compels immediate harvesting for conservation, but with taro, manioc, and the perennial *Cyrtosperma* there is some leeway (since ripening is not involved) because the crops may stand up to a few weeks without spoilage. All products of gardens, however, are on call of the chiefs for festive occasions, but the actual choice of the contribution is made by the gardener. He will attempt to provide taro if he can.

PRESERVATION. The ensiling of tubers or fruits generally requires labor from outside the immediate family because the aim is to complete the preparation process within a day. Crops that are previously harvested have to be brought to the pit sites; other necessities in the prelude to actual ensiling are the gathering of leaf-lining for the pits, the carrying of equipment for peeling and scraping from the village, and the provision of coconut and betel-chew ingredients for helpers. Group labor of this sort is the result of discussion among the men of houses of the same lineage, but the composition of the work-group may include members of other lineages — seemingly on the basis of friendship rather than on more formalized obligations or reciprocity. The timing of such occasions, however, may be modified if the cultivator is called upon by his fishing group to participate in deep-sea canoe fishing, and the composition of the garden group may also be affected in this way.

FOOD UTILIZATION. Food for normal meals depends largely on gardens, as we have observed, but when there is a choice, the senior male of the house is likely to voice his preference. The stores of *ma* are only occasionally used in this way. The chief may ask a member of his lineage for taro, but again this is rare because the landholdings of the chiefs are relatively large and, furthermore, well cultivated because of their own exemplary efforts and the considerable assistance received in everyday garden maintenance. On festive occasions, *ma* can be on the menu as contributions from those without sufficient fresh tubers, but the aim is rather to provide ingredients for the puddings, the product of communal effort, in which groups within designated cookhouses cooperate.

While the influence of authority may be felt in normal food utilization, it is in the recognized aim of food preservation practices, the alleviation of famine, that direct control of production, or rather distribution, passes into the hands of the chiefs. Then all resources, the remains of standing crops, the recognized emergency foods not normally part of meal patterns (e.g. tubers of *Cordyline fruticosa*, sago from *Metroxylon* palm trunks), and especially all the *ma* on the island, are mobilized to meet the situation. I recorded this information in late 1971, during which time I also noted that a chief's leadership qualities were partly evaluated on his performance under such stressful times; while his evaluations of his followers were based on the effectiveness of their contributions, the amount of *ma* reserve that could be produced. Feinberg (1973) was to observe firsthand and record such an occasion in early 1972, in which the sharing out of food by the chiefs was evocative of procedures on ceremonial occasions.

DISCUSSION

This treatment of Oceanic food processing has been a reduction from a consideration of the general distribution of its forms in terms of historical relevance to just two ethnographic examples, geographically close to one another but distinctly different in their purposes of preservation. At this juncture, it is hoped that at least some of the social controls governing production and distribution have been indicated. It is hardly necessary to point out that in this small sample of contrasting agricultural, cultural, and methodological situations, any similarities found cannot constitute rules of social behavior; rather such similarities may be viewed as coming from parts or results of larger sets of greater significance that have been studied.

Food processing is one form of intensification of production method in terms of labor expended per unit of land, population, or produce, which does not increase community production levels. Concoctive preparations of pounded foods, culinary elaborations, in fact tend to result in somewhat more wastage than normal preparation methods. Generally, however, as festive foods, the occasions for their preparation are at the behest of leaders, or would-be leaders where they are nonhereditary. There is some choice in the disposal of preserved food, in the ordinary course of events, but in the main avenues of distribution — the recognized and differing purposes of food preservation in our two examples — the essential roles of leadership again become evident. With distribution systems it might be reasonably expected that close organization of the foundation level of surplus achievement in garden production would be the rule. But, quite unlike modern-day examples of agricultural control in which policy from the top of the hierarchies, communist or corporate-capitalist, is translated into orders at the wheat-field level, there was no evidence of such control in Santa Cruz or Anuta. In both examples, the gardener as an individual recognizes the necessity to produce a surplus from which he will benefit, but the control of which passes largely out of his hands. In other words, this part of the result of his handiwork that HE plans is HIS contribution to a wider communal effort, and exemplifies the notion expressed by Sahlins (1972: 101) of the household unit making provision for surplus for "a public economy; for the support of social institutions beyond the family ...."

Such provision on Anuta is an integral part of the subsistence system, the failure of which would probably result in the collapse of the system itself at the given population level. Thus to Anutans, the *ma*-filled pits represent something like reserve capital, to be expended in time of crisis and to be replaced at the first opportunity. Distribution is the responsibility of the chiefs, a duty that comes with office rather than a means to the attainment of status. Their discharge of the duty, however, is among the factors that govern the people's perception of any chief's qualities.

In the Santa Cruz Islands, the trade cycle is best known for the exchange items, apart from women, representing the specialized developments of material cultures; the underlying subsistence base involved Ndeni as the great provider of processed staple plant food, seeking extra products from agriculture such as pigs, and the larger marine products such as shark and turtle, all significant in traditional ritual. The organization of this trade, as Davenport (1964: 57–94) has noted earlier, was one of the important means by which an individual could elevate himself to traditional leadership and establish a new men's association. Sustained trading success contributed in large measure to the continuity of identity of a men's house and its leadership. In acquiring the valuable trade goods and the "subsistence" items, production, according to ethnographic information and contemporary observation, was in the hands and planning of individuals; but the functional segregation of authority seems to be again manifest in this example because distribution at two levels — the assembling of goods at the local level and the disposal in trade — depended on the acumen of association leaders. The efficiency of production of agricultural products, like the manufacture of feather money, was the function of individuals at the household level often organized into groups, but such organization was not necessarily a step toward political power.

Thus the segregation of levels of decision affecting production is the common factor in the two examples so disparate in other respects. The stimulus for individuals to attain a surplus that will be subject to authority in distribution in one case may be assigned to natural ecology; in the other case it must be assigned to a major SOCIAL aspect of the immediate surroundings of gardeners, the political system. As Sahlins (1972: 135) has expressed it, "political economy cannot survive on that restrained use of resources which for the domestic economy is a satisfactory existence." On a large tropical island of varied resources, such as Santa Cruz, it could have been that the population could have survived with a purely "domestic mode of production" without the development of its flexible political system. Such a view equates survival with calories, and should be tempered with the observation that surviving does not necessarily mean thriving. The present-day depressed atmosphere of Santa Cruz societies cannot be accounted for in calories or low potential production, but in the reduction of population levels and the functional breakdown of social institutions.

In using the term "decision" we obviously encounter a question of accuracy of application in the light of recent conceptualizations of the decision-making processes. Here the term has been used both in production and distribution, but as the functions of different levels in the societies. We turn to the compact summary of analytical bases of study presented recently by Howard and Ortiz (1971: 213–226).

First, in both examples we may look at the decisions on agricultural food production as a contingent series in which "antecedent outcomes affect the possiblity of subsequent outcomes." The difference between such a series and individual decisions, like planting or feast days, seems a fine one, due more to the option of the investigator. An example, divorced from contingent contexts, may be any specific decision in a related series. In the cases presented here, at least the exact events in food elaboration can be thus viewed in isolation, with a change of actors or ego-orientation between the chains of decision affecting production or distribution. In the Anutan example, however, the distribution in circumstances when it passes to the chiefs may suggest that this is hardly decision making because the action of authority for the common good has apparently little option. Even here though, it may be argued that his followers' evaluative judgments of the chief's actions may leave room for presently undocumented options in distribution to alleviate famine.

The context of decision making as a "state of nature" (Howard and Ortiz 1971:217) is closely represented: in the Anutan case, by events outside human control governing surplus production and storage and, irregularly, the distribution of that surplus; in the Santa Cruz example, however, there is a considerable enlargement of scope in the aims of stored surplus because individual choice in favor of storage means one way to enter as a participant in trade or even as one aspiring toward leadership. It would seem unnecessary to make further direct reference to the types and alternatives of decisions of organization and power in the Santa Cruz example as a "product of individual and collective behavior."

The antecedent conditions of opportunity, cost, and values attached to each option that Howard and Ortiz LIKEN to motivation appear to be satisfied in our examples. Also approximated are the conditions of rationality — freedom of action (if varying degrees of freedom are acceptable), perception of the options and their values by the individual, and mutual exclusiveness of the action dependent on a given decision. The abilities of individuals "to rank outcomes according to a scale of preferences" are uncertain, a status that owes as much to the field recording as to any reflection of the cultural situations. Some exemplification of such preferences by Howard and Ortiz (1971: 219), like quantity of resources or political pay-off, have impressionistic resemblances to some of the incompletely recorded situations in Anuta and Santa Cruz.

SUMMARY

The individualistic control at two social levels of agricultural production is accentuated in the examples presented, where elaborations of food are part of the systems. Individual decision and the initiation of household or group action fall to the gardener whose particular crop is concerned, and he must anticipate surplus requirements for which he will be called upon by higher authority. He has greater latitude in field crops than in tree crops, but conversion of surplus to preserved forms ensures a spread of production of both.

The ultimate control, however, is environmental in its broadest sense. Inclement climatic conditions on tiny Anuta can interrupt at intervals the food supply from a continuous cropping pattern and can require the marshalling of preserved resources and the organization of distribution by the chiefs of the island. Thus the necessity for community action curtails the range of individual choice, and that necessity is the restraint that prevents significant consumption of reserves (as a preferred diet change) in normal times. With the greater resources of the larger landmass of Santa Cruz, emergency foods are secondary; natural disasters (damaging cyclones do occur) do not dictate the priority for the production and processing of surplus. Rather the social setting of a traditional interisland trade system formerly provided such an impetus and, moreover, gave a wider choice to the gardener — perhaps in a negative but horizon-widening way — resulting in less gardening and more artifact manufacture, with an option of even "improving" his social position as his aspirations to leadership were expressed in his organizational ability.

Historically the derivations of food preservation processes are obscure. This is especially so with the wide Pacific island distribution of fermentation. It would be ultradiffusionistic to suggest parallels with the mainland Asiatic processes of this sort (not practiced on breadfruit or taro). The extension of the crop range on Anuta and the apparent innovation and importance of food drying, specifically of cooked breadfruit, also extending the range of food preserves on Santa Cruz, may result from earlier intensifications of agriculture to surpluses for vastly different reasons.

REFERENCES

BARRAU, J.

1959 The sago palms and other food plants of marsh dwellers in the South Pacific Island. *Economic Botany* 13:151–162.

1961 *Subsistence agriculture in Polynesia and Micronesia.* Bishop Museum Bulletin 223. Honolulu.

1965a Witnesses of the past. *Ethnology* 4:282–294.

1965b Histoire et préhistoire-horticoles de l'Océanie tropicale. *Journal de la Société des Océanistes* 21:55–78.

BARRAU J., A. PEETERS

1972 Histoire et préhistoire dela préparation des aliments d'origine végétale. *Journal de la Société des Océanistes* 35:141–152.

BROOKFIELD, H. C.
1972 Intensification and disintensification in Pacific agriculture. *Pacific Viewpoint* 13:30–48.

BUCK, P.
1950 *Material culture of Kapingamarangi.* Bishop Museum Bulletin 200. Honolulu.

BULMER, S., R. N. H. BULMER
1964 The prehistory of the Australian New Guinea highlands. *American Anthropologist* 66:39–76.

CAPELL, A.
1968 *A new Fijian dictionary.* Suva: Government Printer.

COENEN, J.
1962 *La préparation du sagou en Nouvelle-Guinée Néerlandaise.* Bulletin du Pacifique Sud.

DAVENPORT, W.
1964 "Social structure of Santa Cruz Island," in *Explorations in cultural anthropology.* Edited by W. H. Goodenough, 57–94. New York: McGraw-Hill.

FEINBERG, R.
1973 "Anutan social structure," in *Anuta — a Polynesian outlier in the Solomon Islands.* Edited by D. E. Yen and J. Gordon. Honolulu: Pacific Anthropological Records.

FIRTH, R.
1939 *Primitive Polynesian economy.* London: Routledge.

FOSBERG, F. R.
1946 "Botanical report on Micronesia," in *Economic survey of Micronesia,* Volume thirteen, part one. Honolulu: Bishop Museum.

FREEDMAN, R. L.
1968 Wanted: a journal in culinary anthropology. *Current Anthropology* 9:62–63.

GREEN, R. C.
1969 "Excavations at Va-1, 1963–1964," in *Archaeology in western Samoa.* Edited by R. C. Green and J. M. Davidson, 114–137. Auckland: Auckland Institute and Museum.

HARDING, T. G.
1967 *Voyagers of Vitiaz Strait.* Seattle: University of Washington.

HONIARA STATISTICAL OFFICE
1970 *British Solomon Islands annual abstracts of statistics 1970.* Honiara: Government Printing Office.

HOWARD, A., S. ORTIZ
1971 Decision making and the study of social process. *Acta Sociologica* 14:213–226.

MALINOWSKI, B.
1966 [1935]. *Coral gardens and their magic* (second edition). London: Allen and Unwin. (Originally published 1935.)

MURAI, M., P. PEN, C. D. MILLER
1958 *Some tropical South Pacific foods.* Honolulu: University of Hawaii.

OLIVER, D. L.

1961 *The Pacific islands.* New York: Natural History Library. (Originally published 1951.)

PIGAFETTA, A.

1969 *First voyage around the world.* Manila: Filipiniana Book Guild.

PUKUI, M. K.

1968 "Poi making," in *Polynesian culture history.* Edited by G. A. Highland, et al., 425–436. Honolulu: Bishop Museum Special Publication 56.

RAPPAPORT, R. A.

1963 "Aspects of man's influence upon island ecosystems: alteration and control," in *Man's place in the island ecosystem.* Edited by F. R. Fosberg, 155–174. Honolulu: Bishop Museum.

1967 *Pigs for ancestors.* New Haven: Yale.

SAHLINS, M.

1963 Poor man, rich man, big man, chief: political types in Melanesia and Polynesia. *Comparative Studies in Society and History* 5:283–303.

1972 *Stone age economics.* Chicago and New York: Aldine-Atherton.

SCHWANITZ, F.

1966 *The origin of cultivated plants.* Cambridge: Harvard University Press.

SERPENTI, L. M.

1965 *Cultivators in the swamps.* Assen: van Gorcum.

SPROAT, M. N.

1968 *A guide to subsistence agriculture in Micronesia.* Saipan: Agricultural Extension Bulletin 9.

STONE, B. C.

1963 "The role of Pandanus in the culture of the Marshall Islands," in *Plants and the migrations of Pacific peoples.* Edited by J. Barrau, 75–82. Honolulu: Bishop Museum.

THOMPSON, L.

1945 *The native culture of Marianas Islands.* Honolulu: Bishop Museum Bulletin 185.

TUETING, L. T.

1935 *Native trade in southeast New Guinea.* Honolulu: Bishop Museum.

VAYDA, P., R. A. RAPPAPORT

1963 "Island cultures," in *Man's place in the island ecosystem.* Edited by F. R. Fosberg, 133–144. Honolulu: Bishop Museum.

WHITE, J.

1971 "New Guinea: the first phase in oceanic settlement," in *Studies in oceanic culture history,* volume two. Edited by R. C. Green and M. Kelly, 45–52. Honolulu: Pacific Anthropological Records 12.

YAWATA, I.

1963 "Rice cultivation of the ancient Marianas," in *Plants and the migrations of Pacific peoples.* Edited by J. Barrau, 91–92. Honolulu: Bishop Museum.

YEN, D. E.

1971 "The development of agriculture in Oceania," in *Studies in oceanic culture history,* volume two. Edited by R. C. Green and M. Kelly. Honolulu: Pacific Anthropological Records 12.

1973a Ethnobotany from the voyages of Mendaña and Quiros in the Pacific. *World Archaeology.*

1973b "Anutan agriculture," in *Anuta — a Polynesian outlier in the Solomon Islands.* Edited by D. E. Yen and J. Gordon. Honolulu: Pacific Anthropological Records.

1973c Arboriculture in the subsistence of Santa Cruz, Solomon Islands. *Economic Botany.*

1973d The origins of Oceanic agriculture. *Archaeology and Physical Anthropology in Oceania.*

Food, Development, and Man in the Tropics

EMILIO F. MORAN

Man's search for food is rooted in habits acquired through a lengthy process of acculturation and an even longer evolutionary history. Man's prehistory is the story of his struggle with the environment, out of which he obtains sustenance. Along with increasing mental skills, man developed more effective ways to harness food energy. The larger populations supported by these more efficient food gathering systems did not necessarily eat better than preceding generations. Development, viewed in aggregate terms, refers to increased total energy, not to its individual allocation. Such was the case in the progress from hunting-and-gathering to sedentary agriculture. The situation repeats itself today. Development is a magic word. Everybody wants to be developed. It is important that in its pursuit managers and agents of modernization consider the meaning of the different habits possessed by traditional peoples.

Man and food have developed a relationship too filled with nuances to be immediately comprehensible to an outsider. "A food habit is not a passing whim or fancy; it is a feature of society and is integrated into a structure of social values that may have nothing to do with the principles of nutrition" (Le Gros Clark 1968:69). Food is prestige and wealth — a mark of what one can afford to buy. It is a means of communication and interpersonal relations. It is an integral part of feasts and ceremonies. Above all, it is tradition, custom, and security (Todhunter 1973:301).

Efforts to change the traditional foods of a human group by outside influences are likely to encounter numerous obstacles. Change in food threatens the security based on customs evolved over generations of experience. Only if the change appeals to the traditional mechanisms of change in a society is its introduction likely to survive one generation. It is important to consider the lifeways of a population in order to discover the clearest path to the betterment of the lives in a group. In other words, if development is going to lead to better lives, it must concern itself not merely with aggregate figures but also with the realities of man's relations to food. One reason why development has so often not meant better life conditions for the masses is due to the imposition of patterns unadapted to the developing area. The result is a breakdown in the traditional system without an equivalent replacement system. Cultures change slowly. An adaptive cultural system resists change even when conditions are ripe for innovation.

This paper tries to show the need to stimulate change using already existing patterns. The tropical Amazon is used as an example of a region with a valuable food staple that can be used to improve the nutritional status of the population, even after that population has been displaced to areas far from rivers rich in protein sources. Brazil is now in the process of development. Its agricultural sector is undergoing rapid change and more is expected. It would be unfortunate if, in the achievement of development, these tropical populations were encouraged to abandon their food habits in favor of those familiar to urbanites and outsiders. Changes in food habits are very costly — they disrupt a basic element of a cultural complex, confuse the individual and lead to combinations of foods that may lower, rather than increase, the nutritional status of the local populations. This situation has been frequently documented among migrants. Manioc is among the most unappreciated foods in the West. Yet, its place in the diet of tropical peoples is too important to premit one to treat it lightly. Manioc can be enriched, simply and cheaply, to improve the protein balance of people who have either insufficient funds for animal protein or are unsure of its supply. Alongside other considerations, this paper wishes to indicate the feasibility of undertaking small rural industries that produce a protein-rich traditional food. This sort of balanced development may lead, then, to both individual and national development through improving man's preexisting relation to some foods while improving its quality and increasing its quantity in aggregate terms.

BRAZILIAN AGRICULTURE

Brazil has a land area greater than that of the United States without Alaska. Fifty-nine percent of this area is made up of the Amazon region. Population density varies from a low of 1.4 persons per square kilometer to the anthill concentrations of São Paulo. Per capita income varies greatly and is high in the industrial south and low in rural Amazonia. The climate is generally tropical but parts of the south are subtemperate. Rainfall everywhere exceeds 40 inches per year. A drought area occurs in the northeast at intervals of ten years.

To this day, Brazil's population is largely rural. A variety of land use patterns are present: small properties, monocrop plantations, ranches, extractivism. Tendencies toward large-sized properties were strengthened by a preference for land as a status symbol among the wealthy and by economies of scale in certain enterprises, notably sugar, coffee, and cattle. Agrarian reform has been attempted time and again through colonization schemes. A recent study documents its history (Tavares, et al. 1972). Failures have been frequent due to the lack of infrastructural support.

Education in Brazil was until recent years largely elitist. Only a small number reached secondary school and from that point on education was geared to the gentlemanly careers of medicine, law, and philosophy. Little support was given to vocational institutions or to the "earth sciences." Much of this is changing but it still affects the development schemes.

Government is based on a strong president with the backing of the armed forces. The military is committed to economic development and national integration. To this end the Amazon region is being rapidly colonized and roads are being built to guarantee Brazilian frontier claims with Spanish-American nations. Money is being made available to credit, research, and development agencies. Large investments are being made by Brazilians and foreigners taking advantage of the new and progressive outlook of development managers.

The major limiting factor on Brazilian agricultural production could be said to be transportation. There is a strong correlation between agricultural productivity and the availability and efficiency of transportation services (Herrmann 1972). The current effort to build roads through the Amazon is an expression of an awareness, in decision-making circles, of this cause-and-effect relationship. Investments in the region have been high and only the potential riches of the area can justify the current investments. Costs of road building in the first portion of the Trans-Amazon highway were as high as U.S.$ 47,064 per mile (Moran 1974a).

Brazil is in a transitional stage of economic development. Industry is growing and is beginning to compete successfully in world markets. Agriculture still employs over one-half of the labor force. Many of these are engaged in sharecropping and subsistence-type farming. Brazilian agricultural output doubled between 1947 and 1965. It is still growing at a rate of over 4 percent yearly, mainly through the opening up of more lands rather than by intensification of areas already farmed. This situation can continue for only a few more years. The last frontier is now open and the vast virgin lands will remain new for only a few brief years. Alternatives to expansion will have to emerge.

Crop land in Brazil increased from 19 million hectares in 1950 to 29 million hectares in 1960. Cropping intensity appears to have reached 25 percent of land in farms (Herrmann 1972:22). Pasture land in Brazil increased from 108 million hectares in 1950 to 122 million hectares in 1960. The states of Mato Grosso and southern Pará are currently being converted into an almost uninterrupted pasture. Forest lands in Brazil have been largely unproductive and only the rubber and Brazil nut products of the Amazon seem to have yielded much — and then it only benefitted a handful of exporters.

Traditional agriculture in Brazil has relied heavily on labor and land inputs to achieve its normal production. Capital inputs have been generally low. Fertilizers have, until now, been used largely in the south, particularly in the São Paulo-Parana areas. Fertilizer responses in Brazil tend to be low. There has been blind acceptance of agricultural technology from temperate areas, with unfortunate results. Inadequate agronomic technology and lack of trained personnel acts as limiting factors on the success of fertilizer use. Brazil's agricultural credit system has suffered from inadequacies for decades. Private lenders, merchants, and lending agents were virtually the only sources of farm credit. Interest rates were prohibitive. The Amazon region is currently enjoying an unusual situation. Tax exemptions, credit facilities, and fiscal incentives have all been created to encourage investment in the area. The response in the first has been excellent and the region's development is a real possibility.

Most of Brazil's agricultural production is consumed domestically. About 70 percent of all cultivated land in 1963–1965 was used for crops other than the six chief export crops. Brazil leads the world in coffee production, and it will soon have a comparable position as a meat exporter. Not much has, however, been accomplished on the level of redistribution of incomes. Increased productivity and economic development do not guarantee that most men's per capita income and living conditions will improve.

MAN AND MANIOC

A major obstacle to personal — as opposed to aggregate — development is the attempt by modernization agents to change the lifeways of traditional peoples without attempting to understand the cultural system which governs their thinking. Temperate zone men when confronte tropical preferences either find these different foods "exotic" or repul Or in a more scientific vein: they test the foods or plants and find them deficient when compared with their own foods and plants. In true evangelical style these men undertake the task of "teaching" tropical peoples the more adequate ways to make a living out of the soil — by growing temperate zone domesticates.

In most circles it is still fashionable to look down upon the tropics and the plant and animal products that come from it. Culture contact between alien cultures brings about a certain degree of disorganization in both, a situation which often causes a defensive reaction leading to the rejection of innovations. It would be much more in keeping with the objectives of science to look at the tropics from within and, to the extent that this is possible, abandon the impositions of our culture and its requirements for "proper living." Culture is man's primary adaptive mechanism — a complex by which he gathers available potential energy from his environment and puts it to use in self-maintenance and growth. But seldom is culture perfectly adapted to its environment. Change occurs in nature as well as in human society. When cultures change they do not abandon their older ways but rather arrive at a compromise between new optimal adaptations to the environment and the traditions gradually accumulated by human groups.

Cultural responses vary depending on what "glasses" one is wearing at the time. The high yields obtained from manioc were seen at one time by colonial administrators in Africa as ideal answers to famine problems. These administrators required, thereafter, that their subjects plant a minimum acreage in manioc (Jennings 1970:64). This foresighted agricultural policy was later criticized on the grounds that it led to the abandonment, by many colonial peoples in the tropics, of other crops in favor of manioc — a situation which some have judged as dangerously risky. In an important clinical study of the disease kwashiorkor, Brock and Autret (1952:62) recommend that "it is essential to encourage, wherever social conditions permit, the production of cereals, which are richer in protein than cassava, or of other roots and tubers, also superior to cassava in protein content." It is somewhat surprising that scientists in one field, without further consultation, go about suggesting radical changes in food habits, unaware of the complexities of change.

The various products resulting from manioc have made this crop nearly indispensable to tropical peoples. The crop spread from Brazil in 1500 and diffused rapidly. It is unsound to advocate a systematic change in the diet patterns of over 250 million people, worldwide. Besides the problems produced it is not certain that the result would be improved nutrition. Cereal grains yield less calories per unit of land, require a higher input of labor, and require more soil nutrients than does manioc. In other words, manioc can free tropical peoples from agricultural labor to devote more of their time to procuring high-quality protein, rather than to spending more of their income and labor in growing cereals alone.

Besides the cultural factors that are likely to work for the stubborn persistence of manioc as a basic staple, research indicates that manioc could turn out to be an important crop in an ecologically deteriorating world (Rogers and Appan 1971). The scarcity of capital in developing nations is a principal obstacle to the transformation of these countries to a modernized agricultural system. In its turn, the technological revolution tends to use pollutants indiscriminately that are inclined to deteriorate the environment. Developing nations are thus caught in a vicious circle: either underdevelopment or economic improvement with accompanying ecological deterioration. It is in this context that food-producing systems with potentialities for efficiently generating nourishment from depleted or disrupted ecological niches, under primitive conditions of economy and technology (due to lack of capital) are bound to become important in the future. It is a blessing that tropical peoples have the means within their own culture to resolve the vicious circle. Manioc has the potential for breaking the circle of doom.

What is needed at this stage is not a bleak outlook but rather an imaginative approach to crop improvement and management. Biological, physical, technological, economic, and social factors are involved that require innovative syntheses. Manioc is outstanding for its rugged ecological adaptations: tolerance to drought, aggressiveness towards pests and weeds, its growth capability in alkaline soils and stiff marine clays with *pH* as high as 9.0, and in acidic soils, sands, and loose laterites with *pH* as low as 5.0. Manioc ranks high as a producer of calories and colonizes successfully especially in areas of depleted resources. It is preadapted to many of the social and ecological factors which have in the past limited the successful functioning of improved agricultural systems.

Foreign aid and development programs sponsored by temperate-zone peoples often show the sort of food bias that we have been discussing. A classic example of this was the introduction of a high-yielding-hybrid corn into Mexico. While the local farmers gradually accepted the new variety, their wives steadily became more opposed to the innovation as it would not make good tortilla meal. Since tortillas constitute the main staple, this was nearly disastrous. In addition, the foreign experts suggested planting the hybrid only, forgetting that the traditional farmer usually planted a number of corn varieties in a single field. The different types of corn were used for a variety of purposes (e.g. foddering, ritual, and human consumption). Each type of corn, moreover, had different ecological adaptations, and thus the farmer could seldom be wiped out by a pest or disease invasion. The innovators did not take the time to study the traditional ways of the population and search for their inner logic before starting. Their actions had serious repercussions on the diet for a while, and eventually the requirements of subsistence led to the abandonment of the new hybrids (Spicer 1967:35–40).

An important element in understanding man's relations to food is the notion that food, like many cultural items, may fall into "categories" that specify the contexts of food use within each society. It is impossible for man to handle the infinite varieties of food in the world. As a result, different societies evolve world-views that segment the world continuum into discrete categories. Not only do all societies segment the "real" world differently, but they obviously choose different criteria by which to define these categories. Sometimes these criteria may be outside or beyond the physical properties of the objects being classified. These categories, it seems, may pertain to any aspect of existence. Some are linguistically marked, while others may simply have labelling terms, which then apply to a whole class of objects or concepts. In other words, one needs to ask the same sort of questions which the "natives" ask in making situational decisions.

Food is particularly important in any culture. It is one of the earliest things learned by a child in the home — what is and is not "food" — its association with disease prevention and curing, its daily consumption with the various associated social rituals, and its role as a reflection of social status of families in the community. It is a major error to look at food only in terms of its nutrient content and of the total calories consumed to do work. Food research should aim at complete understandings of man's relations, monitored by food ideas. Is what people eat a reflection of their status or a reflection of their understanding of the environment? Cultural "memory" has usually aided man in securing an adequate and nutricious food supply. Occasionally, however, this "memory" lags and then injures the overall comfort of man. Left to his own ingenuity, man can probably find in each environment a proper dietetic balance. But since he is seldom left to himself, man must perforce experience the limitations that come from sociocultural restrictions imposed by group force.

Brazilian food habits derive from the three major racial stocks that populated the country: Amerindian, African, and Portuguese. While

Negro influence in the Amazon is not as pronounced as it is elsewhere in Brazil, it is strongly felt in Amazon cities. Nonetheless, many foods were brought over from Africa by Negroes or by the Portuguese who imported them. Sugarcane was an African import to Brazil, as were mangoes, bananas, cashews, yams, watermelons, melons, coconuts, dende oil, guinea hens, and the method of cooking food in a blood sauce. Three African fruits came in and lost their names of origin to become *quiabo*, *maxixe*, and *gerimum* (Cascudo 1966:107).

The Portuguese brought in many familiar domestic animals as a major contribution to the Brazilian diet: beef cattle, goats, chickens, pigs, ducks, geese, and pigeons. They also introduced the use of refined sugar, sea salt, spices, olives and olive oil, garlic, wine, citrus fruits, and raw-distilled rum (*cachaça*). Much later, wheat was introduced in the south of Brazil (Cascudo 1966:107).

Scanning the list of Brazilian food terms one is struck by the large number of Tupi derivatives (Wagley 1964:32). In the Amazon area, Indian influences are strongest. Portuguese interbred with the Amerindian population and adapted to the rain forest after the manner of the Indian — adopting the practices of slash and burn horticulture, the native crops and the methods and beliefs about hunting and fishing. Manioc was the major staple of the Tupi diet. Corn, sweet potatoes, beans, peanuts, squash, cacao, *caruru*, and peppers were among the various local foods used. Apparently no animals were domesticated for food and they depended on hunted game or fish. No fruits were apparently domesticated either, but simply gathered when in season.

The greatest variety of uses often indicates the staple crop, and manioc is a food with a thousand faces. The traditional Amazon population (Moran 1974b) adopted not only the cultivation methods for manioc, but also its processing techniques. While manioc cultivation requires low inputs of labor, processing it requires three to four times the labor cost. The preparation of manioc flour (*farinha*) basically involves the removal of prussic acid and the conversion of the raw tuber into a dry, storable form. There are basically two methods to accomplish this. The first includes peeling, grating, and squeezing the pulp in a tubular basket to remove the prussic acid. Then the mixture is toasted on a large griddle until a coarse, mealy substance is obtained. The second method involves soaking the unpeeled tubers (until a point of near-decay), at which point they are peeled and squeezed to remove the poisonous juice. Then the pulp is roasted as in the first method. It takes a man and his wife a full day to process 30 kilos of *farinha*. This labor input is more than occasional since an Amazonian family of five consumes over two kilos of *farinha* daily

(Wagley 1964:66). Nearly all of the plant is used: the leaves are used in some recipes, the prussic acid is fermented with peppers and gives a vitamin-rich sauce; the flour is used for dough, breads, cakes, and is fried as *farofa*; the peelings are given to the animals. The stem is used to prepare cuttings to plant again, since manioc reproduces vegetatively.

What we see here is a cultural complex rooted in a subsistence system in which manioc occupies the predominant position. It would seem nearly insane to suggest changing this food habit complex, without changing the whole culture and economic system beforehand. There was no reason in the past to consider changing these diets. Population was concentrated on the banks of rivers, where abundant fish were available daily to supplement the carbohydrate staple. But with the current movement to develop the Amazon and the construction of a highway network, the situation changes. The new population in the Amazon will be located near roads, not rivers. This means that the major supplier of proteins will not be available. It also means that populations will have to rely on wild game, known to be limited in numbers. Protein deficiencies lurk in the future. Innovators are already talking of introducing new crops and new hybrids. Will this mean a repeat of the Mexican case cited before? Development agents do not seem to be taking proper cognizance of the traditional ways of the population. A repeat of past errors is possible unless the true potential of manioc is made public and is applied to the new challenges presented by Amazonian development. It seems that a creative approach to manioc, which takes advantage of its tropical ecological adaptations and minimizes the deficiencies in protein content, is in order. The task before food developers and agricultural experts of various kinds is how to manage this food product in a way that will most benefit tropical populations.

MANIHOT ESCULENTA CRANTZ

Manioc has become a pan-tropical staple since its diffusion from the New World in the first decade of the sixteenth century. The Tupinambas made the Portuguese aware of the plant and its products. They, in their turn, took the crop to Cape Verde first and then to Africa and Asia. The manioc products differ widely throughout the world since the Portuguese, who were its agent of diffusion, were only partially aware of the various processes practiced by the aboriginal population. The peoples of Africa and Asia developed new and different uses for the plant. In Nigeria, for example, manioc constitutes the second most important staple, preceded only by yams. Amongst the farm crops it ranks first in tonnage produced, second in total value of the crop, and fourth in total acreage devoted to its production (Oke 1968:227). The most common foods prepared from manioc in Nigeria are *gari*, *fufu*, *lafun* and *kpokpogari*. The process methods differ significantly from those practiced in Brazil and derived from Amerindian technology.

The manioc plant is assigned to the genus *Manihot* and to the family Euphorbiaceae. This woody shrub grows on the average to a height of 5 to 12 feet — though it has been known to attain 18 feet (Jones 1959:5). The leaves are large and palmate, ordinarily with five to seven lobes, on a long, slender petiole. The leaves grow only toward the end of the branches. As the plant grows, the main stem forks, usually into three branches, and these divide, in their turn, in the same manner.

The plant, a dicotyledonous perennial, is cultivated primarily for its large and elongated starchy roots. In Brazil it is known by terms such as *mandioca*, *aypim*, *macaxeira*, and others. The former distinction between bitter (*mandioca brava*) and sweet (*aypim*) manioc has not proved useful botanically and has been abandoned. The invisible characteristics thought to indicate the toxicity of the root vary from place to place and all manioc is now regarded as varieties of *Manihot esculenta* Crantz.

Fresh manioc is primarily a source of carbohydrates and contains very little protein or fat. It is rich in vitamin C and calcium, with significant amounts of thiamine, riboflavin, and niacin. A part of these nutrients are lost in processing. Unfortunately, not many of the processed manioc products have been analyzed for nutrient content (Oke 1968).

Manioc contains a toxic element, prussic acid, which varies from harmless to lethal depending on the amounts of acid present. A root is "sweet" if it contains less than 50 mg. of prussic acid per kilogram of flesh, and bitter if over 100 mg. per kilogram (Bilhous 1952:560–563). Differences in prussic acid have been found between tubers in the same field. The living plant contains no free prussic acid, but like most members of the Euphorbiaceae family, it exudes a latex from small sacs located just beneath the peel or bark when it is cut or bruised. The latex contains cyanogenetic glucoside that begins to break down into prussic acid, acetone, and glucose once the plant is harvested. Cyanogenetic glucoside is highly soluble in water and decomposes when heated to a temperature of 150 degrees Centigrade. The prussic acid is freed by the action of an enzyme, linase, that is present in the plant. Hydrolosis under the influence of linase can be accelerated by soaking the roots in water, by cutting, and by heating. If temperature is allowed to rise above 75 degrees Centigrade, the linase is destroyed and some of the glucoside may not be hydrolized. It was thought at one time that poisonousness was associated with variety and appearance. It has been shown by Bilhous (1952) that the correlation is extremely loose and unpredictable.

Manioc cultivation is largely confined to the tropics. Approximate boundaries can be set at 39 degrees north and 30 degrees south latitudes. It does best at temperatures near 65 degrees Fahrenheit. It shows lack of resistance to cold, its growth stopping at 50 degrees Fahrenheit. Frost can kill the plant. Manioc produces best in areas of abundant rainfall, while surviving under drought conditions. It grows well in a variety of soils and thrives in all except waterlogged conditions.

Manioc is usually planted from cuttings. After the field is burnt, the stalks are introduced into the ground. The cuttings usually chosen come from the center portion of the main stalk and are typically six to twelve inches long. Yields compare favorably with those of other starchy staples. Five to ten tons per hectare can be expected using traditional methods. Under experimental conditions using fertilizer manioc has yielded up to 65 tons per hectare (Jones 1959).

As a staple food, manioc has been criticized on several counts: soil depletion, soil erosion, ease of growing, prussic acid content, and nutritional content. Three of these negative points can be corrected by direct action: leaving stems and leaves in the field, cover-cropping, and manuring; erosion can be arrested by intercropping and contour ridging; prussic acid content can be reduced to safe levels by soaking and heating. Ease of cultivation appears to be more of an asset than a liability.

Manioc leaf protein is clearly deficient in the amino acid methionine and marginal in its content of tryptophane. However, it exceeds in all other essential amino acids, a pattern similar to that of the soy bean, which is usually hailed as one of the most nutritive vegetable proteins (Eggum 1970; Rogers and Milner 1965:312).

Manioc has been used with good results for fattening cattle, horses, hogs, and poultry (IRI 1967). This practice is common in both Nigeria and Brazil. The peels which are thrown to the animals are richer in protein than the flesh and constitute 13 to 20 percent of the whole. This constitutes an important source of food for domestic animals and permits savings in feeds as well as increasing their bulk. Ruminants have been known to accept manioc leaves as a protein supplement (Oke 1968:240). Oyenuga and Opeke (1957) found that cassava stimulated the growth of young pigs better than guinea corn with no ill effect in the carcass quality, as long as it was not more than 40 percent of the dry matter of the feedingstuff. While it is true that manioc is low in protein it yields two to three times more than rice or any other cereal plant. And new processes may lead to improved protein content.

PROTEIN-ENRICHED MANIOC

Enrichment of cassava with single-cell protein has a long list of advantages. It was possibly the speed with which micro-organisms could reproduce that led to recognition of their use as protein sources. Compared with the micro-organisms, the rate of protein production from higher plants is very slow indeed. One can find figures suggesting that the rate of protein production in yeast, for example, may be as much as 100,000 times as great as that by a yearling steer per unit weight of yeast and steer (Shacklady 1972).

It was perhaps the realization that manioc-based dishes could be prepared in essentially the same way — but now with high protein content — that may account for the enthusiasm in research circles for this approach (Strasser, et al. 1970). Recalling what has preceded in this paper, the clear advantages of not having to change the traditional food eating habits of a population are enormous. One of the new processes requires no expensive washing and separation techniques, as in other single-cell processes, thereby aiding the low-capital industries that would emerge. Since industrial production of manioc is just in its preliminary stages in most tropical countries, the incorporation of these enrichment processes could be made a part of their plans. The cost-benefit advantages are clear: this would prevent the importation of costlier protein sources in the years ahead, as well as improve the nutritional status of the population.

In an experiment, three different strains of yeast were grown on hydrolized manioc and the following protein contents were obtained:

Manioc plus *Candida utilis* 35 percent crude protein (dry basis);
Manioc plus *Rhodotorula gracilias* 26.7 percent crude protein (dry basis);
Manioc plus *Hansenula saturnus* 15.5 percent crude protein (dry basis).

The results were encouraging and tests were made simulating industrial conditions in a medium-size plant (Figure 1). The plant would be assumed to produce ten tons per day of a dried yeast product containing 33 percent protein and 15 percent carbohydrate components. A four-hour residence in the propagator was assumed with an allowance for a two-fold volume increase for foaming. The advantages of this method are clear: final product is agreeable to local population, follows a process not far from that of the small *casas de farinha*, and its cost is not exceedingly high. To that we must now turn.

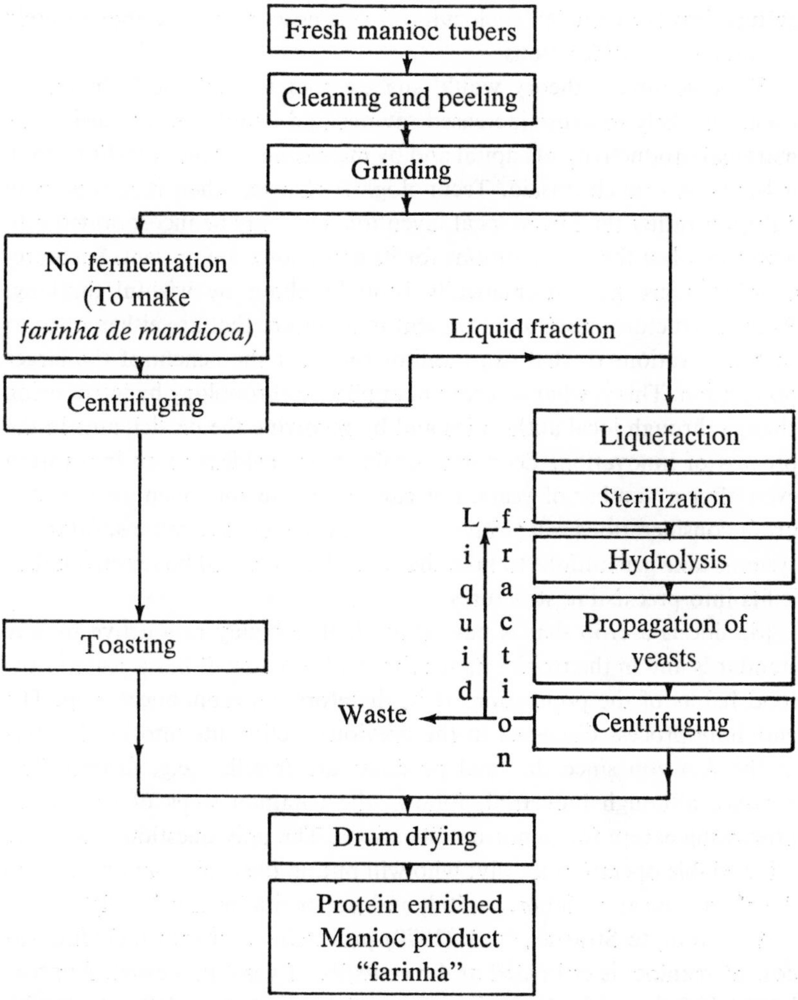

Figure 1. Diagram of the process to produce an enriched *farinha de mandioca* (flour) using yeast. If one were making *Gari* (as in Nigeria) anaerobic fermentation would be incorporated where "no fermentation" is indicated (from Strasser, et al. 1970:115)

THE ECONOMICS OF MANIOC

Any attempt at changing the way things are done involves affecting the structure of traditional agriculture. Farming in most low-income areas of the world is dominated by the isolated small farmer. Labor and capital allocations represent the product of long experience on how to maintain one's livelihood within safe margins. Change and modernization of agriculture involve complex sociocultural processes over and above purely "economic" considerations.

While economic theory would suggest that technological change, of itself, "is likely to cause increased savings and investment by raising the marginal productivity of capital and by increasing income" (Mellor 1967), it leaves too much unsaid. Technological change, when it results from diffusion rather than from local invention, can only be incorporated into a system when the preconditions for its acceptance are present. Such preconditions are not automatically brought about by wishful thinking. Rather, structures need to be present in a culture that are either open to such innovations or that can monitor them for the benefit of the larger population. This is what is meant in applied anthropology by introducing change through local authorities and by involving the participants in the process of innovation. Economic profit is not evident in an innovation even after a number of years, nor can temperate zone men assume that profit considerations will always overcome other considerations. Adaptive systems take generations to take shape, and change will be rejected unless it fits into preexisting structures.

Manioc is a crop that is pan-tropical. It is highly productive by any standards and in the tropics its requirements are few. It has a place in the food habits of the population. It is, therefore, an economical crop. The enriching process discussed in the previous section fits into local habits in the Amazon since the final products are familiar, e.g. *farinha*. The process, although industrial, follows the common steps of traditional processing except for minor modifications. The only question is whether it is a viable operation locally: who will put up the capital and what does the change mean to labor, capital, and per capita income locally?

According to Strasser, et al. (1970) processing cost (not including the cost of manioc) is estimated at 4.5 cents/lb. of yeast processed. Approximately 2.9 lbs. of fresh manioc are required to produce 1 lb. of protein-rich product. This is an excellent yield, as Wagley (1964) estimates that 5 lbs. of fresh roots are needed to produce 1 lb. of *farinha* in traditional processing. Since the enriched *farinha* contains 33 percent protein, the cost of protein is 13.5 cents/lb. This price compares favorably with soybean flour (12–35 cents/lb.), wheat flour (30 cents/lb.), peanut flour (12–17 cents/lb.), fish protein concentrate (20 cents/lb.) and nonfat dry milk (40 cents/lb.). While inexpensive, from such a comparative point of view, it is still more expensive than the unenriched Amazonian staple. Can the population afford manioc at a price of about 20 cents/lb.?

Current prices in the Amazon for *farinha* vary between 7–11 cents/lb. Thus, the protein-rich product costs 9–13 cents more per pound. If the population lives by the river, as is the case in traditional communities, they can fish for their protein. But, if the person is in an urban center or does not produce his own *farinha* nor catch his own fish (as is the case in some new rural Amazon communities), then he will pay 9–15 cents/lb. of fish — depending on the species purchased. Fish catches are down one-half from those of just five years ago (author's field notes 1972). With growing urban populations and displacement of populations from the northeast to the Amazon, such catches are likely to drop even more. With lowered supplies and growing demand, prices can only be expected to go up for fish, as well as meat. Thus, while at current prices the protein-rich *farinha* would fare badly due to the comparable prices of fish, in the next ten years the product can be expected to supply a needed source of nutrients attractive to buyers, who are known to increase their intake of carbohydrates when animal protein becomes expensive. Moreover, in the newly populated areas but by the Trans-Amazonian Highway, fresh fish will not be easily available and game is declining already. Providing a familiar food to supply needed calories and protein is an ideal solution.

If one can accept the "individual economics" above, then the next problem becomes how to finance such an enterprise. Assuming 24 hr./day operation for 250 days/yr. one can expect a production of 5 million lbs./yr. or ten tons per day. Stasser, et al. (1970) estimated costs for major equipment items at U.S.$ 326,000 for a medium size plant with the above productive capacity. While a plant in the Amazon will probably not operate full capacity (less than 24 hour operation) it will call for lower wage costs. Strasser estimated operating costs at U.S.$ 224,000 per year with 20 operators and 1 supervisor at $ 3 and $ 4 per hour respectively. Salaries are considerably lower in the Amazon and this will reduce operating costs and perhaps the cost of processed *farinha.*

It is unlikely that residents of the new *agrovilas* in the Amazon will have sufficient capital to finance even an operation of this modest size. But it is not beyond possibility. Southern Brazilians coming to the region currently are known to have as much as U.S.$ 6,000 in savings. A co-operative in the region could perhaps be organized and advantage could be taken of the incentives provided by the Amazon Development Bank (Banco da Amazonia) and the Agency for Amazon Development (Super-intendencia do Desenvolvimento da Amazonia). Sixty-three agricultural cooperatives were operating in 1972 in the state of Pará and 15 in the state of Amazônas (Cotia 1972). One of them, based in São Paulo but including some subsidiaries in the Amazon region, has a total capacity of over 20 million (U.S.) dollars.

What happens to labor? Manioc takes a great deal of time to process, and requires low inputs for its cultivation. If capital can be diverted into such an industry, low inputs would be spent in cultivation, then the many hours spent in processing the product in traditional *casas de farinha* would be available for other productive activity. The higher nutritional value from the *farinha* would improve local health and caloric balances. Some of the workers would be employed in the factory, while others would be engaged in the necessary marketing operations. Pepper, *guarana*, tomatoes, pineapples, watermelons, bananas, *acai*, and others, too numerous to mention, could be incorporated into more profitable agricultural work that would thereby improve standards of living. By not changing the food habits of the population one avoids introducing them to high costs of new foods while maintaining and improving their nutritional status through enriched manioc products. The results can be expected to be improved health, stable sociocultural change, higher incomes, diversification. The new structure of "rural urbanism" being promoted by the Institute of Colonization and Agrarian Reform includes the formation of small rural industries, and tax incentives and credit facilities have been created to encourage such enterprises (author's field notes 1972). This proposal for protein-rich production can be easily incorporated into this approach to Amazon development.

The feasibility of this project is limited not by the food habits of the population, not by the ability to engage peoples in cooperative efforts, nor by the cost of the final product, but rather by the erroneous conception that manioc is not a good food and that "developed" peoples would steer away from it as soon as their incomes would permit. It is time to start improving food by manipulating its contents rather than by expecting major changes in food preferences. More study is necessary of the categories by which cultures categorize food and food habits (Le Gros Clark 1968). This can then lead to more economical research on those things that can be changed without setting up major barriers to food intake. Imposing food preferences is unenlightened and uneconomical. Food is very close to the world view of peoples and it is an insult to their dignity to consider their food preferences as inferior. It is better to look at the food and see how it can be improved and made a stronger element in their nutritional base. More creative solutions to the world's food crisis are necessary. Manioc has a rare potential as a food in the tropics that should be further researched and improved upon.

REFERENCES

ADAMS, RICHARD

1968 "A nutritional program in Guatemala," in *Health, culture and community*. Edited by B. Paul. New York: Russell Sage Foundation.

BILHOUS, G. G.

1952 L'emploi de la réaction par la couleur de Guignard dans la sélection du Manioc. *Revue International de Bot. Appl. d'Agric. Tropical* (November-December): 560–563.

BROCK, J. F., M. AUTRET

1952 *Kwashiorkor in Africa*. Geneva: WHO.

CASCUDO, CÂMARA

1966 *O folclore no Brazil*. Rio de Janeiro: Casa do Estudante.

COTIA

1972 *Cooperative Cotia: a force for development in Brazil*. Washington, D.C.: U.S. Department of Agriculture.

DE ALBUQUERQUE, MILTON

1969 *A Mandioca na Amazônia*. Belem: SUDAM.

EGGUM, B. O.

1970 The protein quality of cassava leaves. *British Journal of Nutrition* 24(3): 761–768.

HERRMANN, LOUIS

1972 *Changes in agricultural production in Brazil, 1947–1965*. Washington D.C.: Economic Research Service.

IRI

1967 Molasses, cassava and cottonseed meal as supplements to fresh and ensiled sugar cane tops. *Pesquisa Agropecuaria Brasileira* 2. São Paulo: IRI.

JENNINGS, D. L.

1970 "Cassava in East Africa," in *Tropical root and tuber crops of tomorrow*, volume one, 53–83. Proceedings of the 2nd International Symposium on Tropical Root and Tuber Crops. Honolulu, Hawaii: College of Tropical Agriculture.

JONES, WILLIAM

1959 *Manioc in Africa*. Stanford: Stanford University Press.

LE GROS CLARK, F.

1968 Food habits as a practical nutrition problem. *World Review of Nutrition and Dietetics* 9: 56–84.

MELLOR, JOHN

1967 "Toward a theory of agricultural development," in *Agricultural development and economic growth*. Edited by H. Southworth and B. Johnston, 21–60. Ithaca: Cornell University Press.

MORAN, EMILIO F.

1974a Amazon development: the roads to integration. *Modern Government*.

1974b "The regional adaptive system of the Amazon Caboclo," in *Man in the Amazon*. Edited by Charles Wagley. Gainesville: University of Florida Press.

OKE, O. L.
1968 Cassava as food in Nigeria. *World Review of Nutrition and Dietetics* 9:227–250.
OYENUGA, V., W. OPEKE
1957 *Nigeria's feeding stuffs.* Ibadan: University of Nigeria Press.
ROGERS, D. J., S. G. APPAN
1971 Cassava based nourishment generating system capable of functioning in ecologically and economically impoverished areas. *Tropical Root and Tuber Crops Newsletter* 4:13–18.
ROGERS, D. J., MAX MILNER
1965 Amino acid profile of manioc leaf protein in relation to nutritive value. *Economic Botany* 17:211–216.
SHACKLADY, C. A.
1972 Yeasts grown on hydrocarbons as new sources of protein. *World Review of Nutrition and Dietetics* 14:154–179.
SPICER, EDWARD
1967 *The impact of technological change.* New York: John Wiley and Sons.
STRASSER, J., *et al.*
1970 Process enriches cassava with protein. *Food Engineerings* 42:112–116.
TAVARES, V., *et al.*
1972 *Colonização dirigida no Brasil.* Rio de Janeiro: IPEA/INPES.
TODHUNTER, E. NEIGE
1973 Food habits, food faddism and nutrition. *World Review of Nutrition and Dietetics* 16:286–317.
WAGLEY, CHARLES
1964 *Amazon town: a study of man in the tropics.* New York: Knopf. (Originally published 1953 by Macmillan.)

The Origins and Domestication of Yams in Africa

D. G. COURSEY

Although yams are among the most important of African plant domesticates, the origin of the edible yam in Africa and, indeed, elsewhere is a much misunderstood subject. Numerous misconceptions have appeared recently in the writings of Africanists and others concerned with the history of early agriculture, although as early as the publication of Watt (1890) it was recognized that the practice of yam cultivation was indigenous to Africa as well as to Asia and tropical America. This concept was also tacitly accepted in various writings of Burkill (1921, 1939, 1960) and in some of the earliest writing of Chevalier (1909). It has even been implied in otherwise responsible works (Dumont 1966) that yams were introduced in cultivation to Africa from America along with cassava and other crops. The view, expressed in some detail by Murdock (1959), that yam cultivation developed in West Africa only as part of the "Malaysian plant complex" (of yams, aroids, sugar cane, and bananas) reaching West Africa later than 2000 B.P., has gained wide acceptance, in spite of the above-mentioned works of Burkill and Chevalier, those of Davies (1960, 1967, 1968), and the writer's own more recent publications on the subject (Coursey 1967; Coursey and Alexander 1968; Alexander and Coursey 1969). A recent review on the subject of the history of West African agriculture (Havinden 1970) makes no substantial reference to indigenous yam cultivation and appears uncritically to accept Murdock's Malaysian hypothesis of the origin of yam cultivation in the continent. Proper understanding of the subject has been further complicated by differences in the taxonomic systems used for West African yams, there being a consistent difference in this matter between Francophone and Anglophone authors.

In considering the origins of the yams as domestic plants, it is necessary to realize that while some yams were brought into cultivation in the African continent, other species of yams were domesticated at other places in the world; today, yams of Asiatic origin are grown to a substantial degree in most parts of tropical Africa. In the Caribbean area, where African yams are extensively cultivated, these same Asiatic species are also grown. Yams are thus at the same time both African and non-African domesticates. The domestication of the yam has been described from a global point of view in a previous publication (Alexander and Coursey 1969) where it is shown that different species of *Dioscorea* were brought into cultivation independently in three areas of the world: (1) in Southeast Asia, (2) in West Africa, (3) in pre-Columbian tropical America. Different species were involved in these three areas and thus no single Center of Origin of domestication, in the Vavilovian sense, can be ascribed to the yams.

In view of the complexity of the situation, it may be useful briefly to discuss the botany and taxonomy of the yams before proceeding to the main theme.

BOTANY AND TAXONOMY

The yams we are concerned with here are members of the genus *Dioscorea.* This is the type genus, and also by far the largest genus, of the family Dioscoreaceae. It contains several hundred species which occur throughout the tropics, with a few members in temperate and montane regions. The Dioscoreaceae are themselves the principal family of the order Dioscoreales, recently reestablished by Ayensu (1972), although they were formerly (Burkill 1960; Coursey 1967) classified with the Liliales (Table 1). The Dioscoreales are monocotyledons (although they show many features normally associated with dicotyledons, and some species have a nonemergent second cotyledon) which exhibit a number of primitive features compared with most of the angiosperms, for example their inconspicuous flowers.

The Dioscoreales may well have been among the earliest angiosperms to have evolved, and their original appearance may thus have been in what is now Southeast Asia as early as the late Triassic or early Jurassic, the location and time regarded by Axelrod (1970) as that of the origin of the angiosperms. Origin in this area, though at a rather later date (early Cretaceous) is suggested by Burkill (1960). Though no

Table 1 Classification within the order Dioscoreales (after Ayensu 1972)

Order	Family	Genus
Dioscoreales	Dioscoreaceae	*Avetra*
		Dioscorea
		Rajania
		Stenomeris
		Tamus
	Trichopodiaceae	*Trichopus*
	Roxburghiaceae	*Croomia*
		Stemona
		Stichoneuron

fossil records of the genus are available prior to the Eocene, indirect evidence indicates that ancestral forms of *Dioscorea* had achieved pantropic, if not worldwide, distribution before the end of the Cretaceous. In any case they are widely distributed, especially in the tropical regions of the world, and achieved that distribution long before the advent of man. Fairly early in their evolution in geological time, they were subjected to ecological pressures which resulted in the development of an organ of dormancy (usually a tuber, but a rhizome in some of the more primitive species) and a climbing vine which is almost always of an annual nature.

The plant exists entirely as the dormant subterranean organ through the inclement period of the year which, in the tropics, is equated with the dry season. The substantial reserves of food and water contained in the organ of dormancy predispose the plant to attack by both animals and man. For this reason, most species of *Dioscorea* have some form of protection for their tubers which may take the form of alkaloidal or steroidal toxins, spinous development of the stems or even of the roots, or the habit of burying the organ of dormancy deeply in the ground so as to be inaccessible to rooting animals. For more detailed botanical information reference may be made to Waitt (1963), Coursey (1967), Coursey and Martin (1970), Burkill (1960), and Ayensu (1972).

The genus *Dioscorea* occurs today throughout the tropical regions of the world. There are substantial differences related to separation early in the evolutionary history between the New and Old World species. Within the Old World there are also differences between Africa and Asia; but these are considerably less, reflecting the much more recent evolutionary separation of the species of these two continental areas which is believed to have occurred in the Miocene when desiccation of what is now southwestern Asia was occurring. Old World species, apart from a few aberrant exceptions, have chromosome numbers based on ten, whereas the *Dioscorea* of the New World have chromosome numbers based on nine.

The yams which are of economic importance as food crops today, whether Asian, African, or American, have the following general characteristics: The plant grows during the rainy season as a twining vine which extends often for many meters through trees or undergrowth. In cultivation the vines are usually trained on stakes, strings, or wires. These vines, which are annual, bear racemes of inconspicuous white, greenish, or yellowish flowers; the male and female flowers are always separate and nearly always occur on separate plants. The female flowers are followed by dehiscent trilocular capsules, each loculus containing two seeds which are winged for dispersal by wind. At the end of the season of active growth, i.e. the rains, the vine dies down and the plant persists through the dry season in the form of dormant tubers. It is these tubers, the natural storage organs of the plant which enable it to survive the dry season, that are economically useful to man. In all the edible yams these tubers are annually renewed organs. In other species of *Dioscorea* which have not been used by man as food, the tuber is perennial and becomes larger and progressively more lignified from year to year while, as already mentioned, some primitive *Dioscorea* have rhizomatous organs of dormancy. In modern agricultural practice throughout the world, edible yams are propagated vegetatively by means of tuber cuttings or sets which are either small tubers or fragments of tubers. Millennia of vegetative propagation in cultivation have reduced the sexual fertility of many of the cultivars so that they flower comparatively seldom and set fertile seed even less frequently.

In Table 2 are listed the principal species that have been brought into cultivation by man in the three main areas of the world where yams are cultivated. Numerous other *Dioscorea* have occasionally been utilized as food by man in various parts of the world, but are of much less importance: most of these are discussed to some extent by Coursey (1967).

COURSES TOWARDS DOMESTICATION IN ASIA AND AMERICA

Before considering the processes by which domesticates of the genus *Dioscorea* arose in Africa, it may be well to review what is known from other parts of the world, especially Southeast Asia, a region which has

Table 2. Major food yam species (after Coursey 1967; Alexander and Coursey 1969)

	Africa	Asia	America
Major economic spp.	*D. rotundata* Poir [a b] *D. cayenensis* Lam. [b]	*D. alata* L. [a] *D. esculenta* (Lour.) Burk.	*D. trifida* L. f.
Secondary spp.	*D. bulbifera* L. [c]	*D. bulbifera* L. [c]	*D. convolvulacea* Cham. et Schlecht.
	D. preussii Pax.	*D. hispida* Dennst.	
	D. praehensilis Benth.	*D. pentaphylla* L.	*Rajania cordata* L.
	D. sansibarensis Pax.	*D. nummularia* Lam.	
	D. dumetorum (Knuth) Pax.	*D. opposita* Thunb. [d]	
		D. japonica Thunb. [d]	

[a] These species are true cultigens, unknown in the wild.
[b] Some authors regard *D. rotundata* as only a subspecies of *D. cayenensis* (Note 2).
[c] *D. bulbifera* is the only species common to both Africa and Asia. The African form is, however, quite distinct and is sometimes regarded as a separate species, *D. latifolia* Benth.
[d] These are often together known as *D. batatas* Decne and are temperate species native to China and Japan.

been fairly intensively studied. This area has been regarded by several ethnobotanists since Sauer (1952) as a most important area of plant domestication. It is also the area in which some of the *Dioscorea* species now grown in Africa originated.

The principal species of yam of importance in tropical Southeast Asia and those areas, such as Indonesia and the Pacific, which have acquired their agricultural heritage from Asia are *D. alata* and *D. esculenta*. The origins of these species in cultivation have been discussed in considerable detail by Burkill (1924, 1951). Geographically, the ideas put forward are entirely acceptable, but the comparatively recent chronology, suggesting the beginnings of systematic cultivation little more than 2000 B.P., needs considerable revision: the writer did not appreciate the extreme antiquity of vegetative agriculture in Southeast Asia. Recent archaeological evidence (Chang 1967, 1970; Chang and Stuiver 1966; Gorman 1969) has indicated that non-grain-using Mesolithic cultures, which were related to the Hoabinhian ceramic traditions and possessed some knowledge of cultivation, existed in the region of domestication of these *Dioscorea* species at dates around 10,000 B.P. Harrison (1963) has suggested even greater antiquity for Stone Age cultures which had some form of systematic crop utilization in the area.

The most important of the Asiatic yams, *D. alata*, is a true cultigen, unknown in the wild state. It is believed (Burkill 1924, 1951) to have been derived by human selection from wild forms of common origin with *D. hamiltonii* Hook. and *D. persimilis* Prain et Burk., species whose natural ranges overlap in the northern-central parts of the Malaysian peninsula. As has been pointed out by this author, the yams likely to be most useful to man as food will be those native to regions with a fairly prolonged dry season as these will tend to have the largest tubers — tubers which become dormant most deeply and for the longest period and therefore have the greatest suitability for storage. In comparison, because of their almost continuous period of growth, equatorial *Dioscorea* species have little dormancy and, therefore, have much less tuberous development. In a more recent publication the same author (Burkill 1960) follows Haudricourt and Hedin (1943) and Sauer (1952) in supposing that the original cultivation of vegetatively propagated root crops in this area was undertaken by littoral peoples whose staple economy depended on fishing. This may perhaps be true of the Araceae, such as *Colocasia*, which are adapted to cultivation under extremely moist conditions; but as has been pointed out by Barrau (1965a), the vegecultural civilizations which are based on the Southeast Asian development of cultivation contrast fundamentally the production of such aroid crops under littoral or other moist conditions with the production of yams which are associated more with dry land conditions. The introduction of crops, whether vegetatively propagated or otherwise, into cultivation on such a basis has also been criticized by Heiser (1969). In view of this, and also in view of the facts indicated by Burkill (1924, 1951) that yam cultivation in Southeast Asia tends to be associated with upland rather than littoral or riverain peoples, it could be suggested that yam domestication was originally brought about inland, rather than at waterside areas. However, Chang (1970) considers that the cord-marked Hoabinhian ceramics indicate the association of these cultures with littoral or riverain habitats, and the distribution of archaeological material is certainly suggestive of this.

In a more recent publication, Barrau (1970) draws attention to the observation made by Burkill (1953) of the significance of the ritual protection which is afforded to certain *Dioscorea* by the Andaman Islanders — people who within the ethnographic present were without any conventional form of agriculture. On the basis of this and observations of other practices recorded among preagricultural peoples in the Southeast Asian area and among the Australian aborigines, it was suggested that the cultivation of crops such as yams derived initially from ritual protection afforded by gatherers to wild food plants.

After having been brought into cultivation, this species of yam was carried by man far out into the Pacific by the Polynesian migration, which probably originated in southern China and Indochina about 3500 B.P. (Suggs 1960), and later, around 2000 B.P. or more recently, to Madagascar and the East African littoral.[1] As we have indicated elsewhere (Coursey and Alexander 1968; Alexander and Coursey 1969), there is no reason to suppose that this species traveled across Africa in cultivation, contrary to the opinion expressed by Murdock and others. Its distribution in Africa has been mapped by Prain and Burkill (1939) showing that there are substantial areas in the central parts of the continent where it is not known. It was, however, carried in cultivation to West Africa by the Portuguese at an early date after the paleo-Colonial expansion into the Indian Ocean, as there are definite records of it from São Tomé by approximately the end of the sixteenth century (Burkill 1938).

The other principal Asiatic species, *D. esculenta*, appears to have followed roughly the same path to domestication and, subsequently, in cultivation. However, most varieties being less adapted for storage than *D. alata*, it was not so much favored by sea-going people; though it

[1] So little is known of the prehistory of Madagascar that it is virtually impossible to make any useful statement about the origins of agriculture on the island, whether in connection with yams or other crop plants.

It is generally assumed that the island was uninhabited at the time of the Malaysian colonization ca. 2000 to 1500 B.P. It is clearly established that these settlers carried *D. alata* with them as one of their principal food plants. It was an important crop there in 1516 and in 1638 according to historical evidence and until living memory, although now it is largely displaced by cassava (Burkill 1951). It is likely that *D. esculenta* and the Asiatic form of *D. bulbifera* were also brought to Madagascar from Asia.

The indigenous flora of Madagascar is in many ways distinct from that of continental Africa. In particular, the genus *Dioscorea* in Madagascar contains a substantial number of species unknown elsewhere (Jumelle 1922; Jumelle and Perrier de la Bathie 1910; Perrier de la Bathie 1925), and many were formerly used as food. Although some were highly esteemed, none appears to have been greatly ennobled in cultivation, and most retain deeply burying tuber forms. As in mainland Africa, many species are toxic but can be rendered edible by maceration and soaking.

Some of the most important indigenous species are: *D. analalavensis* Jum. et Perr.; *D. antaly* Jum. et Perr.; *D. bemandry* Jum. et Perr.; *D. mamillata* Jum. et Perr; *D. ovinala* Baker; *D. soso* Jum. et Perr. The last two of these were formerly most favored, being nontoxic and of good flavor. The island is also within the range of the African form of *D. bulbifera*.

possibly reached Madagascar at an early date with *D. alata*, it was not introduced in substantial quantities to Africa until late in the Colonial era (Miège 1948).

Various other species of yams of lesser importance in Asia have been considered by Barrau (1965a, 1965b, 1970) and by Haudricourt (1962, 1964).

Although the genus is more widely speciated in tropical America than in any part of the Old World, few of the American *Dioscorea* attained any great importance as crop plants in pre-Columbian America. However, a number of species (notably *D. trifida*) were utilized by Amerindians (Chevalier 1946). This comparative neglect of the genus as sources of food by the Amerindians is probably associated with the abundance of alternative root and tuber crops in the New World (Hawkes 1970), especially cassava and sweet potatoes which are more ecologically flexible and less seasonally yielding than most of the *Dioscorea.* Most of the yams cultivated in tropical America today are of Asiatic or West African origin. Although *D. trifida* is still grown to some extent and is greatly favored, it is regarded more as a vegetable relish than as a staple.

As has been pointed out by Burkill (1960), there has been a general east-to-west movement of the yams in domestication. Thus, Asiatic yams have been transferred in cultivation to both Africa and the New World, African species also being taken to the New World; but there has been little movement in cultivation in the reverse direction. The statement that the American *D. convolvulacea* has been taken in cultivation to West Africa (Dalziel 1937) has not been substantiated. It is believed that *D. trifida* has been grown on a small scale in Ceylon (Waitt 1963), but this is comparatively insignificant. African and American yams have recently been cultivated to a limited extent in New Caledonia and the New Hebrides (Bourret 1972).

COURSES TOWARDS DOMESTICATION IN AFRICA

The Indigenous Origin of the Domesticates

It has already been indicated that the genus *Dioscorea* was of pantropic distribution long before the advent of man, or even of the primates, and that by the Miocene, at the latest, the African members of the genus were isolated genetically from those of the New World and Asia — the desert areas of Arabia and southwestern Asia forming as effective a barrier as the Atlantic Ocean (Burkill 1960).

The majority of the yams grown in Africa today are improved or selected forms of recognizable African species which are known in the wild state in that continent and nowhere else. Asiatic species, mainly *D. alata*, but also to a lesser extent the Asiatic form of *D. bulbifera* and to a much lesser degree *D. esculenta*, are grown, but there is no evidence to suggest that these reached East Africa before the Indo-Malaysian contacts around 2000 B.P. or West Africa prior to paleo-Colonial Iberian contacts later than 500 B.P. This, in spite of such statements as those of Chevalier (1909) that "elle parait cultivée en Afrique depuis une très haute antiquité," or, more recently (1936), "les Noirs, lors de leur migration vers le continent Africain, apportaient avec eux . . . les Ignames de cette espèce" referring to *D. alata*. The range of cultivars of these species found in Africa is extremely limited, compared with what is known in Southeast Asia or the Pacific. The only African cultivated yam unknown in the wild except as an escape is *D. rotundata*, which is a true cultigen, and even this is closely related to known wild African species. It is clearly of African affinity, being so close to *D. cayenensis* that it is sometimes regarded as a subspecies.[2] Yam domes-

[2] A word is needed here on the taxonomic history of the main West African yams, *D. rotundata* and *D. cayenensis*. Confusion initially arose from the unfortunate coincidence that both species were originally described botanically from cultivated material being grown in tropical America, that is, in locations and ecologies remote from their natural habitats. The former species was rather incompletely described by Poiret from Jamaican material in 1813 and the latter from material in Guiana (the specific is derived from the town of Cayenne) by Lamarck in 1789. Subsequently, in 1864, *D. rotundata* was reduced by Grisebach to subspecific status within *D. cayenensis*. This reduction was accepted by Prain and Burkill (1919) and has subsequently been maintained by Francophone writers such as Chevalier (1936) and Miège (1952, 1969). French authors, when referring to *D. cayenensis*, may thus often be discussing material that Anglophone authors would know as *D. rotundata*. In another publication (Burkill 1921), *D. rotundata* was restored to specific status and its identity with the white Guinea yam established, the taxon *D. cayenensis* being restricted to the yellow yam, on the basis of examinations of material in experimental cultivation in Singapore. In his major (1939) study of the African *Dioscorea*, Burkill discusses the species under the general heading of *D. cayenensis* although in his final major work (1960) he again refers to it as a separate species. This separation has also been adopted by Dalziel (1937) and has been fairly generally accepted by Anglophone workers in West Africa. It should be pointed out however that a distinction based merely on the color of the tuber flesh is not reliable as some yellow-fleshed forms of *D. rotundata* and some almost white-fleshed forms of *D. cayenensis* exist. The entire spectrum of cultivated forms as grown in the West Indies has been grouped under *D. occidentalis* Knuth, but this taxon is not valid. Recently, Ayensu (1970) has shown that there are differences in the vascular anatomy of cultivated material of the two types and considers that this warrants a formal separation. Biochemical differences involving the nature of the polyphenolics present in cultivated forms have also been pointed out by Bate-Smith (1968).

Although *D. cayenensis sensu strictu* is widespread in the wild state in West Africa and other parts of the continent, *D. rotundata* appears to be a true cultigen,

tication in Africa depended, therefore, upon indigenous yam species and not upon plant introduction. Similarly, in view of what is now accepted as to the history of man in Africa (G. Clark 1969; J. Clark 1970; Shinnie 1971), it need not initially have depended upon external cultural contacts, although ideas derived from the grain-based agriculture of southwestern Asia influenced the later stages of its progress (J. Clark 1962; Alexander and Coursey 1969). To quote from Burkill (1939) "To the African himself is entirely due the invention of *D. cayenensis* as a crop plant."

Geographical Centers of African Yam Domestication

Wild African *Dioscorea* which are botanically close to the modern cultivated forms are widely distributed in the continent between the Sahara and the arid zones of southern Africa. Maps of the distribution of some of the principal species are given by Burkill (1960). Apart from some differentiation between high-rainfall-adapted forest species and others adapted to drier conditions, there is no very great localization within this very large area.

---

unknown in the wild state like the Asiatic *Dioscorea alata* which it closely resembles. Similarly, it must be presumed to be of hybrid origin. The great similarity in tuber form between some cultivars of *D. alata* and some cultivars of *D. rotundata* has been a further cause of confusion (the growing plants can be readily distinguished by the alate stems of the former and the spinous stems of the latter) as has the fact that both are often referred to simply as "white yam."

Attention needs to be paid to an early and frequently overlooked work of Chevalier (1909) in which a relationship between cultivated yams of the *D. rotundata* type of the West African savanna and the wild species *D. praehensilis* is indicated. In his major African (1939) work Burkill also indicates the probability of *D. rotundata* being a hybrid form between *D. cayenensis* and *D. praehensilis* or perhaps *D. abyssinica* Hochst.

Today, *D. rotundata* is by far the most important of the African food yams, and it exists in a profusion of cultivars, most of which have never been properly documented. However, a substantial number of Nigerian cultivars have been described by Waitt (1965) and some others from the Ivory Coast by Miège (1952). In situations such as this where a large number of vegetatively propagated clonal cultivars exist which have arisen by spontaneous processes in cultivation, it is questionable whether strict Linnaean concepts of taxonomy can be applied. The classificatory approaches adopted for two other food crops which are of high antiquity in vegetative cultivation — that of Simmonds (1966) for the banana or the statistical taximetric approach used by Rogers (1967) for cassava — may well be appropriate. On this philosophy perhaps the most satisfactory way of considering the cultivated forms of the Guinea yams is to regard them simply as members of the *rotundata/cayenensis* group without commitment as to whether this currently represents one or two species, but acknowledging that at least two wild species have contributed

Nevertheless, at the present time, within the ethnographic present, and within the few hundred years that written history has existed in most of Africa, the use of cultivated yams as the principal food crop has been restricted to a comparatively limited part of Africa. This is the area of West Africa between the Bandama River of the central Ivory Coast in the west and the Cameroun mountains in the east, and from the sea, or the coastal lagoons or swamps in the south to the northern climatic limit of yam cultivation (roughly, the 800 millimeter isohyet). This is the ethnobotanical domain originally described by Miège (1954) as "la civilization de l'igname" in contrast to "la civilization du riz" to the west where the upland rice *Oryza glaberrima* Stapf. was traditionally the main nutritional basis of the diet. The concept of the "yam zone" has been investigated further by the present author (Coursey 1965, 1966, 1967; Alexander and Coursey 1969; Coursey and Coursey 1971; Ayensu and Coursey 1972), as has the association of the zone with ethnic boundaries, with the area occupied by people speaking languages of the eastern Kwa linguistic group (Murdock 1959), and with the highest indigenous cultures of the forest areas of Africa, such as the Akan states, Ife, Benin, and Igbo Ukwu (see Map 1). Today, this comparatively limited area of Africa produces more than ninety percent of the yams grown in the continent. This may in part be a reflection of the high population densities in much of the yam zone which, in turn, may well be associated with a long tradition of yam-based agriculture (Shaw 1976). The fact remains that outside the yam zone, yams are proportionately quite minor crops.

On the basis of present-day distribution of cultivation, the writer has earlier (Coursey 1967) suggested a Center of Origin of yam cultivation, in the Vavilovian sense, "on the fringe of the West African forest belt, either within the savannah, or possibly in the Dahomey gap" and that there "may have been a subsidiary centre nearer or in the Congo basin." The first and more important of these would at least approximately

to their ancestry. The contributions of the two (or more) wild species vary from one cultivar to another so that the whole corpus of cultivated material represents in fact a spectrum of forms ranging at one extreme from selected forms of *D. cayenensis* sensu strictu to something approaching pure, but again selected, *D. praehensilis* at the other extreme. The more that the former species has contributed to the ancestry of a particular cultivar, the more it is adapted to forest rather than savanna conditions, that is, to a short dry season and a longer period of vegetative growth; the converse is also true. Further experimental work on this hypothesis is needed, however, in the form of chemotaxonomic studies on a large number of the cultivated forms, preferably in conjunction with work on the photoperiodic response of the same cultivars which may be indicative of their latitude of origin (Ayensu and Coursey 1972).

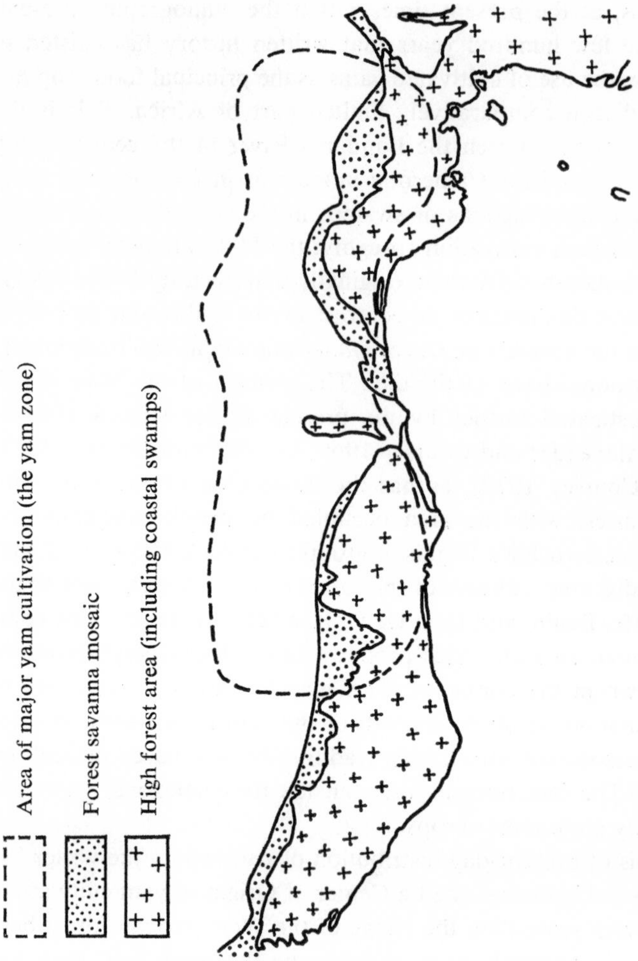

Map 1. Yam cultivation on the West Coast of Africa

coincide with the West African center proposed for various other African crops (Murdock 1959; Wrigley 1960; Portères 1962; Morgan 1962). No comment on the geographical Centers of Origin of yam cultivation in Africa had been made by either Vavilov or de Candolle.

It has been proposed recently (Harlan 1971) that the concept of a geographically compact Center of Origin is only applicable to grain-crop and similar domesticates of the temperate or subtropical regions and that the vegetatively-propagated crop plants of the humid tropical or equatorial regions were domesticated over much larger, diffuse areas or "noncenters." The African yams, on the basis of this concept, originated in cultivation merely somewhere within the African "noncenter."

The use of yams as food is, to a limited extent, certainly a feature of most of the area covered by Harlan's African "noncenter," but the intense concentration of the cultivation of yams, especially of the *rotundata/cayenensis* group, in the West African yam zone needs some further explanation. The use of the more highly ennobled cultivars towards the *rotundata* end of the hybrid spectrum (cf. Note 2) is largely confined to this part of Africa. These yams, in common with other members of the section Enantiophyllum of *Dioscorea*, are nontoxic; the wild forms have tubers which penetrate deeply into the ground and also often have spinous stems, which protect the plants from attack by rooting animals. Most of the yams commonly used in other parts of Africa (apart from recent non-African introductions) belong to other sections — for example *D. dumetorum*, Lasiophyton; *D. preussii*, Macrocarpeae; *D. bulbifera*, Opsophyton; and *D. sansibarensis*, Macroura — which secrete alkaloidal or steroidal toxins to a greater or lesser extent. Such toxins are comparatively simply removed by extraction of water — usually the running water of a stream, after some form of grating, shredding, or slicing — but nevertheless need the conscious application of a detoxification process. It may well be that there is a contrast between separate courses towards domestication that were followed more widely by the toxic yams and the nontoxic Enantiophyllum yams in a more restricted area.

In the case of the *rotundata/cayenensis* group of yams, although it may be incorrect to define a strictly Vavilovian Center of Origin of cultivation, progress towards domestication, the formation and ennoblement of clonal vegetative cultivars, and the emergence of cultigens appear to have taken place in a fairly limited area. If it is accepted that the yams of this group are of hybrid origin, with both forest species (*D. cayenensis* sensu strictu) and savanna species (*D. praehensilis* and/or *D. abyssinica*) contributing to their ancestry, they could only have arisen at the ecotone between forest and savanna, along with what could be termed as "Axis of Origin" generally running in an east to west direction, but dipping southward in the Dahomey Gap.[3]

The use of other species of yam is fairly well diffused over the whole of the African "noncenter," but nowhere else are they of such importance. It has been suggested on linguistic grounds that the cultivation of yams was formerly more widespread, at least in East Africa, and that they have been displaced by other crops, but the evidence is by no means clear (Posnansky 1968; Coursey 1969). It is certain, however, that in times of famine even the most highly toxic yams are used as emergency foods in many parts of Africa, even where yams are not normally cultivated today (Burkill 1939; Coursey 1967). The importance of yams in African cultural history appears, however, to be greatest in West Africa, and most of the discussion here refers to this area.

The Antiquity of Yam Domestication in Africa

Most of what can be said chronologically concerning the domestication of yams in Africa is necessarily highly speculative in view of the limited archaeological data that are available in the relevant parts of Africa, especially with regard to pre-Iron Age times. Not only has comparatively little systematic excavation been undertaken, but both soil and climate are unfavorable to the preservation of archaeological material; and neither parts of yam plants themselves, nor the wooden digging sticks that even today are often used in their cultivation, are likely to be preserved (Alexander 1970; Posnansky 1969).

Until recently, a general impression existed that all African agriculture was fairly recent and was derived largely from external influence.

[3] It has been suggested (Shaw 1976) that the dense populations in the south-eastern parts of the yam zone — approximately the present-day Igbo-speaking areas — are associated with a high antiquity of controlled yam and oil palm exploitation in those areas. Further, there are some rather tenuous indications that at the other end of the zone the western limit of intensive yam cultivation has been moving further westward in comparatively recent times (less than 1000 B.P.) into the area where rice is the dominant staple. It has been pointed out by Harris (1972) that vegecultural systems do not normally expand at the expense of grain-based cultures.

Taken together, these considerations would be consistent with the concept that the earliest domestication of yams occurred at the eastern end of the forest-savanna axis of West Africa rather than elsewhere. It must be emphasized, however, that this is highly speculative and is contrary to the ideas on population movements in West Africa put forward by Flight (1976).

It has been suggested that penetration of the forest zone for permanent settlement was impossible before the introduction of iron tools (J. Clark 1962), and even that modern human populations reached the coastal areas of West Africa only within the last millennium (Ward 1969). It is now becoming established, however, that there is some continuity of cultural tradition in the forest areas of West Africa extending back at least to the Mesolithic (Willett 1971; Ozanne 1971), the introduction of iron around 2500 to 2000 B.P. merely rendering the process of forest clearing more efficacious. It has been established (Gray 1962) that African Neolithic stone axes are quite effective tools for felling moderate-sized trees, while larger areas could be cleared by firing. Evidence from other parts of the humid tropics, such as New Guinea (Powell 1970), shows that forests were cleared effectively by people with only stone tools and fire at least 5000 B.P. Yam cultivation on a systematic basis obviously antedates the historic period on the West African coast. One of the earliest Iberian explorers (Pacheco Pereira 1505) mentions not only the cultivation of yams at various points, but an established trade in yams between Bonny in the eastern Niger delta and yam-growing areas "hundred of leagues" inland at the time of his visits, nearly 500 B.P. From then on there are frequent references to yams by European visitors to West Africa, many of whom emphasize the importance of the crop. The prohibition on the use of iron tools at certain rituals associated with yam cultivation is at least suggestive that it antedates the introduction of iron, but as the West African Iron Age is little more than 2,000 years old, this suggestion provides no indication of a very high antiquity of yam domestication. Indeed, it has been suggested (Baker 1962) that the yams "need not be assumed to have any great antiquity as cultivated plants." A conventional approach based on the views of J. Clark (1962, 1964) is that cultural diffusion from southwestern Asia via Egypt and the Sudan introduced grain-crop agriculture to the West African savanna, sorghum and millet replacing the wheat and barley of Asia and Egypt. The concept of agriculture was then transmitted to hunter-gatherers already inhabiting the northern fringes of the forest, who adopted yams and other tubers (such as *Solenostemon (Coleus), Anchomanes,* and *Sphenostylis*) into cultivation rather than grains. This contact would be dated around 5000 to 4000 B.P.

There is little doubt that such culture contacts and the introduction of iron tools two or three thousand years later played a major part in the development of yam cultivation in West Africa to its present level of sophistication. Somewhat comparable cultural interactions appear to have taken place in all three main areas of the world where yams are cultivated, at approximately the same time, 5000 to 4000 B.P. (Alexander and Coursey 1969).

These interactions can be regarded, of course, as taking place between the differing cultures of Harlan's "noncenters" with their corresponding centers. It has already been seen that in the Southeast Asian "noncenter" there is direct archaeological evidence for Mesolithic cultures based on some systematically controlled exploitation of economic plants. Thus, prior to cultural interactions with grain-crop agriculturalists, the inhabitants of the "noncenter" had progressed substantially beyond the basic hunter-gatherer level towards a symbiotic relationship with their food plants. Even in the absence of archaeological evidence, this is a more satisfactory hypothesis than one based on contact between relatively advanced agriculturalists and primitive hunter-gatherers. Most historic experience of such contacts indicates that they are associated with such severe cultural shock as to lead to the destruction or near destruction of the latter groups or to their assimilation almost without trace, whereas, in fact, in both Asia and Africa high cultures based on vegeculture have emerged (Coursey 1972). Although there is, at present, no clear evidence in Africa of Mesolithic horticultural civilizations comparable to those discussed by Chang (1970) in Asia, similar considerations may well apply, and African yam cultivation can be accepted as having its origins in a culture that developed initially without significant contacts from outside the "noncenter."

In the case of Southeast Asia, Barrau (1970) relates the emergence of symbiotic relationships between man and plant to religiously-sanctioned concepts of protection of edible wild plants, citing Burkill's discussion (1953) of the Andamanese ritual control of the collection of their main food yam, *D. glabra* Roxb., and other important vegetable foods from the wild. These ritual sanctions served to encode culturally the empirically acquired knowledge of the factors necessary to ensure the survival of the food plant species, while continuing to utilize it as a source of human food.

We have used an approach which is virtually identical, even in making reference to Burkill's concepts (1953), in an analysis of the West African New Yam Festival (Coursey and Coursey 1971). This festival is, or was within living memory, the major socioreligious event in the year in the West African yam zone, being the equivalent at once of the New Year and the Harvest Festival in the grain-crop-oriented cultures of temperate western Eurasia. It was held to mark the time when yams of the new crop could first be eaten, that is, the end of the period of ritual prohibition of their consumption, that period which corresponds to the phase of active growth of the yam plant during which it is highly susceptible to damage and, at the same time, would give only a very small yield of tubers. We have suggested that it is a social survival from extremely remote times when the inhabitants of the area were at the gathering stage of development but were beginning to develop some concept of protecting their wild food resources by ritual sanctions comparable to those of the Southeast Asian region (Barrau 1970; Coursey and Coursey 1971). It was also suggested that this concept of protection as a first phase of domestication might date back as far as the end of the terminal Pleistocene, when the contraction of the habitable environment, caused by the expansion of the Sahara, was placing a strain on the reserves of wild vegetable foods — of which yams would have been a most important element.[4]

There is, to date, no rigorous archaeological proof for this hypothesis, but what evidence is available is not inconsistent. Through much of the Congo basin and West Africa, artifacts are found which are described as hoes and as being suitable for the digging of yams and similar subterranean plant materials (Davies 1960, 1967, 1968) deriving from the paleolithic Sangoan and Lupemban cultures, dating from 40,000 B.P. or even earlier.

Evidence is now beginning to appear (Willett 1971) for the development of microlithic industries within the yam zone at dates around 10,000 B.P. — industries which are indicative of an increasing degree of cultural sophistication. Most of the artifactual material found so far is associated with hunting rather than plant-food-collecting activities, but the same applies to the material possessions of hunter-gatherer cultures within historic times, even though such people usually derive a substantial part of their nutrition from vegetable foods.

The Process of Domestication of Yams in Africa

In discussing the antiquity of yam utilization in Africa, we have already

[4] The concepts put forward here were originally developed on the basis of the assumption that the initial stimulus towards domestication of yams in West Africa was provided by the increasing desiccation of the environment at the close of a pluvial period, and the corresponding southward shift of the desert-savanna and savanna-forest ecotones. However, it should be pointed out that not dissimilar pressures on human populations could alternatively have arisen from the northward spread of the forest into the previously inhabited savanna at the onset of a pluvial. Recently developed ideas on the pluvial history of West Africa (van Zinderen Bakker 1976) need to be considered in this content. The rest of the thesis presented here, however, remains unchanged by this alternative concept.

given some indication of the processes involved in the early stages of domestication. As has been indicated by Harris (1967, 1969, 1972), the domestication of vegetatively propagated crops such as yams should not be regarded as a sudden cultural change comparable to the "Neolithic Revolution" of Southwest Asia (Childe 1951, 1952), but rather as a gradual evolutionary process.[5] More detailed examination of this process indicates that it can be divided into the following phases:

1. Hunter-gatherer man from the earliest times, or at least after he had established the controlled use of fire (before 60,000 B.P.), utilized yams of many species collected from the wild in those parts of Africa where they grow.
2. In the period of the Sangoan and Lupemban paleolithic industries (45,000 to 15,000 B.P.), large stone hoes or picks were developed, apparently especially for the excavation of hypogeous plant foods including yams.
3. During this period the first concepts of protecting wild food resources by ritual or other sanctions started to develop. It should be noted that even preagricultural peoples, such as the present-day Bushmen (Schapera 1930), have concepts of protection of wild plant food resources, some of which are systematized in magico-religious concepts. Further, it is established (Campbell 1966) that even Neanderthal man had begun to sublimate individual demands to the needs of the community, again using ritual sanctions as regulators of individual behavior.
4. Beginning around 11,000 B.P., the evidence from Lake Chad (van

[5] In the case of the cereal crops the first major step in the domestication process can simply be identified with a genetic factor – the appearance of th nonshattering rachis. No such simple distinction can be made in the case of the yams. It must also be borne in mind that the domestication process must be much more gradual than with the seed propagated crops, as sexual reproduction is only involved in the initial stages when the plant is still close to the wild form. Once a particular yam has been taken into domestication, it is propagated entirely clonally, and the opportunity for sexual recombination rarely if ever takes place. All plants of a single yam clone are essentially isolated fragments of the same individual plant and should therefore be genetically identical. It is well known, however, that yams are extremely plastic in cultivation, and it is possible that somatic mutation plays a part in this. The only criteria of domestication that can so far be suggested for the yams are: (1) the partial or complete loss of the natural defence mechanisms — toxicity, spinous development of stem or root, or deep-burying habit in the tuber; (2) loss of sexual fertility; and (3) a high degree of polyploidy. None of these, however, are entirely satisfactory. The degree of ploidy has not yet been studied in a sufficient variety of cultivated forms for definitive statements to be made with confidence, although very high polyploids are known. The loss of sexual fertility may be at least in part associated with the juvenility of form that is artifically maintained by the practice of continuous vegetative propagation from small tuber fragments.

Zinderen Bakker 1976) suggests that there may have been a contraction of the West African forest and savanna environments which was favorable both to man and yams. At about the same time the diffusion of more modern types of man (the proto-Negro) of the Kanjeran genetic stock into the West African savanna began (Brothwell 1963). These new human types were associated with the appearance of microlithic industries which may be regarded as indicative of the emergence of a more sophisticated level of interaction between man and his environment (but see Note 4).

5. From the human point of view this process of interaction involved the increasing regularization of the exploitation of plant food resources. At the same time, man was modifying the natural ecosystem and thereby creating new ecological niches, prominent among which would have been middens and the cleared areas around habitations — situations comparable to the "dump-heaps" proposed by Anderson (1952) as the sites of many early plant domestications. In these artifactual environments and, especially, subject to the interest and protection of man, spontaneous hybrid or mutant plant forms were able to survive which would have been eliminated by natural selection processes in the undisturbed natural environment. This was of special relevance in the case of the nontoxic Enantiophyllum yams, ancestral to the yams cultivated today in West Africa. The human populations using wild or semiwild yams originally lived mainly on the savanna between the forest and the Sahara; as this environment contracted and, at the same time, the human populations increased, they increasingly penetrated the forest fringes. Such clearings provided suitable locations for interspecific crossing between savanna species — *D. praehensilis* and *D. abyssinica* — and the forest *D. cayenensis* and for the survival, under protection, of forms superior to both as food plants but less adapted to survival in the wild — the ancestral *D. rotundata.* A parallel exists between this concept of a major step towards domestication occurring as part of human penetration of a nonoptimal environment and the Flannery-Binford model that has been used (Wright 1971) in connection with cereal domestication in southwestern Asia (Shaw 1976).

6. As the greater control of food resources permitted the further expansion of human populations and, simultaneously, as the move into the less congenial forest environment encouraged closer association for mutual protection within a human group, individual human settlements tended to increase in size. This generated further needs for regular food supplies concentrated into limited localities, and the domestication process moved forward from the simple, ritual protection of natural

"stands" of food plants (some of which were already in man-created ecological niches such as middens and disturbed ground) to the removal of wild plants to more convenient, accessible, or advantageous locations in or near settlements. Such an operation has actually been observed within the ethnographic present (Chevalier 1936) with *D. dumetorum* in the Ubangui-Shari: plants were collected for food from the wild, and those not immediately required were replanted near the settlements. This process was described as "protoculture."

7. With increasing regularization of production, yams, by now of partially ennobled forms, became capable of supplying needs sometimes in excess of immediate requirements. The yam tuber, as the dormant phase of the entire plant, is inherently well adapted for storage, and tubers could therefore be reserved for future use. Once the concept of planting had been developed in connection with removal of wild plants to better locations, the idea of replanting a stored tuber, which had begun to sprout at the end of the endogenous period of dormancy, would not be a difficult one to develop.

8. By 5000 to 4000 B.P., after an intervening pluvial period, another period of desiccation occurred causing further population movements out of the Sahara belt. These were now Neolithic grain-crop agriculturalists, already influenced by Southwest Asian cultural patterns. Interaction between these peoples and the yam "protoculturalists," who were fairly sophisticated by now, was possible on a basis of approximate equality, and cross-fertilization of ideas took place leading eventually to the development of a yam-based agriculture in something approaching the present form.

9. With the introduction of iron-working into West Africa around 2500 B.P., penetration deeper into the forest was facilitated. As this human penetration into increasingly humid areas progressed, yams were increasingly favored ecologically at the expense of grain crops. The yam-using ethnic groups were thus able to evolve to higher cultural levels as they had a more adequate, reliable, and generally superior nutritional basis. The more complex societies thus developing, with varying degrees of socioeconomic specialization within a culture, gave opportunities for: increased conscious development of yam-growing practices; the elaboration of associated philosophical notions, enriching the nonmaterial culture; further ennoblement of cultivars; and the exchange of cultivars between groups, facilitating the spread of optimal forms.

SYNTHESIS

The domestication of the yam in Africa may thus be viewed as an essentially indigenous process based on wild African species. Only in its later stages was it influenced by external factors through cultural interactions — Southwest Asian Neolithic culture, the use of iron tools, and the introduction of non-African genetic material.

The initial moves towards domestication did not consist of any traumatic changes comparable to the "Neolithic Revolution" of Southwest Asia but rather of the gradual evolution of a symbiotic relationship between man and yam. At the same time this involved a realization of the physiological nature of the yam plant as needing protection from exploitation at certain stages of its growth cycle and an increasing communalization of control over plant food resources, subordinating immediate individual needs to long-term social ones. These two factors were eventually encoded into a complex of ritual socioreligious sanctions which regulated the behavior of man towards the yam plant in such a way as to facilitate the emergence of stable cultivars and cultigens. A "protocultural" system was elaborated capable of assimilating major external cultural influences when these occurred. The consequence was a complete agricultural complex.

These crucial processes occurred along an axis at the forest-savanna ecotone in the eastern part of West Africa corresponding to the present day "yam zone." It is suggested that the emergence of this symbiotic relationship is chronologically associated with the appearance of microlithic industries in a dry phase ca. 10,000 B.P. This crucial stage in the interrelationship of man and yam could thus be linked with the beginnings of the evolution and diversification of the ancestors of the Negro races.

REFERENCES

ALEXANDER, J.

1970 "The domestication of yams: a multidisciplinary approach," in *Science and archaeology*. Edited by D. R. Brothwell and E. Higgs. London: Thames and Hudson.

ALEXANDER, J., D. G. COURSEY

1969 "The domestication of the yams," in *The domestication and exploitation of plants and animals*. Edited by P. J. Ucko and G. W. Dimbleby. London: Duckworth.

ANDERSON, E.

1952 *Plants, man and life*. Boston: Little, Brown.

AXELROD, D. I.
1970 Mesozoic paleogeography and early angiosperm history. *Botany Review* 36(3):277–319.

AYENSU, E. S.
1970 Comparative anatomy of *Dioscorea rotundata* Poir and *Dioscorea cayenensis* Lamk. *Biol. J. Linn. Soc.*, supplement one, 63:127–136. 136.
1972 *Anatomy of the Monocotyledons*, volume six: *Dioscoreales*. Edited by C. R. Metcalfe. Oxford: Clarendon Press.

AYENSU, E. S., D. G. COURSEY
1972 Guinea yams. *Economic Botany* 26(4):301–318.

BAKER, H. G.
1962 Comments on the thesis that there was a major centre of plant domestication near the headwaters of the River Niger. *Journal of African History* 3(2):229–233.

BARRAU, J.
1965a L'humide et le sec. *J. Polynesian Soc.* 74(3):329–346.
1965b Histoire et préhistoire horticoles de l'Océanie tropicale. *J. Soc. Océanistes* 21(21):55–78.
1970 La région indo-pacifique comme centre de mise en culture et de domestication des végétaux. *J. Agric. Trop. Bot. Appl.* 17(12):487–504.

BATE-SMITH, E. C.
1968 The phenolic constituents of plants and heir taxonomic significance. *J. Linn. Soc. (Bot.)* 60(383):325–356.

BOURRET, DOMINIQUE
1972 Private communication from ORSTOM, New Caledonia.

BROTHWELL, D. R.
1963 Evidence of early population change in central and southern Africa: doubts and problems. *Man* 63(132):101–104.

BURKILL, I. H.
1921 The correct botanic names for the white and yellow Guinea yams. *Gdn's Bull., Straits Settl.* 2(12):438–441.
1924 A list of oriental vernacular names of the genus *Dioscorea. Gdn's Bull. Straits Settl.* 3(4/6):121–244.
1938 The contact of the Portuguese with African food plants which gave words such as "yam" to European languages. *Proc. Linn. Soc.*, London 150(2):84–95.
1939 Notes on the genus *Dioscorea* in the Belgian Congo. *Bull. Jard. bot. Etat. Brux.* 15(4):345–392.
1951 The rise and decline of the greater yam in the service of man. *Advmt. Sci.*, London 7(28):443–448.
1953 Habits of man and the history of cultivated plants in the Old World. *Proc. Linn. Soc.*, London 164(1):12–42.
1960 The organography and the evolution of the Dioscoreaceae, the family of the yams. *J. Linn. Soc. (Bot.)* 56(367):319–412.

CAMPBELL, B. G.
1966 *Human evolution: an introduction to man's adaptations.* Chicago: Aldine Press.

CHANG, K-C.
1967 The Yale expedition to Taiwan and the South-East Asian horticultural evolution. *Discovery* 2(2):3–10.
1970 The beginnings of agriculture in the Far East. *Antiquity* 44:175–185.

CHANG, K-C., M. STUIVER
1966 Recent advances in the prehistoric archaeology of Formosa. *Proc. Natn. Acad. Sci. USA* 55:539–543.

CHEVALIER, A.
1909 Sur les Dioscoréas cultivés en Afrique tropicale et sur un cas de sélection naturelle relatif à une espècce spontanée dans la forêt vierge. *C.r. Hebd. Acad. Sci., Paris* 149(15):610–612.
1936 Contrbiution à l'étude de quelques espèces africains du genre *Dioscoréa. Bull. Mus. Natn. Hist. Nat. Paris,* second series 8(6): 520–551.
1946 Nouvelles recherches sur les ignames ccultivées. *Revue Int. Bot. Appl. Agric. Trop.* 26(279/280):26–31.

CHILDE, V. G.
1951 *Man makes himself.* New York: Mentor Books.
1952 *New light on the most ancient East.* London: Routledge and Kegan Paul.

CLARK, G.
1969 *World prehistory: a new outline.* Cambridge: Cambridge University Press.

CLARK, J. D.
1962 The spread of food production in sub-Saharan Africa. *Journal of African History* 3(2):211–228.
1964 The prehistoric origins of African agriculture. *Journal of African History* 5(2):161–183.
1970 *The prehistory of Africa.* London: Thames and Hudson.

COURSEY, D. G.
1965 The role of yams in West African food economies. *World Crops* 17(2):74–82.
1966 The cultivation and use of yams in West Africa. *Ghana Notes and Queries* (9):45–54.
1967 *Yams.* London: Longmans Green.
1969 Yams in East Africa. *Uganda Journal* 3(1):86.
1972 The civilizations of the yams. *Archeol. Phys. Anthropol., Oceania* 7(3):215–233.

COURSEY, D. G., J. ALEXANDER
1968 African agricultural patterns and the sickle cell. *Science* 160 (3835):1474–1475.

COURSEY, D. G., CELIA K. COURSEY
1971 The New Yam Festivals of West Africa. *Anthropos* 66:444–484.

COURSEY, D. G., F. W. MARTIN
1970 The past and future of yams as crop plants. *Proc. 2nd. Int. Symp. Trop. Root Crops, Hawaii* 1:87–93, 99–101.

DALZIEL, J. M.
1937 *The useful plants of West Tropical Africa.* London: Crown Agents.

DAVIES, O.
1960 The neolithic revolution in tropical Africa. *Trans. Hist. Soc., Ghana* 4(2):14–20.
1967 *West Africa before the Europeans*. London: Methuen.
1968 The origins of agriculture in West Africa. *Current Anthropology* 9(5):479–482.

DUMONT, R.
1966 *False start in Africa*. London: Deutsch.

FLIGHT, COLIN
1976 "The Kintampo culture and its place in the economic prehistory of West Africa," in *Origins of African plant domestication*. Edited by Jack R. Harlan. World Anthropology. The Hague: Mouton.

GORMAN, C. F.
1969 Hoabinhian: a pebble-tool complex with early plant associations in South East Asia. *Science* 163(3868):671–673.

GRAY, R.
1962 A report on the conference. *Journal of African History* 3(2):195–209.

HARLAN, J.
1971 Agricultural origins: centres and noncentres. *Science* 154(4008): 468–474.

HARRIS, D. R.
1967 New light on plant domestication and the origins of agriculture. *Geogrl. Rev*. 57(1):90–107.
1969 "Agricultural systems, ecosystems and the origins of agriculture," in *The domestication and exploitation of plants and animals*. Edited by P. J. Ucko and G. W. Dimbleby. London: Duckworth.
1972 The origins of agriculture in the tropics. *American Scientist* 60(2):180–193.

HARRISON, T.
1963 100,000 years of Stone-Age culture in Borneo. *J. Roy. Soc. Arts* 112(5091):174–191.

HAUDRICOURT, A. G.
1962 Domestication des animaux, culture des plantes et civilization d'autrui. *L'Homme* 2:40–50.
1964 Nature et culture dans la civilization de l'igname, origine des clones et des clans. *L'Homme* 4:93–104.

HAUDRICOURT, A. G., L. HEDIN
1943 *L'Homme et les plantes cultivées*. Paris: Libraire Gallimead.

HAVINDEN, M. A.
1970 The history of crop cultivation in West Africa. *Econ. Hist. Rev*. 23(3):532–555.

HAWKES, J. G.
1970 The origin of agriculture. *Econ. Bot*. 24(2):131–133.

HEISER, C. B.
1969 Some considerations on early plant domestication. *BioScience* 19(3):228–231.

JUMELLE, H.
1922 Ignames sauvages et ignames cultivées à Madagascar. *Revue Int. Bot. Appl. Agric. Trop.* 2(9):193–197.

JUMELLE, H., H. PERRIER DE LA BATHIE
1910 Fragments biologiques de la flore de Madagascar. *Ann. Mus. Colon. Marseille,* second series 8:373–468.

MIÈGE, J.
1948 Le *Dioscoréa esculenta* Burkill en Côte d'Ivoire. *Revue Int. Bot. Appl. Agric. Trop.* 28(313–314):509–514.
1952 L'importancce économique des ignames en Côte d'Ivoire. *Revue Int. Bot. Appl. Agric. trop.* 32(353–354):144–155.
1954 Les cultures vivrières en Afrique occidentale. *Cahiers d'Outre-Mer* 7(25):24–50.
1969 "Dioscoreaceae," in *Flora of west tropical Africa* 3(1):144–154. First edition edited by J. Hutchinson and J. M. Dalziel, revised second edition edited by F. N. Hepper.

MORGAN, W. B.
1962 The forest and agriculture in West Africa. *Journal of African History* 3(2):235–239.

MURDOCK, G. P.
1959 *Africa — its peoples and their culture history.* New York: McGraw-Hill.

OZANNE, P.
1971 "Ghana," in *The African Iron Age.* Edited by P. L. Shinnie. Oxford: Clarendon Press.

PACHECO PEREIRA, D.
1505 *Esmeraldo de situ orbis.* Lisbon. (Translated into English and published by the Hakluyt Society, London, 1937.)

PERRIER DE LA BATHIE, H.
1925 Ignames cultivées et sauvages de Madagascar. *Revue Bot. Appl. Agric. Trop.* 5(46):417–428.

PORTÈRES, R.
1962 Berceaux agricoles primaires sur le continent africain. *Journal of African History* 3(2):195–210.

POSNANSKY, M.
1968 Yams. *Uganda Journal* 32(2):231–232.
1969 Yams and the origins of West African agriculture. *Odu — A Journal of West Africans Studies* 1(1):101–111.

POWELL, JOCELYN M.
1970 The history of agriculture in the New Guinea highlands. *Search* 1(5):199–200.

PRAIN, D., I. H. BURKILL
1919 Dioscorea sativa. *Bull. Misc. Inf. R. Bot. Gdns, Kew* (9):339–375.
1939 An account of the genus *Dioscorea,* part two: Species which turn to the right. *Ann. R. Bot. Gdn., Calcutta* 14:211–528.

ROGERS, D. J.
1967 A computer-aided morphological classification of *Manihot esculenta* Cranz. *Proc. 1st Int. Symp. Trop. Root Crops, Trinidad* 1(1):57–80.

SAUER, C. O.
1952 *Agricultural origins and dispersals.* New York: The American Geographical Society.

SCHAPERA, I.
1930 *The Khoisan peoples of South Africa.* London: Routledge. Research.

SHAW, THURSTAN
1976 "Early crops in Africa: a review of the evidence," in *Origins of African plant domestication.* Edited by Jack R. Harlan, World Anthropology. The Hague: Mouton.

SHINNIE, P. L.
1971 *The African Iron Age.* Oxford: Clarendon Press.

SIMMONDS, N. W.
1966 *Bananas.* London: Longmans, Green.

SUGGS, R. C.
1960 *The island civilization of Polynesia.* New York: Mentor Books.

UCKO, P. J., G. W. DIMBLEBY, *editors*
1969 *The domestication and exploitation of plants and animals.* London: Duckworth.

VAN ZINDEREN BAKKER, E. M.
1976 "Paleoecological background in connection with the origin of agriculture in Africa," in *Origins of African plant domestication.* Edited by Jack R. Harlan. World Anthropology. The Hague: Mouton.

WAITT, A. W.
1963 Yams, *Dioscorea* species. *Field Crop Abstr.* 16(3):145–157.
1965 "A key to some Nigerian variations of yam (*Dioscorea spp.*)." Memorandum 60. Ibadan: Federal Department of Agricultural

WARD, W. E. F.
1969 *A history of Ghana.* London: Allen and Unwin.

WATT, G.
1890 *A dictionary of the economic products of India,* volume three, 115–136. London: Allen.

WILLETT, F.
1971 "Nigeria," in *The African Iron Age.* Edited by P. L. Shinnie. Oxford: Clarendon Press.

WRIGHT, G. A.
1971 Origin of food production in South Western Asia: a survey of ideas. *Current Anthropology* 12(4/5):447–477.

WRIGLEY, C.
1960 Speculations on the economic prehistory of Africa. *Journal of African History* 1(2):189–203.

SECTION FOUR

Cooking Utensils

Coastal Maine Cooking: Foods and Equipment from 1760

ELLENORE W. DOUDIET

Until 1760 the lands east of the Penobscot River (central Maine) were wilderness. Then, peace being established, fear of Indian attack diminished, and when the area was ceded to England, families from the towns near Boston began to move there to settle.[1]

At this time cooking was done in a large open fireplace and in the adjacent brick oven (Gould 1965: 48–52). We may guess that the first thing built in the new home was a chimney of some kind — clay for bricks was available locally. The new kitchen must soon have been the equal of the old. The iron crane, which was an American invention, was not only safer than the old wooden lug pole, which frequently charred and broke (Earle 1893: 130), the crane was more convenient, as it swung forward, allowing the cook to hook her pots on it and to dish out the food in comparative ease. S-hooks were used with the crane and large kettles in which "All the vegetables were boiled together ... unless some very particular housewife had a wrought iron potato boiler to hold potatoes or any single vegetable in place within the vast general pot" (Earle 1898: 56–57). Long-handled frying pans, waffle irons, and skillets (Gould 1965: 76–79) and long-handled forks, spoons, stirrers, and ladles were needed for cooking over a hot fire. Frying pans, skillets — "a kettle or boiler" (Webster 1970[1806]) — toasters, etc. had three legs, so that they could be stood in or near the coals; the large iron kettle which hung from the crane usually also had short legs. Trivets, toasters, and other wrought-iron items could be made by the blacksmith to the housewife's order.

[1] The area being considered includes the present towns of Bucksport, Penobscot, Castine, Brooksville, Deer Isle, and Sedgwick.

Small bakings were done in an iron kettle with a rimmed flattish cover on which coals were placed, the kettle itself also being placed in the coals. Today such a kettle is frequently called a Dutch oven; it was then known as a baking kettle.[2] Large bakings were done in the brick oven. This usually had a flue which joined the fireplace flue a few feet or a few yards up. A hot fire was built in the oven, and, when it was thoroughly heated in an hour and a half or two hours, the carbon which adhered to the rounded top burned away, leaving the bricks clean. The coals were then raked out and the food put in; that which was to remain the longest — beans, for example — was put at the back.[3] In baking bread, sometimes "oak leaves or cabbage leaves were placed on the oven floor to hold the loaves ... in lieu of a pan ... The shovel was sprinkled with corn meal, the loaves put onto it and slid into the oven, and with a quick snap of the wrist the loaves slid off onto the leaves" (Gould 1965: 75). Cabbage leaves were also used in the fireplace, and we read "wrap ... in a green cabbage leaf, lay ... in hot embers and cover as you would to roast an onion" (Rawson 1927: 107).

Until grist mills became available, meal was ground at home.[4] There are two mortars and pestles in the Wilson Museum, Castine, which were used here in the eighteenth century. One mortar and pestle, said to have been "used for pulverizing corn etc. by the first ... family to settle in the town of Penobscot," is hewn from soft wood and could easily have been made locally, though it is thought to have been brought from York, Maine (Plate 1). The other set is lathe-turned and well finished. Both show use.[5]

During the fifteenth and sixteenth centuries, plain, square slabs of

[2] A Castine ledger, D 2, now in the Wilson Museum, Castine, has on page 2:

Nov. 2, 1815		John Lee Dr.		
Bak͡g Kettle	9/	Spider 5/		2.34
Tea Kettle	5/	Bed cord 3/6		1.42
Sett Knives	8/6	pr. Blankets 18/		4.58
doz Pots	4/6	½ doz. Tumblers 4/6		1.50
				9.84

On November 10 of the same year another "Bak͡g Kettle" is listed, such entries continue through the ledger. Another ledger, D 1, has on page 166, for June 1818, "1 Baking Kettle."

[3] On Deer Isle, beans are still baked in an old brick oven; the fire is kept one and a half hours. For bread baked in a (rebuilt) 1780 oven in Castine a two-hour fire is adequate. In another part of Maine the oven heat was gauged by the amount of "oven wood" used.

[4] At about this time in western Maine, "The early settlers endured much hardship, and had many fatiguing jaunts on foot to carry their corn to mill, going five, ten and at one time thirty miles with a bushel of corn on their shoulders. Boys of fourteen had to carry half a bushel" (Allen 1876: 272).

[5] The hewn mortar varies from 9½ to 10½ inches in height; the other is 7½ inches high.

wood (trenchers) were used, replacing the thick slice of bread (tranche) which had served as a plate, and which, "being eaten at the end, saved trouble" (Kerfoot 1924: 14; Pinto 1949: 7). In the sixteenth century circular wooden plates were introduced (Pinto 1949: 7), and in the seventeenth century pewter appeared. Early in the eighteenth century pewter was being substituted for wood in the average English home; America, however, was far away, and trenchers continued in use here until after the American Revolution (Kerfoot 1924: 15, 36). As late as 1775 wooden trenchers were advertised in Connecticut (Earle 1893: 138).

Hash, porridge, and stews were eaten with a spoon and roasted meat with the fingers or a knife. Table forks were rare in the seventeenth and the first part of the eighteenth centuries — not until 1750 to 1780 did forks come into general use in England — (see Figure 1A; cf. Baily 1927: 14; Graham 1973: 32).[6]

These then were the cooking and dining utensils that the settlers brought with them from Massachusetts — kettles large and small, mortars and pestles, long-handled pans of various sizes, iron trivets, and pots and pans with three feet, knives, skewers (Figure 1B),[7] long-handled

[6] "When the use of the fork became general the pointed knife was not needed for spiking the food, and from the latter part of the seventeenth century onwards we find most of the knives with rounded ends. In France the fashion of the rounded blade was supposed to have been started by Cardinal Richelieu owing to the disgusting manners of the Chancellor Seguier, who for reasons of State, was a frequent guest at his table. According to Tallement des Reaux, the Chancellor not only washed his hands in the sauce, but also had a nasty habit of picking his teeth with the point of his knife. This became a cause of annoyance to the Cardinal, who took definite steps to prevent its recurrence by giving orders to his maitre d'hotel that all his knives were to have their points ground down. In 1669 a royal edict of Louis XIV, probably issued with a view to discourage assassination at meal-times, made it illegal for anyone to carry pointed knives, for cutlers to make them, or for inn-keepers to put them on their tables; it also commanded that any existing knives with pointed blades should have their points rounded off. During the eighteenth century the blades were curved and widened out at the ends so that they could be used for eating peas and similar food that would be likely to slip through the wide-pronged fork of the period" (Bailey 1927:8–9).

Fragments of over twenty such wide-pronged forks were found during excavation at the site of the John Perkins House (circa 1763), Castine; other material from the same site has been dated 1790–1850.

"It was not for a long time — not until the 1780's — that the ordinary working Englishman adopted the new device. In the meantime, he ate off his knife; and if he emigrated across the Atlantic he took the old way with him .... By 1784, the fork was 'in' — except among a few diehards who considered it an affectation. (Eating peas with a fork, said one, was as bad as 'eating soup with a knitting needle')" (Graham 1973:32).

As late as 1910 and 1920, individuals in Brooksville and in Penobscot ate peas from their knives — and very neatly.

[7] "Skewers ... were indispensable in preparing a roast ... wrought by hand on the anvil [they] are thin and sharp-pointed with small eyelets by which they could be hung ..." (Gould 1965:72–73). This describes three found at the Perkins House site.

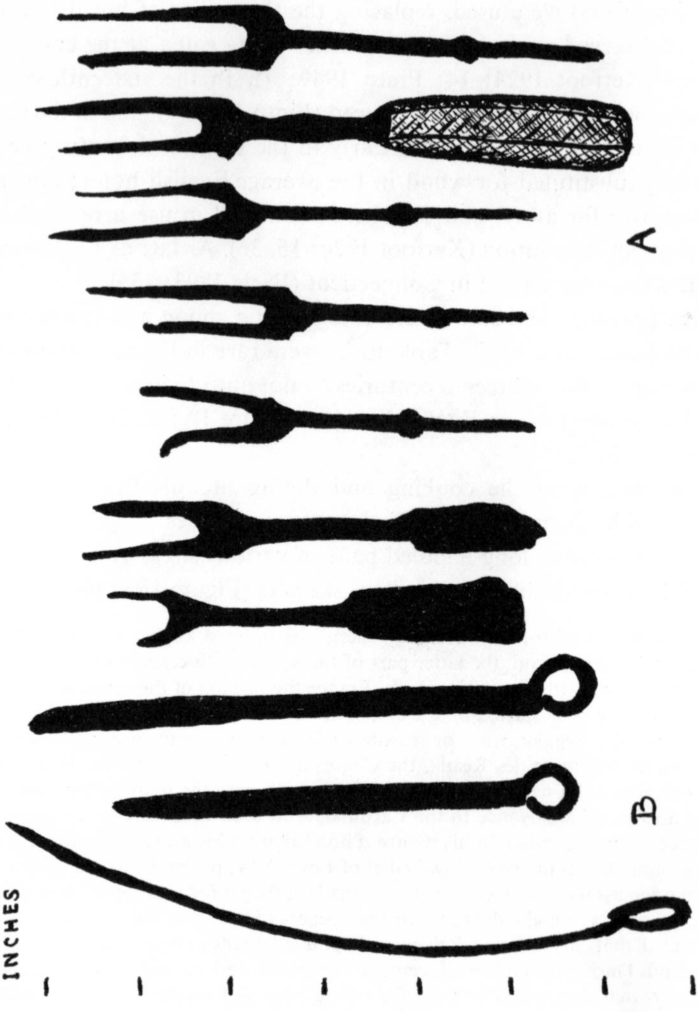

Figure 1. Found during excavation at the Perkins House site. The John Perkins House, built 1763–1783, is now restored on the grounds of the Wilson Museum, Castine. A. Table fork with bone (?) handle and fragments of similar forks. B. Wrought iron skewers

forks and spoons, wooden plates and bowls, some earthenware and china-ware, some pewter,[8] and cherished silver teaspoons (Plate 2).[9] Inasmuch as the settlers came by boat from coastal towns near Boston and landed on the coast or on navigable rivers, they were not restricted in the amount or weight of their goods.

Nor were they then isolated — all traffic was by water, and boats were built almost as quickly as homes. A ledger of the 1760's lists frequent sales of rum and molasses, probably brought from Boston, though possibly directly from the West Indies. Other items may have been produced locally. Frequently listed are Indian meal, corn, coffee, pork, fish, cider, flax, cloth, salt, tobacco, nails, knives, moose meat, and, during 1766, gingerbread. Only one mention of tea has been noted. In 1768 Captain Joseph Young bought a "case knives follkes."[10] Shoppers apparently enjoyed their trips to the store, as entries for mugs of "tody,"[11] flip,[12] and rum are frequent. The impression remaining with the reader is of gallons of molasses and rum and of bushels of Indian meal sold.[13]

Life was precarious in the mid-eighteenth century, "a bad harvest meant death for many," even in England (Pinto 1949: 39). Here in 1775 the weather was so cold that little grain was raised, and some children died of starvation (Buck 1857). A family in Penobscot

> ... were often so scantily supplied with food that ... the children would go to the woods and gather herbs which they would steep and mix with their (Indian) meal ... When they found themselves without anything ... for breakfast, they would ... dig a mess of clams ... (Hutchins n.d.).

In Brooksville, when fishline was unobtainable, a family went into the

[8] Two small pewter beakers and a tankard remain in the Hutchins family, early settlers of Penobscot. A pewter basin with the bottom melted out was found under the eaves of the Perkins House.

[9] A very small silver teaspoon, one of a set that Lydia Hatch Perkins of Castine put in her pocket when she fled, with her children, from the British in 1779, and two similar spoons found in the ground near an old house in Penobscot, are in the Wilson Museum, Castine.

[10] This "case" was probably a container for a knife and fork or for more than one set of knives and forks (Earle 1893: 137).

[11] "Toddy, a mixture of spirit and water sweetened ..." (Webster 1970 [1806]).

[12] Flip, a spiced sweetened spiritous drink with addition of eggs (Brown 1966: 156), or "made of home-brewed beer, sweetened with sugar, molasses, or dried pumpkin, and flavored with a liberal dash of rum, then stirred in a great mug or pitcher with a red-hot loggerhead or hottle or flip dog, which made the liquor foam and gave it a burnt bitter flavor" (Earle 1893: 178).

[13] Ledger of the Wescott store of Castine, now in the Wilson Museum, Castine; the earliest date is 1765.

cedar swamp, stripped bark from the trees, and fashioned it into cod lines and, fishing with these lines in the bay, filled their boat with fish (Limeburner, et al. 1936: 10).

Indian corn was THE important crop, as it could be raised at once, before the land was ready for other crops. A number of cellar holes on a hill in Penobscot[14] testify to the truth of the tradition that early settlers moved there because it was free of frost longer than the river valleys, and corn could mature, though it was an inconvenient distance from the water. "New settlers raised corn at first in all places, and lived on it two or three years ..." (Allen 1876: 271). Corn was served as a vegetable, both fresh and dried, with beans and perhaps salt pork as succotash, or parched and broken as hominy and samp.[15] Corn meal was baked into hoe-cakes[16] and bread, or made into Indian pudding which "was served twice a day in every home" (Gould 1965: 89).[17]

Beans and pumpkins were among the first and the most useful vegetables grown. "Children lived on hasty pudding; and when the corn was cut off by frost they lived on beans. It was 'bean porridge hot and bean porridge cold' with them with little else" (Allen 1876: 271). Pumpkins were served as a vegetable, in pies, with corn meal in bread, and to flavor and sweeten many dishes (Phipps 1972: 112–114). Corn, pumpkins, and beans were Indian crops adopted by Europeans, and here the settlers also grew rye in place of wheat, as rye could be grown further north (Anderson 1952: 162; Earle 1969[1900]: 125).

Fish, both fresh and salt, salt pork, molasses, and rum were usually available, and, with corn, beans pumpkins, and rye, formed the basis of the diet during the early years.

By 1800 families were well established and, although the early crops remained the staples, other crops were also cultivated — peas, beets, turnips,

[14] Wallamatogus Mountain.

[15] Hominy — hulled maize, dried and coarsely ground. Samp — coarse hominy, cooked like hominy by boiling.

[16] Hoe-cakes were made wherever corn was grown; a recipe from South Carolina is very like the following early nineteenth century one from New York State: "To a quart of meal add a teaspoonful of salt and hot (not boiling) water to make a stiff dough, cool with sweet milk, spread on a greased griddle and bake until brown on both sides." Fried in bacon fat, these hoe-cakes are quite good.

[17] Indian pudding (hasty pudding) was corn meal and milk or water — sometimes sweetened and boiled in a bag, sometimes cooked as mush or supawn.

"We set a dish on the hearth holding Injun meal, and from this we took small fingerfuls, and dropped the meal into the boiling pot, a few grains at a time. It took us generally half an hour to get the meal dropped. Then mother always wanted we should stir it for the hour that it cooked. So you see it was quite a long task after all.

When it was done we turned it into a nappy, and served it from that, with milk" (Rawson 1927: 23).

cabbages, carrots, onions, potatoes,[18] and Jerusalem artichokes *(Helianthus tuberosus)*.[19] Tomatoes were unknown.[20] Samphire *(Salicornia europaea)* and goose grass *(Plantago maritima)*[21] were picked on sand or gravel beaches. Milk, butter,[22] cheese, eggs, fish, clams, and lobsters[23] were available most of the time, and fresh meat occasionally.[24] Every farm had an apple orchard, and many grew plums, cherries, currants, and gooseberries.[25]

[18] Potatoes were not considered wholesome, and were little cultivated in the seventeenth and eighteenth centuries (Earle 1893: 153–154). Nor would cooking methods have made them attractive: "To fry Potatoes, Cut them into thin slices, as big as crown pieces, fry them brown, lay them in the plate or dish, pour melted butter, sack, and sugar over them. These are a pretty corner dish" (Carter 1802: 50).

[19] Artichokes growing wild were mentioned in 1832 (Williamson 1966 [1832]: 129), and were cultivated in Bucksport in the 1830's — "Jerusalem artichokes along the border of the cabbage patch" (Brooks 1901: 66). They are not now cultivated, and I have found only one person who is familiar with them.

[20] The tomato was thought, by Europeans, to be poisonous, although in pre-Columbian times it was used as a food in Mexico and South America. Webster's dictionary of 1806 gives no hint that it is edible, identifying it as "the love apple, a species of solanum," whereas Webster's of 1868 describes it as "a garden plant and its fruit." Mrs. Gardiner in 1763 had eleven receipts for ketchup — but no tomato ketchup (Gardiner 1938: 66–71). The introduction of the tomato to one family in the nineteenth century may be typical: "... a new kind of seed ... they produce a vine that bears a beautiful red fruit larger than a plum or an apple, — not at all like either, — but very nice, stewed for sauce or eaten raw. The city folks set great store by them. They call them tomatoes ...." Initially thought to be too acid, the family "learned to dry them, to make catsup of them, to seal them up in bottles; and, in short, the tomato was from this time an institution" (Allison 1877: 258–259).

[21] These are not now generally known.

[22] In view of current thinking concerning butter, it is interesting to read that in the 1830's "It was the custom of the village (Castine) to bribe boys to forbear the use of butter, at the rate of two cents per week; butter, it was held, was bad for a boy's blood ...." (Brooks 1901: 281).

[23] In the first half of the nineteenth century, children in Brooksville waded in the waters of the rocky shores picking up lobsters, which were cooked, shelled, and dried for winter use (information from the granddaughter of one of the children).

[24] As there was no way to keep meat except in cold weather, a butchering was shared with neighbors, who reciprocated in their turn. Most of the meat was dried, smoked, or corned.

[25] Dr. Joseph Stevens of Castine wrote, probably at the time of planting: "Names and situations of Apple Trees set out in our garden — April 24th, 1826. Early Harvest — between the local (?) Old Apple Tree and the Old Cherry Tree. Baldwin — 7 paces N.W. of Great Apple Tree. Ribstone Pippin — 7 paces N.W. of Baldwin — 14 N.W. of Great Apple Tree. A fine fall apple. Pumpkin Sweet — 7 paces N.W. of Ribstone — 21 of G. A. Tree. Early Harvest — 7 paces N.W. of Pumpkin Sweet — 28 of G. A. Tree — Baldwin — 7 paces N.W. of old early apple Tree — N.E. of Baldwin before mentioned — between old early and old Crab — R. Island Greening — 7 paces N.W. of Baldwin — 14 of old Early — N.E. of Ribstone — very fine apple — Keep till January. Hubbardstown Nonsuch — In the lower part of garden — 10 paces S.E. of Black Horse Plumb. Long Island Pippin — S.W. side of the bottom of the Alley. York Russetting — S.W. side of Alley on a line with Ribstone Pippin and R. I. Greening —

Even when crops were plentiful, preservation was a problem up until the twentieth century.[26] With luck, winter vegetables and some apples would keep in a cool but frost-free cellar.[27] Pickles "put down" in crocks (Gould 1965: 138), salted meat, and barrels of cider[28] were also kept in the cellar. Pumpkins were prepared and put in crocks with molasses and spices which preserved them and which were included in the eventual

---

Early Harvest — About 7 paces N.W. of York Russet. S.W. side of Alley — — Baldwin — 7 paces N.W. of Early Harvest last mentioned — S.W. side of the Top of the Alley. Pear Trees — — Jarganelle — between the sumac and a small old cherry tree (black mazzard). St. Michael — between the Jarganelle and an old apple tree — N.W. of Jarganelle 7 paces. St. Germain — 7 paces S.W. of Nonsuch (apple) in lower part of garden — St. Michael — S.W. side of Alley — on a line with two Baldwins — between York and Russetting and a young native plumb Tree — — — Plumb Trees — White Horse — 6 paces S.E. of Jarganelle — Black Horse — 5 paces S.E. of white Plumb — — — Cherry Trees — May Duke — between native plumb and cherry trees on S.W. side of Alley — Mazzard — in front yard — — — Peach Trees — Early Anne — in front yard — N.E. side of steps — Red Rareripe — in front yard — S.W. side of steps — — —" (Stevens 1826).

F. W. Bakeman wrote in 1905: "It is now just about one hundred years since my grandfather and grandmother went into the then new house ... The fields were in high cultivation and the orchards of apple, plum, cherry &c were luxuriant. Even in my day currants and English gooseberries were in greatest abundance."

26 "Household Hint" for June, 1867: "Keep your meat in a dry, cool place, your fish on ice, and your vegetables on a stone floor free from air. Cut your soap when it comes in, and let it dry slowly. Keep your sweet herbs in paper bags, each bag containing only one description of herb. They should be dried in the wind, and not in the sun; and when ordered in a receipt should be cautiously used, as a preponderance in any seasoning spoils it. When oranges or lemons are used for juices, chop down the peel, put it in small pots and tie them down for use. Apples should be kept on dry straw, in a dry place; and pears hung up by the stalk" (Godey 1867: 555).

Warm weather presented more problems. "How to Preserve Smoked Meats in Summer: Take black pepper and grind it very fine, the finer the better; then wash the hams or beef, and rub while damp, thoroughly, with the ground pepper; a sufficiency will adhere to them to safely protect them against the depredations of flies and bugs through the summer" (Godey 1867: 371).

27 "Frosty cellars: Those who are troubled with frosty cellars are informed that by placing a few tubs of water near their vegetables, it will prevent their freezing: such being the attracting qualities of the water, that it will freeze two inches thick, while potatoes placed along side will not be chilled. It would be well to renew the water once a week, as it will in that time lose much of its life (*The Eagle*, February 20, 1810).

28 In early nineteenth-century New England each farm had an apple orchard. "In the month of October the whole population was busy gathering apples under the trees, from which they fell in heavy showers as the branches were shaken by the strong arms of the farmers. The creak of the cider-mill, turned by a horse moving in a circle, was heard in every neighborhood as one of the most common of rural sounds. The freshly pressed juice of the apples was most agreeable to boyish tastes, and the whole process of gathering the fruit and making the cider came in among the more laborious rural occupations in a way which diversified them pleasantly, and which made it seem a pastime. The time that was given to making cider, and the number of barrels made and stored in the cellars of the farm-houses, would now seem incredible. A hundred barrels to a single farm was no uncommon proportion ..." (Bryant 1876: 99).

pumpkin pie.[29] Meat and fish were smoked or salted,[30] dried, and hung in a cool dry place. Apples and pumpkins were peeled, cut, and dried; corn was husked and hung up, frequently in the attic. Apple-paring bees and cornhusking bees were gala events in the autumn.[31] Milk, cream, butter, and cheese were often taken care of in the milk room — a room at the north, the stone floor of which was somewhat lower than the other floors.[32]

In addition to local products, many items were imported. In 1809 the following advertisement appeared in a Castine newspaper:

[29] This was done in the Brooklin-Sedgwick area up to 1900. My own attempt to keep pumpkin this way did not have ideal results. It would probably be better with a larger amount of pumpkin, which would not mean a commensurate increase in molasses and spices.

[30] The kitchen chimney of the John Perkins House, Castine, has a smoke chamber in the second-story section. Two tiers of charred wooden rods once held the meat or fish while it smoked. The chimney was built in the 1780's. Mrs. Gardiner of Boston and Gardiner, Maine, wrote the following in 1763:

"Hams to cure, the New England Way: Let your Pork Legs be cut long and handsome. Scatter a little fine Salt upon them, and then let them lay for two or three Days, rubbing them every Day. Then take more Salt and mix with it Salt-petre, allowing one Ounce of Salt-petre one pound of Salt and one pint of Molasses to each Ham. With this Pickle rub them well, every Day, on each side, for six weeks. Then scatter a little Bran over them and then let them be hung up to smoke, for one month in a Smoke-House, or in a chimney where there is a small Fire but a constant Smoke. One pair of Chops will require the same quantity of Salt, Saltpetre and molasses as one Ham. The month of February is the best Time for laying in your Pork, as you will then have Pork whose Fat is firm, and which has been corn-fed ... The best Smoke for them is raised by fixing Tanners Bark that is sufficiently dry ... Horse Dung is also said to be the best thing to raise a Smoak from for smoaking Hams, Cheeks, Tongues, Beef &c" (Gardiner 1938: 59–60).

[31] "... the task of stripping the husks from the ears of Indian corn was made the occasion of social meetings, in which the boys took a special part. A farmer would appoint what was called 'a husking', to which he invited his neighbors. The ears of maize in the husk, sometimes along with part of the stalk, were heaped on the barn floor. In the evening, lanterns were brought, and, seated on piles of dry husks, the men and boys stripped the ears of their covering, and breaking them from the stem with a sudden jerk, threw them into baskets placed for the purpose. It was often a merry time; the gossip of the neighborhood was talked over ...

Quite as cheerful were the 'apple-parings', which on autumn evenings brought together the young people of both sexes in little circles. The fruit of the orchards was pared and quartered and the core extracted, and a supply of apples in this state provided for making what was called 'apple-sauce', a kind of preserve of which every family laid in a large quantity every year" (Bryant 1876: 101).

Sometimes dried apples were prepared. "The bee was held in the barn ... there were a number of tables set out with pans and knives, and needles and strings. Bushel-baskets of apples stood around the tables ... The men pared the apples and some of the women pared and some strung" (Wilkins 1898: 133–137).

[32] Such a room is known to me in an 1835 home in Brooksville and a still older home in Penobscot.

Salt, Crockery Ware, &c. Just imported in brig Unity, Capt. Lassel, from Liverpool and for sale ... 250 hhds Salt — 9 crates Crockery Ware — 20 pieces Manchester Checks — 6 cases Gentlemen's fine Hats — 6d, 10d and 20d Nails — White Lead.

Also received by the Packet from the West Indies, 12 Hogsheads Rum[33] and Molasses.

Likewise, a general assortment of English and Hardware goods just received from Boston (*The Eagle*, November 14, 1809).

The following month another merchant advertised "English and W. Indies Goods, Crockery and Glass Ware, Corn, Flour, Rice, Pork, Onions, Fish ..."

The wealthier families lived in comfort and some elegance,[34] and company meals, then as now, differed from the daily fare. There was "better living than usual (when there were guests) wine or punch on the table at dinner ... and many nice things for dessert that seemed more proper for Thanksgiving ..." The younger children, however, might have to wait

[33] "Rum, molasses, and salt made the fortunes of the town," has been said so long in Castine that its origin is lost. Certainly these were the most important imports.

In 1750 rum was "in great use with all the English North American colonists ... reckoned much wholesomer than brandy made from wine or grain ... most of [the] soldiers who drank brandy for a time died; but those who drank rum were not hurt, though they got drunk with it every day for a considerable time" (Kalm 1966 [1937]: 325).

Its uses were manifold. The master of a sailing ship took his wife with him to Europe, where she died; he is said to have brought her home in a barrel of rum, for burial in the Castine cemetery.

[34] Surviving homes, furnishings, and records speak for this, as also do advertisements in *The Eagle*. Phebe Perkins' silver spoons and sugar tongs (made about 1805 by a Castine silversmith), her daughter Polly's silver spoons (examples of the silver are in the Wilson Museum), and the large amount and variety of chinaware fragments found at the Perkins House site indicate wealth and some elegance. Most of these shards date from 1790 to 1830.

"The most common china was white or cream ware, undecorated, and would-be cream ware, pearl ware, stone ware and ironstone ... Next in quantity was the printed Blue Staffordshire of 1800–1825. The soft paste china was not only much broken but was flaked from the action of frost, however many of these pieces have been fitted together showing that certain of the Blue Staffordshire plates were printed with scenes of English history. They might ... have been brought to Castine during the War of 1812 when the town was occupied by British troops."

Fragments of a painted-ware saucer (late eighteenth century) were found during the excavation; other fragments of the set were found in the walls of the Perkins House when it was being taken down.

"Recovered during the excavation was a considerable amount of printed Staffordshire in green, light blue, brown, pink or mulberry ... a small bit of canary ware and a piece of red printed Staffordshire mug ...

"There was but little glass ... the bases of two hand blown decanters ... the base of a contact mold blown caster set bottle; an applied handle from a molded lamp or syllabub glass, several pieces from a pressed flint glass sauce dish ... bits of dark green bottle glass ... Most of the items were of molded glass" (Archaeological dig ... 1971).

Plate 1. Mortar and pestle used in Penobscot in 1760's for grinding corn

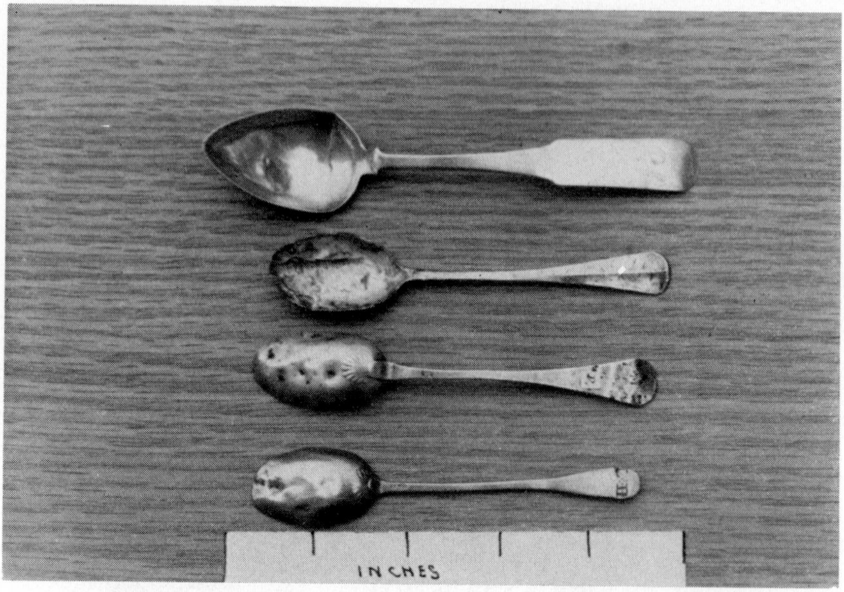

Plate 2. Bottom, one of the teaspoons Lydia Hatch Perkins saved when the British occupied Castine in 1779. Next, two similar spoons found in the ground near an old home in Penobscot. Top, spoon which belonged to Phebe Perkins (1745–1811), stamped B. Mead (Benjamine Mead was a Castine silversmith)

until their elders had dined before they were served (Brooks 1901: 31–32). When a neighbor called, tea, coffee, or wine might be served. For a near neighbor a "plain cotton checked napkin was used. If it was the minister's wife or ... [a] sea captain, a white linen one was used" (Limeburner n.d.: 13). It was the custom, in Castine, of the wife of a master ship builder

> ... in cold weather ... to give her servants a mug of flip and a plate of doughnuts for a luncheon, in the middle of the forenoon of a washing day. Flip was made by stirring in a pitcher a mixture of cider, rum, eggs, sugar, and spices. The stirring was done with a very heavy iron poker called a logerhead, heated to red and whiteness (see also Note 12).

When the parson called at the same hour, he was served Malaga wine and fruit cake (Brooks 1901: 27–28). To men haying in the July sun a refreshing drink of water, molasses, and ginger was taken. "There was always plenty of pie, doughnuts, gingerbread and cookies ... but cake only on company occasions" (Rawson 1927: 76).

The quality of water was important.[35] Even today the well water of various farms is discussed, some being considered excellent drinking water and some inferior.

The fishermen and their families had scanty resources, and an unexpected guest might be given dried beef, toasted red herring, pickles, preserves, bread, saleratus biscuits, and tea, or salt codfish (which was toasted and pounded in a mortar to soften it, then buttered and warmed), tea, and, no doubt, bread or biscuits (Brooks 1894: 148–154).[36] While on board a coasting schooner

> ...the principal diet of the men was "johnny-cake" and fried pork, with a relay of hardtack to fall back upon in case of famine. The johnny-cake was a batter of corn meal mixed with warm water and Saleratus baked in a shallow pan,[37] and eaten with pork fat ... to be out of corn meal was to be without one of the necessaries of life ... (Brooks 1901: 280–281).

[35] In 1763 Mrs. Gardiner wrote, "N.B. Use soft water for old Peas, and hard or Spring Water for young Peas, in making your Peas Soups" (Gardiner 1938: 1).

"Split pease ... in soft water ... To make a good Pease Soup ... To make a White Portable Soup — that you may carry ... in your pocket (use) soft water" ... (Carter 1802: 66–67).

"Boil fresh young vegetables in hard water; a little salt will harden the water at once. Boil dried vegetables in soft water; a little baking soda will soften the water ..." (Corson, et al., 1892 (?): 56).

[36] In another area of New England tea (supper) included bread, butter, tea, and sauce; "no sauce for tea was regarded as very poor living" (Wilkins 1891: 41). Adequate provisions were "plenty of meal an' merlasses, an' some salt fish an' pertaters" (Wilkins 1887: 78).

[37] Homemade johnnycake would have been better: "Old Fashioned Johnny Cake: 1 cup corn meal, ½ cup molasses, 1 teaspoon soda, 1 cup flour, 1½ cups sour milk, 1 egg, ½ teaspoon salt" (Moore 1967: 34).

Another point of view was expressed by a gentleman whose boat was frozen in the ice: "Out of patience, out of tobacco, out of provisions and worst of all, out of rum."[38]

Corn in many forms, rye, beans, pork, salt fish, molasses, and rum remained the staples. Hasty pudding, often the only breakfast or supper dish, was eaten with milk or molasses.[39] Beans baked with pork and molasses, and brown bread of rye, corn meal, molasses, water, and leavening were the Saturday night supper and Sunday morning breakfast.[40]

Beaten eggs, yeast, and soda (with an acid) provided the early leavens. Molasses or sour milk with soda gave excellent results. "Sal aeratus," at

[38] Said to have been written in the diary of Jeremiah Wardwell about 1800.

[39] In the 1830's in Castine a boy's "usual supper [was] hasty pudding and milk" (Brooks 1901: 165). A boy in Penobscot in the 1930's often had corn meal mush with molasses or canned milk for supper.

[40] "Along one side of the storeroom were ranged three bins, with tops that lifted up and served for covers. One of these was for corn-meal, another for flour, and a third for rye-meal. From two of these bins came the materials, every Saturday, for the brown bread that made a part of the Saturday-night supper and Sunday-morning breakfast. Only it was not called brown bread .... It was rye-and-Indian bread, being made of rye and Indian meal. ... 'rine-Injun' really meant rye-and-Indian" (Brooks 1901: 17).

An old-time Brooksville cook wrote these recipes:

"Baked Beans: Pick over one quart of beans on Friday night and put them in to soak in plenty of water. Get up at five o'clock Saturday morning — put about half the beans in the bean pot, add ¼ cup molasses, 1 small onion, ½ teaspoon mustard (dry), and a ½ lb. salt pork, a streak of fat and a streak of lean is best, but if you can get only fat pork add about ½ lb. corned beef, 1 teaspoon salt — — then put in the rest of the beans and place a slice of pork on top. Add water to cover, put them in the oven and bake until supper time. About half an hour before supper remove the cover from the bean pot so the beans will be nice and brown. Of course you will have to add water from time to time while they are baking.

Brown Bread: 1 cup sour milk, 1½ cups corn meal, 2 T. sugar, 1 heaping t. soda, ½ cup molasses, 1 cup flour, 2 T. butter, ½ t. salt. Mix well. If you have a good steamer that fits into your iron kettle, set the dish containing the bread-mixture in the steamer — cover and steam 2 to 2½ hours. If you haven't a steamer put the mixture into a greased 2½ quart lard pail — put something — a brick will do — into the kettle to set the pail on. Have boiling water in the kettle come half way up the pail. Cover. Steam 2 to 2½ hours. Be sure to keep the water in the kettle boiling" (Limeburner n.d.: 11).

Brown bread was also made with yeast. "Raised Brown Bread: 1 pint yellow corn-meal; ½ cup yeast; ½ cup molasses; ½ teaspoon salt; 1 salt-spoon soda; 1 pint rye-meal. Put the corn-meal in the mixing bowl and scald it with boiling water, just enough to wet it; let it stand ten minutes, then add cold water enough to make a soft batter. When lukewarm add the yeast, molasses, soda, salt and rye-meal. Beat it well and let it rise over night, or until it cracks open. Stir it down; put it in a buttered and floured tin to rise again; sprinkle flour over the top. Bake in a moderate oven two hours. Brown bread made by this rule was first tested by the writer thirty years ago, when it was a wonder and delight to watch it as it was put on a wooden shovel and placed in the great brick oven (Corson, et al., 1892 (?): 10).

With present-day corn meal, warm, not boiling water should be used to dampen the meal, or enough should be added at once to make the "soft batter." This recipe makes a moist sweet bread.

that time potassium carbonate or potassium bicarbonate, was available, being made from wood ashes.[41] It was sold as pearlash,[42] refined potash, or wood ashes (Rawson 1927: 69). Later sodium bicarbonate (baking soda) replaced the potassium carbonates and is still used in molasses and sour milk recipes. Yeast, like the Bostonian's hat, was not bought but was something one had, and of which one took great care.[43] Recipes for salt-rising and sourdough bread are rare; in the former, the yeast is inherent in the corn meal[44] or in the potato water (Rombauer and Becker 1962: 569). A great number of recipes are for yeast bread and saleratus biscuit. Later, biscuits were also made with sweet milk, when alum (potassium aluminum sulphate or sodium aluminum sulphate) or cream of tartar were added.[45] Baking powder was not manufactured until about 1865 (Morrison 1904: 54;[46] Kendall 1935: 497–498, 416; Rockett 1971: 74).

A baker provided bread, biscuit (ship's biscuit?), and gingerbread during much, if not all, of Castine's early settlement. In 1809 four sheets of gingerbread at 15 cents a sheet appear on a ledger.[47] It must have been similar to the "sheet of gingerbread" that Lem, "opening the big firkin ...

41 Wood ashes were also used in making soap.

42 Pearlash was advertised in *The Eagle* (1809, 1810) and was noted in ledgers of the early nineteenth century, and later in recipes (Godey 1873: 32, 372, 563).

43 Potatoes and/or flour, water, salt, and sugar form the usual recipe for yeast, but to these ingredients must be added "any good yeast."

44 Salt-rising bread is so called because the yeast is not affected by salt. If corn meal is used, it must, according to Rombauer, be water-ground; however, the recipe below gave good bread when the usual finely ground meal was used. The soda was omitted to make sure all leavening was in the corn meal.

"Salt Rising Bread: 1 pint new milk; corn meal to thicken; 1 gallon flour; 1 tablespoon sugar; 1 teaspoon salt; pinch of soda. Set the milk on the fire and stir in cornmeal to make thick as mush. Set in a warm place all night. In the morning it will be light. Put the flour in a bowl, pour in the mush and mix with warm milk and water, equal parts; add the sugar, salt and soda. Make a stiff batter, cover and keep warm. In an hour it will be light. Work in flour to make stiff dough, let it rise, mold in loaves, put in greased pans, let it rise and bake" (Corson, et al., 1892 (?): 9).

45 Saleratus or "Sour Milk Biscuits: Rub a piece of butter or lard about the size of an egg into a quart of flour. Wet with sour milk into which you have previously stirred 1 teaspoon saleratus that has been dissolved in a little hot water. Use as much milk as you need to make a dough that can be rolled out on your breadboard. Have it about one inch thick, cut with floured biscuit cutter and bake in a very hot oven. It will take practice to get just the right amount of flour and milk. If you use lard, add a little salt."

"Sweet Milk Biscuits: Make the same as sour milk biscuits but add two teaspoons of Cream of Tartar" (Limeburner n.d.: 9).

46 A recipe for baking powder given in an 1890's cook book: "1 ounce super-carbonate soda; 7 drachms tartaric acid (in powder). Roll smoothly and mix thoroughly Keep in a tight glass jar or bottle. Use one teaspoonful to a quart of flour" (Corson, et al. 1892(?): 8).

47 Castine and Penobscot ledgers, now in Wilson Museum, Castine.

took out ... and, breaking it in halves, buttoned under his jacket." It must have been fairly rugged, as it remained buttoned under that jacket while Lem walked several miles and then slept under a haystack; and, though "jammed and crushed," it was eaten the next day "with real enjoyment" (Brooks 1901: 77–82).[48]

In the mid-nineteenth century it was thought important for a girl to be able to make good coffee, tea, johnnycake, saleratus biscuits, doughnuts, molasses gingerbread, brown bread, cookies, apple pie, curd cheese, a boiled dinner, and baked beans, and to fry potatoes and eggs (Limeburner n.d.: 4–5).

At this time the cast-iron cookstove was coming into use, followed by changes in utensils and cooking methods. The long-handled pans and immense kettles disappeared; waffle irons, kettles, and pans were made to fit into the round stove holes when the lids were removed. A Penobscot ledger[49] notes a stove and flat irons sold May 1, 1849; this is the first stove mentioned, although the ledger dates back to 1841. Two stoves were sold in 1850 and five in 1851, of which one is listed as a "cook stove and Furniture — $ 14.00, pipes and elbow @ 10¢ — 1.90." We do not know whether these were all cookstoves, as the term stove was long used for any heating device. "Benjamin Franklin invented what is often called a stove, as early as 1742. This was really a cast iron fireplace ..." (Thwing 1936: 16–1, 17–6).

The first stove in Castine was sent for to Boston in 1838. This "new-fangled contraption" was of great interest to the children, who watched the doors being opened and the drafts adjusted.

With the invention of the cook-stove came a demand for matches to light by scratching. Heretofore, the fire had been raked up at night in the ashes of the fireplace; and when these were uncovered next morning, there were coals ready to light the brimstone matches used by all families at that time. One could not rake up a stove.

[48] Most recipes for molasses cookies will do for sheet gingerbread. The dough is poured on a greased cooky tin and patted flat. One handwritten nineteenth-century recipe from New York State calls for soda, cream of tartar, and alum.

"Molasses Cookies: 2 cups New Orleans molasses, 1 cup shortening (butter or beef drippings), 1 teaspoon cream tartar, 1 cup hot water (put in two cups) — in one cup put two tablespoons soda, in other teaspoon grated alum, — 1 tablespoon ginger, 1 teaspoon salt. Butter & molasses together, then soda water — last alum water."

Another recipe for "Molasses Cookies: 2 cups molasses, ½ cup sugar, 2/3 cup lard, 2/3 cup hot water, 1 tablespoonful ginger, 1 tablespoonful cinnamon, 1 teaspoonful salt, 2 teaspoonfuls saleratus, flour enough to roll out" (*The Hammonton cook book* 1809 (?): 36).

[49] Devereux ledger (Castine and Penobscot n.d.: 276,299,307,352, 365, 371, 373, 380, 334, and 320).

There were other problems: "the bigger boys were obliged to saw and split wood for the new stove. Wood for the fireplace was sawed into two pieces; that for the stove must be cut into three pieces and be split small." The boys also "on baking days built a fire in the big brick oven in which beans, bread, and Indian pudding were cooked" (Brooks 1901: 22–25). One might guess from the latter that, even after the advent of the stove, the brick oven was still used for large bakings.[50]

Until the first quarter of the twentieth century most families had a woodlot; and each autumn a large pile of wood, near the back door, cut and ready for splitting, was the sign of a provident householder. The stove fire would go out at night unless a heavy hardwood stick kept smoldering, but in the morning a fire was quickly started. Fried foods were easily and quickly cooked over the hot fire. Tea stood on the back of the stove, getting blacker and stronger as it stood. More tea and more water were added from time to time. Eventually the teapot would be emptied and the routine repeated.[51]

Though these old-time methods of cooking have largely disappeared from present-day Maine kitchens, the old-time foods have not: tea, coffee, rum, molasses, baked beans and brown bread, salt fish, New England boiled dinner, fried potatoes, fish, clam chowder (made with milk, salt pork, and potatoes), saleratus biscuits, pie, and doughnuts, which were the mainstay of life in the eighteenth and nineteenth centuries, are today the most popular foods.

[50] A handwritten recipe from Massachusetts, probably of this period, suggests the use of either type of oven.

"Brown Bread: Two quarts of Indian meal, one large spoonful of salt, 1 cupful of yeast, ½ cup of molasses, mix it with as warm water as the hands will bear, butter deep pans, wet the hands with cold water to put it in, set it to rise an hour. Bake it in a hot oven 4 or 5 hours. If baked in a brick [oven] it is best to let it remain over night" (from a notebook containing cooking and medical recipes, probably about 1850).

[51] True only of some of the simpler homes; others were very particular to have fresh tea and boiling water.

REFERENCES

ALLEN, WILLIAM

1876 *Now and then.* Collections of the Maine Historical Society 7:271–272.

ALLISON, JOY

1877 Pattikin's house. *St. Nicholas* 4:258–259.

ANDERSON, EDGAR

1952 *Plants, man and life.* Boston: Little, Brown.

1971 *Archaeological dig at the site of the John Perkins house.* Wilson Museum Bulletin 1(20):4.

BAILEY, C. T. P.

1927 *Knives and forks.* London: Medici Society.

BAKEMAN, F. W.

1905 Manuscript folder in the Wilson Museum, Castine.

BROOKS, NOAH

1894 *Tales of the Maine coast.* New York: Scribner's.

1901 *Lem, a New England village boy.* New York: Scribner's.

BROWN, JOHN HULL

1966 *Early American beverages.* Japan: Bonanza.

BRYANT, WILLIAM CULLEN

1876 The boys of my boyhood. *St. Nicholas* 4:99–101.

BUCK, RUFUS, ESQ.

1857 "The history of the town of Bucksport up to 1857." July 4. Manuscript copy in the Wilson Museum, Castine.

CARTER, SUSANNAH

1802 *The frugal housewife.* Philadelphia: Carey.

CASTINE AND PENOBSCOT

n.d. Eighteenth and nineteenth century ledgers from Castine and Penobscott, now in the Wilson Museum.

Cook book

n.d. Untitled notebook containing cooking and medical recipes. Probably written about 1850. Massachusetts.

Cook book and recipes

1830–1880 Untitled manuscript. New York State.

CORSON, GILLETTE, *et al.*

1892(?) *600 selected recipes.* Chicago: Fairbanks.

Eagle, The

1809–1810 Weekly appearing every Tuesday. Castine: Samuel Hall.

EARLE, ALICE MORSE

1893 *Customs and fashions in old New England.* New York: Scribner's.

1898 *Home life in colonial days.* New York: Grosset and Dunlap.

1969 [1900] *Stagecoach and tavern days.* New York: Scribner's. (Originally published 1900.)

GARDINER, ANNE GIBBONS

1938 *Mrs. Gardiner's receipts from 1763.* Hallowell, Maine: Privately printed.

GODEY

1867, 1873 Receipts, etc., in *Godey's Lady's Book.*

GOULD, MARY EARLE
1965 *The early American house*. Rutland: Tuttle.
GRAHAM, J. MAXTONE
1973 Who taught you to eat that way? *Holiday* 53, (1):12.
Hammonton cook book, The
1809(?) (Second edition.) Philadelphia.
HUTCHINS, J. M.
n.d. "Traditions of the Hutchins Family of Penobscot." Unpublished manuscript.
KALM, PETER
1966 [1937] *The America of 1750, travels in North America*. New York: Dover. (Originally published 1937.)
KENDALL, JAMES
1935 *Smith's college chemistry* (third revised edition). New York: Appleton.
KERFOOT, J. B.
1924 *American pewter*. New York: Bonanza.
LIMEBURNER, GRACE
n.d. "How aunt Wealthy learned to cook." Mimeographed manuscript.
LIMEBURNER, GRACE, *et al.*
1936 *Traditions and records of Brooksville, Maine*. Brooksville Historical Society.
MOORE, RILLA LEACH
1967 *Mill Creek, Penobscot, Maine*. Privately printed.
MORRISON, A. CRESSY
1904 *The baking powder controversy*. New York: American Baking Powder Association.
PHIPPS, FRANCES
1972 *Colonial kitchens, their furnishings, and their gardens*. New York: Hawthorn.
PINTO, EDWARD H.
1949 *Treen or small woodware throughout the ages*. London: Batsford.
RAWSON, MARION NICHOLL
1927 *Candle days*. New York: Century.
ROCKETT, FRANK H.
1971 "Baking powder," in *Encyclopedia of science and technology* 2:74. New York: McGraw-Hill.
ROMBAUER, IRMA S., MARION R. BECKER
1962 *Joy of cooking* (tenth edition). Indianapolis: Bobbs-Merill.
STEVENS, J. L.
1826 *Stevens – 1820's*. Manuscript folder in the Wilson Museum, Castine.
THWING, L. L.
1936 The history of stoves. *Chronicle of the Early American Industries Association* 1 (16):1–4; (17):6.
WEBSTER, NOAH
1868 *Webster's high school dictionary*. New York: Ivison, Blakeman, Taylor. (Mainly abridged from the latest edition of the quarto *Dictionary of Noah Webster*, 1868. By William G. Webster and William A. Wheeler.)
1970 [1806] *A compendious dictionary of the English language*. New York: Crown. (Facsimile of the 1806 edition.)

WILKINS, MARY E.
1887 *A humble romance and other stories.* New York: Harpers.
1891 *A New England nun and other stories.* New York: Harpers.
1898 *The people of our neighborhood.* New York: Doubleday and McLure.
WILLIAMSON, WILLIAM D.
1966 [1832] *History of the State of Maine.* (Facsimile of the 1832 edition.) Freeport: Cumberland. (Facsimile of the 1832 edition.)

SECTION FIVE

American Indian Food

Cherokee Indian Foods

MARY ULMER CHILTOSKEY

> ... and maketh the grass to grow upon the mountains, and herb for the use of man.
> Psalm 147:8, *Book of common prayer* (1929 revision)

Peithman in his *Red men of fire: a history of the Cherokee Indians* states in his section on early history:

> During these early days, they lived for the most part by hunting. Game was plentiful and was hunted throughout their domain. Wild fruits, chestnuts and nuts of many varieties grew in profusion and provided food in abundance. These early people eventually became gardeners and in a crude way began to cultivate and grow crops. Maize (corn), squashes and other vegetables were most important foods .Tobacco was grown as a herb and was used as a curative remedy and smoked on ceremonial occasions. Smoking eventually became a daily habit of both men and women (1964:5).

The history of the foods used by the Cherokee people is practically non-existent. Lack of written records might be blamed for this. We may dip into Cherokee lore to get some of the knowledge we seek.

As Hebrew lore tells us that Noah was the first nonvegetarian, the

Much has been written about the Indians of America and most of those writings contain some reference to the methods and foods that have been seen or tasted by the writers. Researchers are familiar with many of these writings.

In this paper, I have tried to share with the reader a bit of my gleanings of more than 30 years of living with the Cherokee Indians of North Carolina — first, as a teacher in the Cherokee Indian Schools and secondly, as wife of a full-blood Cherokee Indian who enjoys the cooking of the older people. It is from him and his brother that I have learned much of what I am sharing.

stories of the "Big flood" and the "Coming of the birds, animals and insects to the earth" might help us learn when the people began to eat flesh. These legends tell that before the flood there were only a few dogs on earth and that they were able to talk to humans — we can hardly imagine anyone eating a talking dog. We know that there were fish in the water during the flood because the man and his wife had fish to eat with their corn while on the raft those many days.

Scientists give no accounts of finding an entirely primitive corn from which the edible grain was developed. When Europeans came to America, the Indians were cultivating and eating corn, a major food item. The Indian corn beads (*Jobii lacrymosii*), which are so popular today as ornaments and were formerly used by the Cherokee people as "medicine," were called by a Cherokee name that meant the "Mother of Corn". Within the past few years a Cherokee woman said that her grandmother grew Indian corn beads to sell to the shopkeepers to use for souvenir items or, as she put it, "to use for fun." The flour corn that the Cherokee in North Carolina still value very highly for its texture and flavor is a bit more primitive than much of the "white man's corn"; it has fewer rows of kernels. What it lacks in numbers, however, it makes up for in flavor.

A favorite medley of Cherokee legends tells about the origin of several of the favorite foods. Parts of these legends have appeared in published form, but I shall present them as they have been told to me and in the manner in which I have told them many times.

When the Great Spirit made the first Indian man — a Cherokee man — and placed him in the best part of the world, all was well for a while. The deer and other animals had been told that they were to share themselves with Man so that he could live well and use the brain that had been put into his body. He had been given a bow and arrow and had been told by the Great Spirit to use it only when he needed an animal. Later as he began to have too much time on his hands, he began to shoot the animals just to see how well he could shoot. This was about to cause the deer and some of the other animals to become extinct. The deer decided to call on the Great Spirit to help with this problem. The Great Spirit came down to counsel with the deer.

The deer said, "Great One, when you sent Man to us, you put a brain in him and told us that he would make the world a better place if we would share ourselves with him. We have shared but he has not done anything to make anything better. Just look at him now; he doesn't have as much sense as the dumbest creature you ever created. He is lying on the ground asleep; he doesn't even build a shelter or hunt a sheltered spot to sleep or rest. The dumbest creature will hunt for a cave, dig a hole, or get under a bush or tree. Now, if this is the best Man is going to do, you might as well take him back with you, he is of no good to us."

The Great Spirit looked at the man who was lying on the ground in the sunshine with his face turned up to the sky, his bow and arrow by his side, fast asleep. He replied, "I certainly didn't mean for him to turn out this way; I must have left something out of his make-up, something important. Now, let me see. Oh! yes, I know. He is lonesome, one can't do his best when lonesome. I'll make him a companion."

So the Great Spirit made a plant to grow straight up above the man's heart, straight up toward the sky, with long green blades coming out from each side, falling gracefully downward. At the place each blade left the stalk, there grew an ear of grain with silks and shucks. At the top of the corn — the first corn — there developed a beautiful creature, Woman — the first woman. Man thought he was asleep and dreaming of this beautiful one.

He said to himself, "Oh! I wish I were awake and that this were real. If I could have this lovely one for my companion, I would be worth something, I would work to build a home and make the world a better place for all."

As soon as the Great Spirit heard this wish, he made the man realize that he WAS awake, that this lovely woman had been created to be his companion. Crawling out from under the stalk (next time you see a stalk of corn look for the place where he crawled out), he arose from the ground, helped the lovely one down, and claimed her for his own. Together they went away to build the first home. But before she left the stalk of corn, she pulled two ears to take with her so that she might have something of her origin. The corn was ripe and she planted some of it in front of her home as we now plant roses and other flowers. She did this every year, not knowing that the corn was good to eat. Early one morning she saw the wild turkey, the sacred bird of things on earth, eating some of the grains. The corn was in the milk stage, so that evening she pulled off several ears and roasted them in the fire to serve to her husband and herself for supper. We might say that "roasting ears" were born that day. We know that from that day forward the corn plant has meant much to the Indian people, Cherokee and others.

Intoxicating liquors have taken their toll on Indian people. Those who observe the present and study the past are inclined to think that the Cherokee background was almost free of alcoholic beverages. The only fermented drink from the past that we are told of is *gun-no-he-nuh* [a drink made from partly cracked corn fermented in water]. This is consumed without being distilled; therefore, the alcohol content is very low. With such a background the present-day Cherokee is hardly able to tolerate much hard liquor without becoming intoxicated.

The Cherokee consider the potato to be almost as important as corn as a food crop. When one grows enough corn and potatoes to last until the next crop, he considers himself a good provider. The history of the potato is a mystery to this day. We do know that the Inca not only grew and ate the potato but prepared the first dehydrated food as a means of preserving the potato, which differed from the other staple crops in that it was perishable. Quoting von Hagen, *Realm of the Incas*, we find:

> *Chuñu* was the first really dehydrated food, and it was prepared in this manner: the potatoes were left outside to freeze, and on the following morning the people squeezed out the water with their feet. The process was repeated on five consecutive days. *Chuñu* may be preserved whole or made into very white, light potato flour, and in this powdery dry state it can last for years. *Chuñu* was one of the principal foods stored in the public granaries throughout the Andes (1961:59).

Many varieties of the squash family have been enjoyed by the Cherokee people. In "hard times" the tender, young gourds have been made into an appetizing dish. The Cherokee had a part in developing the delightful "candy roaster" pumpkin that is indigenous to the southern Appalachian region.

Nuts have always been an important part of the food for winter use. Besides being easily stored, the fat content filled a great need in the Cherokee diet. Families would go through the woods in the fall to gather nuts, making a holiday venture of the chore. Today walnuts and hickory nuts are used in cakes and cookies copied from the white friends, but one long-time favorite that is still frequently made is a mixture of skinned corn, beans, molasses, and milk of both walnut and hickory nuts; pumpkin may be added if one likes. The preparation of the walnut and hickory nut milk is interesting. The nuts are cracked, the largest shells are removed, and the nut meats with the small shells are beaten in the *ka-no-na* [corn beater] until they have the consistency of a paste. This paste is rolled into balls to be used at that time or later. When ready to complete the nut milk, a ball or two will be put into a pot of boiling water and allowed to stand for a few minutes. The hot water causes the oils in the nuts to ooze out; as they rise to the top, the aroma is delightful. When it is ready, the oily, milky liquid is poured into the corn mixture; care is taken not to pour the last of the contents into the mixture for fear there might be unpleasant bits of shell. This dish, *ga-nu-ge*, gets its name from the Cherokee word for hickory nut. This little bit of hickory oil gives the most distinctive flavor to the mixture.

Chestnuts played an important part in the diet of the Cherokee people until the blight began to destroy the trees in the early part of this century. Each fall the local stores get quantities of imported chestnuts, which are quickly bought up by the Cherokee housewives to be made into chestnut bread. Being very much larger than the native chestnuts, these nuts have less flavor; a little sugar is often added to try to make them resemble the old flavor. This bread is made by adding the boiled chestnuts to unsalted cornmeal (Ulmer and Beck 1951: 45). Some varieties of Oriental chestnuts have been planted and are doing quite well in this area, so perhaps the Cherokee people can continue to enjoy the tasty chestnut bread for many years. This bread, eaten with fried fatback or other salty meat, is worth anyone's try. Bean bread is another favorite. Any dried brownish beans are good for this purpose, but the old cornfield bean is the favorite. The bean stalks were formerly kept to be burned, and their ash was then mixed with other ashes to be used when skinning corn. This was to make the corn more easily digestible.

Wild fruits and berries have been chiefly a seasonal food because the chore of keeping them was often insurmountable. One favorite story is the legend of the "Origin of strawberries," which brings in the origin of several other fruits incidentally.

The old people tell that when the First Man and his wife lived in that first home, they were very happy for a long time. One day for no reason at all, so far as the man knew, the wife became angry and stormed out the door with her head held high, walking very fast and hard. The man thought she would cool off and be back in a few minutes, so he kept on with his work of flaking a piece of flint with a deer's antler to make an arrowhead. After a while he realized that she had not returned. He went to the door to see if he might see her and he did; she was just going over the top of the nearby mountain. That old lonesome feeling gripped his heart and he knew he had to catch her. He threw down his work and ran out the door and up the mountain, needless to say becoming more and more tired as he ran. When he got to the top of the mountain, he could see her just going over the next. As fast as he could he went down the mountain and laboriously climbed up the other height, again to see her going over the next. This was more than he could take. He fell down on a rock, buried his head in his hands, and called on the Great Spirit for help. The Great Spirit came, asked the man what he might have done to provoke her anger. Man knew of nothing he had done or had not done.

The Great Spirit told him to rest a little, then come along as fast as he could while he, the Great Spirit, hurried ahead to slow down the angry wife.

When the Great Spirit caught up with the wife, he made the beautiful *Sarvis* tree to grow over her path with its lovely white blossoms hanging down toward her — surely she would stop to admire. But she kept storming ahead. Then he made the pretty red berries to fill the tree, but she was not noticing them. Next he made the bush huckleberries to grow beside her path, but she just swung her arms as she walked, knocking off the berries. Now he decided to be a bit tricky; he made the blackberries to grow across the path, tearing at her skirt and snagging her legs; even the pain of the snags did not slow her down.

Now the Great Spirit saw that he must give more thought and planning to his strategy. What must one do to get over being angry? Oh, yes! One must bow one's head and get down on one's knees. With this in mind he tried to think of a way to get the woman's attention so as to make her do these two things. An appeal to her sense of smell seemed reasonable, because her nose was in the air in a straight line from the ground. So he began to play on her sense of curiosity. He created a tiny plant, close to the ground, bearing a pretty, red, heart-shaped fruit which, when mashed, gave off a most delightful aroma. As soon as she smelled this first strawberry, her curiosity got the best of her. She looked down to see it, bowing her head. It looked like something so good to eat that she immediately went down on her knees to pick one to taste. As soon as the berry touched her tongue, she forgot her anger. Her only thought was to gather some to take to her husband.

She gathered a handful, looked up and saw her husband coming. She ran to meet him; they ate the berries and spent the next few minutes gathering all their hands could hold. While doing so, the man remembered that this little plant saved the best thing in his life — his wife. So he pulled up some of the plants and stuck them in his belt to take home and plant by the doorway among her beloved corn. She, like any housewife, thought only of what she would have for supper. As he stopped outside to plant his little strawberries, she stepped into the house to prepare the meal. It was only then that she thought, "Oh, how foolish I was to become angry and almost lose my home, my love, and my security, and now I do not even remember why I was angry." As she began to prepare the berries to eat, she wished she could keep some around longer. They seemed so fragile, so she looked about to see if she could find some way of keeping them. On the shelf was a small pottery jar with some wild honey in it. The honey keeps for many days without spoiling. She filled the space in the jar with the ripe strawberries.

We might say that on that day strawberry preserves were born. At any rate, all well-meaning Cherokee housewives try to keep strawberries in the house all year round "to insure domestic tranquility." Some may be frozen in the modern manner; others may be dried by a method older than written history, while others may be canned in glass jars as the Cherokee women have been keeping food for more than two generations.

Wild greens are, and have been for times beyond memory, a big part of the Cherokee spring diet. Now, with canning and freezing, these delicacies are enjoyed all year. There was a time when some were dried for winter use. Among the favorites of today are:

1. Ramps (*Allium tricoccum*), a very strong-smelling, onion-like plant growing in the high mountains. If ramps are eaten raw, the eater becomes "socially unacceptable" for a few days while the odor is oozing out through the pores of his skin. But if the ramps are parboiled several times in water before being stirred around in a little grease and salt, and if a few raw eggs are added just before removing from the fire, even the most fastidious may partake. One's health improves with a mess of ramps.
2. Sochani (*Rudbeckia lacianata*), creases (*Barbarea vulgaris*), branch lettuce (*Saxifraga micranthidifolia*), *u-ga-na-s-da* [sweet grass or Solomon's seal] (*Polygonatum biflorum*), *oo-s-te-s-gi* (*Phacelia dubia*), *wa-ne-gi-dun* (*Ligusticum canadense*) and numerous others may, alone or in combination with several others, be parboiled, then stirred around in a little grease and salt before eating with fatback and cornbread.
3. Poke salad (*Phytolacca americana*) is a plant with some poisonous qualities, so eggs and grease are both necessary, after the parboiling, before being eaten. NEVER use the roots of this plant. The mature stems and berries should also be treated with respect.

Tobacco has been with the Indians for many years, and many legends have been told about it. The one that recounts the Great Spirit's instructions about man's using tobacco only when sealing the peace also tells about the smoke in the Smoky and Blue Ridge Mountains and the origin of Indian Pipes (*Monotropa uniflora*). Tobacco has been used for medicine, but nowadays the Indians follow the Europeans in their habit of smoking. A few Cherokee people also chew or dip.

Before the days of canning and refrigeration, the Cherokee people had to rely on the method of drying in order to have many foods "out of season." Even today some of the older women think it strange when younger women serve pickled beans in the summer. Wild greens may be canned or frozen but are considered best when fresh. The time of day for eating certain foods is about the same as for white Americans. Long ago the

Indian ate what he could get when he could get it. Fish soup and mush were breakfast delicacies because the preparation would begin at night when the men and boys came in with a good catch of small fish. These fish were placed before the fire to dry out; the cornmeal was set before the same fire to cook slowly in plenty of water. When dry, the fish would be broken up and placed in a pot of water to simmer all night along side of the mush that was cooking. When the family awakened in the morning, the meal was ready, so breakfast was fish and mush that day. Another morning the family might have to forage afar for food to be cooked later and eaten still later. Cooking was the job of the women. In fact, the word for WIFE means ONE WHO COOKS. But many Cherokee men also are excellent cooks. They will never go hungry just because there is no woman around to cook for them.

Cooking utensils have been varied. Very early the cooking was done in pots of clay into which hot stones were dropped. Later pots were made so that they might be suspended over a fire. Legend has it that the double-woven baskets of river cane preceded the pots. The clay pots may have come about because someone attempted to patch a hole in a basket with damp clay, then used it over the fire which burned off the cane and left the pot watertight. No pottery made today will hold water, if it is made by the low-fire method. The double-woven baskets are not made tight enough to hold water. Spoons, cups, plates, and bowls were carved from wood, buckeye (*Aesculus octandra*) being a favorite. When on a trip, or out on a nut hunt, food was often served on a piece of chestnut bark, cut fresh when needed. Later this was added to the fire to provide a light to enable the campers to make their beds and to keep away the wild animals.

A list of plants native to the Cherokee country which have been used for both food and medicine are given in Table 1. An exhaustive list of plants with their uses for either medicine or food would probably include every plant that grows in this area. This is because the people, when they have been reduced to subsistence eating, have found a way to use almost every plant and animal for food. The items that proved to be poisonous were often used to combat disease and pestilence.

To the Indian the things that the Great Spirit made had a purpose, which was the continued existence of men. Young Chief of the Cayuses surely expressed the Indian philosophy when in 1899 he said:

"I wonder if the ground has anything to say? I wonder if the ground is listening to what is said? I wonder if the ground would come alive and what is on it? Though I hear what the ground says. The ground says, It is the Great Spirit that placed me here. The Great Spirit tells me to take care of the Indians, to feed them aright. The Great Spirit appointed the roots to feed the Indians on.

Feed the Indians well. The grass says the same thing, Feed the Indians well. The ground, water and grass say, The Great Spirit has given us our names. We have these names and hold these names. The ground says, The Great Spirit has placed me here to produce all that grows on me, trees and fruit. The same way the ground says, it was from me man was made. The Great Spirit, in placing men on the earth, desired them to take good care of the ground and to do each other no harm ..." (McLuhan 1971:8).

Table 1. Plants native to the Cherokee country

Name of plant	As food	As medicine
apple *(Pyrus malus)*	raw or baked	bark tea
blackberry *(Rubus nigrobaccus)*	raw or cooked	root or bark tea
cherry *(Prunus serotina)*	drink of berries	bark, syrup, or tea
chestnut *(Castanea vesca)*	nuts	leaf tea
corn *(Zea maya)*	whole or pounded	parched grain, tea of silks
crabapple *(Pyrus coronaria)*	roast fruit	bark tea
creases *(Barbarea vulgaris)*	leaves as salad	leaves cooked
dandelion *(Taraxicum officinale)*	leaves	root tea
dewberry *(Rubus trivialis)*	raw or cooked	tea of roots
honey locust *(Gleditsia triacanthos)*	pulp	bark tea
passion flower *(Passiflora incarnata)*	fruit	tea of fruit or herb
peach *(Prunus persica)*	fruit	tea of leaves or bark
pokeberry *(Phytolacca am.)*	leaves	tea of berries or roots
ramps *(Allium tricoccum)*	plant	plant
Solomon's seal *(Polygonatum biflorum)*	leaves and stems	leaves and stems
spicebush *(Lindera benzoin)*	twigs	twigs
strawberry *(Fragaria vir.)*	fruit	tea of leaves or roots
sumac *(Rhus typhinia)*	red berries	red berries
tobacco *(Nicotiana)*	leaves to smoke	leaves
toothwort *(Dentaria diphylla)*	leaves	tea of plant
wild bergamot *(Monarda)*	leaves	leaves
wild grape *(Vitis)*	fruit	tea of leaves
wild plum *(Prunus am.)*	fruit	tea of bark
wild potato *(Ipomoea)*	roots	tea of leaves

REFERENCES

BARTRAM, WILLIAM

1958 *Travels* (naturalist's edition). New Haven: Yale University Press.

GILBERT, WILLIAM H.

1943 *The eastern Cherokees*. Bureau of American Ethnology 133.

MCLUHAN, T. C.

1971 *Touch of the earth: a self-portrait of Indian existence*. New York: Pocket Books.

MOONEY, JAMES

1900 [1902] *Myths of the Cherokee*. Nineteenth Annual Report of the Bureau of Ethnology.

PEITHMAN, IRVIN M.
1964 *Red men of fire: a history of the Cherokee Indians.* Springfield, Illinois: Charles C. Thomas.

SWANTON, JOHN R.
1948 *The Indians of the southeastern United States.* Bureau of American Ethnology 137.

TIMBERLAKE, HENRY
1948 *Memoirs of Lieut. Henry Timberlake.* (reprinted edition). Marietta, Georgia: Continental Press.

ULMER, MARY, SAMUEL E. BECK
1951 *Cherokee cooklore: to make my bread.* Asheville, North Carolina: Stephens Press.

VON HAGEN, VICTOR W.
1961 *Realm of the Incas.* New York: New American Library.

Wild Foods Used by the Cherokee Indians

REBECCA GRANT

Taken from a transcribed version of the talk given September 4, 1973 at the IXth International Congress of Anthropological and Ethnological Sciences, by Rebecca Grant of Cherokee, North Carolina, herself a Cherokee Indian.

I am going to tell you a little about the foods we eat from nature and the wilds.[1]

In the early spring, we have the *So-chan*, when it comes up, and the cresses. Another wild green is the ramps, bear's garlic (*Allium tricoccum*). It is an ill-smelling plant that comes out of the mountains. If you eat it, nobody will associate with you for two or three days. We also have "poke salad" made of leaves from the pokeberry (*Phytolacca americana*), which is considered poisonous by a lot of people if you do not fix it right. We also have "turkey beans," little beans growing on vines which fall to the ground in the autumn, then come up in the springtime. When they drop to the ground they are just small seeds, but they swell, and by the time they start to grow they are as big as peanuts or bigger. We roast them and eat them like roasted peanuts.

Later, in the summer, there are mountain greens called "Solomon Seal," the bean salad, the angelica. We also dig swamp potatoes, which taste very much like sweet potatoes. When we dig them up, they look like a big old necklace with little ones — all the same size — at intervals of four to five inches, hanging on the root that looks like a vine.

We never are without protein. We eat wild meat — the animals, the

1 Recipes for some of the foods mentioned here can be found in *Cherokee Cooklor* by Mary Ulmer and Samuel E. Beck (1951, The Stephens Press).

squirrels, and the rabbits, but we do not eat them during the summertime, which is forbidden because they have parasites in them. Sometimes we kill bear.

In the fall, we gather [black] walnuts which we use to flavor our succotash and bread. When we make parched corn mush, we flavor it with these walnuts. We also gather hickory nuts and grind them. When we do not grind them, we crack them. After that we take them from the shell and sift them through a basket. Some of the small fragments sift through with the kernels. These we pound with a modern pestle that has a long handle with a heavy top end. I hate this with a purple passion when I have to use it. We pound these nuts and fragments of shell in a mortar until they become the consistency of peanut butter. Then we roll it up in a ball and put it in a bowl, and pour boiling water over it to make a rich drink that looks like cocoa, a very rich cocoa milk. We have something sweet with it.

Mushrooms we pick all through the summer as they come up. We eat the early ones with dried land fish. We take the ginger-looking mushroom that exudes a milky substance and roast it with salt near an open fire. In September the "little bunches" come up, sometimes called "slick-go-downs." These mushrooms are yellow ones that grow in clusters which we cut down and cook. We also have a big tree mushroom, the botanical name I do not know. This one tastes like steak when it is cut up and cooked.

We also used to eat yellow jackets which we dug up until I learned they sting; then we quit. We also ate locusts. I remember one time, when I was eleven years old, it was the last time I saw them come out. My mother cooked some for my brother and me. I couldn't eat one because it looked like a big fly.

In the summertime, we have strawberries, blackberries, raspberries, and huckleberries. Later in the summer, we have the wild grape that grows up in the mountains. In a few places we find the muscadines (*Vitis rotundifolia*), a very fragrant wild grape.

We also dig for crayfish, which have pinchers like a lobster — a very small form of lobster, but they hurt just as bad when they pinch you. We used to cook them. I still like them, if I can get them. When I was young, my Dad used to go seining and catch little minnows which we had to clean the next day. He would bring home two or three gallons of them. We would fry them until they were good and crisp, then make soup. The white people call it chowder — fish chowder. We would have a big pot of mush to go with it. All the old Indians relished this.

Our staple is corn. We have three types of corn that we use. A "dent corn" that is used for cornmeal to make cornbread. Then we have a flour corn, which is Indian maize, that makes our Indian breads such as lye dumplings, and hominy — big hominy. We make parched corn of this. From parched corn we make parched meal. To make parched corn, we put a big pot on [the fire] and sift [wood] ashes into it and then stir and stir and stir with a long paddle until the ashes get hot and fluffy and the corn goes round and round. When we take it off the fire, the corn is all puffy and just as light as a feather. We can either eat it whole or chew it just as you would peanuts, or else you can have it ground into meal. You can carry just a little of this ground meal, which will sustain you to keep you from getting hungry. Just add a little water to it. My father and mother used to pour molasses on the corn while they were pounding it so it would have a sweetish taste. A long time ago, the hunters who were going far away somewhere, and who would stay a day or two, would take some of this parched corn with them.

Then there is the "flint corn," on which we use lye. A lye solution is put into a hopper and the corn dropped into it. The skins come off the corn. This is what we use for big hominy. During the summer, we put some of this hominy in a big jug and let it sit for two or three days. It must be cold. Whenever people are working in the fields, they holler for corn, for this water to drink; we take it out to them. Most of them would rather have the hominy that came out of this drink because it would be a little fermented.

We also use pounded honey locusts (*Gleditsia triacanthos*) to make a drink that is sweet. The honey locust pods look like big old jack beans on the tree. They get brown but are not used until after a frost — a heavy freeze.

Also we gather persimmons, but I do not recall that we ever made anything much from them. I have heard people say they made persimmon beer, a kind of fermented drink, but we never did gather that many at home. My mother used to dry them a little bit and they were real sweet. They were gathered after they fell off the tree because they would pucker your mouth and make you want to whistle if they were not ripe enough.

There was a time to gather everything. We were forbidden to do certain things if the time was not right because it was thought they would hurt us.

SECTION SIX

Food in Tradition

Food and Folk Beliefs: On Boiling Blood Sausage

NILS-ARVID BRINGÉUS

Ethnologists often find that the recorded material in the archives, as well as various kinds of printed descriptions, are remarkably incomplete in describing many aspects of folk life. This is especially true of the descriptions of diet and the preparation of food. This may be due to the fact that work in the kitchen is usually carried out within the inner circle of the family, but a more important reason may be that the woman's work has not been as closely observed as the man's.

Ethnological research has to a great extent been directed towards the study of cultural products and their formal variations, functions, and changes. But food as a cultural product is short-lived, and at best little more than the vessels used in the preparation and serving of food have been preserved and placed in museums. To a lesser extent, ethnologists have directed their attention to the study of cultural behavior. Daily behavior, in particular, has been neglected in favor of customs connected with ceremonial occasions, in the same way that objects in daily use are underrepresented in our museums by comparison with objects marked by status. To some extent the lack of material is connected with the methods of collection. It is only in recent years that we have begun to understand the importance of observation, something which Linnaeus was fully aware of. In addition the informant's or interviewer's evaluations, as well as the climate of the times, may have created barriers to our knowledge. Certain traditions, for example, have been considered so ugly, coarse, or "hayseed" that for these reasons they have never been published.

A Swedish version of this article with detailed references also to recent records was published in the journal *Saga och sed* in 1972. Reports of the records belonging to the maps are kept in The Institute of European Ethnology of Lund, Sweden.

Even worse, we are faced with irreparable damage because the observations cannot always be repeated and the informants who might have helped us are not alive. The areas in which these practices still exist can in some cases still offer us the possibility of glimpsing forms of behavior reported from other places. During an ethnological field seminar in the Carpathians in the summer of 1969 I had the opportunity to observe the importance of the sign of the cross in the baking of bread. The dough was marked with a cross before it was set aside to rise. The loaves were marked with a cross before they were put in the oven. Rising and baking are both processes which can go wrong: the sign of the cross is a universal means which the pious Catholic population made use of on such occasions.

In today's Protestant, highly industrialized Sweden it is impossible to make the same type of observations. However, older records of traditions testify to the occurrence of the sign of the cross in Sweden in similar situations as late as two or three hundred years after the Reformation.

However, the regionally diverse measures which people utilized without being externally influenced, for prophylactic purposes during various types of household work involving risk are of greater interest from an ethnological viewpoint. The examples of this presented in the following pages refer not to baking, but to boiling sausage, which in certain circumstances can also be an activity involving risk.

As early as 1917, in a questionnaire on beliefs and customs connected with slaughtering, the Norwegian ethnologist Nils Lid posed the question: "Were there any special measures that had to be observed during the boiling process so that the sausages would not burst?" This is a good example of a neutrally formulated question, and would have resulted in valuable material if the collection had been carried out systematically. In Denmark, in a questionnaire concerning slaughtering (1944), attention was devoted to various measures connected with the preparation of sausage by the National Museum's Ethnological Investigation. The material received is very enlightening on several points, but it is clear that for certain other traditions it was plainly too late. In order to determine the extent to which the beliefs and measures discussed here are still known, a questionnaire was sent in February 1973 to the informants of the Institute of European Ethnology and the Dialect Archives in southern Sweden. The material received is surprisingly good and suggests that the levelling of tradition has not gone as far as it has in Denmark. However, for certain obscene blessings, the results were negative, possibly because of the collection methods used. Trained fieldworkers would probably have obtained better results. The complex of traditions discussed here has not been studied before, although Nils Lid, who specialized in folk beliefs and methods of slaughtering, has touched on certain traditions (Lid 1924, 1935). Apart from printed sources, recorded material from all the larger Swedish, Danish, and Norwegian ethnological and dialect archives constitutes the basis for this paper.

RATIONAL MEASURES

Blood sausage, which can now be purchased all year round in food shops in the localities where it is eaten, was once freshly prepared at home after the slaughtering of pigs, which took place before Christmas (although there was sometimes another slaughtering during the year). Blood sausage was prepared by beating a mixture of rye flour and rye grains and pig's blood, thinned somewhat with water or small beer; in addition, cubes of pork and pieces of apple — later raisins — were mixed in and the whole was then poured into thick sausage casings. However, these were not more than three quarters filled, because during the boiling process the flour and the grains of rye expand. At the ends of the sausage the skin was tied and fastened by means of a thorn from a sloe bush or a "sausage stick" which was specially cut for the purpose (Vuorela 1961:22ff.). In later times the ends of the sausage were also fastened with a string.

In spite of the precautionary measures observed while filling the casings with the sausage mixture it could easily happen that the sausage split and the contents were wasted. Such a mishap is referred to in a counting rhyme: "Kitta Lorva was cooking sausages, the sausages split and Kitta Lorva drank." In order to prevent this an effort was made to keep the heat under the sausage kettle as even as possible. It was said that "cabbage should be boiled quickly and sausage should be simmered," or "sausage should be boiled as if it were numb, and cabbage as if it were crazy." Another saying had it that "the sausage kettle should be boiled as carefully as a bride treads." There were several stratagems for making sure that the boiling was even and quiet. For example, a small coin might be placed in the bottom of the sausage kettle. When the water was boiling evenly and quietly the coin clattered lightly against the bottom of the kettle. The sausages could also be placed in the kettle with the words "Boil smoothly." The door was to be kept closed to prevent draughts. During the boiling the sausage could also split as a result of the air bubbles formed inside the casing. For this reason a sharp instrument was at hand for pricking the casing. Thorns from the sloe bush are long and sharp and well suited for this purpose.

Blood sausage was often prepared in the large wash-house kettle, or in any big kettle, on the day of or day after the slaughtering. At the Christmas slaughtering it had usually become dark by the time the people were ready to boil the sausage, and it was not easy to maintain an even warmth and watch the sausage. Other precautionary measures were therefore necessary.

TABOOS

In a number of records, from Scania to the middle of Sweden as well as from Denmark (Højrup 1972:104), it is specified that one must keep silent during the boiling of the sausage. THE PROHIBITION OF SPEECH is in and of itself a common prescription in critical situations. However, the fact that the rule of silence was connected with the boiling of sausage seems to depend on immediate associations of identity. Namely, in several records it is stated that one must pinch the lips or keep the mouth shut tight in the same way as one must tighten the sphincter and not break wind. The sausage might also split at the ends and that had to be prevented. The parallel between the sausage casing and the human intestinal canal is very clear. That the taboo on speaking during the boiling of sausage is an old one is shown by a collection of superstitions from western Småland, published in 1774: "When the sausage is placed in the kettle to boil, the persons placing it there must not utter a single word; they must smack the sausages one by one against the side of the wall and put the sausage in the kettle in silence, or else the sausage will split apart" (Gaslander 1895:298). The speech prohibition can also be observed outside the blood sausage area at that time. Thus it is reported from eastern Småland in 1772 that "when the sausage is placed in the kettle, no one can speak, or the sausage will split" (Craelius 1930:64).

It can be seen from Gaslander's description that silence could be combined with magical actions to strengthen its effect, or that it simply constituted a prerequisite for the desired result. From Västergötland it is reported (Sundblad 1881:129) that the housewife first smacked the sausage gently against the side of the stove and then against the edge of the kettle. "While doing this she may not utter a word, for then her actions would lose their effect. This would mean that the sausage would split. Of this she (the housewife) was fully convinced and never omitted them."

If it was not possible to keep silent during the boiling of the sausage the pronunciation of the word *blood* as well as of *blood sausage* had to be avoided. Since the blood obtained at slaughtering was made use of, a substitute name for it was employed. In Scania — with the possible exception of the southwest district — blood was called *röen* [the red one]. This was also the case in those areas of Småland, Blekinge, and Halland that border on Scania, and the corresponding term *ryd* also occurred in older times on Gotland. In immediate connection with this distribution area, in the other parts of Halland, Småland, and Blekinge, as well as on Öland and Gotland and further north, blood was called *svett* [sweat], while sausage, where it was prepared, was called *svettkorv* [sweat sausage]. In Denmark also it is reported (Thiele 1860:226) that during the slaughtering the word *sved* [sweat] could not be pronounced since the animal does not bleed but "sweats." In a similar fashion a sausage made of sheep's blood, as done on Lolland-Falster and Fyn was called *svede* [sweat] (Højrup 1972:103).

The name *svettkorv* suggests that the euphemism was primarily connected with blood and not with the sausage. *Röe* [red] occurs principally in the expression *ta röen* [take the red], i.e. collect the blood during the slaughtering. All such euphemisms have the common property of being used to reduce risks: *tasse* [paw] so that wolves would not attack the cattle; *värme* [warmth] during the preparation of charcoal so that the charcoal stack would not burn; *svett* [sweat] so that the blood would not be drained away at the slaughtering, etc. But as we have seen, the boiling of sausage implied an element of risk and in some places the word sausage was also taboo. From Dalsland it is reported that a boy teased his mother while she was boiling sausage for Christmas. "He leaned over the kettle and said 'I can't wait for the sausage to be ready, Mamma'. The mother was very angry with the boy." I have not found any euphemisms for sausage in Sweden. On the other hand, it was reported from Finland by Wessman in 1925 that when sausage was prepared the word *mullarna* had to be used instead of sausage (Swedish *korv*), or the sausages would split in the oven. In Denmark we find a number of names for blood sausage: "*kerdulter, dingser, tinge, bulökser, vognkjæppe, pusserønter, de grå*" (Feilberg 1894–1904:907; Nyrop 1887:123ff.; Højrup 1972:104). Certain of these names are in the nature of similes. It was clearly desired that blood sausage should be hard like *buløkser* or [wheel spokes] (Lid 1935:65).

Other prohibitions appear to have a partially rational foundation. The demand that the sausage boil quietly and evenly may thus underlie the fact that it was FORBIDDEN TO BLOW ON THE FIRE; this is mentioned in various parts of the country. A similar explanation can also be conceived for the traditions which hold that if a stranger came in, the sausage would come out of the casing. This has to do, as we have seen, with the avoidance of draughts during the boiling of the sausage. In Norway it was even said that sausage should not be boiled in windy weather, "or there will be holes in the skin" (Lid 1924:64). A similar reason may be the basis for the rule that ONLY THE HOUSEWIFE SHOULD BE AT THE STOVE. However, when we find in several reports that MEN SHOULD NOT BE PRESENT there is no longer a rational basis for the taboo. Strangers could not, however, always be prevented from calling while the sausage was being boiled. The belief that the sausage would then split was an old one, mentioned as early as 1773 in Värmland (Fernow 1773:259). In three records from Västergötland it is stated that on such occasions they should be invited to eat sausage in order that the sausages in the kettle should not burst. The same rule was recorded by Rääf (1957:251): "When the sausage is boiling and a stranger comes, he should taste it, or the sausage in the kettle will split." The reason behind this belief can be seen from a Norwegian report:

> In the kitchen one should also beware of evil people's envy, especially old women. They have caused sausages to burst...if you can keep them away from there, that's the best thing you can do. Should anyone arrive in spite of your efforts, one must beware of speaking about what one is cooking, and should they nevertheless catch sight of it or in some other way find out about it, one should share it with them and thereby satisfy them (Storaker 1938:137).

The real reason why a visit from a stranger was undesirable during the boiling of the sausages was thus that they could have evil intentions (*vond hug*). We therefore find this idea linked with, among other things, witches. But in addition anyone who might covet the boiling blood sausages could "fill them with evil thoughts" upon which they would burst (Eidnes 1946:76; Gröttland 1962:88).

It is probable that the visit taboos should primarily be considered against the background of the ancient complex of ideas which is constituted by the traditions of "evil intentions" and "the evil eye" (Lid 1924:83).

That folk beliefs concerning the boiling of sausage can, not infrequently, follow a paradigm is also demonstrated by the idea that BLOOD SAUSAGE SHOULD NOT BE BOILED DURING A NEW MOON but while the moon is on the wane. This belief applied to slaughtering in general, and could by a natural process become associated precisely with boiling the sausage. If the sausages swelled too much during the boiling they would split (Lid 1924:41, 46).

THE SPLEEN AS THE SAVIOR OF SAUSAGE

In a large number of reports it is stated that the spleen of the slaughtered pig was placed in the kettle to prevent the sausages from splitting during the boiling. That this usage is so well attested is due to the fact that the spleen was thereby given a special name. The answers to the questionnaire on sausage show that the custom as well as the name for the spleen are still well known to the older generation. The spleen was called *pölsefrälsare* [sausage savior] in Scania. Most of the reports are located in the southern and central regions of the province, but the term is also known in Breared in southern Halland and in Bornholm. In northern Halland and southern Västergötland the spleen was called *korvafrälsare* [sausage savior]. Other terms which are recorded to a lesser degree are *pölsevaktare* or *korvvaktare* [sausage guardian] (Scania, Blekinge, Västergötland) and *pölsehållare* or *korvhållare* [sausage holder] (Halland, Småland). Two reports have been received from western Scania for *pølsepassare* [sausage guard]. In southern Västergötland there is also record of the term *korvatrösta* [sausage comforter]. The spleen "comforts the sausage so that he doesn't split." On Själland in Denmark the spleen was usually called *pølsepasseren* [sausage guard]. A few reports have been received from Lolland for *pølsevogter* [sausage guardian] and *pølsehyrde* [sausage herdsman]. The terms for the spleen constitute a rather coherent distribution area that includes Själland, Bornholm, the old Danish provinces of Scania and Halland, and southern Västergötland. One report from Blekinge and one from southernmost Småland must be added. Apart from the occurrences marked on Map 1, which refer only to the use of the above terms, the use of the spleen itself is further reported in a number of reports within the same area as well as from Gotland.

That the use of the spleen was also known in northeast Scania can be seen in a report from 1881, in which we find: "When they boil blood sausage they have a custom of putting the animal's spleen in the kettle, so that the sausage doesn't split" (Wigström 1881:157). In Denmark, where the custom has been systematically studied with the aid of a questionnaire from the National Museum's Ethnological Investigations, there are twenty-seven positive and two negative reports from Själland, Bornholm, and Falster, while there are only five positive but eighty-six negative reports from Lolland, Fyn, and Jylland. Since the distribution area includes both Själland-Falster to the west of Öresund and Scania to the east of it, as well as Gotland, we are justified in assuming that the terms as well as the usage reach back at least as far as the period before the mid-seventeenth century, when Scania and Gotland were separated from Denmark.

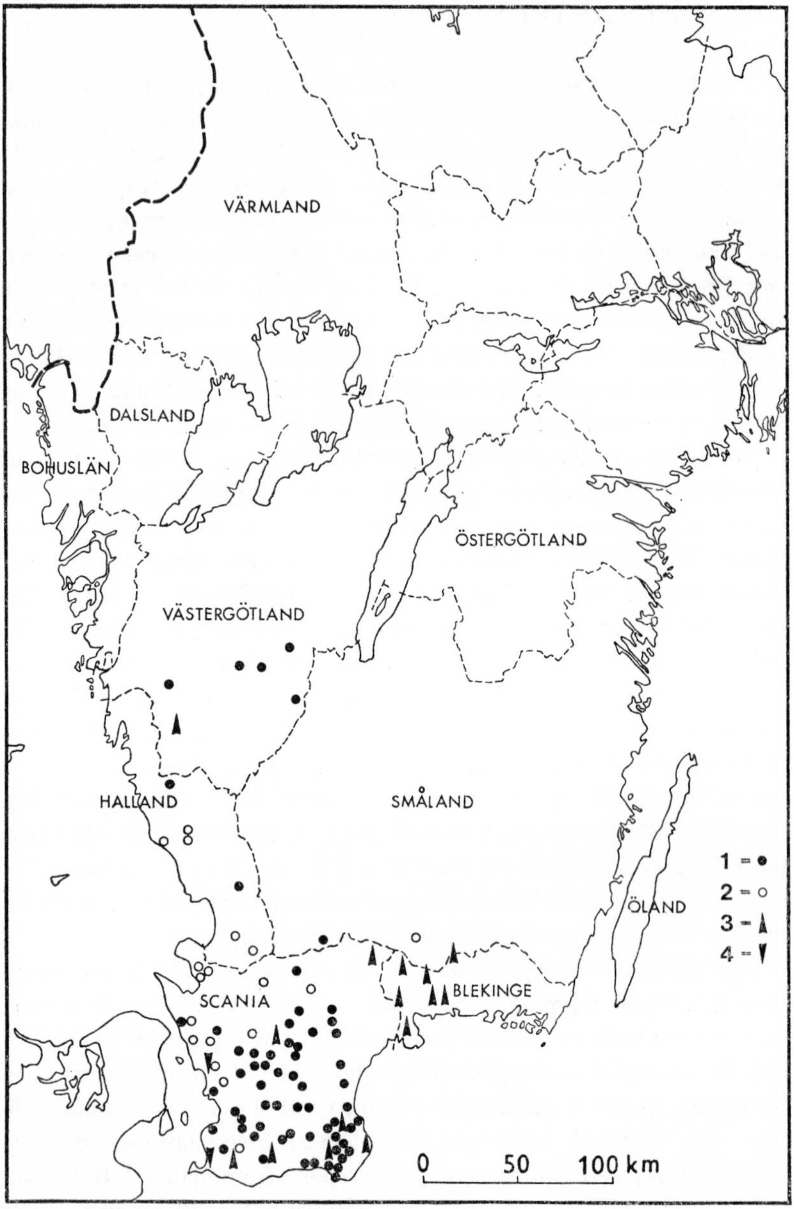

Map 1. Distribution of terms used for the spleen

1. *Pölsefrälsare/korvfrälsare* [sausage savior]
2. *Pölsehållare/korvhållare* [sausage holder]
3. *Pölsevaktare/korvvaktare* [sausage guardian]
4. *Pölsepassare* [sausage guard]

Of the terms given above, "sausage savior" is clearly the oldest. In present linguistic usage the word "savior" is only used in reference to Christ, so that "sausage savior" has something of a blasphemous nature which surely was not the case earlier. For the term "sausage guardian" there exist other linguistic parallels such as "field guardian," "goose guardian," etc. Like these, the "sausage savior" and "sausage guardian" were to ward off damage. The terms *pölsehållare* and *korvahållare* [sausage holder], which we find on the periphery of the distribution area, are clearly connected to another complex of traditions to which I shall return later.

The reports do not provide more detailed information about the form in which the spleen was placed in the kettle. I have the impression that it was generally put in whole. In a report from Västergötland it is stated that "some people cleaned the spleen and scraped it and put it first in the kettle, for the spleen was the 'sausage savior.' Later they gave it to the chickens." In only one report is it stated that the spleen "was cut up."

The question arises here of whether putting the spleen in the sausage kettle was a rational or an irrational measure. The informants do not give any indication of their own opinions or of those of people in general in this connection. Only when we find, in a report from outside the distribution area, that a piece of the spleen should be placed "on the shelf above the stove where the sausages are cooked" is there no doubt that we are dealing with folk belief, assuming that this is not a misunderstanding on the part of the informant.

Ethnologists are well aware of the fact that popular empirical measures should not be underestimated. Great care was taken with anything which could serve as food for human beings. Of the pig's viscera, both liver and lungs were used in the preparation of sausage. Even the gall bladder was saved; use was made of its fat-dissolving properties and of its strong smell (Højrup 1972:102ff.). Nothing similar is known of the spleen, while, on the other hand, informants knew of its function as an oracle: "The spleen is possessed of wonderful power, and by examining it carefully, you could foretell if the winter would be mild or hard. If the spleen was of even width the winter would be early and hard, but if one end was narrower than the other, the winter would be short and mild." Hyltén-Cavallius (1972:340) connects this belief with the heathen use of offerings, according to which "from the slaughtered Christmas pig's liver and spleen the omens could be taken of the winter's length and of its various qualities." Johan Törner (1946:168) took up the same usage in his collection of superstitions from the eighteenth century:

They also use the pig's spleen to forecast the future. If the thickness of the spleen is even throughout, they say the winter will be hard. If it is only thick in the upper part, the end of the winter will be cold. If it is thick in the middle, the middle of the winter will be cold. If the spleen is only thick in the lower part, there will be cold and frost only in the beginning of the winter (Törner 1946:168).

Törner's source is the *Sächsisches und Brandenburgisches Land- und Hauss Wirtschaffts Buch*, published in Nürnberg in 1730, which gives almost the same text. It is thus a question here of a widely disseminated technique of prediction and it may be asked if there is some connection between that technique and the spleen's function as a sausage savior. The origin of the use of the spleen as an oracle is a question which cannot be treated here. Nevertheless, it is clear that the fact that it was used to forecast winter weather is obviously connected with the fact that forecasting winter weather was important at the time of the pigslaughtering for Christmas.

Since biochemists could not, when asked, offer a more concrete explanation for the custom of placing the spleen in the sausage kettle, it may be grounded in some type of association in the same way as the use of the spleen to forecast the weather. One possible indication of this is the fact that as far as I know the sausage savior was only used during the boiling of blood sausage. The spleen is of importance for the production of blood cells, and it is conceivable that this "blood gland" was associated with blood in sausage on the principle that like cures like. (In my opinion, experience of the function of the human spleen in so-called "stitches in the side" as a sort of alarm is not relevant in this connection.) However, I am not sure that this explanation is the correct one.

That the role of the spleen is grounded in folk beliefs is given credence by another circumstance. In an answer in a newly distributed questionnaire about blood sausage an informant says that another medium could be used as a sausage guardian, namely the triangular piece of pork from the place on the pig where the butcher's knife had entered. It was widely believed that this so-called stabbing piece could not be used as food for human beings; this was also true of the spleen.

Irrespective of the origin of this usage of the spleen, we shall see that it was probably rooted in folk beliefs because it constituted an alternative and a geographical complement to other irrational measures with the same purpose.

BLESSINGS

When the sausage was placed in the kettle a "sausage prayer" (Swedish *pölsebön* or *korvabön*), as it is called in some reports, was often recited in order that the sausage should not split. This blessing exhibits a rather fixed pattern and is known in southern Västergötland; there are several reports from central Halland. Most of the reports are in the Folklore Institute in Gothenburg and the greater part of them were written by two professional interviewers between 1928 and 1944. Since the Institute's collection area is considerably greater, there is hardly reason to believe that the picture provided by Map 2 is a result of uneven collection. The attempt to collect new information through the questionnaire that was sent out this year about blood sausage has not produced any results.

Here are several examples of blessings: "Hard as a pole and tough as cunt, you'll hold together and never split." "Hard as a stick, tough as cunt, hold sausage." "Hard as horn and tough as cunt, you must hold and never split." "Hard as flint and tough as cunt, you must hold and never split." "Hard as stone and tough as *kurra* [the head of a flail], all hold, none split." A further variation is "Strong as a wall and tough as skin."

The blessing usually consists of three parts; the first two contain a comparison or a simile with an explanatory function. The first part is "hard as," the second "tough as," and the third contains a direct command: "You must hold and never split." In certain reports the first part is lacking and in some both the first and second parts; it also occurs that the first two are present and the third lacking.

The blessing's main point, "You must hold and not split," is found in twenty reports, while the female sexual organ appears as a simile in nineteen reports. SKIN can be a euphemism for the latter but may refer to skin in general. In addition, *kurra* is a skin. In the report it is stated that "by *kurra* was meant a type of flail head which was made of eelskin, the toughest and strongest of flail heads."

The simile used in the first part of the blessing is more varied. The six reports that have the noun "pole" (Swedish *stötta*) all state that the blessing was pronounced at the same time that the sausage was smacked (Swedish *stötta*) against the side of the stove, which is why the informants clearly understood the contents of the first part to be "hard as a stove's side." By *stone* and *wall* (Swedish *murn*) is meant the top of the stove and the side of the stove; *stick* undoubtedly refers to the sausage stick at each end of the sausage. This was cut from hardwood. By *horn* is probably intended the "sausage horn" (a type of funnel) which was used when stuffing the sausage mixture into the casing.

It is probable that the similes which occur in the first part of the blessing should be taken literally. If the female sexual organ could be mentioned by name, this ought to have been the case with the male organ, without

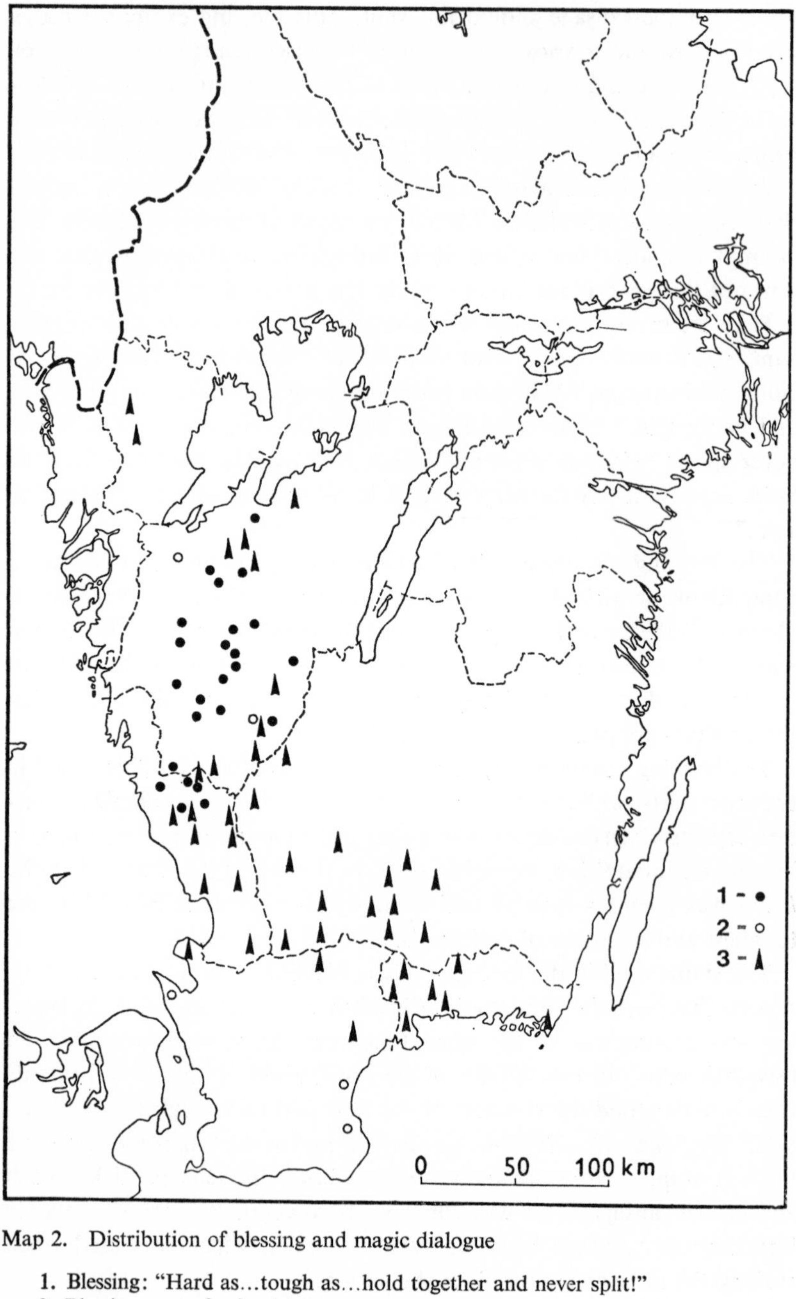

Map 2. Distribution of blessing and magic dialogue

1. Blessing: "Hard as...tough as...hold together and never split!"
2. Blessings not of a fixed type.
3. Magic dialogue: "*Är Hålle/korvhållaren hemma?*"

the use of a euphemism. However, there is some reason to believe that this last possibility should not be completely excluded. In direct significance, the simile in the first part does not offer any parallel to the second part, which would have been natural. There are even reports of blessings where both the male and female organs are used as similes. From Ullasjö in Västergötland is reported: "When they put in the sausage they said: 'Long as a pipe (that is, the bull's penis), tough as leather, long-lasting as cunt'. Many people said this rhyme." In the same province a collector has noted that the sausage was placed in the kettle with the words: "'Stand like a c-ck and not like the skin on a ---', and then they would hold together, my mother told me." A housewife in Scania used to say: "Tough and strong as my cunt and the cockskin and ball skin ..." A woman in southeast Scania used to smack the sausage against the wall with the words "Tough as the skin of a cock," reported her daughter, born in 1852. In the same area a housemaid smacked the blood sausage smartly against the side of the stove with the words: "Tough as balls skin." From Östergötland the formula "Tough as skin" is reported.

Comparisons demonstrate that we cannot completely exclude the possibility that "pole" and "horn" originally referred to the male organ. However, the horn was an attribute of shame; this appeared earlier in certain joking customs in Sweden which referred to the male organ (Danver 1943:183ff.).

In the ancient fire-keeping prayers that were studied by Bengt af Klintberg, mention is made — in various words — of the male as well as the female sexual organ and the blessing concludes with the words "never will the fire slacken in my house" or "God keep my warmth." The last part also constitutes here the blessing's fixed component, while the former is transformed, at times almost beyond recognition. According to af Klintberg the sexual terms have, however, originally

> ... like all elements in a magic spell an exact function, even though it later may have disappeared from consciousness as a result of distortions in the text. In such a case we can interpret the word's function with the help of frequently occurring analogous cases. Their purpose is to PROTECT the embers during the night, when the sleeping human being cannot watch over them (af Klintberg 1971: 238ff.).

Af Klintberg does not discuss the possibility that the sexual terms in the fire-keeping prayers may have been introduced through some sort of association of similar qualities. This is the case with regard to the sausage blessings. The typological and functional analogy between fire-keeping and sausage-boiling prayers clearly allows us to state that the latter are also very old. In itself, the magic charm technique that we meet in the formula "hard as — tough as" has its equivalents in, for example, the blessings for long flax: "Long flax, long flax, long as reins and tough as sinew and white as snow ..." (af Klintberg 1965:97, 132). And the simile technique itself has been known in Sweden since the Middle Ages. We find another simile in the expression "it's as clear as sausage broth." An informant or an interviewer maintains that this is derived from a blessing for sausage boiling: namely, one might have said, "Clear, clear, sausage broth." If the sausages burst the broth became cloudy (Rooth 1971).

Among other things, the fact that the blessings are not rhymed speaks for their relatively great age. There are, however, also examples of very simple rhymed blessings. One such rhyme, which with slight variations appears in four reports, is: *Spricker du itu, ska du få för sju* [If you split you'll catch Hell]. In northwest Scania the houswife might say "Stay in your skin" when she pricked the blood sausage with the thorn of a sloe bush. A similar blessing, with a clearly expressed parallelism, is found in Själland: "Stay in your skin, and I'll stay in mine." No blessings in connection with boiling sausage are otherwise known from Denmark.

The question now is, how did sexual terms function in this connection? Were they used in their capacity as obscenities or only as similes? From a modern point of view certain of the blessings can easily be interpreted as humorous joking poetry. In themselves the terms for "sausage prayer" (*pölsebön/korvabön*) might also give the impression of blasphemy.

It is self-evident that in the past the use of sexual terms for joking or pejorative purposes was not unknown, although in completely different situations than the one with which we are dealing here (von Sydow 1941: 47ff.). In certain situations one could go so far as to exhibit the sexual organs. However, this was not in order to arouse lust but in order to "embarrass" or frighten away beings of various types who attempted to molest a woman. The sexual organ was a shameful organ (von Sydow 1941:68ff.; af Klintberg 1971:239). For this reason various paraphrases for it were used in verbal contexts — in the fire-keeping prayers as well as in the shaming verses of beggar's songs (Strömbäck 1970:40ff.). On the other hand, in sausage prayers the female organ is named directly by its common name, the same name that was otherwise used for the sexual organs of female animals. I am therefore inclined to consider the words as similes of the same type as in the rhymes for long flax. The female organ's great resistance or toughness in the act of parturition and not the attraction of obscenity was the primary reason for its use in this connection. The male organ was not as appropriate as a simile for blood sausage as it was for other kinds of sausage. Another factor which supports my interpretation was the fact that the blessings were recited by the woman who boiled the sausage, who was alone at the oven, and not in order to embarrass a circle of acquaintances. The *Sitz im Leben* of the blessing thus implies that it was used as a simile and only as such.

SMACKING THE SAUSAGE

A tradition that is well documented in various parts of southern Sweden is that THE SAUSAGE SHOULD BE SMACKED AGAINST THE SIDE OF THE STOVE (thirty-seven reports), THE BASE OF THE STOVE (nine reports) or the ANKARTRÄ [a wooden beam above the stove] in the absence of a base (two reports), THE HOOD OVER THE STOVE (four reports) or some other part of the stove. Gaslander mentions this tradition as early as 1774 with reference to Småland, and says that each and every sausage must be smacked "against the wall." Rääf and Hyltén-Cavallius also refer to the usage after this source. From the county of Kalmar, which is outside the true diffusion area, Craelius also reports in 1772 that "when the sausage is placed in the kettle, the first one is struck against the side of the stove."

Another way of preventing the sausages from splitting was to smack them against THE EDGE OF THE KETTLE (seven reports). This tradition is recorded in Västergötland, Östergötland and it is mentioned in 1796 from southern Halland: "When the sausage is first placed in the kettle to boil, they don't want to talk, but smack the sausage smartly against the edge, so that it will not split" (Osbeck 1926:267). The same custom is noted by Rääf (1957:251): "In order that the sausage should not split, they lift him with both hands and strike one end against the stove and the other end against the edge of the kettle."

Reports that sausages are smacked against the stove and/or the edge of the kettle are rather unevenly distributed and it is certain that this reflects an uneven collection of material. However, it is clear that this protective measure was employed in southern Sweden, but not in Scania, Blekinge, or Bohuslän and probably not on Gotland. The absence of reports of this tradition from Scania can clearly be explained by the fact that the spleen was used instead as a sausage savior. I also do not know of any reports from Denmark. In central Halland the tradition displays close geographical ties with Västergötland, with which province there was lively contact.

A parallel to the practice of smacking the sausage against the stove or the edge of the kettle in order to protect it was used when baking; the first loaf to go into the oven was smacked against the side of the oven. Both practices, for bread and for sausage, are reported by Craelius (1930: 61) in connection with the explanation that "the former is certainly because the person who puts the bread in the oven must make sure that it is clean and free of embers, and the latter was a means of finding out if the sausage was too tightly packed, which would necessarily cause it to split during the boiling." These reflections are consistent with Craelius's constant tendency to provide a rational explanation for folk superstitions and thereby contribute to their disappearance. But if the idea was simply to test the stuffing of the sausage, why should only the first one have been smacked against the side of the stove and why in silence, as Osbeck reports?

It is clear that the practice had taken on a ritualized form as early as the eighteenth century. Therefore, pointing to modern parallels in the form of good luck taps will not help us to understand the context of the practice. It would be more correct to seek its counterparts in other prophylactic measures. We may refer here to the fact that an old method of preventing a child from having boils was for the godmother to tap the child's head and feet on the church door at the christening (Rääf 1957:96). A boil can result in the splitting of the skin, as in the case of sausages, where both ends were also brought into contact with the oven or the kettle. A light tap could also be included as a ritual element in certain liturgical ceremonies. It thus seems most appropriate to consider the practice as a sort of tempering in view of the approaching stresses of boiling. As such the practice is clearly rooted in a wider pattern of prophylactic measures.

MAGIC DIALOGUE

In a report from Småland it is stated that: "When they boil blood sausage, there must be two people present. One of them must say: 'Is the sausage-holder home?' The other one must say 'Yes.' This must be repeated three times." This tradition is documented in fifty-three reports. Although an answer to the question is not referred to in all reports, the traditions are nevertheless clearly one and the same. The answers in the questionnaire that was sent out this year demonstrate that the practice is still known to the older generation.

With reference to the person whose presence is inquired after, we can distinguish between two variants which have not been differentiated in Map 2; one of them is represented in the reports in which the *korvhållare* [sausage holder] was asked for (in Halland, *pölsehållare*). In other reports the question reads: "Is *Hålle* home?" Here the personification has thus gone a stage further; Hålle is a person with a name and not simply a "functionary." The spelling of the name varies in the reports, depending on how exactly the pronunciation is reproduced: Håll, Håle, Hålle, Håller, Hållen, Haullen, Höiler, Hel, etc. The distribution is closely connected with the custom of smacking the sausage against the side of the stove and the dialogue is often referred to in direct connection with it. It is also conceivable that the tradition was earlier widely disseminated in Scania for there is a Danish report of it. From Falster it is reported that "the one who is cooking the sausage must ask if 'Hold is in'."

There are thirty-six reports of the variant "Hålle" and sixteen of "sausage holder" (*korvhållare/pölsehållare*). The latter occurs most often in Halland and neighboring areas where we also find *korvhållare/pölsehållare* used as a name for the spleen. Both variants seem to be old traditions. From western Småland where we know that *korvhållare* was traditional, the word is mentioned as early as 1774. If the sausage split open it was said that "the sausage holder isn't home." In a report from Sörmland (Gaslander 1895:198) it is even stated that: "When the sausage is placed in the kettle for boiling, in order that they won't split you should say 'What (who) is the sausage holder now?'"

From a modern point of view we might be tempted to interpret the dialogue as a joke, but this would undoubtedly be a mistake. Even if this might have been the case while the tradition was disappearing, it was certainly not true in older times. In one report it is directly emphasized that "they didn't take the thing as a joke, but in deadly earnest." This is in accord with other behavior and other measures observed in connection with boiling sausage. The ritual character of the dialogue is illustrated by the fact that question and answer are repeated three times; express mention is made of this in many reports. In Halland it was stated that the sausage was smacked against the wall three times, while the person boiling the sausage said at each smack: "Is the sausage holder home? [first smack] Are you home?" The person who had charge of filling the sausage was to answer immediately three times: "Yes of course he's home." The combination of smacking the sausage against the wall and asking a question is a rather natural one. The smacking reminds us of the knocking on a door. The fact that the traditions show a very similar distribution — often occurring in reports from the same area — further emphasizes their affinity.

The reports do not always provide clear information regarding the immediate circumstances surrounding the call or question. Four reports from widely separated places tell us that the words were called up the chimney. One report suggests that the words were asked into the kettle. In both cases there is, of course, no mention made of receiving a natural answer. It is even stated that the cook herself answered:

Before the sausage was placed in the kettle one looked up the chimney and said: 'Are you there, sausage holder?' It was thought that some sort of sound could be heard in the chimney, and the cook took that to mean 'Yes, the sausage holder is here'. She mumbled these words to herself as an answer to her first question.

While this has to do with an answer that was heard, the above report nevertheless shows that there might also be a proper dialogue between two people, for example the maid and the housewife. One informant says plainly that those who answered were "we who stood alongside." In some reports it is stated generally that "someone else" answered. From Halland it was said: "If a stranger came to a place where they were boiling sausage, he was supposed to ask if the sausage holder was home. And then the people in the house answered that he was home, and so the sausage didn't split." However, it is clear that this has to do with an adaptation of a tradition since there could hardly have been strangers calling every time sausage was boiled, while on the other hand there was always anxiety that the sausage should remain whole. In a report from Denmark it is stated instead that "anyone coming in should hop over the threshold and ask if the 'holder' was home," which makes more sense. Question dialogues and sausage blessings have clearly been combined when it is reported that the sausages were laid in the kettle with the words "Stay at home, tough as skin and almost as hard as horn." Another report preserves only the exhortation: "Stay at home, stay here."

I have recently had the opportunity to record two variants used by the informant's mother in Blekinge as late as the 1920's. The first is in a dialogue form: "Is Hel home with his leather trousers on?" after which the woman boiling the sausage herself answered "Yes." The other variant is in the form of a command: "Stay home, while I cook my sausages."

An examination of the reported material makes it clear that the dialogue form is the original one. The question "Is Hålle home?" requires an answer. However, it is more difficult to determine if the variant with the imaginary or with the real answer is the original one. One argument for the latter is an almost century-old report from northeast Scania, in which it is stated that certain people used to "when they were about to place the blood sausage in the kettle, call through the closed door to the cabin" 'Is Hålle home,' upon which someone inside was supposed to answer 'Yes'. This was asked and answered three times" (Wigström 1881: 157).

The thrice-repeated dialogue in connection with boiling the sausage does not constitute unique prophylactic behavior. In Gaslander's description of Västbo (1895:298) we are told that: "When making rennet, the person who is preparing it must ask three times 'What is quicker than fire?' upon which someone else must answer 'Rennet,' and it is believed that milk will curdle faster when making cheese." In this dialogue, which after Gaslander was also reported by Rääf (1957:281) and Hyltén-Cavallius (1972:383), it is clear that rennet is not personified, but the form as well as the situation is rather similar to that for blood sausage. The preparation of cheese also constituted a risk situation for the household. The thrice-repeated and answered question thus seems to follow a pattern which we also find in folk therapy.

For example, in his home district in Småland, Linnaeus reports the following cure for a cough: "The farmer, naked, climbs up in the chimney; the farmer's wife, naked, stands in the fireplace with the child who is coughing. The father calls: mother, are you there? She answers: Yes! Is the child with you? Yes. Is the cough with you? Yes! Pull out the cough in the devil's name!" This was to be repeated three times (Wikman 1968-1969:35).

The thrice-repeated dialogue form has a counterpart in older times, for example when the godmother, before the ride to the christening, asked the parents three times what the child's name was, a custom which I took to be an imitation of the medieval christening ritual (Bringéus 1971:76).

In all probability the sausage-boiling dialogue is rather old. Evidence for this is the fact that it is known both east and west of the Öresund, as is the alliterative form of the question "Is Hålle home?" *Hålle* is a masculine personification of the verb *hålla* [to hold], but we should not for that reason ascribe some sort of animistic intention to the name. Metaphors of this type have often been the breeding ground for fabulous tales and folk beliefs. Hålle became a living being with the same duties as the "sausage savior" and the "sausage holder."

A comparison of the sausage savior tradition in Scania and the southern Swedish tradition of smacking the sausage and magic dialogue reveals unmistakable internal similarities. In both cases it is a question of personification. In one case this has been done with a thing — the spleen — and in the other case with a verb *hålla*. It has never been stated that the spleen was considered as a living being, although it was used for the purposes of prophecy in other contexts. There is equally little reason to consider *Hålle* as some sort of divine being. It is the dominant purpose, the wish for the sausage to hold together, that gives rise to a prophylactic treatment; this in its turn is designed according to a known pattern: personification and magic dialogue.

Even if we previously took into account the possibility that the spleen in the sausage kettle might have had a rational function, the comparison with another complex of traditions shows that this is unlikely. The origin of the magic dialogue is in and of itself easier to understand than how the spleen was brought into this context, but both traditions are variations on the same theme. We can completely exclude the idea that *Hålle* might have been a being which was believed in, but on the other hand we cannot ascribe the tradition to joking stories. Only in one case, which is outside the distribution area, has the tradition developed in that direction. From Öland it is reported that it was usual, when boiling sausage, to ask an inexperienced child to run over to the neighbors and "borrow the sausage holder." This joke could more easily come into being since, during the slaughtering that preceded the sausage boiling, it was usual to send children to the neighbors to borrow a "tail puller" (Eskeröd 1947:43).

Various methods were used in the attempt to keep the sausage from splitting. Among these are the RATIONAL ACTIONS which consisted of not completely filling the casing with sausage mixture, of trying to keep the heat under the sausage kettle as uniform as possible, and of pricking the sausage with a thorn during the boiling. The aim of keeping the sausage whole could also be furthered by TABOOS in the form of prohibiting speech, of opening the mouth or breaking wind, and of mentioning the word "sausage." The placing of a spleen in the kettle, along with the blessings, smacking the sausage, and dialogue are to be considered as various forms of OPERATIVE MAGIC. All these measures must be seen against the fact that boiling the sausage entailed a degree of risk in a time when people were obliged to prepare sausage themselves over an open fire. The boiling of the sausage was very close to being a supernatural situation in which supernatural measures might also be observed.

It may be asked why the complex of traditions treated here has a limited dissemination, being restricted to southern and primarily southwestern Sweden, whereas blood food occurs throughout the country. The explanation for this is to be sought in the technique which was used during the preparation of blood food. Within the distribution areas of the traditions, BLOOD SAUSAGE (*blodpölsa*, *blodkorv*) was the normal form in which blood was used as food. But this is not the only means of utilizing blood. To the west of the Great Belt in Denmark, Højrup mentions soup, porridge, pancakes, and rolls made of blood, the latter called *komber* or *stoddere*. Blood rolls are also known in Norway and Germany (Højrup 1972:103ff.). In Sweden we find BLOOD BREAD (Swedish *paltbröd*) and BLOOD CAKE (Swedish *blodpalt*, *blodklubb*, *blodkams*) (Olsson 1963). None of these require a casing, so that the element of risk associated with the boiling of sausage is not in question. The blood mixture might be poured into the head of a codfish or a haddock or into a fish stomach (Olsson

1958:77ff.) or could be baked as blood bread which was later boiled or soaked in order to be eaten.

This contrast between blood sausage (*blodpölsa/blodkorv*) in southern Sweden and blood cakes in central and northern Sweden clearly has a long history. As early as the beginning of the eighteenth century, the Helsingland priest O.J. Broman (1914:217) wrote: "However, in this country there is a distinction between blood sausage and blood bread or cake [Swedish *palt*, *kams*], in that the former is made with less flour and is put into sausage skins or intestines; while the latter is made by kneading in so much flour that it can be baked as bread, and can without a casing be placed in water to boil, after having been formed in smaller or larger cakes or rolls."

It can be seen from Nils Keyland's description of food in the Swedish countryside that blood bread was a very important food among Swedish peasants from Småland northwards (Keyland 1919:162ff.). On the other hand, in the old Danish provinces of Scania, Halland, and Gotland the blood was used in the form of blood sausage. This was also the case in western Västergötland, where Broman also mentions blood sausage.

Similarly, we cannot immediately account for the east Danish and the south Swedish tradition area against the background of the diffusion of blood sausage. Within this area in older times — before it became more profitable to sell goose blood in towns, where it was used for *svartsoppa* [a black soup made with goose giblets] — goose blood was also used in the preparation of blood sausage. However, this sausage was not cooked in the intestinal casing, but in the tough neck skin of the goose. In this case there was no risk of the sausage splitting and there is no report of prophylactic measures observed in connection with the preparation of this type of blood sausage. Indirectly, we have here clear evidence of the fact that the precautionary measures we have discussed were not connected with blood as a food. Certain taboos, such as smacking the sausage, were not exclusively connected with blood sausage, but could also occur during the boiling of groat sausage, which also swelled while boiling. These precautionary measures were exclusively connected with the fact that the casing might split during the boiling. Such measures are unknown in southwestern Finland, where blood sausage was baked in the oven instead of being boiled over an open fire (Vuorela 1961:20ff.).

In summary, we can state that these prophylactic measures belong to an area in which people made use of blood food in the form of sausage which was boiled in casings over an open fire. This shows us that there is a great deal of rationality underlying magic. Magic is employed when, and only when, it is needed. For blood food, it became necessary when a more developed technique for the preservation of this food in the form of sausage had been worked out. The form and the contents allow the probability of assigning the prophylactic measures as well as the introduction of blood sausage to the Middle Ages, while various forms of blood cakes are of considerably older origin (Olsson 1963).

REFERENCES

AF KLINTBERG, B.
1965 *Svenska trollformler*. Stockholm: Wahlström and Widstrand.
1971 "Magisk diktteknik," in *Folkdikt och folktro*. Edited by A. B. Rooth. Lund: Gleerups.
BRINGÉUS, N.-A.
1971 Barndop. *Fataburen*. Stockholm.
BROMAN, O. J.
1914 *Glysisvallur och öfriga skrifter rörande Helsingland* 3. Uppsala.
CRAELIUS, M. G.
1930 *Försök till ett landskaps beskrivning* (third edition). Stockholm.
DANVER, K.
1943 *Folktraditioner kring vårdagjämningen med särskild hänsyn till kontinentala traditioner*. Lund.
EIDNES, H.
1946 *Tru og tradisjon*. Trondheim.
ESKERÖD, A.
1947 *Årets äring. Etnologiska studier i skördens och julens tro och sed.* Stockholm: Nordiska Museet.
FEILBERG, H.
1894–1904 *Bidrag til en ordbog over jyske almuesmål* 2. Copenhagen.
FERNOW, E.
1773 *Beskrifning öfwer Wärmland* 1. Göteborg.
GASLANDER, J.
1895 "Beskrifning om allmogens sinnelag, seder," in *Nyare bidrag till kännedom om de svenska landsmålen ock svenskt folklif*. Bih. I 3. Stockholm.
GRÖTTLAND, K. L.
1962 *Daglig bröd og daglig dont*. Oslo.
HONKO, L.
1957 Blod. *Kulturhistoriskt lexikon för nordisk medeltid* 2. Malmö.
HYLTÉN-CAVALLIUS, G. O.
1972 *Wärend och wirdarne* 1 (third edition). Lund: Gleerups.
HØJRUP, O.
1972 *Landbokvinden*. Copenhagen: Nationalmuseet.
KEYLAND, N.
1919 *Svensk allmogekost. Bidrag till den svenska folkhushållningens historia* 1. Stockholm.
LID, N.
1924 Norske slakteskikkar med jamføringar från naerskylde område.

Videnskapsselskapets Skrifter II. Hist.-Filos. klasse 1924(4). Kristiania.
1935 Magiske fyrestellingar og bruk. *Nordisk Kultur* 19. Oslo.

NYROP, K.
1887 *Navnets magt*. Copenhagen.

OLSSON, A.
1958 Om allmogens kosthåll. Studier med utgångspunkt från västnordiska matvanor. *Institutet för Västsvensk kulturforskning skrifter* 4. Göteborg.
1963 Kams. *Kulturhistoriskt lexikon för nordisk medeltid* 8. Malmö.

OSBECK, P.
1926 *Utkast till beskrifning öfver Laholms prosteri*...1796. Lund: Gleerups.

ROOTH. A, B.
1971 A simile in Swedish medieval laws of Hälsingland and Uppland. *Proverbium* 16. Helsinki.

RÄÄF, L. F.
1957 *Svenska skrock och signerier*. Med inledning och anmärkningar utgivna av K. R. V. Wikman. Stockholm.

STORAKER, J. TH.
1938 *Mennesket og arbeidet i den norske folketro*. Oslo.

STÖMBÄCK, D.
1970 *Folklore och filologi*. Uppsala.

SUNDBLAD, J.
1881 *Gammaldags bruk. Kulturbilder från Westergötland*. Göteborg.

THIELE, J. M.
1860 *Den danske almues overtroiske meninger*. Copenhagen.

TÖRNER, J. J.
1946 *Johan J. Törners samling af widskeppelser*. Med inledning och anmärkningar utgiven av K. R. V. Wikman. Uppsala and Stockholm.

VON SYDOW, C. W.
1941 Gammal och ny traditionsforskning. *Folkkultur* 1. Lund.

VUORELA, T.
1961 Die finnischen Würsten. *Studia Fennica* 9(4). Helsinki.

WIGSTRÖM, E.
1881 *Folkdiktning, visor, folketro sägner och en svartkonstbok. Samlad och upptecknad i Skåne*. Andra samlingen. Göteborg.

WIKMAN, K. R. V.
1968–1969 Superstitionerna i Lachesis-manuskriptet. Några Linnéanteckningar jämte anmärkningar. *Svenska Linnésällskapets årsskrift*.

Bread in the Region of the Moroccan High Atlas: A Chain of Daily Technical Operations in Order to Provide Daily Nourishment

ARIANE BRUNETON

As is well known, cereals constitute the basis of the diet of the rural populations of northern Africa.

For one particular Berber tribe of the Moroccan upper Atlas region, the Aït Mgun people, who are part of the Infdwak group, it is barley, corn, some millet, and wheat cultivated at high altitudes (2,000–2,500 meters) in the terraced fields of the Tessaout Valley where they live that permit them to survive (see Plate 1). There is as well the minor production of items derived from small farming (goats and cattle), carried on only because of its indispensable nature.

It is in three principal forms, each separate from the others, that these cereals are used in this area. They may be either boiled, made into couscous (with the grain coarsely ground, then steamed), or made into bread; these three uses serving to break up the monotony of life and allowing the people some diversion.

Whether boiled, made into couscous, or made into bread, these three modes of grain consumption have in common a great frequency of occurrence. The ideal schema type of grain use is boiling it as a liquid in the morning, eating the grain in the form of bread at lunch, and then having couscous (either barley or corn) in the evening, alternating with thick boiled products. This schema is, of course, not always realizable due to the precariousness of the resources concerned, and because of the fact that at each meal the essential part of it must be prepared anew. Even if the boiled food contains whey, or if the bread is eaten with melted butter, tea, or a *tagine* of vegetables, or if the couscous is eaten with bouillon, the significant fact is that everything is prepared on the same day when it will be eaten, for immediate use.

This phenomenon is not any less surprising than any of the operations performed upon these cereals in order for them to be usable in any form at all, for this is not done in advance for any product, not even bread. Thus, the chain of successive and necessary operations is carried out for numerous products completely on every new day, each time demanding some two to three hours of work. Indeed, perhaps because of a badly resolved problem of how to store these foods (bread made from barley dries out very quickly), as well as the necessary and careful accounting that these people must make of their cereal reserves, bread must only be made when necessary. Because the constant hunger of everyone is never completely assuaged and because the women's working time must be carefully regulated and divided among several other tasks besides those of cooking — such as care and feeding of the large cattle and woodcutting — this bread is made every day, in every family, according to the precise needs of that day.

Several types of bread have been observed in these mountainous areas. First, there is the round form of bread, from three to four centimeters thick and about twenty centimeters in diameter, whether it be made of barley or more usually wheat; this bread is made, if possible, on feast days. It is called *chleuh* or *agrum* in Berber, and is the bread *par excellence,* leavened and cooked in the oven. There are also two other sorts of bread, which might be called emergency varieties, for their rapid preparation is the consequence of demands made to improvise. There is "bread from the hearth" (*agrum n takat*) also called "shepherd's bread"; (*agrum n'umksa*), bread which may be leavened, and which is also twenty centimeters in diameter, but is rather thick, around five or six centimeters, since it is cooked over hot coals; or "pan bread," (*agrum n'unhdam*) or "unleavened bread" (*agrum arhsis)* which is biscuitlike, since it is made from an unleavened dough that is much less thick (one centimeter maximum) in order to compensate for the lack of leavening, and is cooked on a stone plate or in an earthen pan.

How, then, does the daily work necessary for making bread divide up? Since leavened bread made from barley is the most popular and requires the longest preparation it is what we will discuss most here.

The chain of operations can be divided into two main phases. The first begins with the cereal that is simply beaten and ends with sifted flour that is ready to be kneaded; it includes the set of successive operations of cleaning-separating, pounding, winnowing, mashing, and running through a sieve to yield a sifted product. This is the phase of preparation of the cereal, necessary no matter what may be the final mode of consumption of the grain. This process may be carried out slightly in advance, such as the day before, while the second phase must be performed on the day that the product is to be used. At this point, it is not necessary that the different operations link together in immediate progression; at each stage, the work may in fact be left to be taken up again later. The second phase groups together the operations of kneading, fermentation, shaping, and baking; this phase is peculiar to the making of bread and must be performed in a continuous sequence of events.

It is therefore around the operations of separating and cleaning that the first procedures prefatory to milling are associated. The cereal that has been picked over on the threshing floor and winnowed in the wind, then carried in bags on the backs of the women, has been piled on the ground in a corner of the family room with the grain reserves as well as other provisions, such as dried turnips, onions, sugar, salt, oil, candles, wool, etc. and eventually a large urn or two containing the rest of the corn harvest. The first task, therefore, is to take the small impurities out of the cereal, including pebbles, twigs, and seeds. After having measured out from the reserves the necessary quantity of cereal, representing what will be used for the next day's bread and the evening's couscous or boiled grain (since the farm is set up so that milling is divided in terms of products with different-sized grain, for example fine flour for bread and coarse semolina for couscous), the woman will place herself or her daughter with an esparto-grass plate (*isgwi*) or some flat receptacle before her, with one container full of cereal to be cleaned and another to put it in after the separating process. She picks out with her fingertips the impurities to be thrown out, doing this with remarkable visual acuity, by regularly shaking the mass of grain so as to pour it into one container or the other (see Plate 2).

The separated barley is then poured into a wooden mortar (*afrdu*) in which it is pounded a little at a time with a wooden pestle (*tagart*) which is held in both hands by the standing woman. This pounding, which is not really very complete, has the main purpose of breaking the beard of the barley seeds.

Another cleaning and winnowing process is then necessary. The barley is turned over in the esparto-grass plate, which also acts as a winnower. With rotating movements, and by holding the plate at a slightly oblique angle by its edge, the woman can gather on top the light pieces of the beard. Then, all that is necessary is for the woman to toss up the impurities with a swift jerk, necessarily blowing over the top as well (see Plate 3).

There are no fixed times or places in which these operations are to be performed, but it is usually in the afternoons that women or young girls may be seen separating the grain, their legs stretched out in front of them, the plate resting on top, with another girl standing up and pounding, and yet another seated on a rock holding the edge of her plate with both hands to shake it in the winnowing process. The girls may work together near one another or separately, outdoors or on a terrace if the weather permits, since the kitchens are small and dark and hardly conducive to this sort of work; they then eventually come together in order to share the different operations, if they are all members of the same family working on one and the same mass of cereal.

These operations are indeed the ones that a mother of a family will teach most easily to her daughters, since the work only demands a small amount of physical strength and since there is at this point only a small chance that things will be done wrong. The cleaned cereal is then ready to be pounded and milled. This may be done in one of two ways: either by a handmill or a watermill.

In fact, three water-run mills in Azrzm (the village we have studied here) have been set up across irrigation furrows and function when the output of water is sufficient. One of the mills is called "communal," and the two others belong to private families, one from this village and one from the neighboring one. Protected by a stone shelter, which is not very large, being just about five square meters and rather low as well, a shelter which is closed when unguarded, the water run-mill, (*azrg n waman*) has an apparatus similar to that of the handmill (*azrg*). The only difference is that the watermill is set up to work alone. It is made of two flat millstones, eighty centimeters in diameter and fifteen centimeters thick, that are placed on top of one another and have a hole in the center to let the wooden central axis pass through. This axis, fixed to the top millstone, makes it turn. On its lower end, it has wooden blades against which the water from the furrows strikes, the force increased by being channeled down a small chute. The apparatus handling the pouring of the grain towards the center of the millstone is quite ingenious; it is made of a hopper (*asqar*) a woven wicker sack suspended from the rafters by ropes and pierced with a small hole in its base. The grain which comes out falls into a wooden container which is shaped like an oil lamp — and is thus called a *londil*. The grain then slides to the center of the millstone, towards which this wicker receptacle is slightly inclined. The apparatus that pushes the grain out in a fairly continuous stream is a small piece of wood, the vibrator, or *tasmnqart*, which shakes itself and makes the sack shake as well. It is attached to the sack and rubs against the turning millstone, thus making both move.

The cleverness in this device also leads us to note the following: if the mill stops turning, for lack of water for example, the grain will stop pouring towards the center of the stone, since no movement will be transmitted to it through the immobile vibrator. But on the contrary, if the millstone is turning quickly, the vibrator will move faster, and the quantity of grain pouring through will be greater. It should also be noted that the position of the upper millstone can be regulated so as to provide the desired texture in the milled grain by lifting a wooden lever parallel to the central axis that is connected to the axis.

The woman usually lets the mill function by itself, just glancing at it from time to time and throwing out the gutter-water running around the millstones, produced from the milling process.

Use of the "communal" mill is regulated. Further, it is necessary that the supply be sufficient, that the mill be free at the time it is needed, and that there be a significant amount of grain to be milled (enough for two or three days), so that milling will not only be possible but also worthwhile. Also, when the woman has her own handmill, she often falls back on it.

The handmill is the same sort as that which is used throughout northern Africa and the Sahara region, except that it is not transportable, being fixed to the earth in a specific place, whether it be in the kitchen or in a corridor, always in some sort of covered or sheltered area.

This kind of mill is made of two round millstones, the lower one of which (called *iġrf n waliġ*) is fixed to the ground by clay forming a gutter which serves as a receptacle for the milled product. In the center of the millstone, there is a wooden pivot or *tamrnut* to which a wooden vertical axis is also attached; around this latter axis the upper millstone (*igrf n'ufla*) turns. The upper millstone is hemispherical in shape and is activated by means of a wooden handle (*askwti*) which is a simple stick inserted into the main body of the millstone in an oblique fashion in relation to the stone. Two wooden corners (*akaynu*) serve to steady the vertical axis and the upper millstone, thus prohibiting extraneous movement. They also permit some regulation of the position of the upper millstone over the lower one so as to obtain the desired degree of fineness in milling.

The woman who does this work — for from this stage forward, the adults perform these activities — is seated on the ground, one leg folded under her, and the other stretched out, or with both legs stretched out in front so that the mill can rest between them. On her right, she keeps the plate containing the cleaned barley. A ritual "*bismallah*" spoken in a low voice accompanies the pouring of the first grain into the center of the millstone, just as it will accompany the performance of any other important act. The mill is put into motion by alternating movements of the right or the left hand, one arm always coming along to help the other, and the entire chest area moving forward along with the arm. The millstone is heavy and the work tiring. The milled product, or *izid*, breaks up bit by bit as it goes into the gutter. When the work is completed, the woman gathers up the tiny particles but does not dust the mill off completely, since the cleaning of the mill is usually carried out before the operation and not afterward. After it has been used, it is covered with protective cloths, particularly to keep it from being soiled by the chickens. The job may take from twenty minutes to an hour according to the amount of grain to be treated, from one to four kilograms, as well as according to the degree of fineness of the flour desired and to the energy and speed of the miller.

The milled product thus collected must be sifted and separated into flour and semolina before being used.

It is first poured into a large sieve (*talunt*) made of an iron plate or a punctured goatskin, attached to a wooden circular frame. This will retain the lighter and bigger pieces of bran, which will be set aside as cattle or dog food. The particles that fall onto a sheepskin will then be sifted again with a finer sieve (*atatu*) made of a metal grill placed over a wooden plate (*tazlaft*) which will be used in kneading. The finest flour (*taka*) falls through, while the semolina, i.e. the excess milled product, is retained. The cleaning process ends, if the woman considers it necessary, with a second passage of the flour through the fine sieve. In order to be able to use the semolina for couscous, on the other hand, it is necessary to sift it yet another time.

Doing this, in spite of the care taken, only results in slightly sifted flour, and it is easy to find in the barley bread while eating some small particles of bran shining in the crust and crumbs.

It is with the kneading process that the second phase of operations begins. If by some unusual circumstance the bread is made from wheat and store-bought industrial flour, it is at this stage that the work begins. This is the case even though, by chance or precaution the flour is passed through the fine sieve anyway.

While the cleaning operations performed on the cereal may be carried out outdoors, from the milling process until the cooking stage, the work is more privately carried out under a shelter, in the kitchen, near the oven, where the necessary utensils are readily available.

The first steps of the kneading process take an hour, with a minimum

Plate 1. Azrzm, high valley of Tessaout, 2,000 meters altitude

Plate 2. Separating the barley, outdoors, in the afternoon while a weaving job is being carried out

Plate 3. Winnowing after picking the beard from the barley seeds

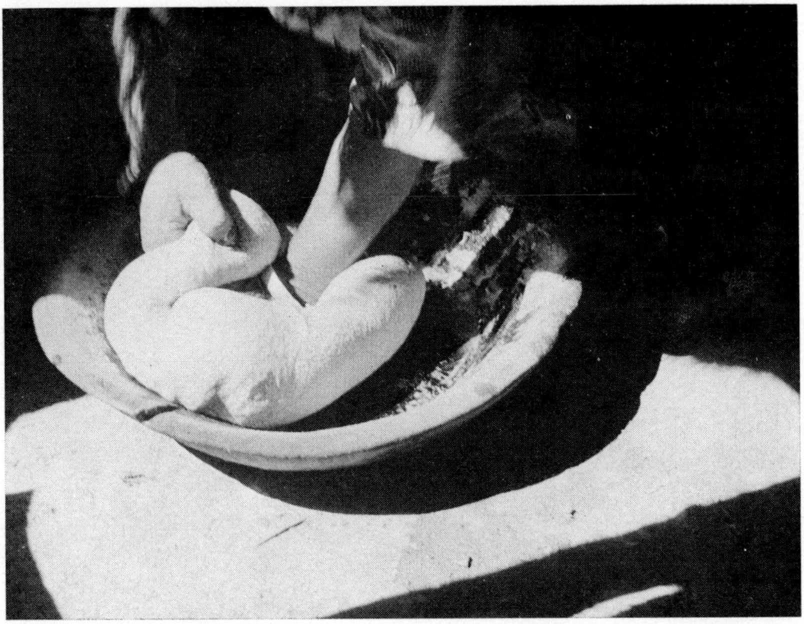

Plates 4 and 5. Kneading in the wooden plate, the *tazlaft*

Plate 6. Baking in the oven, the *afarnu*

Plate 7. Eating: the broken bread is soaked by little bits in the *tagine* sauce

of an hour and a half afterwards, but more than two hours including one hour of rising. It is done in the morning (since the bread is to be eaten at around noon), after milking the goats or chopping the wood, for example. The flour spread over the wooden plate (*tazlaft*) is wetted with lukewarm water. With a small wooden mortar, the woman then grinds the rock salt necessary for the dough. Here as well, there are no provisions of ground salt available. If the woman has not been able to keep a bit of the dough from the preceding day to use as a starter, she must add a packet of chemical yeast along with the salt and water. Then the kneading begins, first with one hand and then more quickly with both. The flour quickly gathers into a ball of dough, and water is added gradually to help the flour stick (see Plates 4 and 5).

The woman kneels to do this work, bent over her plate on the floor. The alternating movements of her hands gather up extra little bits of dough as she kneads, bits that may have stretched out from the mass of dough. When the left fist is sunk into the center of the ball of dough, bringing in the stretched-out part, the right hand stretches another piece out. The rapid rhythm of the process gives the impression that the woman is making a series of envelopes back and forth with her two hands. This kneading, lasting about five or ten minutes, is quite tiring and uses up a lot of breath. It is sometimes done by two people when there is a large quantity of dough to be kneaded, for a wedding, for example. When the job is done, the ball of dough is left to rest in the plate, covered, often in a warm area.

The fermentation process is not a job in itself, but the woman must take it into account in her time allotment since it must take a minimum of forty-five minutes and more often takes an hour or an hour and a half.

With this done, it is just the time to light the oven in order to bake the bread, if the woman is using her own oven. She may also be able to take advantage, as often happens, of the warm oven of a neighbor who has just finished baking, without there being any deliberate organization of work in such a fashion. This is perhaps due to the rather marked degree of individualism of each woman and also to the problems presented by the possible using up by one neighbor of the combustible material (wood) stored in order to be freely usable. Such stoves are rarely made despite the relative proximity of the forest.

The oven, or *afarnu,* having all of the instruments necessary for the baking of bread is far from uncommon. It is the only item used in this process that requires practically no expense at all (the handmill is expensive, around 300 francs, and the different wooden plates or winnowers, woven plates, and sheepskin are not produced in this area); it is made with stones and clay from the area, by the women themselves. They therefore each have one, sometimes even two, one being sheltered in a corner of the kitchen for winter use, and the other uncovered or under branches for summer use. It looks like a large clay mound, fifty centimeters high and eighty in diameter at the base. At its top, there is a round opening of fifteen centimeters in diameter, which serves as a chimney; its draught is regulated by stones that partially cover up the opening; on the side, there is a larger opening reaching to the ground, used for putting the bread in to bake (see Plate 6).

The oven is constructed by modelling the clay to a thickness of ten centimeters over a mound of stones covered with branches. The stones are delicately removed when the clay is dry. The bottom of the oven is made from flat stones resting on pieces of rock salt, whose function, it is said, is to retain heat. The flame is first lighted in the center of the oven.

When the dough has had time to rise and the moment when the oven is warm enough is near, the woman takes the dough that has completely spread over the bottom of the plate and shapes it into round loaves. This operation requires a good deal of room, for the woman must place before her the floured sheepskin (*almsir*) on which the loaves will be shaped. And she must also have at hand the plate containing the dough and the esparto-grass plate, protected with a cloth, on which she will place the loaves as she finishes shaping them; and everything must be placed on the ground.

The woman either divides the entire mass of the dough in advance into round balls that are about the size of grapefruits, and keeps aside enough to make about half a loaf (around 150 grams) for a starter for the next day's bread, or else she takes about a fistful of dough and then rounds it out by rolling it under her hands and tossing it into the air several times. She then flattens it out by rapping it against a corner of the sheepskin and breaking it apart again three more times. The left hand, holding the corner, quickly lifts it, the impulse is passed through the skin, and the dough breaks apart. The right hand then flattens it out again and the pattern is repeated about a hundred times, the woman always being sure to rotate the dough once so that the imprint of her palm is not left on it. The result then obtained after about a minute for each bit of bread is a round loaf that is perfectly flat, and from one to two centimeters thick.

Without any waiting period, the woman then carries the loaves to the oven to be baked. The woman sweeps the fire to the right side and cleans out the space on the left, where the loaves will be placed, already dusted with flour (*asawd*) so that they will not stick. She puts them inside with her hands, or with a small wooden shovel, *tafala* [bayonet] either one, two, or three at a time depending upon the size of her oven, its heat, and her speed in working. The loaves bake and rise all at once. With a stick, the woman turns them so that it is not always the same side that is nearest the flame, which remains burning on the right side of the oven. In three minutes, the batch is done, but the loaves are placed vertically in front of the flame or against the internal wall of the oven to finish browning. Before putting them onto a plate, the woman taps them once to be sure that bits of ashes are gone. They are then ready to be eaten as they are, hot.

Thus ends the chain of operations necessary in the current bread-making process. It is clear that it represents an important job for the woman and that it requires a long time for preparation, estimated to be about two and a half hours if it begins with the cereal and about one and a half hours if it begins with cleaned flour, yielding an average of six to eight loaves.

In order to lessen this inconvenience, we have noticed that it is also possible to make two other kinds of bread, whose preparation is less time-consuming.

The first of these, "hearth bread" (*agrum n takat*), corresponds to the individual demands of someone who arrives too late for the noon meal, the *imkli,* or too late for the evening meal, the *imnsi,* for example, a shepherd returning with his flock in the afternoon. The woman makes this bread then on the spur of the moment with some of the dough that she had placed aside earlier with this in mind (and in these cases the bread will have already risen) or, with some flour and water quickly mixed together, without leavening, a rather thick loaf about five centimeters round will be made, to be placed to cook in the hot coals left from the fire. Although the baking of this kind of loaf is relatively long, about a quarter of an hour, it is a quick solution that, moreover, has the advantage of not monopolizing the flame while something else is cooking.

The other variety, "unleavened bread" or "pan bread" (*agrum arhsis, agrum n'unhdam*) which is also an emergency solution, responds to a demand that is unexpected but also good-sized, such as that brought about by travelers. The operations demanding the most time in the classical preparation of bread, i.e. the rising of the dough and the heating of the oven, are here eliminated. Thus, the bread made quickly will be without leavening and only slightly kneaded, and the baking will be done by placing the biscuitlike dough on a stone plate straddling two others over charcoal, or else on a shard of a pitcher placed on a tripod over the flame. But in order for the baking to be done well and to compensate for the fact that there is no leavening, it is necessary to shape the dough into biscuits that are much finer than ordinary bread, around half a centimeter thick. The shaping therefore takes a longer amount of time, but the biscuits are baked as soon as they are made. They cook quickly, in two or three minutes, burning slightly in certain places. They then retain a convex shape, characteristic of the shard in which they are baked.

The loaves in all cases are eaten quickly after they are baked. In fact, a loaf that is still warm is much appreciated. The criteria for a good loaf of bread, besides its freshness, are that it has risen well and has not been overcooked. Of course white wheat bread is valued and preferred far more than the common barley bread, which has a darker color and heavier texture.

Each adult in the course of a meal will eat the equivalent of about half a loaf of bread, around 150 grams, bread which is brought to the table whole and then broken into four equal parts. It is not a whole piece that is carried to the mouth or soaked in a sauce, but only a small end detached by the right hand from the larger piece held in the left hand. Before the first bite is taken, the ritual "*bismallah*" is always spoken. If a "*tagine*" or a sauce accompanies the bread, everyone dips his piece into the specific part of the plate that is closest to him (see Plate 7). And unfortunate it is for the one who fishes, from the other side of the plate, with his little bit of bread, an onion or part of an egg yolk!

At the end of the meal, all of the crumbled pieces of bread that remain are carefully gathered up by the woman of the family, who goes to give them to those of her children who have not been able to have anything from the first distribution; or else, she stuffs them into her sleeve or sets them aside so as to be redistributed at the first opportunity.

In a general sense, it would doubtless have been interesting in a study such as this to have had more precise data concerning the quantities of cereal treated, for example, in order to follow the successive weight losses of the cereal in the course of the different phases of its treatment; it would also have been interesting to have been able to accompany the description of the different kinds of loaves with a nutritional analysis, and to have better situated the daily consumption of bread according to the particular members of a family and in relation to other forms of cereal consumption.

However, this description should permit, within the framework of studies on eating habits, a comparison with other ethnic and cultural contexts in which there might also be found this sort of chain of operations, which is here carried out daily, as the exclusive job of women, and for one woman in each family group. We could also then extend the comparison to the work necessary for the consumption of cereals in other forms, boiled, as biscuits, as pancakes, in couscous, etc., so as to establish a kind of typology and to allow the study of relationships that hold between them. There might also be established a comparison with the cultural contexts in which bread is still a domestic preparation but involves certain operations, particularly the milling and baking, that are reserved for specialists (in urbanized or semiurbanized areas of northern Africa, for example). Here, there might be some organization of labor as well (such as the weekly preparation of bread among certain peasants of the southwestern part of France).

Another interesting area would be the comparison and study of the gestures involved in the preparation of bread, especially in the kneading and shaping of the loaves, but in such cases, recording by audio-visual techniques would be indispensable.

Finally, for a food such as bread, it might be interesting to note the prime cost or comparative cost, however artificial this may seem, within the different groups in which the product is made.

Sorghum and Millet in Yemen

ANNIKA BORNSTEIN-JOHANSSEN

Yemen, the "Arabia Felix" of Roman travellers, occupies the southwestern corner of the Arabian peninsula, covering an area of about 200,000 square kilometers. The population is estimated at about 6,000,000 inhabitants, comprising small fishing communities along the Red Sea coast, a limited number of seminomadic herdsmen in the east, a town population of about 10 percent, and a majority of settled agriculturalists, most of whom live in the mountain areas. The religion is Islam.

Historical records dating from 2000 B. C. and traditions handed down from even earlier times indicate that Yemen was one of the first areas where agriculture was practiced. The first agricultural settlements were probably along the fertile river beds (*wadis*) where flood water irrigation was practiced. As more land was needed in order to feed the expanding population, agriculture was gradually extended to the mountainsides. Over the course of time a well-balanced system of agriculture evolved, based on terracing and water conservation through an elaborate system of canals and masonry cisterns which controlled run-off waters and diverted them onto the terraced fields. A famous historic example of highly advanced Yemeni agriculture, dating from the first centuries B. C., is the huge Marib dam, which irrigated a large part of what was then the Sabean kingdom.

The Yemen comprises a wide variety of climatic conditions and topography, ranging from the hot, arid plains along the Red Sea coast to high, cool inland plateaux with mountains reaching an altitude of over 3,000 meters. In the east the mountains merge into the vast central

Arabian desert, the Rub al Khali. On the productive terraced farmlands located at an altitude of 500 to 3,000 meters on the westward and southward mountain slopes, the main crop is sorghum (*Sorghum vulgare*), *dhura*, which is grown in rotation with pulses, luzerne, maize, and other cereals. Wheat and barley, grown on the midland and highland slopes, are of less importance. Coffee, named after the port of Mokha from which it was formerly shipped, remains the major export crop although its production has declined in recent decades. The cultivation of coffee suffers from competition with *qât (Catha edulis)*, a narcotic shrub cultivated under the same conditions. *Qât* is more resistant to drought than coffee and it is by far the most secure and profitable cash crop for the farmer. *Qât* leaves are chewed by members of all social and economic strata of the population for their mildly narcotic effects.

In the lower *wadis*, where there is a perennial water supply, a large variety of fruits and vegetables is grown such as bananas, mangoes, figs, dates, lemons, onions, and tomatoes; in the highlands, with less rainfall and lower temperatures, fruit crops are limited to grapes, peaches, and apricots. Small quantities of vegetables are grown only on irrigated land. On the dry Tihama coastal plains, and in the dry valleys on the east, rain-fed crop production consists of drought-resistant varieties of sorghum, bulrush millet (*Pennisetum typhoides*), *dukhn*, and pulses; cotton and maize are grown under irrigation in the permanent surface-flow regions where the major *wadis* discharge their waters onto the plains.

Over three-quarters of the mountain areas and an even greater proportion of the coastal plain are too steep, stony, and arid for agriculture. These areas are used partly for pasture. Livestock holds a vital place in the Yemeni economy because most agricultural operations are carried out with the aid of draft animals. Large herds of cattle are kept for draft, milk, and meat; donkeys and camels are important for transport and draft. Large flocks of sheep and goats supply most of the milk and meat consumed.

The majority of farmers are smallholders, sharecroppers, or tenants who rent land from the large landowners or religious foundations (*Waqf*) which together own most of the cultivated land. Sharecroppers pay between 30 to 60 percent of their crops in rent, depending on the type of crop and whether the land is irrigated or rainfed. In addition a farmer pays a 10 percent religious tax (*zakat*) on all production. The majority of smallholders and sharecroppers live scarcely above subsistence level with only small farm surpluses for sale and small margins with which to survive the periods of crop failure and drought.

Plate 1. Fields are plowed directly after harvesting, and the stumps and roots are carefully collected for fuel and animal fodder
(Highlands; photograph by F. Mattioli, Photo Editor, Information Division, FAO, Rome)

Plate 2. Levelling the soil with a *masabb* before plowing
(Highlands; photograph by F. Mattioli)

Plate 3. The grains are scattered by hand in the furrows behind the plow and are roughly harrowed in by foot
(Highlands; photograph by F. Mattioli)

Plate 4. A home grinding stone for cereals, the *mathanna* (Highlands; photograph by author)

Plate 5. Woman preparing the millet grains for bread on the grinding stone, the *mathanna* (Tihama; photograph by author)

Plate 6. Tihama woman preparing millet dough for bread to be baked in the oven (foreground). Contrary to the practice in the mountain areas, where because of the colder climate the kitchens are always inside the stone houses, in the Tihama area the cooking places are usually outside the light straw huts that are the typical dwellings of the coastal plains
(Photograph by author)

Plate 7. The sorghum bread is flattened by hand and stuck onto the inside wall of the mud oven, the *tannur* (Highlands; photograph by author)

Plate 8. The sorghum porridge, *asid*, is prepared in a clay pot on top of the *tannur* (Photograph by author)

VARIETIES OF SORGHUM

Historically, sorghum has been known in Yemen since the time of the pre-Islamic Himayrite kingdom; it can therefore be safely assumed that it is one of the earliest cultivated crops. The famous eighteenth-century botanist Forskal, in his *Flora of Arabia*, noted that several wild varieties of sorghum existed and concluded that it is probably native to Yemen.

Several varieties of sorghum are cultivated and named in Arabic according to their colors. The most common and cheapest type is the red sorghum (*hamre*) a goose-necked variety with a compact panicle and with two subtypes, *lahmani* and *a'alesi*. Yellow sorghum (*safre*) and white sorghum (*baithe*) which has three subtypes, *shahethi*, *kadani*, and *jameli*, are the most sought-after varieties for baking bread. At lower altitudes a variety with an open panicle, called *ghareb*, is common.

Sorghum is cultivated not only because of its high yields of grain,[1] but also for its considerable yield of animal fodder and material for fuel. Vegetation is very scarce and every part of the plant is carefully collected and put to use. The stems and leaves are fed to animals in dry seasons when pasture is lacking and the roots are used as fuel.

AGRICULTURAL CYCLES AND METHODS OF CULTIVATION

The season for planting and harvesting the sorghum varies according to rainfall from area to area. In the midlands and highlands a short rainy season normally occurs in the early spring months from March to April. There is a longer, more plentiful rainy season in the summer months from July to September.

Between November and April the land is plowed several times and prepared for run-off water during the spring months. The Yemeni farmers calculate agricultural cycles by stellar constellations; the last plowing before planting is established by the position of the star *al neisan* in April. In any field large enough for a plow to be turned, wooden plows, called *hali* or *batleh*, are used. These plows have an iron cap which is driven forward; they are pulled by oxen or camels (Plate 1). The topmost terraces of the steep mountainsides are often so

[1] Yields of sorghum are estimated to be 1.5 metric tons per hectare (average for the country) and over 2.5 metric tons per hectare in good irrigated soils (FAO 1960).

narrow that hand cultivation with a mattock is necessary. Harrows are not used but by stirring the soil several times it is made fine enough for the crops to be sown. For levelling and consolidating the soil an apparatus consisting of boards dragged by camels, donkeys, or oxen (a *maharr*) is used with a driver standing on the board. A smaller implement of the same type, the *masabb*, operated by two men (Plate 2), is used in fields too narrow for animal draft; it is also used for piling up small banks of earth around the fields before irrigation.

In the highlands planting is started about two weeks after the spring rains, a date established by the position of the star *al aleb* at the beginning of May. The grains are sown by means of a funnel and tube, or are scattered by hand in the furrows behind the plow and roughly harrowed in by foot (Plate 3). If enough moisture has been conserved, or if the land is irrigated, sorghum is often interplanted with cowpeas or field beans mixed with the cereal grains and sown through the same drill. During growth the plants are thinned out and weeds are removed; these are used as animal fodder.

About three months after planting the cowpea pods are harvested and the plants pulled up. This is also the time of *sharf*, the cutting of the leaves from the sorghum stems, a period which in the highlands is established by the star *'allan*. In October and November, the sorghum cobs mature and are handpicked for threshing. Afterwards, the tall stems are cut off a few centimeters above the ground with a sickle, (*sherim*), and used either as green fodder or tied in bundles and piled up in conical stacks to dry for later use as dry fodder. Some fields are plowed immediately, but in many places the stubble is left until winter. Stumps and roots are always carefully collected for fuel.

In areas with an adequate water supply a second crop of sorghum may be planted in January and harvested in summer, but in the highlands, where most fields are rain-fed only and where rainfall is scarce and irregular, only a single crop per year is normally grown.

The harvested sorghum cobs are collected on a stone-paved threshing floor (*al jern*), which is used communally by the entire village. Cobs are left to dry for some time and then threshed by beating with a wooden stick (*al malidj*). Another method of threshing, less common and used mainly for barley and wheat, consists of leading two oxen or donkeys which drag a large stone over the grains. Winnowing is done by throwing the seeds in the air, thus separating the grains from husks, or by using a special winnowing basket. The grain is stored in an earthen pit dug in the ground inside the house (*al madfen*); each family normally possesses one. The *madfen* is an excellent storage place; it keeps the grain well protected from humidity and insects for long periods of time.

WORK PATTERNS

The average farmer usually does not cultivate more land than he and the members of his family can handle. In the mountain areas both women and men work in the fields and are helped by older children, few of whom go to school. The men undertake the heavier tasks such as ploughing, levelling the soil, and threshing, while all the other work is done by men and women together. A special task for the little boys is to chase birds from the fields. Sitting on high wooden structures in the middle of the field, they spend the whole day from early morning onward hurling stones with a leather sling and singing as night falls: "Little birds, the sun has now set and it is time for you and me to go to bed."

In the areas where the land is insufficient to support the population, there is an important temporary migration of men from the villages to towns for work. The families remain in the villages and, in addition to the women's heavy work load of taking care of the home and children and fetching water, the rsponsibility for farm work is also left in their hands.

It is interesting to note, however, that in some parts of the Tihama lowland women never participate in agricultural work desipte the similar social organization and ethnic origin of this group as compared to the people of northeastern Africa, where women bear a large part of the responsibility for farming. Thus most farm work is done on a family basis except by the larger landowners who hire workers during the busy season. During *sharf*, harvesting and threshing work teams are sometimes organized on a village basis, called together by the village barber (*mezaien*).[2] The landowner pays each person participating in the work in kind with food during the days of work, and also by giving a certain amount of leaves, straw, or grain, depending on the season.

[2] The *mezaien* belongs to a castelike group and has many important functions in the village. He is barber and butcher, acts as messenger between families and tribes in conflict, circumcises boys, and attends marriages and other ceremonies. The wife of the *mezaien* has similar functions in the women's domain, e.g. preparing the bride for a wedding. The *mezaien* ranks low in the social structure and intermarriage with other groups is prohibited. The *mezaien* is rarely paid directly for his services but receives a certain contribution in kind from each farmer in proportion to the farmer's production and to the services the *mezaien* has rendered.

Each agricultural season has its own songs and proverbs. For example, there is a proverb of the period of *sharf*, which falls in the middle of the sorghum cycle when the animals are well fed from green sorghum leaves, that says: "Don't be deceived by the animals of *sharf* and the girls of the feast" (i.e. they may look fat and beautiful during this time but don't be sure it will last). The working songs during *sharf* are often improvised dialogues between groups of men and women; a woman foresinger (*al nasheda*) sings a leading theme, referring to a happening in the village or to an incident taking place at the moment, the other women fall in with the theme and the men respond in chorus, improvising their reply. Or the farmers harvesting the sorghum sing their praise to God:

Good morning, O Naji, good morning friends and neighbors.
Tell me the story of the seeds, and what God wants with your fields
What he wants with the sorghum.
We have paid the *zakat* and made our prayers,
And now see the grace of God.
We have charged the soil with fertilizers,
And see here the second harvest.

SORGHUM AND MILLET IN THE DIET

A proverb speaks of sorghum as "the knee of the year" and it is indeed the basic component of the diet of the Yemeni farmer. Sorghum and millet together represent almost 80 percent of all cereal production and comprise the most important sources of calories and protein in the Yemeni diet.[3]

Cereals are prepared as porridge and bread, neither of which is ever absent from the daily menu. Pulses and vegetables are eaten when available. Vegetables, however, which need a lot of water for cultivation, are especially scarce and are eaten only during the short vegetable seasons. Small quantities of milk and butterfat form a regular part of the diet. Other animal products such as meat and eggs are expensive items reserved for the better-off families who can afford to eat them regularly and for special occasions such as marriages and other celebrations. The same is true for fruits, except in the relatively rich fruit

[3] Food consumption data do not exist for the country. According to the official statistics, based on estimated production, cereals alone contribute about 75 percent of total calorie intake and about 70 percent of total protein intake. Sorghum and millet thus contribute about 60 percent of total calories and 58 percent of total proteins in the diet (UNDP 1973).

regions in the lower midlands, and grapes during the grape season in the highlands. A common and nutritionally important Yemeni dish is the *helbe,* a sauce prepared from the protein-rich fenugreek seeds which are widely grown throughout the country.

Preparation of Bread and Porridge

Preparation of bread is a laborious task which occupies much of the women's time. The kitchens are small, dark, and poorly ventilated, (by means of a hole in the ceiling above the ovens), and thus very hot and smoky when the fires are lit. A mud bench along the wall contains one or two *tannurs* [cone-shaped, topless ovens made of baked clay or mud] which are used both for cooking and for baking bread. The kitchen windows are kept small in order to prevent anyone from looking into this exclusively feminine domain.

Kitchen utensils consist of clay pots of different shapes and sizes, and cheap aluminum pots. The *berme* and the *jefne*, two medium size clay pots, are used for boiling meat and porridge; the *madhalle*, a hard stoneware pot, is used for baking dishes directly on the fire. For serving and stirring the food, wooden rods and spoons are used. Cutlery is not commonly used. Food is eaten only with the right hand and with the help of bread dipped into the common dishes served in pots and on trays on the floor.

No meal is complete without bread, not only by reason of its bulk and tastiness, but also because of its convenience for picking up other food. The typical loaves are flat and round and only slightly leavened. Bread tastes best when fresh from the oven, because it contains no fat or milk and therefore soon becomes stale.

The grain is ground into a fine flour on a large grinding stone (the *mathanna*) which most families possess (Plate 4). In the Tihama a smaller roller stone is common (Plate 5), on which the millet, soaked overnight in water, is rolled several times to obtain the required consistency. In many areas, home milling is being replaced by local machine mills, thus relieving the women of this hard, time-consuming task.

Bread dough is prepared by using a piece of dough from the preceding batch of bread as a starter. This is mixed with flour, salt, and water and left overnight to rise. The risen dough is divided into pieces and shaped into rounded balls which are quickly pressed and shifted between the palms of the hands (Plate 6), and thus shaped into a widening circular loaf. When the dough is thin it is flipped onto a pillow (the *makhbaze*) and stretched into an even circular shape. It is then stuck quickly onto the inside wall of the hot *tannur* (Plate 7) and baked for about one minute until slightly brown. Instead of using the *makhbaze,* the ball may be stuck directly onto the side of the *tannur* and flattened there by hand.

The typical sorghum loaves are *jehein* [small, round loaves baked in the *tannur*] and *lehueh* [a spongy pancakelike bread baked on a metal disc placed on top of the *tannur*]. The *lehueh* is a typical Ramadan bread which is also often used for preparing the dish *shufut*. This dish is made by soaking the *lehueh* in soured skimmed milk *(laban)* spiced with thyme and other green herbs. Another common sorghum bread is *gafue*, similar to *jehein* but with ground lentils added to the dough.

At lower altitudes, millet predominates over sorghum as the main cereal. The millet loaves, *kidr* and *fadayer,* are prepared in the same ways as the sorghum loaves but are smaller and thicker, due to the smaller ovens used in these areas. The millet dough is often slightly fermented to give a dark, sour bread.

Millet and sorghum flours are often mixed, and maize flour may be added. Barley and wheat may be used separately or mixed together, but are never mixed with millet or sorghum. Ground lentils or the flour of other beans or peas may be added to sorghum and millet flour for baking bread. This is not done with breads made of wheat and barley.

If bread is regarded as a necessary part of a complete meal, the porridge *(asid)* is even more essential: "without a daily pot of *asid* a man cannot work" says the song. *Asid* is prepared by adding sorghum flour to boiling water and stirring it continuously over a hot fire for about half an hour until the right consistency and smoothness have been obtained. *Asid* (Plate 8) is often eaten by making a hole in its center into which *madid* [a thin gruel made of skimmed milk and wheat or barley flour, and served with melted butterfat] is poured.

CHANGES IN FOOD HABITS

The basic foods of the rural population are thus bread, *asid*, *madid*, *helbeh*, and whatever fresh fruits and vegetables are available in season, plus very limited amounts of meat and eggs. Food habits in the towns are generally more varied than in the rural areas, due to the greater availability of foods in the urban markets and the higher purchasing power of the townspeople, except among the poorest sections. Meat and eggs are more frequently consumed, and a much larger variety of fruits and vegetables are available all year round at the town markets. Imported wheat and rice are replacing the local cereals in part, which is unfortunate in view of the lower protein and mineral content of the polished rice and the low extraction of the wheat flour. The influence of the Turkish occupation of the country at the beginning of the century and of the recent influx of Adenese and other foreigners can be seen in the greater variety of dishes and spices in urban cooking. *Asid,* which is tiresome and time-consuming to prepare, is regarded as heavy "peasant food" and is being replaced by rice. Local bakeries are now marketing modern loaves of white wheat bread, which are finding an expanding market among foreigners in restaurants, schools, and hospitals, and in some Yemeni homes.

Changes in food habits which are taking place in Yemen are recent, however, and the traditional food still remains, if only for special occasions. No town housewife with self-respect will deprive her family of fresh homemade bread from the *tannur,* and an important criterion of a girl's suitability for marriage is still her ability to bake bread, a skill acquired only through years of training in the kitchen. A marriage feast is unthinkable without a pot of *asid,* prepared from white sorghum (which is preferred in taste to the red variety). Townswomen, when asked about food preferences during pregnancy, usually refer to good old village foods like asid and sorghum bread, which they say are "safe," "give strength," and "contain vitamins," (the common expressions used to indicate strength-giving properties in foods). Even for the townsmen, sorghum still remains the "knee of the year," the Yemeni "lever" for work and feast.

REFERENCES

FAO
1960 *Report on the FAO mission to Yemen* (C-1792). Rome: Food and Agriculture Organization.

UNDP
1973 *County brief for the Yemen Arab Republic.* Sana'a: UNDP.

The Breads of Mani

MARGARET LOUISE ARNOTT

Bread is of such importance to man as a defense against hunger and as a symbol of food that a day has been set apart to commemorate it. On October 3, 1972 (*Philadelphia Inquirer*, October 1, 1972), the President of the United States, along with other world leaders, proclaimed the fourth international celebration of the "Day of Bread," and a variety of special events marked this occasion. On December 13, 1972, the Federal Republic of Germany issued a special stamp imprinted "Bread for the World" (*Philadelphia Inquirer*, November 19, 1972: 9 K).

Throughout Greece bread is the staple daily food of most of the rural and urban population. It is looked upon as holy, is never wasted, and, moreover, is an integral part of festival occasions. The people of Mani make breads which have a character quite different from those made in other parts of Greece. Therefore, in this paper, I propose to describe these breads and discuss their function because technological development is causing many customs to disappear. Remote as the Maniots are, they have not escaped these ravages; hence much of the reasoning behind the customs is lost and young housewives are becoming careless in carrying on the traditions. With food playing a major role in the thinking of the 1970's, every aspect of its use in the life of mankind needs to be examined. Frequently, in areas where food is scarce, festival occasions provide an opportunity for augmenting the normal diet. Mani is one of these districts.

A region of the southern Peloponnesus covering the slope of Mount

The material presented in this paper was collected between 1953–1957 and was checked and up-dated during visits in 1966 and 1972. Much of the material about Mani bread was gained with the assistance of Stavros Scopeteas, a native of Exohorian.

Taygetos, Mani is hard to reach because of its rugged mountain terrain. It is a district inhabited by the descendants of people who took refuge in these mountains at the time of the Slavic invasion. Mani was the first district to gain the right of self-government from the Turkish overlords, and its robust independence helped to nourish the seeds of the Greek Revolution of 1821. Here, too, the law of the clan flourished so that even today blood feuds are not unknown among the Maniots. Like all mountain peoples, they are noted for their individualism, their reserve, and their questioning of the stranger, but once he has been accepted, their loyalty and hospitality know no limits. The customs of these mountaineers, unlike the customs in other areas of Greece, vary little from village to village.

Greek breads are generally of two shapes — round or long and narrow, the round breads being either ring-shaped or solid flat loaves. Festival breads, too, are usually found in both the round and long loaf; however, the breads of Christmas and the New Year are generally solidly round, while the breads of Easter are made in a variety of shapes.

Christmas breads, known as Christ's Bread(*χριστόφωμο*) have a deep religious and agricultural significance. In the southern part of Greece these loaves are spiced, decorated with a hooked cross made of dough, and have walnuts in the shell embedded in them. The cross is the traditional symbol always found on it and the nuts are gathered and set aside especially for this bread. Nuts used for this purpose are said to be symbolic of the fruits of the earth or of the "virginity of the Virgin," or that they will bring "good luck." In some sections of the Peloponnesus, white eggs are used to form the cross,[1] eggs being the symbol of fertility. In some farming areas in the north of Greece Christmas breads are decorated with dough designs of house and farm implements (see Arnott 1955), while other areas use the church seal as decoration.

The breads that the Maniots make at Christmas have a use and character quite distinct from those of the rest of Greece. Here breads are made for the animals as well as for the family. The breads dedicated to the livestock are molded to represent each small animal that is owned, and it is believed that should one animal be forgotten it will sicken and die. The models are about seven inches in height and are perfect in every detail. Not only are images made of the animals, but models of the shepherd with his bag, staff, and dog are included, as well as the hens and one singing bird (see Plate 1). These small dough figurines are made from the same dough as that used for the family Christmas bread, but instead of being baked after they are shaped, they are boiled in oil. The completed

[1] District of Kalavryta, 1954.

figures, called *Perthedoules* (περδικοῦλες), are given to the children who assemble them on a small table or shelf and eat them some time before the New Year.

Because the animals are thus individually depicted, no note is taken of them when the family Christmas bread is decorated. On this bread only representations of birds and fruit can be found, together with walnuts in the shell. Here nuts are "for good luck"; they have been especially selected in the fall when the nuts are gathered and at that time have been carefully scrubbed and stored for the Christmas festival bread.

While not technically bread, mention should be made of a Christmas Eve pastry called *lalangia* (λαλάγγια).[2] Made from a mixture of flour, water, and eggs, the dough is shaped into strips ten to fifteen inches long, having the thickness of a common pencil. These strips are twisted around a finger and then dropped into hot oil, thus producing various irregular shapes. The *lalangia* are eaten with cheese. At the same time, pieces of meat are roasted over the coals. This custom is practiced to annoy the mischievous creatures who live on the earth from St. Philip's Day, November 14, the beginning of the pre-Christmas fast, until Epiphany, January 6. (On this last day all waters are blessed and the priest, carrying a cross and holy water, goes to each village house to bless it.) These little creatures are called *tsilikrota* (τσιλκροτά) and are visualized as small beings with tails, who go about to tease women, little girls, and boys, or old men. The pastries are made on Christmas Eve in retaliation, as it is believed that the delicious smell which ascends the chimney makes the little creatures jealous, angry, and hungry. Then it is thought that the *tsilikrota* scream down the chimney: "Grandfather give us meat even if it is not baked" (*παωοῦ τστσί καί ἄς είν' κι' ὠμό*).

In other parts of Greece these imps are known as *kalikantzari* (καλικαντζάρι) and are placated in various ways. In Greek Macedonia a special bread is made for them (see Arnott 1955: 244).

Throughout Greece, New Year breads, called Breads of St. Basil, (*βασιλόπητα*), while also having a religious character, each contain a coin which introduces the secular side of the occasion by foretelling the future. In parts of Epiros[3] not only is a coin baked in the bread but also a piece of straw. When the bread is cut, whoever finds the straw in his piece has good luck for his animals, while the man who finds the coin has luck for himself.

The Maniots take further note of the animals at the New Year when

[2] Asimina Scopetea, personal communication, January 5, 1972.
[3] Amelia Papachristidou, personal communication, Ioannina, Epiros, April 1955.

they make a tongue (*Γλῶσσα*) for each animal they possess. These are made in the shape of the animal's tongues and are very fragile because they are formed of a thin batter fried to a crisp in deep hot oil. When they are eaten by the family, the tongues are dipped into honey and covered with chopped nuts. It is hard for the small children to understand why only the larger animals are represented. Occasionally they insist that the tongue of the chicken be represented too, and mothers have difficulty in making them understand that the tongues of chickens are too small. It is at times like these that children are regaled with the folklore and legends of their nation, while enjoying the gastronomic pleasures of sampling the festival dishes.

Easter breads vary both in method of preparation and in shape, but are usually decorated with red eggs. Some say these loaves must be long and twisted to contrast with the New Year *pitta*,[4] while others insist they must be round to symbolize eternity; still others shape them like dolls or serpents and use them for special purposes. Although the rule is not unvarying, in general the New Year *pitta* is made of unleavened dough, while the breads of Easter called *tsoureki* (*τσουρέκι*) are usually made of a rich, sweet, risen dough.

Again, the Maniots have distinctive designs and customs for the breads of this season. Throughout all areas of Greece, it is customary for godfathers and godmothers to exchange gifts with their godchildren at Easter. In Mani, on Easter Day, or on Easter Monday the godchild receives an especially made *kouloura* (*κουλούρα*), twenty to thirty red and white eggs, wine, cheese, and sometimes a lamb. These gifts are sent to his parents so that all may enjoy a good feast and a happy Easter. The first year after the baptism the *kouloura* is made as large as possible. A special construction to widen the mouth of the oven is often necessary to bake it, as it is usually from one and a half to four feet in diameter. Each year the size will diminish until the last to be given, generally during the fourteenth year, is only twelve to fifteen inches in diameter. The *kouloura* which is sent the first year is not only elaborately designed and extremely large, but it is also decorated with roses.

The *kouloures* for gifts are of two shapes: male (Plate 2) and female (Plate 3). The male shape belongs to men and boys and is in the form of a horseshoe because men are intended to be generals, to go to war, and to live in the open on a horse or working with horses — ideas not incompatible with the Spartan ideal. On the other hand, the female shape, for women and girls, is that of a ring, the common shape of the daily bread,

[4] A general name given to all round breads, cakes, or pies.

because the women must remain at home to be the makers of bread.

Easter *kouloures*, or bread rings, are so-called because they are always open in the center and are made either on Great Thursday or on Great Saturday.[5] They are made of regular bread dough and are not sweet, as is usual for Easter breads, but instead are spiced so that they have an aromatic fragrance which sometimes scents the whole room. Oil is used in the kneading instead of water. After the breads are formed into their respective shapes, they are decorated. First a cross of dough is laid over the center opening. If the *kouloura* is very large, a double cross is used, but if it is small, only a single cross is made. In the center of this cross, set into a nest of dough, is a Great Thursday-dyed red egg. When the *kouloura* is a large one, similar red eggs are used at the ends of the cross as well as at its center. Sometimes this is the only decoration on the bread, but usually there are also other dough designs. On large *kouloures*, where more than one egg is used, there must always be an odd number of eggs — three, five, seven, or nine.

Eggs dyed on Great Thursday, the traditional day for dying Easter eggs, are considered to have greater efficacy than those dyed on other days. These eggs are dyed early in the morning, at the time the Great Thursday liturgy is being sung in the church, and, therefore, they are believed to have the church's special blessing — hence, the use of a Great Thursday-dyed red egg on the *kouloura* given to the godchild. Eggs such as those used on the Easter breads are placed before the icons and are given as gifts. In some places eggs laid on Great Thursday, especially by a black hen, are held to have particular powers.

The cross on the male *kouloura* has the appearance of an open eight rather than of a cross. On the lower loop is a wreath of laurel leaves of dough, the victor's crown, while at the upper end are flowers, each with a clove at its center. At the top center of the horseshoe is a sitting dove of dough with eyes of cloves, and in the remaining space around the horseshoe are dough pears and figs. Cuts are made with scissors on the inner edge of the horseshoe and on the top of the cross, while the undecorated spaces are sprinkled with sesame seed.

There is no mistaking the cross which covers the center of the female *kouloura*, for it is definite in shape. The center of this cross also has a dough nest containing a Great Thursday-dyed red egg, while the ends are decorated with clove-centered flowers of dough of the same type as those on the male *kouloura*. Sitting doves with clove eyes occupy the spaces between the cross ends, all of them bound together with a rope of dough.

[5] In Greece, Holy Week, the last week of Lent, is called "Great Week." Each day of this week is therefore preceded by the word "Great."

Again cuts are made with scissors on top of the cross and the undecorated portions of the bread's surface are sprinkled with sesame seed.

Sometimes these *kouloures* are given at Christmas. In that case, walnuts in the shell are used instead of red eggs. Occasionally, the child's initials replace the fruit and flower decoration made of dough. In any case, the godchildren wait anxiously for their *kouloures* which they show to each other, to see who has the best, before eating them.

The Easter bread made for the family also takes the *kouloura* or ring shape. Each member of the family has his own *kouloura* which is hung on the wall and eaten only by him. Moreover a *kouloura* is made for each member of the family who is away from home, and it is either sent to him or, if the distance is too great, it is hung on the wall and eaten "for his health" by other members of the family while they are gathered together. Then the family speaks of his absence, of the work he is doing, and of his childhood activities.

When the Easter *kouloures* are made on Great Thursday, a special small *kouloura* is made "for the happiness of the house." It is hung on the wall near the household icons, is kept throughout the year, and then is burned and replaced by a new one. This house *kouloura* seldom if ever has a red egg for decoration, as is customary with the other Easter breads. Instead a special ornamentation of dough decorates it, and there is always a cross on it.

Widows, or those in mourning, do not make Easter *kouloures* or dye red eggs, nor do they make Christmas breads for a period of three years.[6] Instead, they are supplied by their relatives or neighbors, thus frequently the bereaved have more food than they normally would have.

When Name Days[7] are celebrated in Mani, small round loaves stamped with the church seal, called *Prosforo* (*πρόσφορο*), are taken or sent to the church "for health." They are given to the priest with an offering of bread and a bunch of flowers. After the service the breads are cut in small squares and given to the congregation. From the special offering, a larger square is cut, wrapped in paper, and given to the person presenting the breads. This square of bread is taken home and eaten by the one whose Name Day is being celebrated. Twenty years ago, it was the priest who brought this piece of bread to the house, but little by little this practice has been disappearing.

[6] Recently the period of mourning has been reduced to one year, but some persons still hold to the three-year period.

[7] Name Day celebrations take the place of birthday celebrations. It is customary to entertain on the day dedicated to the saint whose name one bears. The day usually begins with attendance at the church service and ends with the reception of friends who call throughout the day to wish *Hronia Polla* (*χρόνια πολλά*).

On the Patronal Festival of the church, five large, round, spiced, sugar-coated breads, weighing six pounds each, are brought and placed on a table in the center of the church. These breads, called *artos* (ἄρτος), are given by people who have made a vow when petitioning for a special blessing, or they are bought by the church. At the conclusion of the service, the priest comes to the table, blesses the breads, then cuts them in pieces. These pieces, called *ipsoma* (ἴψωμα),[8] are distributed to the congregation, who eat them when they are fasting.

Because it is thought that bread has power, many superstitions are connected with it. Mani is not exempt. To give them strength, men going to war are given a piece of bread to be carried in their knapsacks.[9] Usually when Maniot men go to the fields in the morning, they carry a piece of bread in their pockets, or in a special bag, to protect them from harm throughout the day. This piece is kept separate from the lunch bread and is eaten only upon their safe return from the fields at night.[10] Sometimes, to protect children, a small piece of bread is put under their pillows when they sleep. Because bread represents power and is sacred, to see a loaf in a dream is interpreted as a good omen.[11] In other Peloponnesus districts a woman who has had a bad dream will get up, go to the door, and throw a piece of bread over her shoulder to break the spell.[12]

While breads are used at festival events in every area of Greece, the customs which surround their use in Mani are different, but vary little within the district. In each case they have a significance peculiar to Mani. In some instances, they are definite additions to the daily diet, but all are surrounded with rapidly disappearing tradition. Studies need to be made of festival occasions to determine how they contribute to the diet of the people who practice them. In many instances these practices are being dropped because of the high cost of living, because of disinterest or the speed of modern living, or because of the introduction of foreign, less nutritious, status foods. Bread, where used in festivals, should be observed with particular interest because of its nutritive value.

[8] After the Liturgy, small squares of bread called *antidoron* (ἀντίδωρον) are given to the congregation. The name changes on the Patronal Festival.

[9] Asimina Scopetea, personal communication, August 1972.

[10] Stavros Scopeteas, personal communication, March 1955.

[11] Asimina Scopetea, personal communication, August 1972.

[12] John Christofilakis, personal communication, Krokee (Lebetsoba), Sparta, April 1956.

REFERENCES

ARNOTT, MARGARET
1955 Ein griechisches Weihnachtsbrot. *Schweizerisches Archiv für Volkskunde*. Basle.
Philadelphia Inquirer
1972a October 1.
1972b November 19, page 9.

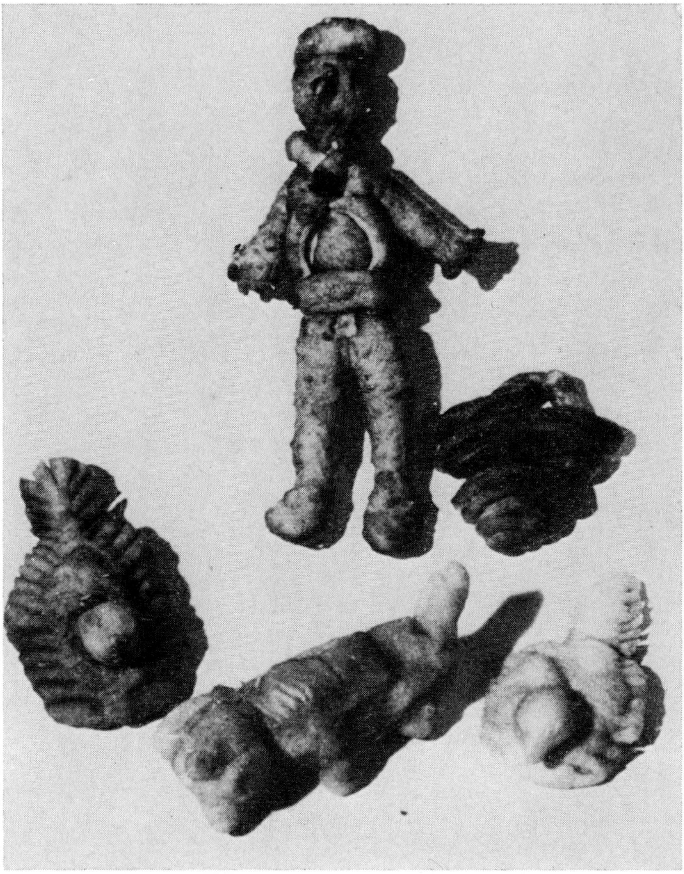

Plate 1. Perthedoules

Plate 2. Godchild's Easter kouloura-male shape

Plate 3. Godchild's Easter kouloura-female shape

Bread in Some Regions of the Mediterranean Area: A Contribution to the Studies on Eating Habits

HÉLÈNE BALFET

The data on which this paper is based were collected within the framework of a collective survey undertaken by a team of researchers (Musée de l'Homme, C.N.R.S., the University) on the theme "cultural unity or diversity in the Mediterranean area."[1] One of the revealing factors chosen for this study was cooking; thus documents on bread, among other things, were collected, not systematically throughout the Mediterranean area, but first in a few regions in which other surveys had been or are being carried out jointly. This initial study demonstrates a number of common features within the regional diversity which will be described below. However, it should be pointed out that this is only a partial and hypothetical presentation. The present state of the work in particular does not enable us yet to confirm either the Mediterranean specificity of these features or their continuity over the whole area. The regions studied included Mediterranean France (Languedoc and Provence), Italy, especially the southern part, Turkey (various parts), Malta, the Maghreb (various parts, in towns and country areas), and a few observations on Corsica, Lebanon, and Syria.

We will deal with two problems successively: the various qualities of the bread made and consumed, and bread's role in terms of nourishment.

[1] The author is indebted to the scholars of this team who took part in the discussion of this paper and particularly to the following for access to their personal notes: P. Boratav (on Turkey), A. Bruneton (on Morocco), R. Cresswell (on Lebanon), M. de Fontanes (on Languedoc, Italy, Greece), S. Ferchiou (on Tunisia), J. Fribourg (on Spain), and G. Ravis-Giodani (on Corsica).

QUALITIES OF BREAD

Examination of various products known as bread, which are eaten together (and are more or less interchangeable) in each of the regions considered, prevents us from using a restrictive definition. We cannot here give this term a meaning which will not enable it to cover everything known as bread in any one part of the Mediterranean area. Additionally, almost everywhere where there are various types of bread, there is one term which, even if it applies specifically to one of these types, also serves if all the types of bread are meant, or if simply "bread" in a wider sense is meant (see the following section).

To justify not restricting our definition — unlike other definitions — to either the wheat composition, or the fermentation, or the baking, or shape or thickness, we will give a few examples showing a very wide range for certain regions — especially wide when the bread is effectively a basic food and when all or part of its production can be counted on to be in the home.

In North Africa, in the mountainous Kabylie region, one finds (apart from the European-type bakery bread which is more and more widespread): (1) leavened bread in discs of two to three centimeters in thickness, usually called bread (*agrum*), baked in a special dish in the fire, first on one side and then the other side; (2) griddlecakes, the same shape or rectangular, unleavened, and considered as "spare" bread, quickly prepared and eaten at once; (3) griddlecakes similar as far as the dough is concerned but supplemented with a few aromatic herbs or a little oil; (4) fine griddlecakes or pancakes made with the same dough but kneaded better and stretched into thin discs and baked on a platter; (5) the same but more pliable and cooked under a lid.

Furthermore, the nature of the constituent, wheat or barley or often a blend of both (and among the poor or in periods of demand, blends of other flours, acorn flour for example, with the cereal mixture), introduces into each form of bread a number of sometimes very fine grades, which helps to break the monotony of an apparently uniform food.

Even now, in Tunisia, in one large village one can find leavened bread made in loaves by craftsmen, leavened bread in thin round discs baked in a special oven (*tabuna*), and griddlecakes (*kesra*) baked in a dish (*tajin*). Sometimes these griddlecakes are garnished with a vegetable stuffing inserted between two layers of dough before baking (the baking process is the same as for the simple griddlecakes, first on one side in the *tajin* and then the other). The same dough, well-kneaded, stretched into very fine slices, folded over several times, and baked in the *tajin*, forms a kind of pliable pancake which can be stuffed with other food.

In certain regions of Lebanon every ten to twelve days in the winter and every four to five days in the summer, the women prepare a pancake bread with a fermented dough stretched into fine discs which are pressed against the wall of an oven (*tannur*). Elsewhere (in the north) there are collective ovens with bedplates (*fours à sole*) where several people can bake leavened bread which keeps for several days; smaller and thinner loaves, garnished with various seasonings according to the season, are baked for immediate consumption.

The same tradition is found in Europe: when large round loaves of bread were prepared and baked in a home or collective oven which was not lit often, the oven was used at the same time for baking fancy loaves, supplemented in various ways and intended to be eaten that same day while they were warm.

Similarly in the Bolu region of Turkey a thin and improved bread (*pide*) is prepared so that it can be baked quickly at the beginning of the day's baking and is eaten the same day; the big round loaves are baked slowly so that they will keep for one or two weeks and are not started on until twenty-four hours have elapsed. If needed, bread in flat cake form is prepared quickly and baked on a metal plate. The same plate also serves to prepare a "thin bread" (pancakes) either from day to day as required in the summer or in large quantities in the autumn. (In the autumn the bread is softened by sprinkling it with water just before it is to be eaten.)

Elsewhere in Turkey, where they use a *tabuna*-type of oven called the *tandir*, up to ten different varieties of bread are found, all made of leavened dough and varying according to the composition, thickness, i.e. the consistency and especially the order in which the loaves are loaded into the oven and the baking time. Also in Turkey, there are two ways of preparing stuffed bread, either baked like *tandir* bread or on a plate depending on the regions, *etli pide* [flat meat loaf] and *börek*, baked in the home or at the bakery.

The latter type of preparation, already mentioned for North Africa and Lebanon, is also found in Malta with the *ftira*, a loaf stuffed with olives, tomatoes, and anchovies, especially prepared as a lenten meal. It is found again in France and Italy, where the *pizza* presents, in addition to the type which is widespread today, various traditional forms, some of which are very similar to the Kabylie onion and herb griddle cakes, others having a stuffing between two layers of dough. There seems to be no doubt that these different preparations have their place here, if one considers not only that they are made of bread dough, but also that they often have the same names as the bread on which they seem to be an improvement involving a whole range of intermediate preparations (a few spices, a little oil).

It can be seen from these examples that by adopting the most commonly used criteria (wheat flour, fermented dough, oven baking) for defining bread throughout the Mediterranean area, one would miss out on a large portion — and sometimes even the totality — of what is known and referred to as bread. We shall therefore try to find a more all-encompassing definition for *a food made of a dough produced with flour* (cereal flour in most cases), *kneaded before being baked* (which distinguishes it from gruels), *and baked when dry* (which distinguishes it from boiled or fried pastas). However, there is still ambiguity as to the distinction between bread and pastry, which is generally marked in vocabulary and usage, but nearly always with a more or less wide margin of inaccuracy.

Within this assemblage some divisions can be made according to various criteria:

1. fermented or unfermented doughs (often complementary);
2. form and thickness in loaves, in more or less thick plates, in sheets;
3. rigidness or pliability;
4. composition (wheat, barley, mixture of cereals, other flours);
5. additives, if any (seasoned or garnished bread); which enables us to define the traditional meanings of:

1. BREAD (French: *pain*) (in the strict sense): leavened dough, in loaves and by extension leavened dough in more or less thick slabs;
2. GRIDDLECAKE (French: *galette*): unleavened dough in fairly thick slabs, or in thin slabs, or in sheets — but not pliable;
3. IMPROVED DOUGH, leavened or unleavened (with oil or butter, kneading . . .);
4. PANCAKE (French *crêpe*), pancake bread: leavened or unleavened dough in pliable thin sheets.

These divisions are of course mainly meant to aid (and not to confine) the subsequent collection of information. For the data collected demonstrate the value of complete lists, by region, with the names and conditions of making and eating, and also the frequency or rarity, the subassemblages found locally, etc. This type of research has not yet been started in certain areas of the Mediterranean region.

The above discussion especially emphasizes the two points of fermentation and baking, to which a few remarks can be added.

As to baking, it is usual in the regions we studied to see the coexistence of at least two devices which can be provisionally listed as follows:

1. An oven proper, with a bedplate on which the bread is placed while the fuel is pushed back to the side, and with thick walls to keep and radiate the heat. They are sometimes used by individuals but often are used collectively. Because they take a long time to heat, they are especially designed for baking a large amount of bread.
2. The *tabuna*, *tannur*, and *tandir* type ovens: these have a cupola construction with the base frequently dug out of the ground; they always have two openings, one at the base to maintain the ember fire and one at the top, which is fairly large, through which the "loaves" — which are always flat — are put into the oven. They are placed against the wall and must be withdrawn before they fall from the wall into the embers.
3. A dish which has a lid and which is placed on a fire.
4. A simple dish placed on a fire: unless the loaf is in very thin sheets, it has to be baked successively on both sides.
5. Sometimes (in North Africa) a special dish for baking leavened bread is used: the base, which has uneven relief on the bottom side, isolates the slab of dough from the hot surface and enables it to rise without burning.
6. A metal plate which is placed on a fire is suitable for baking thin sheets of dough (pancakes).

As for fermentation, it is interesting to examine on one hand the complementary relation found in several regions between "leavened bread" and "unleavened bread," and on the other hand the importance attributed to leaven and the symbolic value attached to it. In relation to leavened bread, which has to be kneaded several times before being baked and which must be left to rise in a warm place, unleavened bread — in North Africa as in the Near-East (cf. biblical quotations in the days of the patriarchs and of the Exodus) — plays a very precise role: it is a special kind of bread and the bread of hospitality *par excellence*; it is prepared quickly, on the spot, while traveling, and is especially intended for unexpected guests. Everywhere, the leaven consists of a portion of dough taken off before forming the loaves and kept carefully until the next kneading, into which it is incorporated. Leaven is regarded as having a hidden power which acts mysteriously as it mixes itself with the dough. For ancient Israel, and more generally in the ancient world, it is at the same time a symbol of deterioration, of corruption. (More research is planned on the survivals, if any, of these notions.)

THE ROLE OF BREAD IN NOURISHMENT

In all the Mediterranean regions, the role of bread is extremely important and has been so for a very long time. It was — and has remained so nearly everywhere until today — THE food.

This is true quantitatively because bread occupies the primary place among the corn-base preparations which in fact play a dominant part in the nourishment of all the groups. It is also true of bread as the symbol of food, of life itself — the "daily bread," "man does not live by bread alone . . ." — These expressions testify to this symbolic value. Offering bread and water is a gesture of hospitality which must be performed even to an enemy if he is hungry and thirsty — one cannot, without disgrace, turn against a man from whom one has accepted bread. We should also deal with bread offerings, and more generally with bread's place in the rituals of the three religions which share the Mediterranean area, and also in what is left of the earlier farming rituals (for instance in Algeria bread is broken on the plowshare when a field is plowed for the first time). And we must also consider that it commands more respect than any other food: one never throws it away; one carefully picks up all uneaten bits; and even the passer-by who finds a piece of bread on his path will pick it up and leave it in a visible place (Guinaudeau 1964). In several regions (North Africa, Italy), bread, if its traditional form allows it, is never cut with a knife but broken; a gesture or a blessing generally precedes the slicing of round loaves. (Systematic research on survivals of these traditions, as they are applied to the various types of bread, should be carried out before the progressive replacement of household loaves by more anonymous products makes them go out of use.)

There are two main ways of eating bread: either as a meal on its own or to accompany a meal.

Bread as a Meal

As the evening meal is frequently the only cooked one, bread (whether garnished or not, or accompanied or not) is the the essential part of the meals eaten during the day, and especially of those eaten outside the home. This applies both to the European regions and to North Africa, and more particularly to two regions in which extreme diversity and fanciful ideas seem to prevail — Malta and the Lebanese mountains.

The relation between the bread itself and the "tasty" element of it (which is always supplementary and quantitatively not important) naturally varies according to the economic possibilities, the seasons, and the regional customs.

The simplest way is that the bread is eaten alone. All types of bread can be eaten this way. This leads to the category of loaves or griddlecakes especially baked to form a meal which is very rich in possibilities: the bread can simply be prepared just in time to eat it fresh, as pliability or crunchiness make it tasty in itself; it can also be kneaded more thorougly with a little oil or a few aromatic grains or herbs; and at the other extreme, really complex culinary preparations can be made in three main forms: (1) kneading with grains of sesame and aniseed, mint, oil and onions (North Africa), pork fat and scrapings (Languedoc), oil and rosemary, eggs, ewe cheese (Tuscany and Umbria pizza); (2) the dough can be split in half and stuffed with a preparation of minced meat or cottage cheese and onions (the meatloaf and *börek* of Turkey), of mutton fat, pimentoes, and spices (*magluga* griddlecake in the Mzab), with a very spicy sauce (*mtabga* in Tunisia), with pork fat and scrapings, fish, seasoned herbs (Corsican *bastela*, Italian *pitta*), anchovies and olives (Maltese *ftira*), and finally: (3) griddlecakes made of dough which has been covered with a garnishing and baked in an oven (pizza, tarts, etc.).

More frequently, the seasoning is added inside or on the bread after it has been baked, in the traditional styles of the sandwich and the "tartine" or slice of bread. In several regions, as we have shown, there is a well-established tradition of eating such a midday meal in slightly different forms according to the nature and the consistency of the bread used for the purpose — *pain bagnat* in Province, *pan bagnato* in Italy, a Tunisian or Maltese sandwich (round rolls cut in two, sometimes without the white of the bread, which serve as containers for a kind of spicy salad). In Lebanon as well, the thin and pliable sheet of bread is split and filled; in Turkey they prepare, with the same sort of pancake bread, sandwich rolls filled with cheese, onions, hard-boiled eggs, etc. This custom is always found in places where the place of work is far from the home, but never, to my knowledge, where the men and children take sandwiches not only to work or to school but also frequently to the nearby square or coffeehouse, as in Lebanon or Malta.

Finally, even in outdoor meals, one also finds that the piece of bread and the accompanying sausage, cheese, olives, or dried fruit, are brought separately to the place where they are eaten and then combined at each mouthful.

Bread as Part of a Meal or Accompanying Dishes

Two specifically different methods are used when bread forms part of a meal.

Bread as such is eaten with a dish. We must note here that although this is the most widespread mode of eating bread today in the food habits of the Western countries, the traditional association between the two elements has been extensively modified. This can be demonstrated by the definition given at the beginning of the nineteenth century by a Languedoc-French dictionary (Boissier de Sauvages 1971) for the terms *pitanzâ* and *pitânzo*. The first term means to take sparingly, to take very little of one thing, and hence to eat bread with the dishes of a meal "so that one spares the dish and it simply serves as a vehicle for the bread, which must be the main food"; *pitânzo*, called *compain* or *pousse-pain* in other provinces, is "any sort of dish which is usually eaten with bread." As for Provence, we have fifteenth-century evidence (cf. Stouff 1970) of this type of relationship between bread and what is called there *companagium*, as shown in a contract entered into between a Marseille abbey and a laborer, the latter undertaking to cultivate a garden for the abbey in exchange for which the abbey supplied his bread, his wine, and his second wine and soup every day, as well as *companagium* for the eight main holidays (we know however that at the time the *companagium* was a daily feature at the tables of the upper classes). These concepts are found again in southern France with expressions denoting the "tasty" meals "making you eat bread."

What is meant here in particular is the "ragout" type of dish, whose spicy and abundant sauce is scooped up with bread broken into pieces and held in the fingers; sometimes, too, the pieces of a pliable bread (in Lebanon, Turkey, North Africa) help to catch and hold in the fingertips the pieces of food which the various guests take from the common dish. Bread can also be used as a support on which the kebab or piece of grilled meat (in various regions) or *figatelli* (in Corsica) is placed so that the meat can be eaten conveniently without losing any juice.

The last method of using bread described here — a method used quite frequently — is when bread becomes part of the actual composition of the dishes. The bread cut into slices on which a broth is poured; formerly this broth was called a soup, before the term covered all sorts of soups, with or without bread. Especially in Europe the bread in soups occupies an important place, either as the only substantial element (as for example in garlic soup, known at least in Italy, Provence,

Languedoc, Corsica, and Spain in very similar forms and with very similar names), or when it is added to various fresh and/or dried vegetables, sometimes in such quantities that "the spoon, when put into it, must stand upright" (in Corsica and Languedoc).

Slices of bread placed in a dish can also have the abundant sauce from stew-type dishes poured over them, the sauce consisting of vegetables, meat and/or fish; at least one of these dishes, the *bouillabaisse*, is well known all over Mediterranean France, but one also finds others elsewhere. Two original forms may be mentioned: in Algeria, particularly in the Aurès region, a thin griddlecake reduced to crumbs in a dish is covered with a very spicy sauce (*merga*) in which mutton meat or fat and various vegetables are cooked; in southern Italy the daily meal is a dish consisting of dried bread (*freselle*) sprinkled, according to taste and the season, with oil and raw tomatoes or with a hot sauce with tomatoes and various aromatic herbs.

Sliced bread, griddlecakes, or broken or crumbled pancakes also form the basis of sweet dishes that are very frequently prepared, particularly in North Africa, for midday meals eaten by women and children, for visits, or for holidays; fairly thin griddlecakes are ground to pieces and kneaded with honey, sugar, fruit, curdled milk, etc.

Finally, we should mention a Moroccan dish which occupies position within the available literature which seems to be isolated but which may belong to the same family as preparations encountered elsewhere: the *bsila*, a "puff" pastry dish made of fine pancakes, which are cooked beforehand, and then used to separate layers of meat and fruit stuffing, all rebaked in the oven and served burning hot. We probably have now only to find intermediate forms enabling this very elaborate dish to be connected to other puff pastry dishes (in pastry) and to certain "stuffed breads," in particular the Turkish *börek* and the Corsican *bastella*.

Any sort of conclusion seems to be premature at the end of such a paper, whose purpose is to present the research which is under way and to contribute to a working session on bread, by providing documents and open questions for discussion.

REFERENCES

BONI, A.
1970 *Les cuisines régionales d'Italie*. Paris: Planète.
BOISSIER DE SAUVAGES, M.
1971 *Dictionnaire languedocien — français*. Geneva: Slatkine Reprint. (Originally published 1820.)

DES VILLETTES, J.
1960 La vie des femmes dans un village maronite libanais: Aīn el Kharoubé. *Institut de Belles Lettres Arabes* 90:209–222. Tunis.

GAUDRY, M.
1929 *La femme Chaouīa de l'Aurès*. Paris: Geuthner.

GOBERT, E. G.
1955 Les références historiques des nourritures tunisiennes. *Cahiers de Tunisie* 3:502–542. Tunis.

GUINAUDEAU, Z.
1964 *Fès vu par sa cuisine*. Rabat: J. E. Laurent.

KÖSE, MÜRSEL
1965 Tandir (à Kars). *Türk Folklor Araştirmalari* 9(189):3714–3719. Tunis.

MAKAL, M.
1963 *Un village anatolien*. Paris: Plon.

STOUFF, L.
1970 *Ravitaillement et alimentation en Provence aux 14e et 15e siècles*. Paris: Mouton.

WESTPHAL, A., *et al.*
1935 Articles on *levain* and *pain*. *Dictionnaire encyclopédique de la Bible*. Valence: Imprimeries Réunies.

Dietary Aspects of Acculturation: Meals, Feasts, and Fasts in a Minority Community in South Asia

JUDIT KATONA-APTE

Acculturation implies a process whereby a minority ethnic group assimilates into a dominant group in a culture-contact situation. To determine the extent of this assimilation, it is necessary to examine the important aspects of the daily existence of the acculturating community: these are language, religion, clothing, diet, etc. In this paper, this examination will be restricted to food habits.

The Marathi speakers, a minority community now living in Tamilnad, India, provide the focus for the examination of the process of acculturation on food habits. An analysis of their food habits requires some prior knowledge of the overall dietary patterns of Indians, especially of such concepts as meals versus snacks, feasts, and fasts. Therefore these are discussed briefly before examining the effects of acculturation.

Anthropologists rarely consider the study of food habits as important for the understanding of a culture. Nevertheless food habits contribute significantly to the identity of a society because of their relationship with other aspects of the culture.

For instance, food habits are often closely associated with religion. "Fish Fridays," Kosher kitchens, and the bread and wine that symbolize the body and blood of Christ are all part of the Judeo-Christian beliefs. Examples from Mohammedanism are the pork taboo and Ramadan, when no food is allowed from sunrise to sunset.

Hinduism, in this respect, is extremely complex. The number of special days requiring some form of observance varies from fifty to a hundred and fifty or more. All of these days are marked either by feasting or fasting by some segment of the population. While all do not celebrate every holiday, most observe so many that this becomes an important aspect of the daily life of all Hindus.

MEALS AND SNACKS

In India, a clear distinction is made between snacks and meals. In the American context there is not so much of a separation because such foods as hamburgers, pizzas, and sandwiches confuse the issue. The Indians do not have cooked food items that could be considered either a meal or a snack. Even the language reflects this difference. Many Indian languages have separate verbs to distinguish between eating a meal or a snack.[1]

Consuming a meal is a very important event in the daily life of an Indian. Often, it is the only pleasurable occasion in the struggle for survival. A person may hungrily await a meal and feel satisfied afterwards, even though the meal may be insufficient both in quantity and quality. Psychologically, the concept of a meal is all-encompassing and important to the average Indian, irrespective of its substantive value. Thus a feast of many courses or a meal of just the staple and a single side dish are considered equally important by him.

Nibbling and/or snacking, as we know it in the West, is not done in India. However, foods made of grains, legumes, sugar, and salt, and hot drinks such as coffee and tea are eaten between meals. In South India the term *tiffin* is applied to these foods. Snacks are not consumed at will, or when one is hungry; they are eaten only at specified times during the day, or possibly when visitors appear. What the British call "tea" — food served between the noon and evening meals — would be a snack, or *tiffin*, in India. These foods are consumed for breakfast in the morning and in the afternoon when the breadwinners return from work; the afternoon *tiffin* is to tide the family over from the morning meal, which may be served anytime between 8 A.M. and 2 P.M., to the evening meal, which is served around 8 P.M. Of the low-income population in South India, many have only one meal a day and *tiffin* for the second meal. Often the *tiffin* will consist of only coffee or tea.

The difference between a meal and snack food is determined by the use of the staple. Usage of the staple is not enough to constitute a meal; the staple has to be prepared in the acceptable accustomed form. For instance, in the south where rice (*Oryza sativa*) is the sole staple, the rice has to be boiled unbroken, and served with at least one side

[1] For example, Marathi, Gujarati, Kannada, and Tamil, just to name a few.

dish. Broken rice, fermented rice, rice flakes, rice flour, etc. are considered *tiffin* items. In the parts of the north where wheat (*Triticum aestivum*) is the staple, all wheat preparations that are not unleavened bread are snacks; this includes farina, semolina, cookies, and savory items made of wheat flour.[2]

Tiffin or snacks can be more substantial than meals. For example, the author was apologetically offered *tiffin* instead of the evening meal at the home of a South Indian professor. The *tiffin* consisted of soup, chicken curry, fried unleavened bread, salad, vegetables, legumes, and sweets. Because of the absence of boiled rice, however, it could not be considered a meal. Yet boiled rice and *rasam* [a very thin peppery soup] is considered to be a meal. Unleavened bread and a raw onion is a meal, but a mixture of farina and vegetables is only a snack.

FASTING

The notion of fasting, including its form, function, and relevance to the average Indian has not been adequately described by anthropologists or other behavioral scientists. It is often mentioned in studies dealing with the religion or culture of India (Dubois 1906; Stevenson 1971; Gupte 1916; *Census of India* 1961), but the form and nature of fasting, the whys and whens, and the impact it produces on the dietary habits of the population have not been explained. In the Western world, due to Judeo-Christian influences, fasting means not eating for a specified period of time. But fasting can have a different meaning in other religions and cultures.

In India, fasting is an extremely complex matter, varying according to religion, caste, family, age, sex, and degree of orthodoxy. There are gradations in fasting, both in terms of its frequency and its severity. A person who fasts more frequently may fast less severely than the one who fasts only occasionally. A more religious person is likely to fast more often and more severely than the one who is not so religious.

The frequency of fasting is determined by the degree of religious attitude and by personal choice. Some fasts, such as *amavasi* [new moon day] and *ekadasi* [the eleventh day of both the new and the full

[2] The terms RICE and WHEAT as used in this paper also include millet such as *Pennisetum thyphoideum, Sorghum vulgare, Zea mays,* and *Eleusine coracana.* Rice and wheat are often used as short forms for "rice food" or "wheat food." Wheat and millet prepared as unleavened bread are labelled wheat, and rice and millet boiled in water are both labelled rice.

moons] are common to most Hindus. Then there are weekly fasts — fasting one day of the week — to show goodwill toward a favorite god or goddess, to appease a god or goddess, or to either avoid or bring about a specific event; these days are determined by astrology. Such a fast may be undertaken to help oneself or a member of one's family, or to indicate preference for a particular deity. Most gods and goddesses of Hinduism are assigned a specific day of the week (as well as a specific day of the year).

Hindus fast to receive rewards, such as a male offspring, or to ward off evil. As an example, a description by Abbé Dubois (1906: 706) of *ekadasi* is given below:

> Ordinary food may be taken on the twelfth day in the afternoon, but not before, on pain of forfeiting for a hundred generations all the blessings which should flow from these ceremonies.
>
> Those who faithfully observe the fast of the *Eka-dasi* in the manner described will make sure of salvation. If any one has killed a Brahmin or a cow, taken away the wife or property of another, committed fornication with the wife of his *guru*, drunk intoxicating liquors, caused abortion in a pregnant woman; all these and other similar sins, no matter how numerous or heinous they may be, will be entirely absolved by the fast of the *Eka-dasi*, and by sacrifices offered to Vishnu on that day.

There are numerous fast days during the Hindu calendar year. For example:

> The days of the new and full moon are fast days, as also the tenth, eleventh, and twelfth days of each lunar month... on the tenth and twelfth days one meal may be taken, on the eleventh day... no meal at all is allowed. To fast on these three days has a special merit.... The feast called Sivaratri... no one must eat or drink... for the whole twenty-four hours.... On the ninth day of the lunar month *Cheitra*.... Brahmins may take only one meal in the day, and that without rice; they may eat peas, cakes, bananas, and coconuts.... On the eighth day of the month of *Sravana* they are forbidden to take any food at all.... They must also fast on the anniversaries of the ten *Avatars*.... on the days called *manuvadi, yugadi, sankranti*; on the days of eclipses; at the equinoxes, solstices, and the conjunction of planets, and on other unlucky days; on the anniversary of the death of father or mother; on Sundays and several other days during the year (Dubois 1906: 270–271).

If one starts counting, a startling revelation is made. There could be many more fast days during the week than nonfast days. For instance, *ekadasi* and *amavasi* are likely to be in the same week. In addition, a person may fast on Saturday for Hanuman [the monkey god]. This accounts for three days. He may also fast on Mondays (for Shiva) to save a son from harm. There may also be one of the innumerable

Hindu holidays that week, such as *Bogi* [eve of the harvest festival] when fasting is traditional. Altogether, this amounts to five fast days in a week.

If one fasted in the sense understood in the Western world, it would be physically impossible to survive. But fasting among the Hindus ranges along a continuum from total abstinence as in the Jewish Yom Kippur to a partial restriction of diet as in the Catholic no-meat Fridays, to abstaining from specific foods only as is the case with Lent.

The foods allowed during fasting vary from nothing to all but one item in the diet. At one extreme is the person who fasts by not eating nonvegetarian foods on fast days; then there are those who eat everything except the staple prepared in the accustomed form, and eat the staple prepared in other forms. Some eat one regular meal and substitute other foods for the second meal; such substitute foods could be anything from another form of the staple to sago (*Manihot esculenta*), fruits, milk, and nuts. Others may eat nothing but the one meal on fast days. For example,

> ... they return home and keep a fast, ... eat no cooked grain or rice, they are allowed mangoes and unlimited sweets made of milk ... (Stevenson 1971: 51).

Or

> ... fasts in some degree during the day, eating only fresh dates, milk, or sugar, but no grain, or flour, or anything made of flour. The very strict, however, will not even eat fruit, ordinary salt, red pepper (black is allowed), or betel leaf (areaca nut is admitted) ... (Stevenson 1971: 289).

Thus, because a person is fasting, it rarely means that he is going without food. The foods allowed are prepared with taste and variety; after all, much fasting is done on the eves of holidays which are joyous occasions. There is a Marathi proverb which states that on fast days one eats twice as much as on other days, while still claiming to be fasting. In South India, *tiffin*, as described earlier, is substituted for meals by those who do not eat the accustomed meals on fast days.

Purity is also an important consideration while fasting. After all, a fast symbolizes cleansing of the body:

> For men and women at all social levels, what is eaten affects their personal purity and therefore their roles in social interaction. With whom and from whom they take food has social consequences ... (Mandelbaum 1970: 200).

Purity in Hinduism is a continuum from extremely pure to extremely defiling. Thus those foods that are closer to the pure are more permissible than those which are at the low end. For example, rice, if boiled in water, is unacceptable for fasting; but if boiled in milk — a product of the cow — it is acceptable. (It is possible here to "cheat" by boiling the grain in water and then sprinkling it with milk, a practice to benefit the aged and ill.) Foods fried in *ghee* [clarified butter] are near the pure end of the scale. Thus, sweets are eaten for fasting, since traditionally they are prepared with *ghee*.

Stephen Tyler (1973: 78) explains pollution and its relation to food:

> Food itself is subject to classification on the basis of its relative purity, depending on who handles it in preparation, how it is prepared, how and by whom it is served. Some foods have special purity, either inherently (milk) or by the process of preparation (fried foods). Further, fried food can be more or less pure depending on the kind of oil used, clarified butter (*ghi*) being best. Fried food, known as *pakka* food, is less vulnerable to pollution than food prepared in water or baked (*kachcha* food). Similarly, raw (or unprepared) food still in a husk or shell is less susceptible to pollution than food that has been husked or shelled. A Brahman, for example, can accept an unpeeled banana or unhusked coconut from an untouchable, but will not accept the exposed flesh of these fruits. Similarly, food served in clay utensils is more prone to pollution than food served in brass utensils. In general, the more food departs from its raw or unprepared state the more important becomes the question of its manner of preparation, serving, and consumption. Leftover food is defiled unless it has been consumed by a deity or holy man. Alcohol and meat are inherently polluting and no manner of preparation can remove their impurity.

On fast days Hindus are more careful and will not eat food which may be part of their dietary on other days. Even if one meal is consumed and the other substituted, the most common practice, "polluting" foods are avoided for the whole fast day. The consumption of yeast bread, for instance, is rapidly spreading in India because of its low cost and convenience (no need for preparation). But it is considered a pollutant by those who associate it with Christianity, since bread was introduced by Christian missionaries. In some areas this is also true of chicken and eggs. Many who consume nonvegetarian foods daily will avoid doing so on fast days. Ready-made foods bought from shops are less pure than homemade ones. But *ghee*-fried foods from the outside are purer than boiled foods prepared at home.

Legumes, if first soaked in water and then ground, are acceptable; but if ground first and then mixed with water, they are unacceptable. Vegetables and legumes are avoided by some, but not by all. Again some others will avoid certain vegetables such as onions and garlic because these are considered to be aphrodisiacs. New World vegetables are taboo because they are not mentioned in the *Vedas* [sacred texts of

Hinduism]. Fruits which can be peeled, milk, nuts, spices, tea, and coffee are acceptable.

It should be pointed out that some of these restrictions are observed regularly by the very orthodox; others will resort to them only as they are necessary for observing religious practices — as exemplified by fasting.

FEASTS

There are eighteen major festivals in the year for Hindus, (Dubois 1906:567) not including such special events as marriage, thread ceremony, death ceremony, etc. All kinds of festivals are celebrated. They are important from a nutritional point of view, since they involve feasts.

Feasting is a way for food to spread among a larger segment of the population. In rural areas (80 percent of India is rural) all members of the community will eat generously on festive occasions. For many in the lowest economic segments, these are the only times that they consume adequate quantities of food. This is possible because of the still-surviving feudal system; landowners and others with wealth are responsible for helping the poor celebrate the festivals. Gifts of food are given to those who work for others by their employers. Often, grain which can be stored for future use is given.

At marriages and similar festivals, the person offering the feast will make sure that even the lowest castes are given food, though they may not be included among the guests. The foods eaten at festivals are not so much different from everyday foods as they are plentiful and various. The staple is the same, but the side dishes are more numerous and are accompanied by sweets and other delicacies.

Some foods such as coconut (*Cocos nucifera*), *ghee*, turmeric (*Curcuma domestica*), betel nuts (*Areca cathecu*), and certain fruits have a special significance for all religious and sacred occasions. Other foods are associated with particular festivals; for example, sweets, rice flakes, and *karita* (*Cucumis pseudo-colocynthis royale*) with *Divali* [festival of lights], a rice dish called *Pongal* for the harvest festival *Pongal* in South India, milk for *Naga Panchami* [a snake festival], and the sacrifice of a ram, buffalo, or goat for *Dasara* [festival for weapons].

Some foods are believed to be symbolic, representing certain important concepts. For instance, rice is a symbol for abundance and fertility, banana (*Musa paradisiaca*) for fertility, betel leaves (*Piper betel*) for auspiciousness, *ghee* for purity, betel nut and coconut for hospitality, sacredness, and auspiciousness, and mango (*Mangifera indica*) for sacredness and auspiciousness. Margaret Stevenson (1971: 265) describes Gujarati New Year's Day and the significance of salt for that day:

> But the best of all things and the luckiest of all is salt, called on this day, even by Gujaratis, *sabarasa*, the essence of everything; so how can man buy better, than by buying salt on New Year's day in the morning? Salt, too, mixes easily with all things, and salt is always pleasant to all men, so men are symbolically advised to be pleasant to all, and to mix in friendly fashion with everyone during the coming year ....

ACCULTURATION

The group under discussion here migrated from Maharashtra to Tamilnad several generations ago. There are approximately 50,000 Marathi speakers concentrated in a few districts and in the capital city of Madras. Data for this paper came from depth-type interviews and observations of those living in Madras (the largest segment, about 10,000, live in Madras). There are three major caste groups in the Marathi population in Madras: Brahmin, Tailor, and Mahratta (Apte 1974); each is approximately evenly represented in the sample.

To the eye of an outsider, the Marathi speakers appear to have assimilated considerably into life in South India. When questioned, they claim to be South Indians. They speak Tamil as any native, dress as other South Indians, and seem to eat South Indian foods. But in the home and among relatives they speak Marathi, they marry other Marathi speakers only from South India, and they celebrate Maharashtrian holidays and festivals. And on closer examination, their food habits do differ from those of other South Indians.

They claim to eat like the South Indians and mention typical South Indian foods as proof: *idli* [rice and legume patty] *dosa* [rice and legume crepe] and *payasam* [vermicelli-milk sweet] for special occasions. These foods are not part of the diet in Maharashtra. However, they also eat foods that are part of the common diet in Maharashtra. For example, they tend to eat boiled rice for the morning meal and *chapatis* [unleavened wheat bread] for the evening meal. In the old culture[3] both wheat and rice are served at both meals, or only rice

[3] The terms "new culture" and "old culture" used in the discussion of the Marathi-speaking community of Tamilnad refer to Tamilian and Maharashtrian cultures respectively.

is served at one of the meals. In the new culture, wheat is not served for a meal. For festivals, old culture sweets such as *puran poli* [stuffed unleavened wheat bread] *laddu* [round sweet ball] *srikant* [sweet soured cream] or *pedha* [small patty of cream and sugar] are prepared.

There are other differences also. While eating off the plantain leaf — more often done in South India than North — Tamilians use the leaf horizontally with the point of the leaf to the left. Maharashtrians use it vertically with the point at the top. Marathi speakers in Tamilnad use it horizontally, but are not especially careful about which way it points.

The concept of staple, and snack or *tiffin*, has also changed among the Marathi speakers. To South Indians, wheat preparations are *tiffin*, as they are to Marathi speakers. One of their favorite snacks is *puri masala* [deep fried unleavened bread with peas-potato vegetable]; in the old culture this combination is part of a meal.

Three aspects of the dietary acculturation of Marathi speakers in Tamilnad are particularly significant:

1. Old-culture diet is maintained while celebrating festivals from the old culture, and it is combined with diet from the new culture for celebrating festivals from the new culture. Festivals of the old culture, such as *sankrant* [harvest festival] and *holi* [spring equinox], though absent in the new culture are celebrated by the Marathi speakers. Foods reminiscent of the old culture such as *poli* [flaky unleavened bread] and *til laddu* [sesame sweet] are prepared on these occasions. Typical South Indian specialties, with the exception of *payasam*, are not mentioned in the preparations for these festivals. When new-culture festivals such as *Pongal* and *Ugathi* [Telugu New Year] are celebrated, they seem to use the relevant South Indian foods such as *pongal* for *Pongal* and *pachadi* [a kind of chutney] for *Ugathi* along with their old-culture foods.

In South Indian festivals, a sequence of flavored rices is served, such as lemon (*Citrus medica*) rice, *sambar* [pureed legumes with vegetables] rice, yogurt rice, etc. The Marathi speakers serve similar dishes, except that instead of mixing the rice with the lemon, *sambar*, or yogurt, they serve the rice alone and the other ingredients as a side dish, just as it is done in the old culture. For special old-culture occasions, mixed rices such as *masala bhat* [rice with vegetables and spices] or *sakhar bhat* [sugar rice] are not served by the Marathi speakers.

2. Those aspects of the old-culture diet which are suitable and convenient to the new-culture environment (both ecologically and cultur-

ally) are maintained. The diet of the Marathi speakers, while not quite like that of the new culture, fits into the new culture without difficulty. While adopting items that are plentiful in the new culture, they do not necessarily prepare them according to the cooking practices of the new culture.

Ecologically, adaptation to a boiled rice staple may be preferred since wheat does not grow in South India. Millet is common to both areas, but when used it is prepared in the manner of the new culture. Vegetables and fruits which are plentiful in the new culture are preferred. Thus sweet limes (*Citrus aurantifolia*) and a larger variety of plantains (*Musa sapientum*) are consumed. In addition to lemons and mangoes, pickles are prepared from gooseberries (*Phyllanthus emblica*) that are plentiful in the south.

In the daily dietary, the unleavened bread and boiled rice combination as staple has been replaced by boiled rice alone as staple. Certain vegetables such as snake gourd (*Trichosanthes anguina*) are avoided by many for religious (rather than health) reasons. In the old culture the vegetables avoided are mainly onions (*Allium cepa*) and garlic (*Allium sativum*).

3. The Marathi speakers, instead of accepting the new-culture diet totally, adopt some facets of it. The result is a partial adaptation to new-culture habits. These adopted facets, however, would be unacceptable to the old culture.

In an acculturation situation, cultural traits mix. The result of such a mixture is like neither that of the old nor of the new culture. Often, however, this mixture of cultural traits is considered as characteristic of the minority group. Some of these new traits are compromises, though not looked upon as such by their practitioners. For the change in dietary habits to be acceptable to the dominant culture, it does not necessarily have to be patterned after the dominant group.

Dietary habits are adopted according to both content and cognitive labelling of the new culture. For instance, eating wheat in the evening, closer to the old-culture dietary, becomes a new-culture trait as soon as it is labelled *tiffin*; then it is immediately acceptable to the new culture.

The highest point of dietary adjustment of the Marathi speakers is the transformation of their choice of fast foods. In South India, *tiffin* is an acceptable substitute for meals when a person is fasting. While *tiffin* corresponds in form and terminology to snack foods in Maharashtra, snack foods are not necessarily allowed for fasting there. In the old culture, no form of the staple may be used while fasting; that includes rice, millet, and wheat. Also avoided are legumes and most vegetables, such as onions, cabbage (*Brassica oleracea*), cauliflower (*Brassica oleracea)*, eggplant (*Solanum melongena*), squash (*Cucurbita pepo*), gourds (*Momordica charantia*), green beans (*Phaseolus vulgaris*), and cucumbers (*Cucumis sativus*).

The most common forms of *tiffin* in Tamilnad are *idli* and *dosa*, both prepared of rice and legumes and eaten with *sambar* made of legumes and vegetables. *Tiffins* are also made of wheat, *puri* or *uppuma* [farina mixture with spices and vegetables] for instance.

The most important cultural distinction with regard to food patterns between Maharashtra and South India lies in the foods consumed for fasting. Tiffin is allowed in the south, but comparable snack food items are not part of the fasting in Maharashtra. The consumption of *tiffin* items during fasting by the Marathi speakers in Tamilnad would not be acceptable to their old culture.

SUMMARY

While the main purpose of this paper was to discuss the relevance of dietary habits to the acculturation of Marathi speakers in Tamilnad, it was necessary to first describe certain important cultural concepts such as meals, snacks, fasts and feasts in India. This was followed by an examination of the changes which have occurred in the food habits of Marathi speakers in Tamilnad. It appears that (a) the daily eating habits have become more like those of Tamil speakers; (b) certain aspects of the old-culture diet which are suitable to the food habits of the new culture have been retained; (c) also retained are the old-culture habits of food preparation and consumption for the celebration of festivals from the old culture; and (d) the most significant degree of assimilation has occurred with regard to food habits during fasting.

REFERENCES

APTE, MAHADEV L.

1974 Voluntary associations and problems of fusion and fission in a minority community in South India. *Journal of Voluntary Action Research* 3(1).

Census of India
1961 *Fairs and festivals in Maharashtra,* volume ten, part VII B. Delhi: Manager of Publications.

DUBOIS, ABBÉ J. A.
1906 *Hindu manners, customs, and ceremonies* (third edition). Oxford: Clarendon Press.

GUPTE, RAI BAHADUR B. A.
1916 *Hindu holidays and ceremonials.* Calcutta: Thacker Spink.

MANDELBAUM, DAVID G.
1970 *Society in India.* Berkeley: University of California Press.

STEVENSON, MARGARET
1971 *The rites of the twice-born* (second edition). New Delhi: Oriental Books Reprint Corporation.

TYLER, STEPHEN A.
1973 *India: an anthropological perspective.* Pacific Palisades, California: Goodyear.

Notes on Different Types of "Bread" in Northern Scotland: Bannocks, Oatcakes, Scones, and Pancakes

GRITH LERCHE

From my fieldwork in the north of Scotland, especially Caithness, in September-October 1970 I should like to draw attention to a very important element in the Scottish diet: the most commonly eaten types of "bread," the oat and barley breads, which are known as "oatcakes" and "scones." The big round oatcake, before it is quartered, is called a "bannock." The "oatcakes" (pieces of a bannock) are also called "farls." The "scones" are made of wheat flour or barley meal.

The word "oatbread" was used by older people in Caithness for the pieces of the bannock, and in northeast Scotland they also say "oatbread" or simply "bread" (Fenton 1971b: 156). The varieties of scones eaten daily are flour scones, dropped scones — also called pancakes — and bere scones made of bere meal, which is coarse milled barley of the type called BERE or BIG in Scotland (*Hordeum Hexastichon*). In Scotland amongst the rural population generally, the iron griddle or gridded BRANDER until recent times took the place of the oven, and the bannock took the place of the loaf.

It is my intention to give the recipes and the baking processes as they were actually done by Mrs. Marian Calder in Dunnet near Thurso far north in Scotland. Background information concerning eating habits in the Calders' house will be given, together with details of which meals the various types of bread were eaten at, the times of day when the meals were taken and the principal constituents of the meals. Some historical notes are added to show the Scottish bread culture in comparison with the continental bread culture.

The Calder family consists now only of James Calder and his wife Marian, both more than sixty years old. Their croft, Westside Cottage, at Dunnet Bay was Mrs. Calder's home as a child. There is electricity, television, radio, and telephone. The croft is on eleven and one-half acres with eight fields in a six-shift rotation, growing potatoes, turnips, hay and grass, with barley and oats as the two cereals. Mrs. Calder had a kitchen garden in front of the house and an enclosure behind with onions, leeks, carrots, potatoes, rhubarb, and cabbage. When I visited them at the end of September they had cut their turves or peats for the winter supply, the onions were in boxes, a fish was drying on the wall outside. There were still some potatoes and cabbage in the kitchen garden. Mrs. Calder had many hens and thus also eggs. They have not had pigs since the war, but a butcher's van passes on fixed weekdays. They had just got a new cow so they would soon start milking again and churn their own butter. Every Thursday a grocer's van comes so they do not need to go to town very often. On one occasion Mrs. Calder bought from the grocer's van from nearby Castletown: ½ lb. Danish butter, 1 lb. coarse and 1 lb. white salt, soap, 1 kg. flour, a package of sliced bread from "Barretts" in Inverness, and some self-raising flour. She has a recipe book with recipes of the usual Scottish dishes; she had written it herself. She has always taken part in the meetings of the SWRI (Scottish Women's Rural Institute) where members can win prizes for good bakery, etc. Mrs. Calder has a rather modern kitchen with an electric stove and an electric oven, but this is never used when she bakes her oatcakes, scones, and pancakes. Her husband likes them only when made on the griddle over the peat fire, so she bakes at the fireplace in the living room.

Mrs. Calder's recipe for OATCAKES:
2 handfuls of oatmeal (4 oz.)
1 teaspoon of melted dripping
1 teaspoon of salt
pinch of baking soda (i.e. bicarbonate of soda)
enough water to make a stiff paste

This quantity of dough gives the best results since the dough will stiffen when made in bigger quantities. Mrs. Calder bakes oatcakes once a week. She usually makes four bannocks a week, but if her peat fire is not good enough she only makes three bannocks. Each of them is quartered, so she normally gets sixteen oatcakes.

In many recipes boiling water should be used, but she uses "normal water," lukewarm (McNeill 1963: 183; 1965: 74; Fitzgibbon 1970: 102). As dripping she sometimes uses the melted fat from sausages.

It gives the oatcakes some taste, she says. The ingredients are mixed in a bowl and kneaded thoroughly with her hands. She then flattens the dough out on the wooden baking board dredged with oatmeal, and does not use a rolling pin or "bannock-stick" which is used by many (see Plate 1). The bannock, which is now 28 cm. in diameter and about 1½ cm. thick, is quartered before it is placed on the griddle. Mrs. Calder's griddle is made of aluminium; she has used it for ten years. She still has the old iron griddle. The oatcakes were often burnt on the old griddle, she told me. When the griddle is hot enough after having been heated over the peat fire, hanging from a crook, the bannock is put on. It is baked about 4 minutes and is then turned with a modern flat fish-spoon (see Plate 2). Earlier Mrs. Calder used a wooden spoon; from other districts some very beautiful cast iron, heart-shaped bannock spades or oatcake turners are preserved (Grant 1961: 194). After about 2 minutes baking on the other side the oatcakes are taken off the griddle and placed against a wooden toaster in a slanting position in front of the peat fire for another five minutes. From Inverness-shire some very nice stone toasters are preserved (Campbell 1950: 139; Grant 1961: 195). Those made of wood are also called "bannarack" (McNeill 1963: 183; Grant 1961: 195; Campbell 1950: 139). It takes Mrs. Calder about half an hour to make the weekly portion of oatcakes. Mrs. Calder's mother always used the words "oat-bannock" for the big one and "oat-bread" for the small oatcakes. Oatcakes may be baked in a slightly different way by other housewives, and in the book of recipes by McNeill the oatcakes are baked on the one side until they curl up at the edges and then the other side is only toasted slightly before the fire (McNeill 1965: 74).

Besides oatcakes Mrs. Calder made scones every week. Mrs. Calder distinguished between PLAIN SCONES made of plain flour, BERE SCONES made of the bere meal, and "FRO SCONES." This is Mrs. Calder's explanation: usually I have seen the word in the dairy terminology, the first syllable is in the combination "fro-stick," a stick for making frothed milk. For the "fro scones" Mrs. Calder prefers buttermilk instead of sweet milk (i.e. fresh milk): for her scones she never uses sugar, syrup, or butter, which are mentioned in most recipes for scones, but the egg is her own idea.

Recipe for SCONES:
1 cup of flour (½ 1b.)
½ teaspoon of baking soda
pinch of salt (fine)

½ teaspoon of cream of tartar
1 egg
buttermilk and/or sour milk

The egg is whipped and some buttermilk and/or sour milk is added. The wet and dry ingredients are then mixed and kneaded into a soft dough. The baking board is dredged with flour and the dough is beaten out on it and shaped into a rather flat, round cake which is cut into pieces. The diameter is 26 cm. and the pieces are 8 cm. wide and 2-2½ cm. thick. When I watched her, she cut the big scone into eight pieces (see Plate 3). Without the egg this scone type is called "white bannocks" or "soda scones" in some recipe books (McNeill 1965: 70).

Mrs. Calder's bere meal scones always have cream of tartar and soda, but often she leaves out the egg. In recipes these are of course normally called "barley bannocks" (McNeill 1965: 70). Earlier, when they grew their own barley she made bere scones regularly, now only occasionally.

Recipe for BERE SCONES:
1 handful of bere meal (2 oz.)
½ handful of "flour meal"
pinch of salt
½ teaspoon of baking soda
½ teaspoon of cream of tartar
buttermilk and/or sour milk

All the ingredients are mixed together with a spoon in a bowl, and the flat-shaped big scone cut into four pieces is placed on the hot griddle to be baked.

The bere scones are baked about four minutes on one side and then turned and baked about three minutes on the other side. It depends a little on the fire. Mrs. Calder sometimes lowered the griddle if she found the heat was not strong enough. Bere scones are about 1½ cm. thick, thus a little thinner than flour scones.

Of a dough much like that for scones Mrs. Calder makes PANCAKES. They are often called tea pancakes, dropped scones or Scots crumpets in recipes and in shops (McNeill 1965: 73; Fitzgibbon 1970: 85).

Recipe for PANCAKES:
3 teacups of "flour meal"
a pinch of salt

1 heaped teaspoon of baking soda
1 teaspoon of cream of tartar
1 spoonful of sugar
1 egg and a little cold water whipped together
sweet milk

This dough or batter contains sugar and has the consistency of thin cream, so when the ingredients are mixed together for five minutes in a bowl, the batter is dropped on the hot greased griddle in large table-spoonsful. Four pancakes are baked at a time on the griddle. The pancakes are baked about two minutes on each side. In half an hour Mrs. Calder baked eighteen pancakes from this portion. They are 1½ cm. thick and their size is 10-12 cm. This is the ration for the week for her and her husband. Earlier, when there were more people at home, they went to the mill twice a year with oats. They got four bolls of meal (1 boll = 10 stones) and baked twice a week.

By looking through the listed daily meals and what is eaten at the meals by the Calders, it is evident that the oatcakes, scones, and pancakes are a very important part of the daily food, even if also some bought, sliced white bread is eaten.

DAILY MEALS AT THE CALDERS'

7:15 they get up, drink a cup of tea at once, and eat some oatcakes.

10:30 porridge and milk.

13:00 they drink a cup of tea and have something to eat: scones, oatcakes, "plain bread" (i.e. sliced loaf), homemade rhubarb jam, butter and cheese are all put on the table.

16:30 they have dinner. When I was there they had potato soup (Tattie soup), then pancakes with rhubarb jam, biscuits, cookies, oatcakes, and scones.
The dishes vary: potato and fish — cod or haddock or fresh herring, boiled or fried. Soup of pork or beef, mince, stew, cabbage and pork, black and white pudding which are bought at the butcher.
White pudding is: meat, onion, oatmeal, suet, pepper, and salt mixed. It is bought half-cooked from the butcher and only has to be heated in hot water or fried.
Black pudding: the Calders have made it themselves from pig's blood.

Other ingredients are onion, barley meal or flour meal mixed, fat, pepper, and salt. It is ready to slice and fry. Potatoes are eaten with this. This dish is mostly eaten during the winter. In the spring potatoes are peeled before cooking. When they get old they are often served mashed. During the winter they are often cooked with the skins on.
20:00 they have supper. Tea and bread of all kinds (white bread, oatcakes, scones, pancakes).

On Sundays they do not eat porridge for breakfast but, instead, have a boiled or scrambled egg, with bacon.

The daily consumption of bread and cereals is rather big. This is not only a habit of the Calders: visits to other farms in Caithness showed that it was all the same. The family Rosie at Freswick had oatcakes, which they told me were earlier called oatbread, and bere and flour scones at each meal. The family consisted of two elderly sisters and a younger nephew. They owned two crofts with twenty acres. They bought the flour meal for the scones (in fact, they did not like this flour). Their flour scones were made on the griddle over the fireplace and they were quartered. The bere scones were made in the modern kitchen. They did eat porridge for breakfast.

Two elderly sisters, aged fifty-six and sixty-two, live at the farm Corr in Latheron. The farm has 102 acres; in 1956 they got electricity, so they have TV and radio. There are many cows, sheep, and chickens on the farm. They bake their own scones and oatcakes in bigger quantities than Mrs. Calder, and often twice a week, since the family frequently came from the town for the weekends.

At this farm they make oatcakes with a rolling pin and bake them on an aluminium griddle; this is not placed over the open fireplace but on the coal range. They do have a modern electric stove with an oven. When the oatcakes are toasted it is done in the oven for five minutes. Earlier they toasted the oatcakes on a special invention — an iron toaster which could be hung in front of an open hatch on the coal range. There are thus stone and wooden toasters for the fireplace; the middle stage, i.e. coal range toasters, and then the modern way of toasting in the electric oven or on the grill of the oven. I would not be surprised if the toasters for sliced white bread were used for the oatcakes sometimes too!

The Keith sisters at Corr have not grown their own barley and oats for the last forty years. At that time the cereals were milled at Firth Mill. They do make bere scones as well as flour scones and pancakes. The sisters distinguish between "plain scones" without egg and sugar and "richer scones" with egg and sugar. They make their own marmalade of gooseberry, rhubarb, and wild raspberries.

THE DAILY MEALS AT THE KEITHS' AT CORR:

8:00 they get up and have a cup of tea.

"On top of the day" i.e. 12:00, they have breakfast — porridge and a cup of tea.

13:00 another cup of tea, oatcakes, scones, jam, and butter. (They churn their own butter and they make their own white cheese with caraway seeds.)

18:00 they have soup, broth, "tatties," "different sorts of meat, never out of tins."

22:00 they have a cup of chocolate, tea, or coffee before they go to bed. Usually they have a pancake too.

I did not meet a housewife who baked real loaves, even though I visited many farmhouses where they had electric ovens. In fact all the housewives have electric ovens, but for some reason some do not like the taste of oatcakes and scones baked in the oven. They are better when made on the hot griddle over the peat fire. In many families, they baked their own oatcakes and scones, but in others they bought all their bread, also oatcakes and scones, even if the same family took the trouble to churn their own butter in a plunge churn and made their own white cheese — I refer to the sisters on a farm in Houstry. There is a big market for different sorts of scones and oatcakes, to judge by the large quantities sold in the bakery shops of the small towns; some bakers have made the baking of oatcakes into quite an industry. The names of some of the oatcake "factories' 'in Scotland are: Paterson's Griddle Oatcakes, Nairn's Scottish Oatcakes, Simmer's Scottish Oatcakes, Stewart's Oatcakes, Turriff Forbes' Oatcakes, Hand-made Morayfirth Oatcakes, and Stocken's Oatcakes, Stromness, Orkney.

The public taste in the countryside up to quite recently has been to live on one's own crop, according to the remarks above and according to records and books (Grant, for instance). The cereals grown in Scotland have almost exclusively been barley (especially the six-rowed bere) and oats. These two cereals stand the cold and humid climate of Scotland better than wheat and rye. Wheat has been grown but is mostly imported. Bread baked from wheat was eaten in Edinburgh in the fifteenth century; "Maynebread" and four kinds of wheat bread were eaten in Scotland in the sixteenth century. There have been numerous bakers in later centuries who also baked bread from wheat and used wheat flour for the Scottish types of bread, cakes, and shortbread. Even large loaves of rye have been eaten in the eighteenth-century "Ankerstock" and rye was also used for bread in the sixteenth century for the poor people (McNeill 1963: 178). These data must refer mainly to Edinburgh and other towns.

In the eighteenth century, bread as we know it today, white wheat bread, was not yet part of the ordinary Scottish diet (Plant 1952: 99). It is important to understand, when using older records, whether they are referring to town conditions or rural conditions. In Scotland there has also been a perceptible difference between the way of life and customs of the Highlanders and people from the moorland districts in contrast to the Lowlanders. For instance, Lowlanders who lived on the fertile parts were content to make their bannocks of mixed barley, peas, oats, and rye. The Highlanders found mixed cereals disgusting (Plant 1952: 100).

Barley and oats are sown in the spring; even then they are able to take the best advantage of the short Scottish summer since they have a short period of growth. The flour made from these two cereals does not contain gluten, so the ripening action of the lactic acid in the gluten of the flour, which takes place during fermentation in a loaf of wheat or rye, does not occur in bread of oats or barley. Barley and oat bread stay rather flat during baking and do not rise; therefore it has no effect to bake for instance oat cakes and bere scones in an oven. They will be just as well baked on a hot griddle, though it is otherwise with the wheat and rye loaves.

Since most of Scotland lies north of the climatic northern border for the growing of wheat and rye, the cereals are oat and barley. The Scottish farmers did have problems with their crop. It had to be dried: on many farms and at ruins of farms in deserted villages in Caithness I saw the big beehive-shaped stone drying kilns built at the end of the barns (Plate 4). Even if it was for use in whiskey or for bread, the crop had to be dried to be safely stored in the winter. Those who did not have a kiln and whose needs were small dried the corn over the fireplace. On the continent there was always a large, built-up baking oven for drying the cereals, for instance in Denmark (Højrup 1964: 141).

The elements to be noted in discussing the traditional rural bread culture in Scotland are: the cereals grown, the need for drying the crop, the lack of baking ovens, the drying kiln, and the method of baking on a griddle over the fire. The two main points, the crop grown and used for bread, and the baking methods, each help one to deduce what kind of bread culture one would expect to find among a rural population in a given area. If one knows that the cereals grown are oats and barley, then it can be realized that the farmers' wives had no need of an oven since the bread had to be a kind of flat bread. Groups other than farmers who also traditionally make a flat bread are the Bedouins and Lapps. They do not have to be content with oat and barley, for they have a choice, and since they buy their flour they often use wheat; but since they are used to moving around, the old types of big, heavy, fixed baking ovens did not suit their unsettled way of life.

These observations on some aspects of the Scottish diet will, I hope, stimulate my colleagues to carry out similar observations in other countries and other regions while there is still time to do it. In a few years' time it will be more and more difficult to carry out fieldwork in one's own country or in the Western world, to record, for instance, bread baking as it has been done for generations. More and more bought, factory-made, white loaves are eaten all over the world. The transition from the traditional local bread diet to the "sandwich" diet we will have an opportunity to study somewhere, also in the future. It is also important to record the traditional eating habits of the present time, since it has taken normally three generations to change eating habits; but now everything changes rapidly as a result of the very urbanized ways of life, much traveling, and the import of food, fresh fruits, and exotic delicacies etc. from all over the world.

REFERENCES

CAMPBELL, ÅKE

1950 *Det svenska Brödet*. Stockholm: Svensk Bageri.

FENTON, ALEXANDER

1971a Hafer- und Gerstenmehl als Hauptgegenstand der schottischen Forschung. *Ethnologia Scandinavica*.

1971b "The place of oat-meal in the diet of Scottish farm servants in the eighteenth and nineteenth centuries," in *Studia ethnographica et folkloristica in honorem Béla Gunda*. Edited by J. Szabadfalvi and Z. Ujváry. Debrecen: Kossuth Lajos University.

FITZGIBBON, THEODORA

1970 *A taste of Scotland in food and pictures*. London: Pan Books.

GRANT, I. F.
1961 *Highland folkways.* London: Routledge and Kegan Paul.
HØJRUP, OLE
1964 *Landbokvinden.* Copenhagen: Gad.
MC NEILL, F. MARIAN
1963 *The Scots kitchen: its lore and recipes* (second edition). London and Glasgow: Blackie and Son.
1965 *Recipes from Scotland* (seventh edition). Edinburgh: Blackie and Son.
PLANT, MARJORIE
1952 *The domestic life of Scotland.* Edinburgh: Edinburgh University Press.

Plate 1.

Plate 2.

Plate 3.

Plate 4.

Biographical Notes

MARGARET LOUISE ARNOTT is presently Assistant Professor at the Philadelphia College of Pharmacy and Science and is President of The International Committee for the Anthropology of Food and Food Habits. She has lived, studied, worked, and published in Greece. Bread and its uses is her special field of research.

HÉLÈNE BALFET (1922–) is Ethnologist at the Centre National de la Recherche Scientifique. She has worked at the Musée de l'Homme in Paris since 1950 and at the Université de Provence (Centre d'Etude et de Recherche Ethnologique sur les Sociétés Méditerranéennes) since 1969. Her research interest includes both comparative technology and the ethnology of Mediterranean societies. She has done fieldwork mainly in the Maghreb and the south of France.

SANDOR BÖKÖNYI (1926–) is Member of the Archaeological Institute of the Hungarian Academy of Sciences and Lecturer of Archaezoology at Eötvös Loránd University, Budapest. He was Founder and till 1973 Curator of the Archaeozoological Collection of the Hungarian National Museum. He received his M.V.D. in 1960 and his D.Sc. in 1969. His primary interests are the study of the Holocence fauna, animal domestication, diffusion and history of domestic animals, and animal husbandry as a human occupation in the Near East and southeast and Central Europe. Recent publications are: *Data on Iron Age horses of Central and Eastern Europe* (1968); *The development and history of domestic animals in Hungary* (1971); *History of domestic mammals in Central and Eastern Europe* (1974); *The Przevalsky horse* (1974).

ANNIKA BORNSTEIN-JOHANSSON is Sociologist at the University of Stockholm and is at present working with a FAO Nutrition Project in the Yemen Arab Republic.

GLORIA BOXEN (1947–) was born in Toronto, Canada. She studied at the Faculty of Food Sciences, University of Toronto (B.Sc. in Food Sciences, 1970, M.Sc., 1972). Her special research interest is in changes in nutritional behavior.

NILS-ARVID BRINGÉUS (1926–) was born in Malmö, Sweden. He received his Ph.D. at the University of Lund in 1958. He has been Assistant Professor 1958–1967 and Professor of European Ethnology since 1967. He is Editor of *Ethnologia Scandinavica* and is a member of the editorial Board of *Ethnologia Europaea.* His research interests include agricultural implements, food, customs, and folklore.

ARIANE BRUNETON (1944–) studied sociology, ethnology, ethnographic film, and Berber language in Paris (Sorbonne — E.N.L.O.V. — Audiovisual Department of the Musée de l'Homme, fifth section of Ecole Practique des Hautes Etudes). She did her first research (1967–1971) in Morocco, especially on diet and food habits, and was Associated Expert in the Nutrtion Division of the FAO (Rome) from 1970 to 1971. Since 1972 she has done research in rural France on both the food habits and women of that area.

MARY ULMER CHILTOSKEY (1907–) was born in Marengo County, Alabama. She obtained her B.S. in Elementary Education from Livingston University in 1934 and her M.A. in Social Studies from George Peabody College for Teachers in 1940. She taught for eighteen years in the public schools in Alabama and for twenty-five years in the Cherokee Indian schools in North Carolina before retiring in 1967. Her special interests are Cherokee lore — foods, legends, history, etc. She has assisted in the publishing of two books: *Cherokee cooklore* and *Cherokee words with pictures.* She is presently working on *Cherokee plants, their uses.*

D. G. COURSEY (1929–) was born and studied in London. He joined the Colonial Agricultural Service and worked in Nigeria (1951–1964), most of his research being concerned with yams and cassava. His work on yams was continued at the University of Ghana (1964–1966), where he extended his interests in root crops from the purely agricultural to the sociological and prehistorical aspects. In 1966 he returned to England, where he now works for the Ministry of Overseas Development and is mainly concerned with agricultural advisory work in the developing world. He is author of the standard monograph on the yam and of about sixty other papers.

ELLENORE DOUDIET (1913–) was born in Binghamton, New York. She studied techniques and restoration of paintings at the Art Students League, New York (1932–1934) and engineering at N.Y.U. (1942–1943). She has been Director of the Wilson Museum, Castine, Maine, from 1946 to the present and was President of the Maine Archaeological Society, 1969–1970. Since 1971 she has been President of the Castine Scientific Society.

GAETANO FORNI (1926–) was born in Milan, Italy. He studied agrarian and zootechnical sciences at the University of Milan (Agr. Dr., 1951). Then he specialized in paleoethnology (paleoeconomics, paleotechnology, paleobotany, paleozootechnics) and also in the relations among economics, society, and religion. At present he is Coworker for the prehistoric section of the Rivista di Storia dell'Agricoltura (edited by the Accademia dei Georgofili, Florence), Founder-Member of the National Institute for Agriculture History (University of Milan) charged with the anthropological-agrarian museology, and Founder-Member of the International Association for the Study of Prehistoric and Ethnologic Religions (Capo di Ponte, Brescia, Italy) which strives to promote an interdisciplinary dialogue between art historians, ethnologists, historians of religions, museologists, philosophers, prehistorians, and other categories of scholars. His main publications are: *Dio, religione e agricoltura* (1957); *Due forme primordiali di coltivazione* (1961); *Domestikation, Tierzucht und Religion* (1961); *Scoperta della tecnica di coltivazione e religione dei coltivatori* (1962); *Homo ludens, homo creans e le origini delle tecniche* (1966); *Origini dell'agricoltura africana e sua evoluzione sino alla colonizzazione europea* (1969); *La pianta domestica: elemento ecologico, fatto culturale e documento storico* (1970); *Di alcuni particolari aspetti del problema dell'origine dell'agricoltura* (1971); *Musei agricoli e musei di storia dell'agricoltura, musei etnografico-folcloristici chiusi e all'aperto* (1974); *Relazioni tra religione, società, economia e ambiente: un problema di antropologia storico-ecologico* (in press); *L'ethnozoologie en tant que branche de l'ethnologie* (in press).

REBECCA GRANT (1917–) was born on the Cherokee Indian Reservation, Cherokee, North Carolina. She attended the Cherokee Indian schools through the tenth grade. After rearing eight children, she earned her GED diploma in 1970. Her knowledge of native plants and their uses for foods came from her parents. Today she still gathers, prepares, and regularly eats many of the wild plants that grow around her home.

MERVYN DAVID WALDEGRAVE JEFFREYS (1890–) retired from the British Colonial Service, Nigeria, as Assistant Judge and from the University of the Witwatersrand as Senior Lecturer. A Rhodes Scholar (1910) and M.A. Oxon (1924), he holds the Diploma in Social Anthropology (1928) and a Ph.D. in Cultural Anthropology (London, 1934). Interested particularly in African studies including lobolo, the early use of maize, polygamy, divine Umundri kingship, twin cults, and the origin of the Hottentot culture, he has published over four hundred articles, mostly in scientific journals. A bibliography of his work up to 1971 was compiled by David Allan Stone, published by the University of the Witwatersrand, Johannesburg.

NORGE W. JEROME (1930–) was born in Grenada, West Indies. She received her B.S. from Howard University in Nutrition and Dietetics in 1960, an M.S. from the University of Wisconsin-Madison in Human Nutrition and Experimental Foods in 1962, and a Ph.D. in Human Nutrition and Social Anthropology from the University of Wisconsin-Madison in 1967. She has been on the faculty of the University of Kansas Medical School since 1967. Her special interests include nutritional anthropology, epidemiology and ecology of malnutrition, and food exchange and dietary substitutions in high- and low-income countries. She is an Associate Professor of Human Ecology at the University of Kansas Medical School.

JUDIT KATONA-APTE (1943–) a native of Hungary, received her B.A. in Anthropology and is currently a doctoral candidate in the Department of Nutrition at the University of North Carolina School of Public Health. She is specializing in nutrition and anthropology and has done fieldwork in India and in the United States. Her interests and publications focus on medical and nutritional anthropology, methodology, acculturation, and nutritional adaptation.

MAGDALENA KRONDL (1924–) is an Associate Professor at the University of Toronto. She has studied nutrition at London University

(B.Sc., 1944). In 1950 she received her Ph.D. in Anthropology at Brno University in Czechoslovakia. Her publications were the first in the area of food consumption patterns. She was the first author of the Czechoslovak Food Composition Tables. Her current research interest is in nutrition behavior.

GRITH LERCHE (1941–) is Scientific Assistant of the Royal Danish Academy or Sciences and Letters' Commission for Research on the History of Agricultural Implements and Field Structures and Secretary for the International Secretariat for Research on the History of Agricultural Implements at the National Museum of Denmark. She obtained her M.A. degree in 1967 from the University of Copenhagen. Besides much fieldwork and expeditions within and outside of Europe, e.g. excavations of the Viking ships at Roskilde; archaeological excavations at Bahrain; and ethnological research in New Guinea, Iran, India, Syria, Scotland, Finland, and Czechoslovakia, she has published studies on timber constructed farm and town buildings, bread culture, plowing implements, spade cultivation and harvesting methods. She is co-editor of the journal *Tools and Tillage: A Journal on the History of the Implements of Cultivation and Other Agricultural Processes.*

EMILIO MORAN (1946–) received his B.A. in Spanish American Literature from Spring Hill College (1968), his M.A. in Brazilian History from the University of Florida (1969), and his Ph.D. in Anthropology (1975) with a dissertation on socioecological adaptation along the Trans-Amazon Highway. He has also received certificates in Economics, Tropical Agriculture, Ecology, and Latin American Studies. His special interests include human adaptation to new environments, the study of agricultural systems with a view to the maximization of production, and the application of energetics to the study of man-environment interactions. His recent publications include: "Energy flow analysis and *Manihot esculenta* Crantz" (1973); "The adaptive system of the Amazon Cabuclo" (1974); and "Farmers and extractions: men and culture in two Amazon towns" (1975).

NANCY POLLOCK (1934–) was born in England. Educated at Colorado College and the University of Hawaii, she is currently Senior Lecturer in Anthropology and Coordinator of Pacific Studies at Victoria University, Wellington, New Zealand. She is author of several papers on ecological, diet, and general social anthropological topics pertaining to fieldwork data from Jamaica and the Marshall Islands in the Pacific.

LUIGI SAFFIRIO was Official of the Hygiene and Public Health Department of the City of Turin. Now retired from that post, he is Scientific Collaborator of the Egyptian Museum of Turin for studies in cultural Anthropology and prehistory. His publications are: "L'alimentazione umana nell'Egitto preistorico" (1965, *Aegyptus* 45: 20–55; 1966, *Aegyptus* 46: 26–59); "Food and dietary habits in ancient Egypt (1972, *Journal of Human Evolution* 1: 297–305); "L'alimentazione umana nell'antico Egitto (Thinite period, Old Kingdom and first intermediate period)" (1972, *Aegyptus* 7: 19–66).

VISHNU-MITTRE (1924–) was educated at the University of Punjab, the University of Benares, the University of Lucknow, and Cambridge University. His major studies were paleobotany and palynology and his research interests have been in palynology, plant taxonomy, floral history and paleoclimates, environmental archaeology, origins of agriculture, and geomorphology. He conducted his fieldwork in several parts of India, and in Ceylon, Nepal, and the English Fenlands. Some typical publications are "Studies on the fossil flora of Nipania, Rajmahal Hills, Bihar" (1956–1959, *Palaeobotany* 2: 75–84; 5: 96–99; 6: 31–46, 82–112; 7: 47–66); *Evolution of life* (with M. S. Randhawa, Jagjit Singh, and A. K. Dey, 1969, New Delhi: Publication Directorate, CSIR); "The beginning of agriculture: palaeobotanical evidence from India" (in *Evolutionary studies in world crops: diversity and change in the Indian subcontinent*, edited by Joseph Hutchinson, 1974, Cambridge University Press). He also edited *Late Quaternary vegetational developments in extra-European areas* (1974, Lucknow: Birbal Sahni Institute of Palaeobotany). He is presently at the Birbal Sahni Institute of Palaeobotany, Lucknow.

CHRISTINE S. WILSON received her B.A. from Brown University in Biology in 1950 and her Ph.D. in Nutrition from the University of California at Berkeley in 1970 after the study of public health nutrition and nutritional biochemistry at Harvard School of Public Health and Vanderbilt University, respectively. Her dissertation was an ethnographic study of diet and health in a Malay fishing village. Similar research was subsequently carried out among Mexican Americans. She is currently Lecturer at the University of California at San Francisco and, as Senior Nutritional Scientist for a private firm, is preparing an evaluative manual on nutrition intervention programs for preschool children in developing countries. Her publications and special interests are in the area of nutritional anthropology, and she is particularly interested in trying to bring the two disciplines of nutrition and anthropology closer together.

DOUGLAS E. YEN (1924–) was born in New Zealand. After receiving his B.A. and M.A. in Agricultural Science from Massey University, he was appointed Plant Breeder at the Crop Research Division, Department of Scientific Research, Lincoln, New Zealand, in 1948. He transferred as Officer-in-Charge of the Vegetable Station of the same division at Otara, Auckland from 1953–1966, during which time he began ethnobotanical research. In 1966, he was appointed Ethnobotanist at Bishop Museum, Hawaii. His publications include papers in plant breeding and ethnobotany, the most recent being the monograph, *The sweet potato and Oceania* (1974). In 1975 he received his D.Sc. from the University of Auckland.

Index of Names

Index of Subjects